THE POEMS OF
MS JUNIUS 11

BASIC READINGS IN ANGLO-SAXON ENGLAND

CARL T. BERKHOUT, PAUL E. SZARMACH,
AND JOSEPH B. TRAHERN, JR., *General Editors*

OLD ENGLISH SHORTER POEMS
Basic Readings
edited by Katherine O'Brien O'Keeffe

BEOWULF
Basic Readings
edited by Peter S. Baker

THE ARCHAEOLOGY OF ANGLO-SAXON
ENGLAND
Basic Readings
edited by Catherine E. Karkov

THE POEMS OF MS JUNIUS 11
Basic Readings
edited by R. M. Liuzza

ANGLO-SAXON MANUSCRIPTS
Basic Readings
edited by Mary P. Richards

CYNEWULF
Basic Readings
Robert E. Bjork

OLD ENGLISH PROSE
Basic Readings
edited by Paul E. Szarmach

THE POEMS OF MS JUNIUS 11

Basic Readings

edited by

R. M. Liuzza

ROUTLEDGE
New York and London

Published in 2002 by
Routledge
29 West 35th Street
New York, NY 10001

Published in Great Britain by
Routledge
11 New Fetter Lane
London EC4P 4EE

Routledge is an imprint of the Taylor & Francis Group

Library of Congress Cataloging-in-Publication Data

The poems of MS Junius 11 : basic readings / edited by R.M. Liuzza.
    p. cm. — (Basic readings in Anglo-Saxon England ; vol. 8)
  ISBN 0-8153-3862-7
    1. Caedmon manuscript. 2. English poetry—Old English, ca. 450-1100—
History and criticism. 3. Christian poetry, English (Old)—History and criticism.
4. Manuscripts, Medieval—England. 5. Manuscripts, English (Old) I. Liuzza,
R. M. II. Series.

PR1624 .P64 2001
829'.1093823—dc21

                                                                2001044216

Contents

Preface of the General Editors

Basic Readings in Anglo-Saxon England (BRASE) is a series of volumes that collect classic, exemplary, or ground-breaking essays in the fields of Anglo-Saxon studies generally written in the 1960s or later, or commissioned by a volume editor to fulfill the purpose of the given volume. The General Editors impose no prior restraint of "correctness" of ideology, method, or critical position. Each volume editor has editorial autonomy to select essays that sketch the achievement in a given area of study or point to the potential for future study. The liveliness and diversity of the interdisciplinary field, manifest in the Annual Bibliography in the *Old English Newsletter* and in the review of that Bibliography in the *Year's Work in Old English Studies*, can lead only to editorial choices that reflect intellectual openness. BRASE volumes must be true to their premises, complete within their articulated limits, and accessible to a multiple readership. Each collection may serve as a "first book" on the delimited subject, where students and teachers alike may find a convenient starting point. The *terminus a quo*, approximately the 1960s, may be associated with the general rise of Anglo-Saxon studies and a renewed, interdisciplinary professionalism therein; other collections, particularly in literature, represent the earlier period. Changes in publication patterns and in serial-acquisitions policies, moreover, suggest that convenient collections can still assist the growth and development of Anglo-Saxon studies.

This volume is the first in our series to be devoted to the study of a single manuscript, published in 1655 by Francis Junius and the first of the four great codices of Old English poetry to appear in print. Roy

Liuzza has collected twelve previously published essays to which he has added a detailed update of one (by its author) and an original essay commissioned for this volume. The first three essays deal with manuscript as a whole—one surveying and commenting on past criticism, one advocating a salvation history of the sort found in Augustine's *De catechizandis rudibus* as the manuscript's organizing principle, and a third examining various examples of paronomasia, which provide a vehicle in the four poems for discovering the congruence between language and divine truth. These essays are followed by two on *Genesis*, two on *Exodus*, three on *Daniel*, and two (including Janet Schrunk Ericksen's original contribution to the volume) on *Christ and Satan*. Liuzza's informed and succinct summaries of each essay in his Introduction will provide both the novice and the experienced scholar ease of access to the wide variety of essays as well as a sense of how they contribute to one another.

The General Editors would like to thank Professor Liuzza for his willingness to organize this volume and add it to the collections already published in the series.

Carl T. Berkhout
Paul E. Szarmach
Joseph B. Trahern, Jr.

Introduction

R. M. LIUZZA

MS Junius 11 in the Bodleian Library at Oxford, written around 1000, contains poems on biblical subjects, untitled in their manuscript but called by modern editors *Genesis*, *Exodus*, *Daniel*, and *Christ and Satan*. The manuscript was the first Old English poetic collection to be printed, by its owner Franciscus Junius in 1655;[1] Junius believed that the poems were written by Cædmon, the inspired poet and innovator of Old English Christian poetry made famous by Bede's *Ecclesiastical History* iv.24. It is now commonly accepted that the poems in the manuscript are not by Cædmon; in fact, each is probably by a different author. Yet the poems were collected and arranged in one manuscript, a fact which allows and encourages us to consider them as a group and raises the possibility that the meaning of one poem may be illuminated by the study of its manuscript companions. The physical context of these poems, in other words, may be our best clue to their interpretive context. This collection, which gathers together 13 essays on the Junius poems, presents an opportunity to read each poem in light of the others.

"In many respects we are in no position yet to examine these pieces," Geoffrey Shepherd wrote in 1966; "We do not know enough about Anglo-Saxon literary activities, and we have not yet acquired modern critical techniques adequate for the analysis of their work."[2] Shepherd's discouraging opinion was based on the evidence of what he calls "successive recomposition," the reuse of older materials in later texts. The most dramatic example of this is the interpolation of a long fragment of a translated Old Saxon poem (now called *Genesis B*) into the narrative of *Genesis A*. Smaller interpolations may have been common—parts of the poem *Daniel* appear in the Exeter Book *Azarias*, and there is no scholarly consensus on which poem should be considered "original." The corporate character of authorship in such texts baffles our expectations of textual integrity and blunts our tools for deciphering poetic meaning. Indeed, the poems in Junius 11 challenge our critical faculties in many different ways. The manuscript is one of only two MSS in Old English entirely devoted to poetry—the other is the Exeter Book—and the only surviving poetic manuscript with illustrations.[3] The sequence of its texts indicates that it was compiled deliberately, but its compiler, audience, and purpose are all unknown. The dramatic rewriting of biblical narrative found in these poems raises provocative questions of source that are not yet resolved; the bold blend of traditional Germanic form and biblical and patristic content hints at an equally intriguing complexity of style and audience. The poems in the Junius MS are both historical and allegorical, native and foreign, familiar and yet strange. They challenge, but they do not quite defeat, the critics who have sought to explain them; the essays in this collection, approaching these poems from many different directions and situating them in many different contexts, suggest that Shepherd's pessimism was, happily, overstated.

Joyce Hill's "Confronting *Germania Latina:* Changing Responses to Old English Biblical Verse" (1992) opens the collection with a brief survey of the history of criticism on the Junius poems. Hill frames this history in terms of an opposition between "Germania"—an interest in native, vernacular, pagan and secular traditions—and "Latina," a focus on the learned Christian background of Old English poetry. Scholars of the nineteenth century, Hill notes, were less interested in Christian Anglo-Saxon culture than in the traces of paganism and northern history they saw in works such as *Beowulf* and *Widsith;* thus they left the Junius 11 poems in a state of relative neglect. Later works of mid-twentieth-century criticism, most notably Bernard Huppé's 1959 *Doctrine and Poetry*, read the poems in the light of Augustinian and patristic exegesis and argued that their diction and meaning were built on a foundation of learned allusion and imagery.[4] While this shift of interest certainly enriched the study of the poems, Hill argues that "Both sets of assertive certainties . . . confidently bring to bear upon a given text a body of extratextual assumptions which tend to generate a self-confirming reading" (6); both tend relatively to ignore manuscript and contextual evidence in favor of a reading that is, in an important sense, predetermined by the critical assumptions the reader has brought to the work. Hill urges a more balanced approach to these poems, one that reads not strictly allegorically but typologically, respecting the historicity of the narrative while recognizing Old Testament events as prefigurations of the life of Christ. Her essay suggests that the tension in the poetry itself between native and Latin elements, vernacular style and Christian content, is adumbrated in the criticism of the poetry.

It has always seemed clear that the poems in Junius 11, though composed by different authors, were brought together purposefully. What have been less clear are the nature of that purpose and the intention of the organizers. Earlier attempts to explain the unity of the contents of Junius 11 turned to the liturgy, especially the liturgies of Lent and Holy Week; J. R. Hall's "The Old English Epic of Redemption: The Theological Unity of MS Junius 11" (1976, revised for this volume with an added "Retrospective") argues that the manuscript's organizing principle is that of a poetic outline of salvation history not unlike Augustine's *De catechizandis rudibus* and Wulfstan's *Sermo 6*. Hall demonstrates the considerable similarity between these historical narratives and the episodes in the Junius poems, and suggests that the compiler of Junius 11 (or a compiler of a manuscript from which Junius 11 was copied) selected the contents of the manuscript to illustrate the major moments in the history of salvation. Hall's argument is an important recognition that literary analysis, the study of the meanings of individual texts, is inseparable from codicology, the study of the whole book. Though the poems were written separately, they were read in sequence; our understanding of their meaning in their Anglo-Saxon context must begin with an understanding of the use and meaning of the manuscript in which they have survived.

For medieval readers, the Bible was a text of inexhaustible richness and meaning. The Latin text had been studied and reread for centuries, its nuances examined and interpreted, its grammar and syntax probed for hidden meanings; any translation, as Ælfric worried in his *Preface to Genesis*, would convey only the *nacedan gerecednisse*, the "naked narrative." Roberta Frank points out in "Some Uses of Paronomasia in Old English Scriptural Verse" (1972) how the authors of the Junius poems used the resources of their language to suggest some of the depth of the biblical text. If the nature of things is captured in their names, as medieval writers such as Isidore of Seville believed, then wordplay might be an effective hermeneutic for discovering the meanings hidden in the world and the course of history. Frank points out many instances of plays on words, serious puns that, to the medieval mind, resonated with deeper meaning. The authors of the Junius poems exploited sound associations to create or replicate etymological puns in both Latin and English, and called upon all the resource of alliterative verse, which tends to link words strongly across the caesura, to create couplings of sense as well as sound. Frank finds significant plays on words in such pairs as "word / weard / weroda," "Daniel / dom" (playing on Jerome's etymology for the name), "Sion / seon" (again reproducing the etymology given by Jerome), and near-homonyms such as "God / god" and "mann / man." Far more than a decorative device or a clever embellishment, Frank argues, wordplay and sound association were a vehicle for discovering the congruence between vernacular language and divine truth. "That Daniel's name and its Hebrew interpretation," she notes, "converged so gracefully in Old English verse—with an alliterative inevitability missing in the Latin translation—might have seemed to the poet to confirm the fitness of his native tongue to transmit biblical truths" (77).

Eric Jager's "Tempter as Rhetoric Teacher: The Fall of Language in the Old English *Genesis B*" (1988) explores the character of Eve through a detailed comparison of her language and that of the Tempter who entices her to eat the forbidden fruit. Examining not only the elements of the Tempter's persuasive speech but also the extent to which Eve's discourse imitates and echoes his, Jager argues that Eve is literally the Tempter's "instrument" and student in the art of rhetoric; her perversion of language is the first indication of a fallen nature: "Eve's changed perceptions result from her changed terms of reference for understanding the world of her experience. She has exchanged God's terms for the Tempter's" (113). Jager places the study of the poem's diction in the service of an understanding of character, discourse, and the relation between perception and moral truth.

Though critical interest in *Genesis B* has been strong, relatively less attention has been paid to the poem that surrounds it, *Genesis A*. Andrew Orchard's "Conspicuous Heroism: Abraham, Prudentius, and the Old English Verse *Genesis*" (1994) focuses on an often-neglected part of *Genesis*, the battles of Abraham and the kings of Sodom. Noting its "exuberant expansion of the biblical source" (120) and its characteristic use of heroic diction and imagery, Orchard praises the artistry of the poet who managed to evoke a whole realm of heroic conflict out of a few verses of the biblical text. The passage's traditional diction and style place it alongside such works as *Beowulf, Maldon,* and *The Battle of Brunanburh,* but Orchard notes that Abraham's battles, as in the patristic commentaries on the biblical source, have an allegorical significance as well and are not merely type scenes added to make the narrative livelier. Building on a suggestion of Bernard Huppé, Orchard examines the elements of *psychomachia* in the martial episodes in *Genesis A;* he finds strong parallels to the work of the *Genesis* poet in Prudentius, "a useful analogue for the way in which a poet steeped in heroic tradition can interpret and elaborate a promising piece of scripture" (130). Orchard's work suggests that even the most "traditional" or "Germanic" elements in the poem may be the product of a rich cultural fusion between Latin and vernacular literary and intellectual traditions.

Exodus is widely regarded as one of the densest and most difficult of Old English poems; its complexity of diction and extravagance of metaphor, and the compact frenzy of its language and style, have led more than one critic to assume the poem is damaged, misarranged, or otherwise imperfect. James W. Earl's "Christian Tradition in the Old English *Exodus*" (1970) searches in the poem itself for an avenue toward interpretation. Writing at a time when the critical consensus on *Exodus* favored reconstructive surgery to smooth out its abrupt transitions, Earl looks instead to the traditions of Christian exegesis on the biblical story to explain the narrator's frequently strange and occasionally baffling juxtapositions and metaphors. The exodus, Earl notes, is not only a model of earthly life, it is a type of baptism; the crossing of the Red Sea symbolizes all the passages—from death to life, sin to redemption, bondage to freedom—implicit in the sacrament. Earl also notes the number of ways in which the Red Sea crossing (the only extended narrative in the poem) is made to represent the whole of the biblical story of Exodus and the conquest of Canaan, and to contain explicit and implicit references to the cross of Christ and the harrowing of Hell as well. Read against the rich tradition of biblical and liturgical commentary, Earl argues, the poem is much more coherent than is usually thought, and its most complex passages are seen to have a unity of image and theme.

Looking in more detail at one such crux in the poem—an apparent digression on Noah, Abraham, and Solomon, delivered just as the children of Israel are crossing the dry sea bed—Stanley Hauer's "The Patriarchal Digression in the Old English *Exodus*, Lines 362–446" (1981) proposes a number of reasons why the passage fits in the larger context of the interpretation of *Exodus*. Thematically the episodes recall how God helps those in need, rewards the faithful, and honors His covenant with His chosen people. In terms of imagery, the sailor Noah is linked to the Israelites, consistently referred to as "sailors" or "seafarers" in the poem; Abraham, for his part, is a wanderer and exile like Moses and the chosen people. At the same time each story within the digression is a foreshadowing of Christ. Hauer demonstrates that the apparent digression is "a skillfully introduced and poetically effective subplot reinforcing through its parallels much of the significance of the material in the main story" (182).

One example of the sort of density of detail achieved by the poet of *Exodus* is found in a passage describing the tribes of Israel marching into the sea; Judah, first in the host, is led by a banner (*beacen*) on which is a golden lion. Charles Wright examines this image in "The Lion Standard in *Exodus*: Jewish Legend, Germanic Tradition, and Christian Typology" (1994; revised for this collection) and finds its roots not only in the Germanic tradition of animal standards, but also in the traditions of biblical exegesis. The image is suited to a native narrative style but may also derive, Wright points out, from the learned Christian tradition. Moreover, the Lion of Judah has a "well-established Christological interpretation" and stands in opposition to the banners of the Egyptian host; the *segn* of Judah is typologically the same as the pillar of cloud (also called a *segn*), a prefiguration of the Cross, the standard of Christ. Wright's explication of the knotty threads of this image suggests the complex web of typology and tradition in the poem, its merger of heroic language and biblical exegesis, Old Testament narrative and spiritual allegory.

The biblical book of Daniel is a rather sprawling work of mystical prophecy and apocalyptic history; the Old English poem *Daniel* narrows and focuses the action by limiting its scope to the first five books of the biblical account. Moreover, as Robert Farrell argues in "The Structure of the Old English *Daniel*" (1968), it achieves unity and balance by concentrating on a few themes which are adumbrated by carefully chosen repetitions. The poet forecasts the destruction of Babylon—a parallel to the destruction of Jerusalem depicted at the beginning of the poem—and constructs the forces which cause these two destructions as an opposition of faith and faithlessness, law and lawlessness, wisdom and folly, God's *cræft* and the devil's cunning. Farrell demonstrates how the repeated key words create the structure of opposition that conveys the poet's message: The kings of Babylon, like the Jews, fell because they turned to evil deeds, pride and drunkenness. Farrell argues that the Old English *Daniel* is by no means a mere paraphrase of the biblical text or a clumsy interpolation of narrative and lyric, but "a moral poem with clearly evident lessons, a climatic order of events and a skilful development of themes" (223).

Earl R. Anderson's "Style and Theme in the Old English *Daniel*" (1987) emphasizes the historical and political concerns of this complex poem rather than its moral or didactic elements. Anderson argues that common medieval historiographical ideas—among them, the notion that the Hebrews as *populus dei* lost their favored position through sin and were superceded by the *populus christianus*—are woven throughout the poem. Beginning with a close comparison of the "Song of Azarias" in *Daniel* (lines 279–361) and the related text *Azarias* in the Exeter Book and a survey of the poem's biblical and nonbiblical roots, Anderson explores the poem's interest in the concept of the *populus Dei* whom God protects and punishes, and who may lose their favored position through sin and suffer God's correction at the hands of other nations. God's transfer of power from one nation to another, the *translatio imperii*, is, Anderson argues, the central theme of the poem.

Antonina Harbus, however, argues in "Nebuchadnezzar's Dreams in the Old English *Daniel*" (1994) that the focus of the poem is rather the spiritual development of the king whose visions are interpreted by the young Daniel. "*Daniel* deals specifically with the pride and humbling of Nebuchadnezzar," Harbus argues, "and when the narrative does not concern him, his failings—pride and drunkenness—are reflected in other characters, such as the Israelites in the opening scene, and Belthazzar at the end of the poem" (261). Though the king's dreams are related in far less detail than they are in the biblical story, they are retold so as to focus on the king's relation to the dream rather than the prophet's; Daniel's role in the narrative is systematically diminished, and "[t]he result is more a psychological portrait of redemption than a tale of prophecy" (262). Shifting the focus of the story from a prophetic history to a psychological study of pride and atonement, Harbus argues, is one way the poet has refashioned the biblical text for his contemporary audience.

Considerable controversy surrounds the interpretation of the evidence of the last quire of MS Junius 11. Debate over the construction of Junius 11 has arisen not only because of the condition of the codex but because of the apparent incongruity of its last text.[5] *Christ and Satan* is the only explicitly New Testament poem in the Junius collection; in contrast to the other Junius poems, it is predominantly liturgical rather than narrative in its construction. Critics continue to disagree over its structure, purpose, and unity. Ruth Wehlau's "The Power of Knowledge and the Location of the Reader in *Christ and Satan*" (1998) is a succinct and convincing analysis of one of the poem's major themes, knowledge and identity: learning and remembering who one is, and the dependence of these activities on a right relationship to God. Wehlau shows that through repetition and wordplay God's omniscience is contrasted to Satan's deception and ignorance; the Temptation of Christ is presented in the poem as a contest of knowledge—Satan fights to unmask Christ in His human form, and is sentenced in defeat to measure the depth of Hell and, in effect, learn to know himself. Faced with the negative example of Satan, the human reader is urged to *gemunan* "remember" and recognize the history of salvation, to distinguish between false words and true, and to use the memory of Christ's saving sacrifice as a weapon in the battle against Satan. Building on Wehlau's observations, Janet Schrunk Ericksen's original contribution to this volume, "The Wisdom Poem at the End of MS Junius 11," suggests that *Christ and Satan*, in its emphasis on the power and intelligence of God, may be read as a type of wisdom poetry, "not a genre but a content category" embracing many different kinds of literature. Ericksen links the poem to various monastic dialogues such as the *Collectanea pseudo-Bedae*, *Adrian and Epictitus*, and *Solomon and Saturn*; all contain lists of revealed things that were used in "contemplating the bounds and extent of human and divine wisdom, and in encouraging the pursuit of wisdom." Human wisdom stands between divine omniscience and satanic falsehood, and the pursuit of right thinking and the perception of God's power evident in nature are among the poem's most powerful messages. If the poem were recognized as a piece of wisdom literature, Ericksen argues, its readers may have approached it differently and with different expectations than the other narrative poems in Junius 11; this may explain the poem's marginal status in Junius 11, "part of and distinct from the rest of the manuscript" (317).

Echoes of the Old Testament may be found everywhere in Anglo-Saxon culture: in religious writings, laws, collections of gnomic wisdom, vernacular poetry—even the heroic world of *Beowulf* is set, more or less, in an Old Testament context. The Junius poems are a dramatic example of the depth to which vernacular and Latin traditions were interlaced among the Anglo-Saxons. The essays in this collection suggest a number of approaches to the issues of manuscript context and textual authority, problems of source and analogue, questions of readership and audience; individually and collectively, they offer the reader a deeper and richer understanding of these individual poems, of their unique material context, and of Anglo-Saxon culture.

NOTES

1. Franciscus Junius (sometimes called "Francisci Filius" or "F. F." to distinguish him from his kinsman Franciscus Junius, "Francisci Nepos" or "F. N.") was born in Heidelberg in 1591, son of the theologian Franciscus Junius the elder, and raised in Calvinist Leiden, where he attended university. After a failed early career in a fractious country church near Rotterdam, he served as librarian and tutor to the Arundel family for several decades. In addition to his work in Latin and Hebrew, Junius was interested in the Germanic languages, notably Frisian, Gothic, and Old English; in this he was a pioneer of comparative philology. Junius' edition of the manuscript is *Caedmonis monachi Paraphrasis Genesios ac praecipuarum Sacrae pagina Historiarum, abhinc annos MLXX* (Amsterdam, 1665; a reprint is ed. Peter J. Lucas, Early Studies in Germanic Philology 3; Amsterdam/Atlanta, GA 2000). Junius died in 1677; much of his manuscript collection—including transcripts and early printed books with annotations—is in the Bodleian Library at Oxford. He bequeathed his collection of Gothic, runic, and Anglo-Saxon types to Oxford as well, where they were used to print, among other important works, George Hickes's *Thesaurus* (Oxford, 1705). For Junius' life and work see the essays in Rolf Bremmer, ed., *Franciscus Junius F. F. and His Circle* (Amsterdam, 1998).
2. Geoffrey Shepherd, "Scriptural Poetry," in E. G. Stanley, ed., *Continuations and Beginnings: Studies in Old English Literature* (London, 1966), 1–36, p. 11.
3. Considerations of space and expense have not made it possible to include discussions of the illustrations in this anthology; readers may wish to seek out Barbara Raw, "The probable derivation of most of the illustrations in

Junius 11 from an illustrated Old Saxon *Genesis*," *Anglo-Saxon England* 5 (1976), 133–48; Thomas Ohlgren, "The Illustrations of the Cædmonian Genesis: Literary Criticism Through Art," *Medievalia et Humanistica* 3 (1972), 199–212; and Catherine Karkov, *Text and Picture in Anglo-Saxon England: Narrative Strategies in the Junius 11 Manuscript,* Cambridge Studies in Anglo-Saxon England 31 (forthcoming, Cambridge UP).

4. B. F. Huppé, *Doctrine and Poetry: Augustine's Influence on Old English Poetry* (New York, 1959).

5. See Hall's and Ericksen's essays in this collection, and for a detailed consideration of the evidence see Peter J. Lucas, "On the Incomplete Ending of *Daniel* and the Addition of *Christ and Satan* to MS Junius 11," *Anglia* 97 (1979), 46–59, and the counterarguments of Barbara Raw, "The Construction of Oxford, Bodleian Library Junius 11," *ASE* 13 (1984), 187–207; rpt. in *Anglo-Saxon Manuscripts: Basic Readings*, ed. Mary Richards (New York, 1994), 251–75.

Acknowledgments

I would like to thank all those who have helped in the preparation of this volume, especially Janet Ericksen, J. R. Hall, David Johnson, and Paul Szarmach. For permission to reprint, I would like to thank the authors of the individual essays and the editors of the following journals and presses:

Joyce Hill, "Confronting *Germania Latina*: Changing Responses to Old English Biblical Verse." Reprinted from *Latin Culture and Medieval Germanic Europe. Proceedings of the First Germania Latina Conference held at the University of Groningen, 26 May 1989*, ed. Richard North and Tette Hofstra (= *Mediaevalia Groningana* XI. Groningen, 1992), 71–88. © 1992 Egbert Forsten Publishers. Used with permission.

J. R. Hall, "The Old English Epic of Redemption: The Theological Unity of MS Junius 11." Reprinted from *Traditio* 32 (1976), 185–208, revised by the author for publication in this volume. The original essay is copyright © 1976 Fordham University Press, and is used with permission.

Roberta Frank, "Some Uses of Paronomasia in Old English Scriptural Verse." Reprinted from *Speculum* 47 (1972), 207–26, by permission of the Medieval Academy of America. Copyright © 1972 Medieval Academy of America.

Eric Jager, "Tempter as Rhetoric Teacher: The Fall of Language in the Old English *Genesis B*." Reprinted from *Neophil* 72 (1988), 434–48. Copyright © 1988 Kluwer Academic Publishers. Used with permission.

Andrew Orchard, "Conspicuous Heroism: Abraham, Prudentius, and the Old English Verse *Genesis*." Reprinted from *Heroes and*

Heroines in Medieval English Literature: a festschrift presented to Andre Crépin on the occasion of the sixty-fifth birthday, ed. Leo Carruthers (Woodbridge, 1994), 45–58. © 1994 the author. Used with permission.

James W. Earl, "Christian Tradition in the Old English *Exodus*." Reprinted from *Neuphilologische Mitteilungen* 70 (1970), 541–570. Reprinted with the permission of the Modern Language Society of Helsinki.

Stanley R. Hauer, "The Patriarchal Digression in the Old English *Exodus*." Reprinted from *Studies in Philology* 78 (1981), 77–90. Copyright © 1981 by the University of North Carolina Press. Used with permission of the publisher.

Charles D. Wright, "The Lion Standard in *Exodus*: Jewish Legend, Germanic Tradition, and Christian Typology." Revised for publication in this volume; the original appeared in *Archiv für das Studium der neueren Sprachen und Literaturen* 227 (1990), 138–145. This version © 2001 the author.

Robert T. Farrell, "The Structure of the Old English *Daniel*." Reprinted from *Neuphilologische Mitteilungen* 69 (1968), 533–59, by permission of the Modern Language Society of Helsinki.

Earl R. Anderson, "Style and Theme in the Old English *Daniel*." Reprinted from *English Studies* 68 (1987), 1–23. © Swets & Zeitlinger. Used with permission.

Antonina Harbus, "Nebuchadnezzar's Dreams in the Old English *Daniel*." Reprinted from *English Studies* 75 (1994), 489–508. © Swets & Zeitlinger. Used with permission.

Ruth Wehlau, "The Power of Knowledge and the Location of the Reader in *Christ and Satan*," reprinted from *The Journal of English and Germanic Philology* 97 (1998), 1–12. © 1998 by the Board of Trustees of the University of Illinois. Used with permission of the University of Illinois Press.

List of Abbreviations

ASE   *Anglo-Saxon England*

ASPR   *Anglo-Saxon Poetic Records*, ed. G. P. Krapp and E. V. K. Dobbie, 6 vols. (New York, 1931–53)

CCSL   *Corpus Christianorum, Series Latina* (Turnhout)

CSEL   *Corpus Scriptorum Ecclesiasticorum Latinorum* (Vienna)

EEMF   *Early English Manuscripts in Facsimile* (Copenhagen)

EETS   Early English Text Society (London)

ELN   *English Language Notes*

JEGP   *Journal of English and Germanic Philology*

MÆ   *Medium Ævum*

MLN   *Modern Language Notes*

MLQ   *Modern Language Quarterly*

MP   *Modern Philology*

N&Q   *Notes & Queries*

NM   *Neuphilologische Mitteilungen*

PG   *Patrologia Graeca*, ed. J.-P. Migne, 168 vols. (Paris, 1857–68)

PL   *Patrologia Latina*, ed. J.-P. Migne, 221 vols. (Paris, 1844–64)

PMLA   *Publication of the Modern Language Association*

RES   *Review of English Studies*

SP   *Studies in Philology*

Confronting *Germania Latina*: Changing Responses to Old English Biblical Verse

JOYCE HILL

This essay first appeared in *Latin Culture and Medieval Germanic Europe. Proceedings of the First Germania Latina Conference held at the University of Groningen, 26 May 1989*, ed. Richard North and Tette Hofstra (= *Mediaevalia Groningana XI*. Groningen, 1992), 71–88.

The phrase "Germania Latina," whilst capturing the essence of what the present papers variously set out to examine—the coming together of Germanic and Latin (Christian) cultures in medieval north-west Europe—pinpoints with equal effectiveness the two extreme positions from which scholars in the nineteenth and twentieth centuries have approached the vernacular poetry of Anglo-Saxon England. What can be characterized as the "Germania approach" sees in the poetry, even the biblical poetry, the survival of the essential Germanic spirit, evidenced in vocabulary, formulaic structures, verse form, and those scenes and episodes which—so the critics claim—testify to the heroic ethos of the Anglo-Saxons. The "Latina approach" by contrast, in its most extreme form, assumes a patristic context for both poet and audience and thus advocates a pan-allegorical exegetical reading in which, to use the metaphor of Chaucer's Nun's Priest, the "fruyt" is the spiritual meaning and the poetic form merely the "chaff" which encases it. The emphasis on Germania held sway in the nineteenth and early twentieth centuries; the pan-allegorical reading, the "Latina approach" in its most exaggerated manifestation, is a product of the period after 1950. Neither stance has ever dominated to the exclusion of all others, but each has dominated in its turn sufficiently to shape the course of Old English literary schol-

1

arship, which is why each deserves consideration in this present context. What we understand as Germania Latina, as manifested in the vernacular poetry of Anglo-Saxon England, has at different times been determined not so much by the poems themselves as by the assumptions that critics have brought to bear upon them. The result is that the critics find what they seek and promote a literary-critical response pattern which, for a generation or more, prompts others to do likewise. The effect, more often than not, is that in place of enquiry critics display the "assertive certainty" which Hirsch has identified as characteristic of the critic who "has been trapped in the hermeneutic circle and has fallen victim to the self-confirmability of interpretations."[1] My purpose in the brief compass of this paper is to attempt to understand and to characterize the two major "hermeneutic circles" that have dominated the reading of Old English poetry in modern times and to identify some of the approaches which, in recent decades, have begun to establish the bases for a more sensitive and balanced response, a response which I hope will further our understanding of the fusion of Germanic and Christian cultures in Anglo-Saxon England.

Beowulf would be as good a basis for the discussion as biblical poetry, the elegies as satisfactory as the verse saints' lives. But since the limitation of space requires a firm focus, I shall concentrate on the biblical poems which make up the Junius manuscript. The work done on these poems illustrates my theme very clearly and, above all, their survival as a collection making up one single codex allows me, in the generally contextless world of anonymous and undatable Old English poetry, to consider finally how clues to a reading of the poems may be gleaned from the context provided by the manuscript itself.

MS Junius XI, now in the Bodleian Library Oxford, is datable palaeographically to the first half of the eleventh century.[2] It is one of the four major codices of Old English verse and, in common with the other codices, is an anthology of works by different authors of different dates. All the poems in it are thus copies. The first poem, the longest extant in Old English after *Beowulf*, is *Genesis*, which is made up of two texts: *Genesis A* and, embedded in it at lines 235–851, *Genesis B*, which is a translation into Old English of an Old Saxon original. *Genesis B* presents at length an imaginative account of the Fall of the Angels and an account of the Fall of Man; *Genesis A* deals more briefly with the Fall of the Angels and then works through the book of Genesis as far as Abraham and Isaac, but it has lost much of its description of the Fall of Man, hence no doubt the incorporation of the *Genesis B* material. The second poem, *Exodus*, treats only chapters 13 and 14 of the Old Testament book, although of course it alludes to material beyond this; it is thus concerned principally with the escape from Egypt, the wanderings in the desert, and the crossing of the Red Sea. The third poem, *Daniel*, utilizes material from Daniel chapters 1–4, ending with Belshazzar's Feast; it is probable that the ending of *Daniel* has been lost, although not all scholars agree on this point.[3] Last comes a text which is given one title by modern scholars, *Christ and Satan*, although it is debatable whether it is one poem or three; certainly it falls into three parts: the Laments of the Fallen Angels, Crucifixion to Last Judgment, and the Temptation of Christ.[4] At the end *of Christ and Satan* (229) the scribe has written "FINIT LIBER .II. AMEN." As a result scholars have questioned whether the supposedly missing end of *Daniel* has a corresponding note, "FINIT LIBER .I." This detail, important though it is, will necessarily remain a matter for dispute, but the note following *Christ and Satan* has prompted discussion about what the recognition of separate books within the codex tells us about the history of the compilation of the manuscript, the intention of the compiler of the codex as it now stands, the purpose for which the anthology was made, and consequently the way in which the contents may have been read, at least in the eleventh century in this anthology form.[5] These are issues to which I shall return below. Here, in concluding the survey of the manuscript, there are two more basic points that need to be made. Firstly, it is a high-status anthology, being elaborately illustrated—uniquely of Old English poetic manuscripts—by ambitious line drawings handsomely laid out, although in fact the sequence was not completed. Secondly, although usually referred to now as the Junius manuscript, as catalogued in the Bodleian in honour of the famous Dutch scholar who first published its contents in Amsterdam in 1654, it has for long been known as the Cædmon manuscript, a title based on the now discredited supposition that the poems were the compositions of the cowherd Cædmon, whose miracle is recorded in Bede's *Historia ecclesiastica*.

The poems were first published, as noted, above, in 1654. But it was not until the nineteenth century that the corpus of Old English poetry began to be studied systematically for philological and literary critical purposes, and this study then flourished at first more in Germany than in the English-speaking world. The development of this early phase, dominated by the "Germania approach," was well documented twenty-five years ago by Eric Stanley, in a series of articles in *Notes and Queries* entitled "The Search for Anglo-Saxon Paganism."[6] From this ample stock of quotations I cite that by Greverus in 1848 as an example of the prevailing cast of mind:

> ... the form in which it [*sc.* Anglo-Saxon poetry] is presented is rough indeed, yet full of primitive strength, even though it has been muddied and weakened by the influence of Christian clerics, and been deprived of its magnificence and of its pagan soundness to the core.[7]

Stanley characterizes the Germanic bias as "a prejudice which turned into a predilection."[8] The circumstances which gave rise to it were largely extratextual. It was the era of foundation work in philological study, which in some respects tended to emphasize the common Germanic antecedents on a linguistic level, thus foreshortening the passage of time and so encouraging a response to the meaning and connotation of word and phrase which depended on recognition of their putative early Germanic pre-Christian significance, rather than a recognition of possible semantic shifts over centuries, including possible specialization within a given language.[9] More obviously, perhaps, the bias of Germania was fostered by the upsurge of Germanic nationalism in which national identity was in part established by reference to the Germanic past, a past which could be held to be "pure" only to the extent that it was not influenced by the Mediterranean world. Old English poetry came into the calculation, as did Old Norse, for various complex reasons, chief among them being that greater Germania provided a better counterweight to the Mediterranean world than Germany could do alone, and because, with insufficient suitable material surviving in Old High German and Old Saxon, it was necessary to lay claim to the underlying traditions of Germania by penetrating what was thought to be the more productive materials in these cognate languages.

The effects on Old English literary scholarship were profound and long-lasting. Philological research of the kind that I have mentioned was energetically pursued and generated a confidence that poems could be dated which, given the predispositions of the time, usually turned out to be relatively early, a confidence that has since been thoroughly undermined.[10] It was firmly held then, however, and helped to sustain an apparently logical framework which conditioned the response to Old English Christian poetry. The sustaining logic, not usually spelled out, seems to have been: if early, then not long postconversion; if not long postconversion, then uneducated and naive; if naive, then not worth taking too seriously. And so the poems could be dismissed, as they frequently were, as at best dull paraphrases, deserving of comment only for a few passages, which critic after critic cites as evidence of a persistent Germanic spirit surfacing in defiance of the Christian subject matter.[11] The effusively condescending and partial remarks made by George K. Anderson in *The Literature of the Anglo-Saxons*, published in 1949 and reissued in a revised edition in 1966, demonstrates that the attitude was still finding expression well into the present century.[12] Anderson's position is not so very different from that of Francis Blackburn, who, in 1907, attempted to win over the readers of his student edition of *Exodus* and *Daniel* by declaring in a devastatingly patronizing tone:

> The audience for which the poet sang was different [*sc.* from the audience of 1907]. Would not our estimate be greatly changed if we could bring to these stories, as men did then, the interest and curiosity of children?[13]

It is hardly surprising, then, that *Beowulf*, *Widsið*, and the fragmentary remains of *Waldere* and *Finnsburh* attracted more investigative and editorial attention than the supposedly naive and inept religious epics. Their legends, their underlying myths, their heroic code, were minutely examined and intricately related to the legends, myths, and heroic code of the Germanic world at large, and along with this research came editions and commentary. By comparison the religious epics were neglected and the assumption that there was nothing much to say about them became largely self-perpetuating. It was not until 1978 that Doane produced the first full-scale critical edition of *Genesis A*;[14] *Exodus* was first given a critical edition by Edward B. Irving in 1953,[15] *Daniel* by R. T. Farrell in 1974.[16] *Christ and Satan*, always the odd one out in the codex, was provided with a critical edition by Clubb somewhat earlier, in 1925. But the greater attention given to these poems in present times has generated another edition, by Finnegan, published in 1977, and a book-length, would-be edition by Sleeth in 1982.[17] The high level of interest in *Exodus* has also stimulated a further edition, that by Lucas published in

1977,[18] and a reconsideration by Irving, who has responded to the changing critical climate by publishing accounts of his new thinking in articles in *Anglia* in 1972 and in the John C. Pope festschrift in 1974.[19]

The biblical poems are obviously catching up, but the fact that they have lagged so far behind for so long has had an adverse effect not simply on our appreciation of them, which needs rounded critical editions, but also on our understanding of the vernacular poets' responses to the meeting of the two cultures of Germania and Latina. The publication of these editions is both a response to new critical enquiry conducted in other publications, and a stimulation for further enquiry within a broadly similar tradition, so that the cycle of scholarly activity which I have already pointed to in respect of heroic poetry is now repeated for major poems in the Christian tradition. But it is a repetition with a difference, since the emphasis is now on "Latina" rather than "Germania."

What, then, has produced this shift of interest? The cynic might offer the unflattering reason that it is because the biblical poems, along with a number of other Christian texts, constituted the sole remaining "new territory" in the limited surviving corpus, so that critics were driven rather than drawn to them. If there is a grain of truth in such an explanation, it does not, of course, invalidate the work done, nor diminish the need for it to be done, if the extant corpus is to be properly understood. And alongside it other more positive reasons can readily be brought forward. To a very large extent the shift reflects important developments in related fields of study, which show the impact of the church on Anglo-Saxon society, the intellectual and religious influences to which the Anglo-Saxons responded, their standards of learning, and the books available, whilst increasing study of the corpus of mostly ecclesiastical vernacular prose has also shifted the emphasis away from preoccupations with Germanic elements, and has enabled critics to see the extant poetry in a wider literary perspective.

For some critics, although in fairness it should be noted that it is not true of all, the approach to Old English poetry through Christian, specifically patristic, traditions provided a new set of certainties, and these, whilst ideologically opposed to those of the earlier "Germania" approach, parallel them in many respects. Both sets of assertive certainties, for example, confidently bring to bear upon a given text a body of extratextual assumptions which tend to generate a self-confirming reading, and both operate on the basis of what Stanley B. Greenfield has castigated as "the fallacy of homogeneity,"[20] by which all Old English poems are regarded as being fundamentally the same in cultural orientation, inspiration, and intent, either by design or by accident.[21] For the Germania-orientated critics of the nineteenth and early twentieth centuries this was not always made explicit, but for the patristic-orientated critics of the pan-allegorical school,[22] determinedly pursuing a Latin-based reading of the Old English poetic corpus, the assumption of intellectual and inspirational homogeneity is made explicit, since it is central to their argument.

This method of reading medieval literary texts is not confined to Old English poetry, but the development of this approach in the Old English field, led by B. F. Huppé, matches chronologically its development elsewhere.[23] Huppé's chief publications have been *Doctrine and Poetry: Augustine's Influence on Old English Poetry* (New York, 1959), which deals—albeit lopsidedly—with the poems of the Junius manuscript,[24] *The Web of Words: Structural Analyses of the Old English Poems Vainglory, The Wonder of Creation, The Dream of the Rood, and Judith* (Albany, 1970), and the *Hero in the Earthly City: A Reading of Beowulf* (Binghamton, 1984).[25] One may add to these, of course, numerous articles by Huppé and others, and several books, of which perhaps one of the weightiest has been Margaret Goldsmith's *The Mode and Meaning of "Beowulf"* (London, 1970).

The foundations upon which Huppé builds his interpretative process, as he explains in *Doctrine and Poetry*, are Augustine's pronouncements upon the reading of Scripture in *De Doctrina Christiana* and his comments on the way in which non-Scriptural writings, including pagan and secular literature, may reveal Christian truths, most usually if read figuratively from the predetermined Christian stance. Huppé believes that this constitutes a poetic theory and, in tracing the persistence of the Augustinian tradition through such medieval writers as Isidore, Vergil of Toulouse, Bede, Alcuin, Rabanus, and Scotus Erigena, he seeks to demonstrate that the early Middle Ages had a well-developed and widely disseminated theory of composition and reading, which, as far as non-Scriptural texts were concerned, alluded in hidden or not so hidden ways to the teachings of the church, and whose meanings could be laid bare by the same processes of essentially allegorical exegesis which were used to penetrate the Scriptural canon. To the extent that these assumptions are sustained by what is felt to be an inescapable logical framework, we may point once again to a methodological, although not ideological, parallelism with the Germania-oriented critics. In the present case the logic runs something like this: If the poems are written (sometimes even demonstrably derived from texts circulating in written form), they must be the product of the literate element in society; the literate element is made up of professional churchmen, who are heirs to the patristic tradition; such men are not going to produce or allow to be copied poems which run counter to their own ideologies and thought processes. And so we find that this logic not only leads to the theory of homogeneity within the Old English poetic corpus, which is what Stanley Greenfield was referring to when he used the phrase "the fallacy of homogeneity," but that it leads also to an assumption of a much more wide-ranging homogeneity, namely that there is a fundamental homogeneity between the vernacular poetry of Anglo-Saxon England (seen as homogeneous within itself) and the Latin, essentially patristic, traditions of the medieval church.

Stanley Greenfield, in *The Interpretation of Old English Poems*, published in 1972, argued effectively against the assumption of homogeneity and cited Hirsch, from whom I have also quoted, in drawing attention to the danger of operating within a hermeneutic circle. As Greenfield notes:

> It is not sufficient for an interpreter to say "Look, here is a similar passage from the Bible or one of the Fathers" and then build a superstructure of interpretation upon this precarious foundation.[26]

Yet, as he demonstrates, that is frequently what Huppé, Goldsmith, and others actually do. Rather, Greenfield argues, the critic should first take care to establish what constitutes valid interpretation, given the historical context.

D. W. Robertson, writing chiefly on Middle English, Bernard Huppé, and others argue, of course, that this is precisely what they are doing: identifying the contemporary perspective and using it to compose valid criticism.[27] But the self-contained nature of their identification and its application is evident, and their apparently logical assumptions which generate their assertive certainties are open to challenge on several fronts. In his various books Huppé fails to demonstrate, for example, that all literate Anglo-Saxons could match Bede's familiarity with the

Augustinian tradition, nor does he demonstrate that vernacular poets had access to or familiarity with the enormously wide range of Latin works upon which his exegetical interpretations of the poems depend. And if one may well feel doubtful about the poets, there must be greater doubt about the audiences, even allowing for the fact that one needs to know less to interpret an allusive poem than to compose it. Above all, he does not demonstrate that Augustine's statements actually constitute a poetic theory applicable to vernacular poetry. We do well to remember, in any case, that this tradition was not the only one which commented upon the literary process, for, as Philip Rollinson pointed out in 1970,[28] Isidore had clearly developed theories about different kinds of literature, naturally including Scripture (for which his position was Augustinian), but ranging also from history to fiction and fables, with many subdistinctions, and these, as Rollinson observes, perfectly well accommodate the variety of surviving Old English poetry, without the need to subject it all to the reductive processes of *allegorosis.*

The pan-allegorical school is, of course, the extreme manifestation of the shift to the Christian (Latina) approach to Old English poetry, and there have always been those who have opposed it even whilst they have been responsive to the growing understanding of the place that Old English poetry has within the Christian culture of Anglo-Saxon England, just as there were those who, in earlier generations, did not dismiss the Christian dimension out of hand as being irrelevant or naively represented.

As early as 1912, for example, at a time when F. W. Blackburn was being so patronizing about *Exodus* and *Daniel*, J. W. Bright argued that *Exodus* owed its inspiration to the liturgical calendar and that its sources were the Old Testament lections for Holy Saturday, read for their typological significance.[29] Not surprisingly, perhaps, given the climate of opinion of the time, this suggestion was not systematically investigated. But by the middle of this century things had changed. In 1960 Cross and Tucker, for example, had argued that a typological reading was signaled by the poet of *Exodus*,[30] and in 1968, in his essay on "Scriptural Poetry," Geoffrey Shepherd felt confident enough to argue that, since there was an obvious correspondence of subject matter between all the Old Testament poems of Junius XI and the Holy Saturday readings, there could be "little doubt that MS Junius 11 is to be related to the lectionary of the Anglo-Saxon church."[31] Bright's tentative suggestion regarding *Exodus*, which had not been taken up in 1912, had been extended to the other poems by M.-M. Larès in 1964,[32] and the suggestion that there is a liturgical rationale in the codex now tends to be expressed in surveys of the poetry.[33] In fact neither Bright nor Larès is quite accurate enough liturgically for their arguments to be accepted precisely as they stand, nor do they amount to proof that the liturgy is the actual source, either for *Exodus* or for the whole sequence of Old Testament material in the Junius manuscript.[34] But this angle of approach has had two valuable results: It has stimulated the identification of details within the texts which reveal typological awareness on the part of the poets—executed in different ways and with varying effect in the three Old Testament poems, but present in them all; and it has encouraged consideration of the manuscript itself as an interpretative reading context for the poems, at least for those who encountered the poems in this anthology form in the eleventh century.

Typology, unlike allegory, is based on historical correspondences and is thus related to the Bible's own historical emphasis. Recognition of this as the figurative dimension does not lead, as an allegorical reading often does, to the dismissal of those often expansive passages in the Old English biblical poems which present a vivid, often culturally adjusted realization of a particular event, nor does such a reading require a minutely detailed exegesis derived from a wide range of Latin scholarship, for the typological correspondences are relatively simple and were, moreover, more readily accessible to the potential audience for vernacular poems than the intricate details of patristic exegesis.[35]

Close attention to the texts themselves has led to other discoveries: that the biblical poems show a detailed familiarity with the Bible far beyond the portions of Scripture that they are ostensibly paraphrasing; that they present their particular events in the context of an understanding of God's plan for mankind; that they each have, again in various ways and to varying degrees, an exemplary moral dimension, concerned with the conflict of good and evil, obedience and disobedience, pride and humility—an exemplary dimension that embraces *Christ and Satan* as well as the Old Testament poems, and compatible not so much with an allegorical interpretation as with an historical and typological one. There has emerged, too, a sense of the positive identity of each as a unique poetic creation, different even in the execution of those elements that they seem to share, and different also in style, even within the confines of a common Old English verse form.[36] Thus scholars are increasingly confident that these poems stand firmly within the Christian tradition, to which they respond in ways that are seen to be sophisticated, not naive, although it is noticeable that most critics sustain this confidence without recourse to the assertive certainty of homogeneity, which a sensitive examination of the poems dispels, and also without recourse to the once well-established certainties about early date, etymological word meanings, and the equation between formulaic verse structure and non-literate composition, which have all been called into question, if not thoroughly undermined, since the mid-century.[37]

If, however, a healthy degree of uncertainty has established itself, as a corrective to the two tightly drawn hermeneutic circles that I have characterized earlier, there is one new certainty that has emerged: a certainty that the manuscript itself is a form of evidence. Not, of course, that Junius XI can provide evidence of the intention of each of the poets, or of the way in which the original audiences received the respective poems, whenever, wherever, and for whoever they were written, but that the manuscript can be indicative of the intention of the compiler and of the way that he at least read the poems and intended them to be read. Investigation of this point is not simply a matter of detecting a rationale in the organization of the manuscript's subject-matter, although it is partly that; it is also, as Barbara Raw has shown in two masterly studies published in *Anglo-Saxon England*, volumes 5 and 13, a matter of investigating the manuscript as an artefact.[38] Her analyses both of the illustrations and of the manuscript's construction show that there was an illustrated text of the Old Saxon *Genesis* available in England, from which the Junius manuscript's illustrations were copied and from which, therefore, it was possible for someone to choose to translate a suitable passage to make good a copy of the Old English *Genesis* (*Genesis A*), which had lost its description of the Fall of Man,[39] and that *Christ and Satan*, the "Liber .II.," although not part of the compiler's original plan, was not a separate manuscript added to the manuscript of Old Testament poems, as some have thought, but became part of the compiler's revised plan very early on, and was copied for the most part on vellum already prepared for the last gathering of the original manuscript before the manuscript was sewn and bound for the first time.[40] She is able to show that the end of *Daniel* is missing, thus making more concrete the possibility that there was a terminating note, "FINIT LIBER .I.," corresponding to the "FINIT LIBER .II." note after *Christ and Satan*. If, in addition, we take account of the fact that the manuscript throughout has numbered divisions which are sequential (where they occur) and that, as Thornley has shown,[41] it is carefully punctuated for recitation, as if it is a liturgical manuscript, we can reasonably conjecture that, at the time of its compilation at least, the poems were brought together for reading aloud in a formal ecclesiastical context.[42] And we can thus also deduce that there was at least a moment in time, in the early eleventh century, when some Anglo-Saxons read these poems as an interlocking scheme, one which could be perceived morally (tracing the patterns of disobedience and obedience which shape the sequence of fall and redemption), typologically (with the Old Testament material of the first book anticipating the more directly presented redemptive patterns of the second), liturgically (in the echo of Lenten, Passiontide, and Easter texts), and as an epitome of Christian history, which Hall proposes as the generic model for the manuscript's compilation.[43]

Yet, if this is a certainty, it is a certainty based on what we can know and to some extent can test; it is not the apparent certainty of what we wish to assert. Different in kind from Raw's manuscript analysis but having a similar validity and usefulness are two studies published recently in *Anglo-Saxon England*, one by Alfred Bammesberger which shows how corruptions in the texts of *Genesis* and *Exodus* were caused by the scribal incorporation of marginalia,[44] and the other by Paul Remley, which is able to demonstrate what version of the book of Genesis the poet of *Genesis A* used.[45] These studies, like the work on the manuscript itself, proceed by examining what is actually there for us to examine, and they produce genuine advances in knowledge, not simply about the poems themselves, but also about the Christian culture of Anglo-Saxon England and the poems' place within that culture. It is work of this kind which allows us to move forward and which, in recognizing both the possibilities and the limitations of the evidence, constitutes the only sound basis for the scholar's confrontation with Germania Latina.

NOTES

1. E. D. Hirsch, Jr., *Validity in Interpretation* (New Haven and London, 1967), 166.
2. For a complete facsimile of Junius XI, see *The Cædmon Manuscript of Anglo-Saxon Biblical Poetry, Junius XI in the Bodleian Library*, ed. Israel

Gollancz (Oxford, 1927). For a summary description, see N. R. Ker, *Catalogue of Manuscripts Containing Anglo-Saxon* (Oxford, 1957), 406–8. The codex as it stands was compiled over a period beginning perhaps *ca.* 1000 and being completed (insofar as it is complete) in the second quarter of the century. Scholars of art history and of the written texts are not in agreement among themselves or with each other about whether a more precise dating is possible and, if so, what that date might be.

3. R. T. Farrell, in his edition *of Daniel and Azarias* (London, 1974), argued forcefully that the extant text of *Daniel* is complete. Ker, in his *Catalogue of Manuscripts*, 407, had argued that it was not. The case for a lost ending has since been developed by Hall, Lucas, and Raw, whose varied but complementary evidence seems conclusive: J. R. Hall, "The Old English Epic of Redemption: the Theological Unity of MS Junius 11," *Traditio* 32 (1976), 185–208, at 186 [reprinted in the present volume]; P. J. Lucas, "On the Incomplete Ending of *Daniel* and the Addition of *Christ and Satan* to MS Junius 11," *Anglia* 97 (1979), 46–59, at 52; B. Raw, "The Construction of Oxford, Dodleian Library, Junius 11," *Anglo-Saxon England* 13 (1984), 187–207.

4. The three major studies of *Christ and Satan* review and develop the debate about the poem's unity: *Christ and Satan: An Old English Poem*, ed. M. D. Clubb, Yale Studies in English 70 (New Haven, 1925); R. E. Finnegan, ed., *Christ and Satan: A Critical Edition* (Waterloo, Ontario, 1977); C. R. Sleeth, *Studies in "Christ and Satan"* (Toronto, 1982).

5. G. P. Krapp, in his edition of *The Junius Manuscript*, ASPR 1 (New York, 1931), thought that "the conclusion of DANIEL, now missing in the manuscript, ended with *Finit* or some other indication that the original design or instructions of the copyist had been carried out. GENESIS, EXODUS, and DANIEL would thus have constituted Liber I in the eyes of the person who added CHRIST AND SATAN, and who called his addition Liber II" (xii). G. Shepherd, in his essay on "Scriptural Poetry" in *Continuations and Beginnings: Studies in Old English Literature*, ed. E. G. Stanley (London, 1966), 1–36, believes that "a rubric concluding Book I occurred but has been lost at the end of *Daniel*" (33) and argues for a reading of the manuscript as a whole in such a way that this detail is significant in directing attention to an ecclesiastical rationale. J. R. Hall, "The Old English Epic of Redemption," 185–7, is firmer still. Farrell, however, in his edition of *Daniel and Azarias*, believes that nothing is missing from the end of *Daniel*, that it is "quite possible that the scribe of the first three poems never considered his work a 'first' book" (33), and that "the notation at the end of *Christ and Satan* may represent only the viewpoint of one of the

scribes who copied this added text, as he completed it" (32–3). Even if Farrell is right, however, the existing scribal note tells us something about how the collection was understood by at least one Anglo-Saxon who, in recording his response, prompted others to view the collection likewise.

6. E. G. Stanley, "The Search for Anglo-Saxon Paganism," *Notes and Queries* 209 (1964), 204–9, 242–50, 282–7, 324–31, 455–63; 210 (1965), 9–17, 203–7, 285–93, 322–7. Reprinted with corrections, indices etc. as a monograph, *The Search for Anglo-Saxon Paganism* (Cambridge and Totowa, 1975). References here are to the 1975 monograph.

7. Ibid., 32. The translation is Stanley's. The German original, with bibliographical details, is given in 126 n. 87.

8. Ibid., 122.

9. Stanley devotes a large part of his study to this predilection for seizing upon the putative early Germanic pre-Christian significances and treating them as if they remain unchanged throughout the Anglo-Saxon period. The instance that he deals with most fully is *wyrd*, showing finally that scholars now appreciate that the word underwent a major semantic shift. The work of the Dictionary of Old English in Toronto has made modern scholars aware of nuances of meaning and of semantic shift, and the Dictionary's *Microfiche Concordance to Old English*, compiled by A. diPaolo Healey and R. L. Venezky (Toronto, 1980), provides evidence for word usage on a scale far beyond anything available earlier. As noteworthy examples of sensitive modern semantic analysis, one may cite H. Schabram, *Superbia: Studien zum altenglischen Wortschatz* (Munich, 1965); and D. H. Green, *The Carolingian Lord: Semantic Studies on Four Old High German Words* (Cambridge, 1965). This last, despite its title, has much to say about shifts in the usage of words for "lord" in Old English as well as in Old High German, since Green makes extensive use of cognate languages (thus showing how, in contrast to some of earlier word studies, cognates can help refine the identification of variations of meaning in place and time). An invaluable starting point for investigating the development of word study is A. Cameron, A. Kingsmill, and A. C. Amos, *Old English Word Studies: A Preliminary Author and Word Index* (Toronto, 1983).

10. The presence in poems of what appear to be early or non-West-Saxon forms are recognized now as being characteristics of a literary *koiné*, rather than sure indicators of original date and place; see K. Sisam, *Studies in the History of Old English Literature* (Oxford, 1953). The difficulty of arguing for date on the basis of linguistic forms is made abundantly clear by A. C. Amos, *Linguistic Means of Determining the Dates of Old English Literary Texts* (Cambridge, MA, 1980).

11. The most frequently cited passages in the Junius manuscript poems are

the war of the kings in *Genesis* (1960–2095) and the destruction of Pharaoh's army in *Exodus* (447–81). Satan's lament in *Genesis B* is also often commented upon, to the exclusion of the rest of the poem, but this is as much to draw a parallel with Milton's Satan as to highlight the Germanic sentiments.

12. G. K. Anderson, *The Literature of the Anglo-Saxons* (Princeton, 1949; rev. 1966), 112–23. It should be clear that I cite Anderson because he perpetuates what most scholars now consider to be an outdated and unacceptable point of view. Of course I do not mean to suggest that the investigation of the Germanic dimension in the early literature of northwest Europe is in itself an unprofitable undertaking; on the contrary, much can be learnt when the investigations are sensitively carried out in a genuine spirit of enquiry, as is illustrated elsewhere in this volume.

13. *Exodus and Daniel*, ed. F. A. Blackburn (Boston, 1907), xxii.

14. *Genesis: A New Edition*, ed. A. N. Doane (Madison, 1978).

15. *The Old English Exodus*, ed. E. B. Irving, Jr. (New Haven, 1953).

16. See note 3.

17. For Clubb, Finnegan, and Sleeth, see note 4.

18. *Exodus*, ed. P. J. Lucas (London, 1977).

19. E. B. Irving, Jr., "New Notes on the Old English Exodus," *Anglia* 90 (1972), 290–324; E. B. Irving, Jr., "Exodus Retraced," *Old English Studies in Honour of John C. Pope*, ed. R. B. Burlin and E. B. Irving, Jr. (Toronto, 1974), 203–23. Another telling sign of the modern interest in this poem is the recent publication, notwithstanding the editions of Irving and Lucas, of *The Old English "Exodus": Text, Translation, and Commentary*, by J. R. R. Tolkien, ed. Joan Turville-Petre (Oxford, 1981), which presents material prepared by Tolkien for a series of lectures delivered to a specialist class in the 1930s and 1940s.

20. S. B. Greenfield, *The Interpretation of Old English Poems* (London and Boston, 1972), 9.

21. For the scholars of the pan-allegorical school the homogeneity exists principally by design, since the poets knowingly conform to patristic patterns of interpretation. For nineteenth- and early-twentieth-century scholars of the Germanic school, however, the homogeneity was assumed to be the result of the accident of place and time.

22. The name "pan-allegorical school" was first applied to the critical tradition under discussion by Charles Donahue in *Critical Approaches to Medieval Literature: Selected Papers from the English Institute, 1958–1959*, ed. with a foreword by D. Bethurum (New York, 1960), 61, in the course of his "Summation" (61–82) to the published debate between E. T. Donaldson and R. E. Kaske on "Patristic Exegesis in the Criticism of

Medieval Literature," a critical approach that, although still novel, was already making a dramatic impact, to the satisfaction of some and unease of others.

23. For Middle English literature, as for Old, the tradition of patristic interpretations begins in the 1950s, and it is with the impact of this tradition on Middle English literature that the debate noted above is principally concerned. Two of the chief publications in this field were D. W. Robertson and B. F. Huppé, *Piers Plowman and Scriptural Tradition* (Princeton, 1951), and D. W. Robertson, *Preface to Chaucer* (Princeton, 1953). Early articles exploiting and debating this tradition are noted in *Critical Approaches*, cited in note 22.

24. B. F. Huppé, *Doctrine and Poetry: Augustine's Influence on Old English Poetry* (New York, 1959). Despite the wide-ranging title, Huppé deals only with Cædmon's *Hymn* and the Junius poems. Cædmon's *Hymn* (9 lines) is discussed on 99–130; *Genesis A* on 131–216; and *Exodus*, *Daniel*, and *Christ and Satan* in the course of his concluding "Conjectures," 217–39.

25. Huppé is not alone in using his own translation as a basis for interpretation, but his book on *Beowulf* is a particularly clear example of how such a method intensifies the "hermeneutic circle" and virtually guarantees the "self-confirmability" of his reading of the poem. For discussion and illustration, see my review, *Anglia* 105 (1987), 136–40.

26. S. B. Greenfield, *The Interpretation of Old English Poems*, 23. See also M. Alexander, *Old English Literature* (London, 1983), 104: "Yet it is often difficult to assess the propriety of a particular allegorical interpretation, since by its nature allegory asserts the primacy of a level of meaning which is hidden and to some extent arbitrary."

27. D. W. Robertson argues in general terms for reading literature from a historical perspective in "Some Observations on Method in Literary Studies," *New Literary History* 1 (1969), 21–33. Greenfield, in *The Interpretation of Old English Poems*, 4–5, quotes from pp. 30–1 of Robertson's argument, noting with approval the insistence on historically valid criteria, but he goes on to comment: "Yet it is not so easy, as we shall see, to arrive at a consensus as to the realities of the past which are appropriate and valid for the specific work under analysis" (5).

28. P. Rollinson, "Some Kinds of Meaning in Old English Poetry," *Annuale Mediaevale* 11 (1970), 5–21.

29. J. W. Bright, "The Relation of the Cædmonian Exodus to the Liturgy," *Modern Language Notes* 27 (1912), 97–103.

30. J. E. Cross and S. I. Tucker, "Allegorical Tradition and the Old English *Exodus*," *Neophilologus* 44 (1960), 122–7.

31. G. Shepherd, "Scriptural Poetry," *Continuations and Beginnings*, ed. Stanley, 24.

32. M. -M. Larès, "Échos d'un rite hiérosolymitain dans un manuscrit du Haut Moyen Âge anglais," *Revue de l'histoire des religions* 165 (1964), 13–47. It is worth noting that Bright's ideas were referred to by some scholars in the 1940s and 1950s, thus preparing the ground for the acceptance of liturgical influence and for the new investigations referred to in this paper. See, for example, the approving comments by C. W. Kennedy, *The Earliest English Poetry* (Oxford, 1943; repr. with a new foreword by James P. Pettegrove, Totowa and London, 1971), 177–80, and *Early English Christian Poetry* (London, 1952), 15–16. For a more measured consideration of Bright's hypothesis at this time, see *Exodus*, ed. Irving, 14–15.

33. For example, C. L. Wrenn, *A Study of Old English Literature* (London, 1967), 103–4; T. A. Shippey, *Old English Verse* (London, 1972), 137; S. A. J. Bradley, *Anglo-Saxon Poetry* (London, 1982), 10. Since Bradley's volume was commissioned to replace the earlier Everyman Library collection of translations by R. K. Gordon, *Anglo-Saxon Poetry* (London, 1926, rev. 1954), it is instructive to compare Bradley's comments on the Junius manuscript poems with those by Gordon.

34. See the caveats brought forward by Irving in his edition of *Exodus*, 14–15, "Exodus Retraced," 205–6; by Lucas in his edition of *Exodus*, 59–60; and by Hall, "The Old English Epic of Redemption," 187–9.

35. Critics have consistently commented on the concrete realizations of the Junius manuscript poets, which, as T. A. Shippey notes in *Old English Verse*, 140, distinguish them from those medieval minds for whom "Scriptural history no longer possessed 'any reality . . . only signification.' " It is a characteristic which some will see as harmonizing more with typology, firmly rooted in the reality of the historical event, than with patristic allegory, which tends to give priority to the signification. On the value of typology as a basis for reading *Exodus*, see Irving, "Exodus Retraced," 209–20, in the course of which Irving coins the useful phrase "heroic typology" (216). On typology and allegory in general, as well as in relation to this poem, see also *Exodus*, ed. Lucas, 55–9.

36. Ample evidence in support of these generalizations is to be found in the editions and studies of the Junius poems so far cited. To these should be added E. R. Anderson, "Style and Theme in the Old English *Daniel*," *English Studies* 68 (1987), 1–23 [reprinted in the present volume]. Other articles dealing with details in the texts have contributed greatly in recent decades to our understanding of the Junius manuscript poems; see S. B. Greenfield and F. C. Robinson, *A Bibliography of Publications on Old*

English Literature to the End of 1972 (Manchester and Toronto, 1980) and the annual bibliography in *Anglo-Saxon England*. For a recent attempt to distinguish different poetic styles in the longer poems on "scientific" grounds, see D. Donoghue, *Style in Old English Poetry: The Test of the Auxiliary* (New Haven, 1987).

37. For dating, see note 10; for word-meanings, see note 9. The equation between formulaic verse structure and nonliterate compositions, which if true would have profound implications for our understanding of Old English Christian poetry, bas been systematically undermined by A. C. Watts, *The Lyre and Harp: A Comparative Reconsideration of Oral Tradition in Homer and Old English Epic Poetry* (New Haven, 1969).

38. B. Raw, "The probable derivation of most of the illustrations in Junius 11 from an illustrated Old Saxon *Genesis*," *Anglo-Saxon England* 5 (1976), 133–48; "The construction of Oxford, Bodleian Library, Junius 11," *Anglo-Saxon England* 13 (1984), 187–207.

39. Gollancz, *Cædmon Manuscript*, liii, had suggested that *Genesis B* was first added to *Genesis A* in the present manuscript. The argument was further developed by B. J. Timmer in his edition of *The Later Genesis* (Oxford, 1948), 14–15. The second of Raw's articles brings forward evidence which suggests that this view cannot be sustained.

40. In the second of her articles, Raw further supports her argument for the planned inclusion of *Christ and Satan* by bringing forward evidence that space was provided for at least four and probably six full-page illustrations in this poem, showing that "it was intended to resemble the other poems in the manuscript in decorative appearance," a fact which "supports the view that it was copied into the manuscript as a continuation of the three Old Testament poems rather than being bound in after a separate existence" (196). For the argument that *Christ and Satan* was originally a separate manuscript, see Lucas, "On the Incomplete Ending of *Daniel* and the Addition of *Christ and Satan* to MS Junius 11," 52.

41. G. C. Thornley, "The Accents and Points of MS Junius 11," *Transactions of the Philological Society* (1954), 178–201, with a "Note on Dr Thornley's Article" by J. R. Firth, 201–3, and a bibliography, 203–5.

42. The provenance of the manuscript is not certain, but it is most likely to be Canterbury, probably Christ Church. This is the traditional assignation, on stylistic grounds, and because it fits the entry of "Genesis anglice depicta" in Prior Eastry's early-fourteenth-century catalogue. Lucas, however, in his 1977 edition of *Exodus*, 1–6, argued for Malmesbury Abbey. This was firmly rejected by R. Thomas, "Identifiable books from the pre-Conquest library of Malmesbury Abbey," *Anglo-Saxon England* 10 (1982), 1–19, at

16–18, who favored the traditional provenance of Christ Church. Raw favors Canterbury for artistic reasons: "The probable derivation of most of the illustrations in Junius 11," 135–6.

43. Hall, "The Old English Epic of Redemption."

44. A Bammesberger, "Hidden glosses in manuscripts of Old English poetry," *Anglo-Saxon England* 13 (1984), 43–9.

45. P. G. Remley, "The Latin textual basis of *Genesis A*," *Anglo-Saxon England* 17 (1988), 163–89.

The Old English Epic of Redemption: The Theological Unity of MS Junius 11

J. R. HALL*

This essay first appeared in Traditio *32 (1976), 185–208. Translations in square brackets have been supplied by the editor. Updated references in square brackets in the notes have been added by the author.*

I

Anglo-Saxon scribes were compilers and organizers as well as copyists. Each major Old English literary manuscript gives evidence of editorial planning. The *Beowulf* codex was apparently designed as a collection of marvelous tales; the Vercelli Book as a collection of legendary and homiletic matter; and the first three poems of the Exeter Book (*Christ I, II,* and *III*) were arranged in proper chronological sequence.[1]

MS Junius 11 reflects a similar approach toward book making.[2] Like the *Beowulf* and Vercelli manuscripts, the volume is limited to works on the same general subject, in this case biblical material; and like the first three pieces of the Exeter Book, the poems in Junius 11 are placed according to the chronology of the scriptural history they contain. But Junius 11 differs from these other codices in that it provides special bibliographic evidence pointing to a special unity of content. The sections, or fits, of the Old Testament poems are numbered in a continuous series: *Genesis,* [I]–XLI; *Exodus,* XLII–XLVIIII; and *Daniel,* L–LV. Because such continuous enumeration otherwise occurs only in single poems—*Beowulf, Elene,* and the extant part of *Judith*—the implication is clear that the Old Testament works in Junius 11 were in a particular sense considered as a single entity.[3]

The final poem, *Christ and Satan*, is copied as a work separate from the first part of the codex. The New Testament poem does not continue the series of sectional numbers of the earlier poetry but begins its own set of twelve.[4] In addition, the colophon of the work (p. 229) reads "Finit Liber II. Amen." Since the time of Francis Junius scholars have interpreted these words to mean that the Old Testament poetry was regarded as Liber I and *Christ and Satan* as Liber II.[5] Unfortunately, the concluding folio of *Daniel* is lost, making it impossible to know for certain if there was a corresponding *explicit* to the first part of the manuscript. It does seem reasonable to assume, however, that this was the case.[6] A comparable division is found in the only complete copy of Ælfric's treatise "On the Old and New Testament," preserved in MS Bodleian Laud Misc. 509. On fol. 13lv, where Ælfric's consideration of the Old Testament concludes, the codex reads "Explicit de veteri testamento. Incipit de novo testamento."[7] The two-part division of Ælfric's treatise parallels the arrangement of the Old and New Testament poetry of Junius 11 into two books, each with its own set of numbering.

Though distinct units, Liber I and Liber II were treated as integral parts of the volume in two important respects. Textual accents are used in Junius 11 to an extent unmatched in other Old English literary manuscripts. In his meticulous study of the Junius accents, G. C. Thornley has concluded both that the same principles of accentuation are employed throughout the volume and that the accents were written as a guide to public delivery.[8] The same can be said of the metrical punctuation in the codex. Evidently inserted to assist in reading aloud, the points marking off half-verses are, as George P. Krapp notes, "used with remarkable regularity and correctness throughout the whole manuscript."[9] Statistical analysis confirms Krapp's observation. The text copied by each scribe shows a high percentage of correctly pointed hemistichs: A (pp. 1–212), 96%; B (pp. 213–15), 95%; C (pp. 216–28), 94%; D (p. 229), 95%.[10] Such consistency and excellence of metrical punctuation is unparalleled in the three other major Old English codices.[11]

The unitive bibliographic features of Junius 11 invite consideration of the volume as a special collection of scriptural poems which, like the later Middle English plays constituting a biblical cycle, were compiled and organized by an editor or editors according to a definite plan.[12] In fact, previous scholars have suggested various organizing principles for the manuscript. Though each of these suggestions is valuable, none of them provides a satisfactory solution. My purpose is to examine the question in depth and to furnish a detailed answer.

II

The majority of proposals advanced by critics to explain the compilation of Junius 11 center on the Paschal liturgy. As an hypothesis, this approach is reasonable because *Christ and Satan* in part deals with the Crucifixion, Harrowing, and Resurrection; yet the liturgical systems of Old Testament material cited by scholars to account for the contents of Liber I are inadequate to explain this part of the manuscript. T. A. Shippey refers to a resemblance between *Genesis*, *Exodus*, and *Daniel* and the readings for Holy Saturday in the Old Jerusalem tradition.[13] But of the twelve readings listed in the *Leofric Missal*, the only such ritual in this tradition known to have been present in England during the Anglo-Saxon period, only five correspond to material in Junius 11.[14] The parallel that M.-M. Larès draws between Liber I and the Old Jerusalem lections for Holy Week cannot claim even this much agreement: only eight of the more than thirty readings have counterparts in the Old English manuscript.[15] Barbara Raw notes that there is a correspondence between Liber I and certain subjects of the *Liber Responsalis* for the Sundays from Sexagesima to Easter,[16] but the subjects of five of the eight Sundays have no parallel in the Old Testament part of Junius 11. Two other scholars, Geoffrey Shepherd and C. L. Wrenn, associate Liber I with the readings of the lectionary of the Anglo-Saxon Church for the season of Septuagesima.[17] Less than half of the lectionary material, however, corresponds to that in Junius 11.[18]

The failure of these proposals to explain adequately the organization of the manuscript suggests that the principle behind the compilation, though related to the Paschal liturgy, is to be found outside the liturgy itself. The proposals of the two remaining critics do not concern the liturgy at all. Though neither critic points to a possible source or particular tradition that might have guided the Junius editor, both scholars clearly identify, in a way the previous scholars do not, what seems to me to be the controlling idea behind the compilation. Over sixty years ago Hardin Craig alluded to the question in discussing a subject mentioned above, Corpus Christi cycle drama:

It is evident that a parallel exists between the cycles of plays and the great
religious epics of the Middle Ages. The conception of an epic of redemp-
tion had long been in existence. The contents of Junian MS XI show just
the features needed to make of the drama as developed within the church
a complete cyclical presentation of man's fall and redemption.[19]

I believe that Craig is correct to identify Junius 11 as an epic of redemp-
tion and to do so without reference to the liturgy. He fails to develop the
point, however; and, buried amid a discussion of cycle drama, his state-
ment apparently has been ignored till now. Yet Alvin A. Lee has recently
made an observation similar to Craig's. In discussing the Anglo-Saxon
view of history, Lee points out that the poems in Junius 11 "set forth the
overall biblical structure" of the story of redemption.[20] Like Craig, how-
ever, Lee is only incidentally concerned with the unity of the manuscript
and does not pursue the point.

III

But evidence that Junius 11 does comprise a nonliturgical epic of
redemption is readily available. In past centuries scholars had little trou-
ble in explaining the constitution of the volume. Observing the high cor-
relation between Cædmon's topics outlined by Bede and the contents of
Junius 11, these scholars believed that the poems were a collection writ-
ten by Cædmon himself.[21] It would be hard to find a critic today who
credits Cædmon with the composition of the Junius poems; moreover,
major stylistic differences among the works seem to indicate that each
was composed by a different author.[22] Though the older scholars evi-
dently erred in their ascription, I believe that they were correct to associ-
ate Cædmon's subjects with the material in the Old English volume. The
relationship between the two sets of topics is not authorial, however, but
theological. After describing the manner in which Cædmon was granted
the art of song, Bede says that Abbess Hilda ordered the poet to be
taught the course of sacred history, *series sacrae historiae*. What Bede
means by the term is evident from his subsequent outline of the poet's
biblical themes, for Bede immediately goes on to state that Cædmon
turned what he was taught into verse:

At ipse cuncta, quae audiendo discere poterat, rememorando secum et
quasi mundum animal ruminando, in carmen dulcissimum conuertebat,

suauiusque resonando doctores suos uicissim auditores sui faciebat.
Canebat autem de creatione mundi et origine humani generis et tota Gen-
esis historia, de egressu Israel ex Aegypto et ingressu in terram repromis-
sionis, de aliis plurimis sacrae scripturae historiis, de incarnatione
dominica, passione, resurrectione et ascensione in caelum, de Spiritus
Sancti aduentu et apostolorum doctrina; item de terrore futuri iudicii et
horrore poenae gehennalis ac dulcedine regni caelestis multa carmina
faciebat.[23]

[But he held in memory all that he was able to learn by hearing, and like a
clean beast chewing the cud turned it into the sweetest and most pleasant
songs, so that his teachers became his audience. He sang of the creation of
the world and the origin of the human race and all the story of Genesis, of
the exodus of Israel from Egypt and the entry into the promised land, and
of many other stories of sacred scripture; of the incarnation of the Lord,
the passion, resurrection, and ascension into heaven, of the coming of the
Holy Spirit and the teaching of the apostles; he also made many songs
about the terror of the coming judgment and the horrible torments of hell
and the joys of the kingdom of heaven.]

The course of sacred history for Bede, then, signifies a select pattern of
scriptural events from Creation to the Last Judgment. It was in this tradi-
tion of understanding history that Cædmon was educated and in light of
which he composed, a tradition central to the theology of the Middle
Ages. As S. J. Crawford noted in 1925 in commenting on Bede's descrip-
tion of the poet's work, "it is significant that what may be termed Cæd-
mon's 'Confession of Faith' follows the order of the Classification of
Topics which was traditional in Western Europe from St. Augustine to St.
Thomas Aquinas."[24] That the material in the Junius Manuscript approxi-
mates[25] Cædmon's set of biblical subjects suggests that the course of
sacred history is the organizing principle behind the compilation.

IV

To confirm this hypothesis, it is necessary to show that the contents
of Junius 11 can actually be read as an epic of redemption. Here Bede's
list, a bare outline of sacred history and not an explanation of it, cannot
serve as a guide. The treatment of salvation history in Augustine's *De
catechizandis rudibus*, however, provides an interpretation of the
redemption which goes far in explaining the unity of the manuscript. In
addition, Augustine's survey of biblical events is closer in some ways

even than Cædmon's topics to the contents of Junius 11.[26] Significantly, Augustine's little treatise, written for a Carthaginian deacon as a guide in instructing prospective catechumens, had a profound influence on monastic education for a thousand years. According to Joseph P. Christopher, Bede and Alcuin used the treatise as a textbook.[27]

It is quite possible that the editor of Junius 11 was directly acquainted with *De catechizandis rudibus* and, within the range of his choice of material, compiled the manuscript accordingly. The importance of Augustine's work for understanding the Old English volume does not hinge upon this possibility, however. It seems reasonable to assume that an editor wishing to organize such a poetic version of salvation history would not have needed Augustine's treatise itself to guide him. The outline of redemption in *De catechizandis rudibus* was a traditional one in Anglo-Saxon England. Not only is Bede's list of Cædmon's subjects a variant of Augustine's outline,[28] but Wulfstan's Sermo 6, composed during the same period in which Junius 11 was copied, is also structured on a similar Augustinian pattern of salvation history. Like the address in *De catechizandis rudibus*, Sermo 6 was evidently written as a model to be used by priests in their instructing.[29] Wulfstan reveals no firsthand knowledge of Augustine's treatise. His homily will be important for showing that Augustine's treatment of the history of redemption may admit modifications and still retain its fundamental scope, purpose, and character.[30]

Before making a detailed comparison between the versions of salvation history in the model addresses and the contents of Junius 11, it is necessary to stress the different nature of these two types of work. As a catechism, Augustine's address has two basic components, *historia* and *theoria*. The former term refers exclusively to the narrative of God's dealings with man—sacred history proper; *theoria*, on the other hand, refers to the teacher's running explanation of these events, a blend of typological analysis, doctrinal commentary, and exhortation.[31] Though Sermo 6 shares with Augustine's discourse these two features, Wulfstan's *theoria* is much shorter and less complicated. The Anglo-Saxon homilist shows no interest in typology, and his doctrinal exegesis lacks Augustine's complexity. Despite these dissimilarities, Sermo 6 is the same kind of work as Augustine's.

The Junius poems obviously belong to a different genre. Though passages of explanation and exhortation occur in them (especially in

Christ and Satan), the poems are basically narrative, not catechetical; one would not expect to find *theoria* in them comparable to that in the model addresses. A second major difference between the material in the Old English codex and the homilies involves the question of proportion. Junius 11 is a full-length book, more than twelve times longer than Wulfstan's sermon and more than five times longer than Augustine's. Each Junius poet usually treats in rich detail the *historia* which the two homilists, because of the nature of their work, must summarize.[32] Unlike the homilists, who survey the whole course of sacred history, each poet concentrates on a limited amount of scriptural material and graphically portrays, often in epic terms, the working out of God's plan: The task of the homilists was to condense the whole; that of the poets, to detail a part. Likewise, in assembling his codex the Junius editor did not have to tailor its length to suit the conditions of a sermon meant for a single occasion.

The difference in genre between the model addresses and the Old English poems results in differences in their respective contents which make it impossible to determine for certain if the editor of Junius 11 selected and arranged the works according to the tradition of the course of sacred history begun in *De catechizandis rudibus*. A glance at the accompanying chart will show, however, that the basic narrative structure of the material in the manuscript does correspond well to the outlines of salvation history used by Augustine and Wulfstan. If the contents of Junius 11 can, in fact, be explained by the theological concepts employed by the homilists, this correspondence is more likely the product of design than chance.

V

Starting with the exhortation that men should praise God, the *Genesis A* poet alludes to the Creation of the Heavens and goes on to describe the Fall of Lucifer and the rebel angels, their infernal punishment, and the Creation of the World in six days (1–234).[33] At this point, the interpolation of *Genesis B* begins, with its own story of the revolt in heaven—which, in the context of *Genesis A*, serves as a reprise—and its famous version of the Fall of Man (235–851).[34] In perfect narrative sequence, *Genesis A* now resumes with God's discovery of the guilty pair and their expulsion from Eden (852–964).

Augustine, *De catechizandis rudibus*	Wulfstan, Sermo 6	Old English MS Junius 11
Creation	Creation	*Gen. A* 1–14, 92–168, 206–34
	Fall of Lucifer	*Gen. A* 15–91
Creation of Man	Creation of Man	*Gen. A* 169–205
Fall of Lucifer		*Gen. B* 246–441
Fall of Man	Fall of Man	*Gen. B* 235–45, 442–851, *Gen. A* 852–964
Cities of God and Man	Abel and Cain	*Gen. A* 965–1245a
Sinful World	Sinful World	*Gen. A* 1245b–84
Noah and the Flood	Noah and the Flood	*Gen. A* 1285–1554, *Ex.* 362–76
Resumption of Evil (Idolatry)	Resumption of Evil (Idolatry)	*Gen. A* 1555–1701 (Ham, Tower of Babel)
Abraham: Fatherhood	Abraham: Fatherhood	*Gen. A* 1702–2936, *Ex.* 353b–61, 377–88, 397–446
Crossing the Red Sea		*Exodus*
Mosaic Law and Journey	Mosaic Law	*Ex.* 1–7, 516–64
Paschal Lamb		cf. *Ex.* 33–53 (Tenth Plague)
Prosperity in Canaan		*Dan.* 1–16
King David	King David	cf. *Ex.* 389–96 (King Solomon)
	Corruption of Israel	*Dan.* 17–32
Captivity and Exile	Captivity and Exile	*Dan.* 33–78
Conversion of Pagan Kings		*Dan.* 79–674 (Nebuchadnezzar)
	Fall of Babylon	*Dan.* 675–764 . . .
Return to Israel	Return to Israel	Loss at end of *Daniel*?
Christ: Life	Christ: Life	*CS* 665–729 (Temptation)
Death	Death	*CS* 493–511, 545–56
	Harrowing	*CS* 365–511 (*passim*)
Resurrection	Resurrection	*CS* 512–44
Ascension	Ascension	*CS* 557–68a, 579–96
Pentecost		*CS* 668b–78
Growth of the Church		
	Antichrist	
Last Judgment	Last Judgment	*CS* 597–664
Admonition	Admonition	*CS* 1–364; cf. 665–729

Wulfstan and Augustine deal with these major events, though in different order. Wulfstan starts with the Creation of the World, continues with the crime and punishment of Lucifer, and relates the Creation and Fall of Man (24–52). Augustine, on the other hand, turns directly from the Creation of the World to that of Man, and considers the rebellion of the wicked angels in discussing Adam's Fall (18.29–30).[35] Augustine's narrative order is comparable to that of *Genesis B*, where the two Falls are directly related, with no intervening account of Creation as in *Genesis A* (Creation in six days) or in Wulfstan's sermon (Creation of Man). Also noteworthy is Augustine's teaching that God, by His nature, is eminently praiseworthy (18.30.6). This doctrine recalls the introductory lines of *Genesis A*, which, in the tradition of Cædmon's *Hymn*, contain a similar idea.

After the poet describes the consequences of Adam's Fall, he relates the story of Cain and Abel, noting along the way that the fratricide was the proximate cause of the growth of evil among men (965–1054). In treating the offspring of Cain and Seth, the poet implies a nonbiblical antithesis between the two family lines to suggest that Cain's descendants typify the City of Man and Seth's the City of God (1055–1245a).[36] This antithesis culminates in the identification of the "sons of God" and "daughters of men" of Genesis 6.4 as the sons of Seth and the daughters of Cain; it is the corruption of Seth's offspring by Cain's which so angered God that He sent the Flood (1245b–84). The poet next tells the tale of Noah and the ark, and details the reintroduction of evil into the world through Ham's sin and the building of the Tower of Babel (1285–1701).

The homilies of Wulfstan and Augustine together account for the major themes in this portion of *Genesis A*. Similar to the Old English poet, Wulfstan implies that it was Cain's fratricide, inspired by the devil, which gave impulse to the spread of evil throughout the entire world. Wulfstan goes on to tell his hearers that this burgeoning wickedness occasioned the Flood (53–69). Augustine also points out that the sinful condition of the world precipitated the deluge. But instead of directly referring to the fratricide as a chief factor in the growth of evil among men, he introduces the topic of the Cities of God and Man (19.31.2–5). Underlying this doctrine, however, is the distinction, as in *Genesis A*, between Abel and Cain and the family lines of Cain and Seth; for in *De civitate Dei* (15.1, 8, 22) Augustine emphasizes that Abel was the first man to belong to the heavenly City and Cain the first to belong to the earthly, and that after Abel had been murdered, Seth and his descendants carried on the line of the good until, corrupted by Cain's daughters, they too deserved to perish in the Flood. A similar substitution of a general lesson for specific material from the Book of Genesis occurs when the homilists take up the question of man's fall into wickedness after the deluge. Neither Augustine nor Wulfstan directly refers to the sin of Ham and the Tower of Babel. Instead both teachers are content to characterize the main vice of this period as idolatry, a characterization which evidently derives from a theological reading of the two events in question or of nonbiblical episodes closely associated with these events.[37] The two homilists and the poet are in full agreement that this portion of sacred history is notable for the resumption of evil in the world.

After the *Genesis A* poet treats of the Tower of Babel, he embarks upon a subject which occupies him for the rest of his work, the story of Abraham from his election to the sacrifice of Isaac (1702–2936). The main recurrent theme of this part of the poem, in accord with the Book of Genesis itself, is that Abraham, by the faith he shows throughout his adventures, is to be the father of a blessed race which is to possess the land of Canaan. Thus, Lee says that here *Genesis A* "recounts the birth of the Israelite people, through Abraham's exile, the Covenant, and the sacrificial foreshadowing of the sacrifice of Christ"[38] Lee's last phrase refers to the sacrifice of Isaac. And, indeed, that the poem concludes with this event reinforces the point that the major theme of the tale of Abraham is his fatherhood through faith. It was through Isaac that the obedient Abraham would gain his literal posterity; and it was through Christ, Whom Isaac prefigured, that this posterity would be blessed and, in a spiritual sense, come to include all believers.

It is significant that just as *Genesis A* does not continue the narrative of the Book of Genesis past the story of Abraham, so neither does Augustine nor Wulfstan discuss the remaining material on Isaac, Jacob, and his sons.[39] Moreover, though it is beyond the scope of the homilists to deal with specific episodes from the Abraham story, both emphasize Abraham's fatherhood. Like the *Genesis A* poet (1702–10a), Wulfstan begins by identifying Abraham as a descendant of Noah's most blessed son, Shem (98–100).[40] Wulfstan then explains why Abraham is important: "And of ðam mæran Abrahame comon heahfæderas, and of his mæran cynne eac coman þa witegan þe cyddan Cristes tocyme. . . . And of ðam sylfum Abrahames cynne com eft Iudea cynecynn" (100–2, 105–6). [And from the famous Abraham came the patriarchs, and from his famous race also came the prophets who proclaimed the coming of Christ. . . . And from the same race of Abraham came later the Jewish royal line.] Augustine says that, although many turned to wickedness after the Flood, some good men still sought to do God's will. One of them was especially chosen by God:

> Ex quibus Abraham pius et fidelis dei seruus electus est, cui demonstraretur sacramentum filii dei, ut propter imitationem fidei omnes fideles omnium gentium filii eius futuri dicerentur. Ex illo natus est populus, a quo unus deus uerus coleretur, qui fecit caelum et terram; cum ceterae gentes simulacris et daemoniis seruirent. (19.33.11–12)
>
> [From among these, Abraham, a pious and faithful servant of God, was chosen, that the mystery of the Son of God might be shown to him, so that through the imitation of his faith, all the faithful of all nations might be called his children in the future. Of him was born a people, by whom the one true God who made heaven and earth should be worshipped when other nations served idols and evil spirits.]

In his concern with Abraham's faith as well as his fatherhood, Augustine is in fundamental agreement with the *Genesis A* poet's treatment of this part of sacred history.

The first forty-one numbered sections of the Junius Manuscript constitute *Genesis*; with section forty-two, *Exodus* begins. The principal theme of the Abraham story in *Genesis A* is that the faithful patriarch is to be the father of a chosen people who are to inhabit Canaan; in *Exodus* this promise is realized. The poet makes it amply apparent that the Israelites under Moses are the offspring of Abraham and, as such, are delivered to the Promised Land. In the introduction to *Exodus*, the narrator says that Moses was granted special power by God to win a homeland for *Abrahames sunu* (18b). Later, with the chosen people pinned against the sea by the advancing Egyptian host, Moses exhorts the Israelites to trust in *Abrahames god* for deliverance (273b). When the sea divides and the chosen people are crossing over, the poet shifts his narrative backwards in time. After emphasizing that each of the tribes had one father (353b–61), the poet gives a brief account of Noah and the Flood and of the sacrifice of Isaac (362–446). The purpose of the latter story, which echoes the conclusion of *Genesis A*, is to show that the ori-

gin of the race of Israel, and its destiny to dwell in the Promised Land, is
the direct result of Abraham's trust in God even to the point of sacrific-
ing his own son. Finally, after the Israelites have crossed the sea, Moses
assures them that if they continue their own trust in God, He will grant
them joyful rule of the land of Canaan, as promised long ago (549–64).[41]

Wulfstan's treatment of this portion of sacred history agrees with
the *Exodus* poet's in stressing that Moses was a great lawgiver. On the
other hand, Wulfstan does not consider the crossing of the Red Sea. It is
nevertheless instructive to observe that the connection which the
homilist establishes between Abraham and the chosen people, like the
connection between *Genesis A* and *Exodus*, centers on Abraham's
fatherhood. Speaking of the race founded by Abraham, Wulfstan says,
"ðam sylfan cynne God sylf sette lage 7 Moyse bebead þæt he hy be
ðære lage wisian scolde. Se Moyses wæs Godes sylfes gespeca, and se
Moyses wæs eac þæs rihtcynnes [i.e., of Abraham's race]" (102–5) [for
that same race God himself established a law and commanded Moses
that he should guide them according to the law. This Moses was God's
own spokesman, and Moses was also a direct descendant of that race (of
Abraham)]. Augustine's connection between Abraham and the chosen
people at the time of Moses also focuses on Abraham's fatherhood. After
he says that from Abraham the chosen people were born, Augustine
explains that those Israelites who lived a spiritual life prefigured the
Church. Then, to introduce the story of the Egyptian Exile, Augustine
simply states, "Populus ergo ille delatus [est] in Aegyptum" (20.34.1)
[that people then was brought down into Egypt]. The link Augustine
makes between Abraham and Israel in Egypt is the same as that which
joins *Genesis A* and *Exodus*: The chosen people under Moses are Abra-
ham's descendants.

Augustine's consideration of this part of salvation history also pro-
vides close parallels to *Exodus* itself. Like the author of the Old English
poem (8–32), Augustine makes the point at the start of his account that
Moses received special power from God to deliver the chosen people
(20.34.1). After contrasting Israel's miraculous crossing of the Red Sea
with Egypt's destruction there, Augustine compares the story of Noah
and the ark with the scene at the Red Sea, concluding that "Vtrumque
signum est sancti baptismi, per quod fideles in nouam uitam transeunt,
peccata uero eorum tamquam inimici delentur atque moriuntur"
(20.34.3) [Both of these are signs of holy baptism, through which the

faithful pass into new life, while their sins, like enemies, are done away with and perish]. The same sacramental typology also helps to link the two events in the Old English poem, though the *Exodus* poet of course leaves the point implicit.[42] It should be noted in addition that Augustine describes Baptism in military terms. According to John F. Vickrey, the martial imagery used by the poet in his account of the crossing was similarly intended to suggest the spiritual warfare of Baptism.[43]

Augustine goes on to consider the Mosaic Law, given to the chosen people on their march through the desert.[44] He makes two major points: first, that the Old Law symbolizes spiritual realities pertaining to Christ and the Church; second, that the journey itself also contained signs having great figural import. Augustine postpones discussing the figural dimension of the journey, however, because he says that such a treatment would be too time-consuming for his catechetical address (20.35.8 to 36.9). After describing the miracle at the Red Sea, the *Exodus* poet, in his treatment of the Mosaic Law, also distinguishes between the letter and spirit of Scripture. After he pictures Moses teaching his people, the poet points out that each law which God gave the patriarch on the journey can still be found in Scripture. If the Spirit will unlock the mystery of Moses's teaching, we will gain wisdom and not lack God's instruction.[45] Next, implicitly giving a spiritual interpretation of the Exodus itself, the poet characterizes our earthly life as an exile which, though sorrowful, will end happily when the Lord Himself comes to lead us to heaven (516–48). The parallel between Christ leading man from his earthly exile to heaven and Moses leading the chosen people from their exile in Egypt to the Promised Land is clear; elsewhere Augustine himself presents a similar figural reading.[46] In *De catechizandis rudibus*, Augustine, like the Old English poet, acknowledges the need for spiritual interpretation of the Mosaic Law and of the Exodus; the main difference is that the poet actually suggests such a reading of the Exodus, whereas Augustine refrains because such a treatment is beyond his present scope.

Augustine next discusses the kingdom that the Israelites established in the Promised Land. The only historical figure which either he or Wulfstan mentions for the period between Moses and the next major phase of sacred history, the Babylonian Captivity, is David. For Wulfstan, David is important as an ancestor of Christ (108–9). For Augustine, David is important not only for his lineage but also because his kingship in the earthly city foreshadowed Christ's in the heavenly Jerusalem (20.36.11–12).

Though Junius 11 contains no material directly on David, *Exodus*—in a glance ahead to the time when the chosen people are established in the Promised Land—provides a close parallel. In speaking of the hill to which Abraham led Isaac, the poet says that at that same place the great temple was later constructed (389–96). It is noteworthy that the poet does not call the builder of the temple, Solomon, by name, but instead refers to him as *sunu Dauides* (389b). This epithet is richly ambiguous: "Son of David" is not only a fit patronymic for Solomon, it is also a traditional title for Christ (see, e.g., Matt. 1.1). The aptness of such a reference to Christ becomes clear when it is recalled that the Fathers viewed the temple as a figure of the Church or of the heavenly Jerusalem.[47] The typological aspect of these lines provides a correspondence to the two homilists' consideration of this part of sacred history. The poet both calls attention to David's lineage and implies that the spiritual rule of Christ was prefigured during this same period.[48]

I have said that the *Exodus* poet's treatment of Solomon and the building of the temple anticipates the time when the chosen people are established in the Promised Land. Their prosperity in Israel, which implicitly includes the construction of the temple (later mentioned in the poem), is the first subject of *Daniel*. *Exodus* ends at fit forty-nine in the manuscript with the chosen people rejoicing in their liberation from Egypt; *Daniel* begins at section fifty with the poet's statement that the Israelites lived happily in Jerusalem after Moses had led them out of Egypt (1–7).[49] But the next portion of *Daniel* shows how the chosen people engineer their own downfall. The Israelites, after prospering under divine guidance, turn from God to the devil, and He allows a great Chaldean army to conquer the land. Jerusalem is wasted, Solomon's temple plundered, and Israel abducted to Babylon for slavery (8–78).

The explanation in *Daniel* for the Babylonian Captivity, that Israel abandoned God and so God abandoned Israel, is not found in the corresponding part of the biblical book. Wulfstan's account of this period of sacred history, however, accords well with the first portion of the poem. Like the poet, Wulfstan interprets the conquest and Babylonian Exile of the chosen people as resulting from their shift of allegiance from God to the devil. Speaking of the royal line of Israel, the homilist says:

Sume hy wurdon æt nyhstan swa þurh deofol ahyrde þæt hi næfdon to
Gode naðer ne lufe ne ege swa swa hy scoldan, ac ðurh deofles lare unriht
lufedon ealles to swyðe. And at nyhstan þæt folc ða wearð swa wið God
forworht þæt he let faran hæþenne here 7 forhergian eall þæt land; 7 ðone
cyningc Sedechiam þe þa wæs on Iudea lande man geband, 7 ealle þa
duguðe þe on þam earde wæs man ofsloh oðþon gebende 7 lædde hi ut of
earde. (112–20)
[There were some in the end so hardened by the devil that they had neither
love nor fear of God, as they should, but through the devil's teaching
loved unrighteousness all too greatly. And finally that people became so
cursed by God that He let a heathen army attack and plunder all that land;
and the king Zedekiah who was in Judea was bound, and all the nobles
who were in that country were slain or bound and led out of the land.]

The treatment of the Babylonian Captivity in *De catechizandis rudibus*
differs from the account in Sermo 6 in that Augustine's interpretation is
almost wholly figural.[50] After the Israelites reached the Promised Land,
they reigned in an earthly way according to the measure of their desire.
The city built by the chosen people, however, is a type of the heavenly
Jerusalem, whose citizens "sunt omnes sanctificati homines qui fuerunt,
et qui sunt, et qui futuri sunt; et omnes sanctificati spiritus, etiam
quicumque in excelsis caelorum partibus pia deuotione obtemperant
deo, nec imitantur impiam diaboli superbiam et angelorum eius"
(20.36.10) [are all the sanctified men who were, who are, and who will
be; and all sanctified spirits, even as many as are obedient to God with
pious devotion in the highest parts of heaven, and do not imitate the
impious pride of the devil and his angels].[51] This passage, with its dis-
tinction between serving God in piety or the devil in pride, recalls the
opposition at the beginning of *Daniel* between the early Jerusalem
which obeyed God (1–16) and the later one which was seduced by pride,
turned to demonic deeds, and chose the devil's power (17–32).

Augustine extends his typological analysis when he considers the
nature of Babylon. As Jerusalem symbolizes the fellowship of the
blessed, so Babylon betokens the fellowship of the wicked. The capture
of Jerusalem and the Exile signify that the true members of the Church,
citizens of the heavenly Jerusalem, were to be under the power of the
kings of this world. At the present time Christians are to serve faithfully
those temporal lords who do no evil, yet at the Last Judgment the City of
God will be separated from the Babylon of this world (21.37.2–9).

According to Lee, this same set of ideas is at work in *Daniel*. The poem
has three time references. First, it pertains of course to the time of the lit-
eral events in the Book of Daniel; second,

> it concerns the Church in that period of sacred history between the First
> Coming of Christ and the Parousia, during which the faithful elect are to
> continue their witness, even risking martyrdom, and during which repen-
> tance, as for the Babylonian king, is still possible; finally, especially in the
> symbol of Nebuchadnezzar's great image in the plain of Dura (a tradi-
> tional figure for the coming of Antichrist), *Daniel* has an eschatological
> time reference, to those events associated with the separation of the two
> cities during the Last Judgment.[52]

Unlike the initial part of *Daniel*, the rest of the poem, though frequently
differing in detail and emphasis, follows the narrative of the first five
chapters of the biblical book. Owing to the loss of a leaf in the manu-
script, however, the poem ends imperfectly before its final episode, the
fall of Babylon, is quite finished.[53] Neither Wulfstan nor Augustine takes
the time to enumerate specific events which occurred during the Captiv-
ity. Nevertheless, Augustine does say that during the Exile Babylonian
kings, stirred by miracles occasioned by the presence of the Israelites,
came to know and worship and order worshiped the one true God
(21.37.4). According to students of *De catechizandis rudibus*, Augustine
is referring here, first, to the conversion of Nebuchadnezzar through the
episodes of his initial dream, the fiery furnace, and his exile, and second,
to the conversion of Darias through the incident of Daniel in the lions'
den.[54] Though it is unlikely that the poem contained the last episode in
its missing material, the conversion of Nebuchadnezzar is the controlling
theme of the second part of the work. Referring to lines 104–674, Fran-
cis C. Brennan says, "Here the poet is concerned with the long spiritual
education of Nebuchadnezzar, who seeks understanding and wisdom but
lacks the humility to achieve it completely. His development involves
three distinct episodes."[55] These episodes are the same to which Augus-
tine alludes, the last of which leads to the king's permanent conversion.

An episode in the history of Israel mentioned by Wulfstan and
Augustine but lacking in *Daniel* is the return of the chosen people from
Babylon to Jerusalem. Reference to the event might have been made,
however, in the lost ending to the poem. To support this possibility, it
may be noted—and this is clearly seen in Wulfstan's account of the

episode (122–5)—that it was the fall of Babylon which led to the repatriation of the chosen people. It is quite possible that, together with the rest of the material on the fall missing at the end of *Daniel*, the return of the Israelites may also have been mentioned. The poet would have had good reason to maintain the link between the two events; the end of the Exile would have fittingly completed a narrative begun with Israel's banishment.

But the lack of the episode, as the manuscript stands, does not impair the intelligibility of the course of sacred history in Junius 11. For the progression of God's dealings with man can be understood as a series of great time blocks which build toward the next major event in sacred history, the coming of Christ. When he is about to introduce this subject, Augustine pauses to note that five ages of the world are now completed. The first is from Adam to Noah; the second, from Noah to Abraham; the third, from Abraham to David; the fourth, from David to the Babylonian Captivity; the fifth, from the Captivity to the coming of Christ. With the advent of Christ, the sixth age begins (22.39.1–3).[56] According to the pattern of the world ages, then, the most significant event immediately before Christ's coming is the Babylonian Exile. The return of the chosen people to Israel is not a critical episode.

The reason is that the repatriation of the chosen people, as Augustine makes clear, did nothing to reconcile them to God. Significantly, Augustine's characterization of the Israelites after their return precisely agrees with the *Daniel* poet's description of them before their Babylonian Exile. The poet relates how the chosen people at first prospered in Jerusalem but then, falling into sin, were punished by God. This same set of elements—prosperity, carnality, punishment—appears in Augustine's description of the Israelites after the Exile. The chosen people, he says, were permitted to return to Israel and to rebuild the temple, but to teach them that their true deliverance was to be spiritual and not carnal, God allowed the country again to come under foreign oppression (21.38.15). The chosen people returned to Israel but not to God; morally, they still needed what the *Daniel* poet shows they lacked before they even left their land: spiritual deliverance.[57]

The distinction between carnal and spiritual deliverance is fundamental in understanding the theological organization of Junius 11 into two parts, Liber I and Liber II. With Adam's fall man had doomed himself to eternal separation from his Creator. Though God had selected certain persons—Abel, Seth, Noah, Abraham, Moses, Daniel, and the three young men in the fiery furnace—for a special relationship with Him, the chosen people and mankind as a whole, enslaved by carnality, remained alienated from God. Thus Augustine says that during the time of the Old Covenant a true spiritual life was known only to a few (22.40.5). What man needed was a moral example, someone to deliver him from carnality by showing how a true spiritual life should be led. This is the reason given for Christ's coming in *De catechizandis rudibus*: "omnia ergo bona terrena contemsit homo factus dominus Christus, ut contemnenda monstraret; et omnia terrena mala sustinuit, quae sustinenda praecipiebat: ut neque in illis quaereretur felicitas, neque in istis infelicitas, timeretur" (22.40.6) [the Lord Christ, when He became man, despised all earthly good things, in order that He might show us how these things ought to be despised; and He endured all earthly ills, by which He showed how they ought to be endured; so that we might neither seek happiness in the former, nor fear unhappiness in the latter]. Then, in a series of brilliant paradoxes beginning with the virgin birth and culminating in the Crucifixion, Augustine emphasizes that Christ as man set an example of unworldliness, though as God the whole world belonged to him (22.40.7–10).[58]

Wulfstan likewise stresses that Christ is true God and true man, and also points out that He showed us the right way to eternal life (160–92). But the Anglo-Saxon homilist includes an additional aspect of the redemption. Moral liberation was not the only kind of spiritual deliverance needed by man alienated from God. Compounding the moral chaos in the present world was Satan's lordship over all men, good as well as evil, in the next.[59] Wulfstan emphasizes that, until the coming of Christ, "næs æfre ænig mann on worulde swa mære þæt he on an ne sceolde to helle swa he forðfaren; 7 þæt wæs ærest for Adames gewyrhtum" (158–60) [there was never any man in the world so great that he did not have to go straight to hell when he perished; and that was first because of Adam's deeds]. It is the twofold spiritual deliverance by Christ as man and God—deliverance from the world and deliverance from hell— which forms the basis of Liber II in MS Junius 11, *Christ and Satan*.

The first part of the poem, called the Lament of the Fallen Angels (1–364), serves as a backdrop for this twofold deliverance. On the historical level, the Lament reminds the reader why hell came to be created and details its acute sufferings, sufferings to which the human race became subject because of Adam's sin and from which Christ would come to deliver man.[60] On the moral level, the Lament shows why obedience to God throughout sacred history has been so difficult; Satan, in revenge for his punishment, is engaged in an ongoing conspiracy to cause strife on earth.[61] Furthermore, in its treatment of the fallen angels' disobedience, the Lament dramatizes how not to act toward God.[62]

The second main division of *Christ and Satan* is called, after its beginning episode, the Harrowing of Hell. In his homily Wulfstan states that Christ "mid his agenum feore mancynn alysde of deofles gewealde 7 of helle wite" (157–8) [with his own life redeemed mankind from the power of the devil and the torment of hell]. Behind Wulfstan's simple statement, as the Old English poet portrays it, is high Christian drama. Christ's entry into the underworld sends the demons into panic, but the human captives rejoice. After binding the Satanic forces, He leads the blessed company to heaven (365–467). With Adam's race freed from the devil's power and hell's torment, half of man's twofold spiritual deliverance is accomplished.

This part of the poem also concerns man's moral liberation. In an address to the souls He has conducted to heaven, Christ recounts His creation of the world, His sorrow that Adam's sin brought mankind to hell, His virgin birth, and His sufferings and death on the cross (468–511). The point of this speech is to stress the profound love that God has for His creatures. A bit later, to make explicit the moral implications of God's concern for humankind, the poet emphasizes that it is each person's duty to repay Christ the love He demonstrated in dying for man's salvation (545–56). Augustine makes the same point in a rhetorical question: "Quis autem non redamare affectet iustissimum et misericordissimum deum, qui prior sic amauit iniustissimos et superbissimos homines, ut propter eos mittere unicum filium . . . pro eis et ab eis posset occidi?" (22.39.4) [Who would not earnestly long to return the love of a most just and merciful God, who has already loved the most unrighteous and proud men so much that He sent His only son for them . . . to be capable of dying for them and by them?]. The idea is also found in Wulfstan's homily (195–6).

The third main division of the poem, the Temptation in the desert (665–729), effectively completes the subject of man's moral deliverance. Wulfstan points out that Christ, in His earthly life, hungered and thirsted and, in other respects, was like us in all things but sin (160–71). The Temptation shows that Christ underwent not only physical discomfort but even temptations, and triumphed over them. In a passage quoted above, Augustine says that Christ despised the good things of earth and endured the bad as a lesson for us. The Temptation offers the classic example of how man is to reject worldliness and endure physical hardship: He is to take Christ as the model for his moral life.[63] In particular, the third temptation, in which Christ rejects all the wealth and power on earth (679–709), provides an apt illustration of Augustine's teaching that Christ chose a life of poverty and shunned political power to instruct us not to become attached to the things of this world (22.40.7–9). Just as Christ's victory over Satan at the Harrowing reversed the first grave consequence of Adam's Fall, the devil's captivity of man's soul in hell, so Christ's victory over Satan in the Temptation reversed the second grave consequence of the Fall, the devil's captivity of man's heart on earth, and redeemed mankind from moral chaos.[64] Liber I presents a twofold problem; Liber II furnishes a twofold solution.

For a reason that will be considered later, the poet places the Temptation last. He deals with the rest of the events of salvation history, which, chronologically, come after the Temptation, in the second main section of the poem. After the poet relates the Harrowing, he describes the Resurrection, the Ascension, and Pentecost, and concludes this part of his narrative with an account of the Last Judgment (512–664). With one exception in each case, both homilists give the same episodes in treating this portion of sacred history.[65] Wulfstan omits mention of Pentecost in favor of describing the time of the Antichrist (201–5), and Augustine speaks on the Growth of the Church after discussing the Descent of the Spirit (23.42 to 24.44).

The absence of either one of these episodes in Junius 11 does not impair its course of salvation history. Consideration of the Antichrist is often omitted from treatments of salvation history, as it is, for example, in Augustine's. An account of the Growth of the Church may also be regarded as optional. Not only does Wulfstan give a comprehensive survey of salvation history without dealing with the subject, but later in his life Augustine himself apparently ceased to view it as a necessary or proper part of sacred history.[66] *Christ and Satan* contains all the essentials of the story of redemption in *De catechizandis rudibus*. The poem also includes an account of the Harrowing, an episode not considered by Augustine in his present work; but this event, mentioned in the Apostles' Creed throughout the whole Latin West by the turn of the ninth century,[67] complements rather than contradicts the Augustinian view of the redemption. In placing stress on the moral aspect of the redemption and on Christ's dual nature, the *Christ and Satan* poet is in fundamental accord with Augustine.

Both homilists conclude their addresses with an exhortation. Wulfstan's is a brief plea to love God wholly and to keep His laws for a heavenly reward (214–7). Augustine's admonition touches on a number of points. He urges his hearers to maintain their faith in the final resurrection, three times warns against the devil's temptations, instructs his audience to beware of bad example, and contrasts the joys of heaven with the pains of hell (24.46–49). Such admonitions are, of course, not a part of sacred history as such; rather, they are lessons for man's moral life derived from reflecting upon the story of redemption. In a sense, the final episode of *Christ and Satan* serves as a tacit exhortation. The picture of Christ defeating the devil in the wilderness is a picture that speaks by itself, needing no commentator to point out the moral. The Temptation says implicitly what Augustine says outright: that each person should combat and conquer Satan's blandishments.[68] By placing the Temptation last, the poet leaves the reader with an example from Christ's life which, unlike the Crucifixion, Harrowing, and Resurrection, can be followed daily.[69]

Otherwise, in theme and in technique, the Lament of the Fallen Angels is closer to the admonitions of Wulfstan and Augustine. After detailing Satan's infernal punishment, the narrator twice directly addresses his hearers, assuring them that if they serve God they will avoid such sufferings and live in everlasting glory with the saints (189–223, 279–314). After referring to the torments of hell, both Wulfstan (209–17) and Augustine (25.47.5–7) make exactly the same plea to their audience. The Lament also provides parallels to Augustine's warnings to avoid bad example and to beware of the devil. In the Lament Satan is pictured as the archetypal sinner, whose example must not be followed in any respect. He is also depicted as man's chief enemy, who would be only too happy to bring human souls down to his own level of misery. In intent, content, and method, the Lament follows the medieval homiletic tradition.[70]

VI

Despite differences between the *historia* in Augustine's sermon and Wulfstan's, the Anglo-Saxon's outline of salvation history is within the tradition of that in *De catechizandis rudibus*. Likewise, the differences between the contents of the two homilies and the subjects of the Old English volume—differences which largely result from the generic distinction between a book of poetry and a sermon—should not obscure the fact that there is a notable resemblance between the pattern of episodes and themes contained in the homilies and the material in Junius 11. This resemblance can be seen in greater relief on considering how much material the Bible contains and how little of it is actually included in the works under discussion. Many versions of salvation history are possible, from St. Stephen's brief treatment in Acts (ch. 7) to Augustine's extensive treatment in *De ciuitate Dei*. That the contents of Junius 11 regularly correspond to and can usually be understood in light of the course of sacred history begun in *De catechizandis rudibus* seems to be no accident. The probable inference is that the editor both planned his book according to the course of salvation history and selected his poems according to this particular tradition.

APPENDIX

Lacking a statement from the man who commissioned the copying of Junius 11, it is impossible to determine for certain if *Christ and Satan* was included in his original plan for the volume. The available evidence makes it probable, however, that such was the case. I have dealt with the question at length in my dissertation (11–49); here I may only outline the reasons for this conclusion.

First, it is likely that the manuscript would have been considered incomplete in containing a progressive series of only Old Testament poems. The chief value of the Old Testament for Christians resides, of course, in the groundwork it provides for the coming of Christ. Without *Christ and Satan*, the story begun in *Genesis*, *Exodus*, and *Daniel* terminates abruptly and inconclusively. There is no evidence at all that the Old Testament quires had been bound by themselves, before *Christ and Satan* had been copied for the volume. Second, the selective interpolation of *Genesis B* into *Genesis A* seems best explained by the presence of *Christ and Satan* in the original design for the manuscript. Satan's conquest of mankind in *Genesis B* is dramatically answered by Christ's conquest of Satan in the final poem in Junius 11. The counterpointing is probably not accidental. Finally, analysis of the metrical pointing and sectional numbers provides a strong basis for thinking that each of the poems in Junius 11 was copied from the same exemplar. (If so, the credit for organizing the series of poems belongs to an earlier editor.)

The reasons given for believing that *Christ and Satan* was added to Junius 11 as an afterthought are tenuous. Some have dated the copying of the New Testament poem at a generation later than that of the Old Testament poetry, but a significant majority of scholars place the writing of both parts of the volume at about the same time. Moreover, an artist who was contemporary with the Old Testament scribe seems also to have worked in Liber II. It has been additionally argued that the Old Testament portion was planned as an artistic book, while no such purpose is apparent in the second part of the manuscript. This view oversimplifies the data. Examination of the manuscript shows that the originally ambitious plans for the volume had to be abandoned before Liber I itself was finished; the lesser artistic merit of Liber II may have been simply the last phase in the gradual breakdown of a once elaborate scheme for a codex of both Old and New Testament poetry. Even so, an excellent case can be made that an intelligent system of illustrations, similar to those designed for Liber I, had been intended for *Christ and Satan*. The original intentions of the editor for an elegantly decorated codex of salvation history may not have been implemented, but it is likely that at least the contents of the volume agree with what he had planned from the outset.

NOTES

*This paper is a revision of my earlier treatment of the subject in my doctoral dissertation, "The Old English Book of Salvation History: Three Studies on the Unity of MS Junius 11" (University of Notre Dame, 1973). I am very grateful to my adviser, Professor James F. Doubleday, for his valuable criticism of this material in its original form. Another version of this paper was read before the Medieval Club, University of Illinois at Champaign-Urbana, in November 1973. For helpful advice on the present version, I should like to thank Professor Carl T. Berkhout of the University of Notre Dame [now of the University of Arizona]; Professor Joan M. Wylie Hall of Saint Mary-of-the-Woods College [now of the University of Mississippi]; and Professor John P. Hermann of the University of Alabama.

1. For the *Beowulf* Manuscript see, e.g., Paul B. Taylor and Peter H. Salus, "The Compilation of Cotton Vitellius A XV," *Neuphilologische Mitteilungen* 69 (1968), 199-204 [and Andy Orchard, *Pride and Prodigies: Studies in the Monsters of the "Beowulf"-Manuscript* (Cambridge, 1995)]; for the Vercelli Book see, e.g., George P. Krapp, ed., *The Vercelli Book*, ASPR 2 (New York, 1932), v; for the Exeter *Christ* see, e.g., Robert B. Burlin, *The Old English* Advent (New Haven, 1968), viii [and Bernard J. Muir, ed., *The Exeter Anthology of Old English Poetry: An Edition of Exeter Dean and Chapter MS 3501* (Exeter, 1994), I, 23–27].

2. The codex, also called the Junius or Cædmon Manuscript, is held by the Bodleian Library, Oxford. I should like to thank the librarian for permission to examine this volume and the other Bodleian manuscript mentioned below, Laud Misc. 509. A complete facsimile of Junius 11 has been edited by Israel Gollancz, *The Cædmon Manuscript of Anglo-Saxon Biblical Poetry* (Oxford, 1927).

3. On this point see also Francis A. Blackburn, ed., *Exodus and Daniel* (Boston, 1907), xxii; Charles W. Kennedy, *The Cædmon Poems* (London, 1916), xi; and C. L. Wrenn, *A Study of Old English Literature* (London, 1967), 104.

4. Only four of the twelve sections are actually numbered. Similarly, over 40% of the sections in the Old Testament part of the manuscript lack numbers.

5. Francis Junius, ed., *Cædmonis Monachi paraphrasis poetica . . .* (Amsterdam, 1655), 91. Junius' statement is quoted and accepted by Benjamin Thorpe, ed., *Cædmon's Metrical Paraphrase of Parts of the Holy Scriptures* (London, 1832), 263; Karl W. Bouterwek, ed., *Cædmon's des Angelsachsen biblische Dichtungen* (Elberfeld, 1849), 164; Merrel D. Clubb, ed., *Christ and Satan* (New Haven, 1925), 137; and Gollancz xlix. Following the manuscript, Junius, Thorpe, and Bouterwek print the Old Testament poems as one work and the New Testament poem as another. Likewise, the codex is described as having only two "articles," by N. R. Ker, *Catalogue of Manuscripts Containing Anglo-Saxon* (Oxford, 1957), 406–7, 543.

6. See Geoffrey Shepherd, "Scriptural Poetry," in *Continuations and Beginnings*, ed. E. G. Stanley (London, 1966), 33.

7. This writing is in red and thus distinct from the brown of the text. Except for a few capitals of proper names, red ink is otherwise used only for the *incipit* to the treatise.

8. "Studies in the Versification of the Old English MS. Junius 11: An Investigation into the Use and Function of the Accents and A Consideration of the Poetical Rhythms and their Relation to Sense and Style" (diss. University of London 1950) especially 191–3, 213, 216(a), 381–3, 400–1, 405. Apparently accents were made by both the original scribes and by correctors; there is no evidence that the various accent-writers had different purposes.

9. *The Junius Manuscript*, ASPR 1 (New York, 1931), xxii. All textual citation of the Junius poems is from this edition.

10. My calculations. Except for a few debatable instances, the standard used for proper pointing is the division of half verses in Krapp's edition. An omitted or a misplaced point is counted as an error. These figures may not exactly represent the percentages of correct pointing when the volume was first copied. Like several accents (see Thornley 183–4), some of the points may have faded away entirely; as it is, some points in Liber II, where they are usually lighter than in Liber I, can barely be seen. In cases in which there is uncertainty if a particular mark is a point, I have usually assumed that the mark was intended as such. From my examination of the text under natural and ultraviolet light, at least 90% of the points appear to have been inserted by the original scribes, but no certainty is possible.

11. For statements contrasting the consistent and accurate pointing of Junius 11 and the sporadic pointing in the three other major OE codices, see Blackburn xv; Gollancz xxi; and George P. Krapp and E. V. K. Dobbie, ed., *The Exeter Book*, ASPR 3 (New York, 1936), xxi. As for individual poems, so far as I know only the *Menologium* and *Maxims II*, in MS Brit. Mus. Cot. Tib. B. i fols. 112–115ᵛ, are comparable to the poems in Junius 11 in the excellence of their metrical punctuation. I wish to thank the librarian for permission to examine this volume.

12. Not all scholars agree, however, that *Christ and Satan* was originally intended as part of the volume. See the Appendix below.

13. *Old English Verse* (London, 1972), 137, 207–8, and cf. 143. For support, Shippey refers to Larès's study, cited below. But because Larès is concerned with Holy Week, not just Holy Saturday, Shippey's exclusive reference to the Easter Vigil constitutes a different proposal.

14. *The Leofric Missal*, ed. F. E. Warren (Oxford, 1883; rpt. Farnborough, Hants., 1968), 97–8. The *Missal* was not produced in England but imported from France sometime during the tenth century. In England, the standard set of Holy Saturday readings in the late tenth and early eleventh centuries was the Gregorian (two of its four readings correspond to material in Liber I); see my article "Some Liturgical Notes on Ælfric's *Letter to the Monks of Eynsham*," *Downside Review* (forthcoming) [published in 93 (1975), 297–303, at 301–3; and Christopher A. Jones, ed. and trans., *Ælfric's Letter to the Monks at Eynsham* (Cambridge, 1998), 200, n. 228. As Jones notes, the recently published edition of the Winchcombe Sacramentary gives further evidence of the twelve-lection set of Holy Saturday readings in late tenth-century England: see Anselme Davril, ed., *The Winchcombe Sacramentary (Orleans, Bibliothèque municipale, 127 [105])*, Henry Bradshaw Society 109 (London, 1995), pp. 83–85].

15. "Échos d'un rite hiérosolymitain dans un manuscrit du haut Moyen Age anglais," *Revue de l'histoire' des religions* 165 (1964), 13–47. For a complete list of the Old Jerusalem Holy Week readings, see John Wilkinson, cd. and trans., *Egeria's Travels* (London, 1971), 266–70, 276.

16. "The Story of the Fall of Man and of the Angels in MS Junius 11 and the Relationship of the Manuscript Illustrations to the Text" (MA. thesis University of London 1953), 16–9, 196–7. [See also Barbara C. Raw, *The Art and Background of Old English Poetry* (London, 1978), p. 1.] For the subjects of the *Liber Responsalis* for the Sundays of Sexagesima, see *PL* 78, 748–64.

17. Shepherd 24; Wrenn 103–4.

18. The lectionary tradition followed in England during the late tenth and early eleventh centuries was that of *Ordo librorum XIIIA* (ed. Michel Andrieu, *Les Ordines Romani du haut moyen age* [Louvain, 1948], 2.481–8), of which two English copies are extant. The first, preserved in MS Corpus Christi College, Cambridge, 190 fols. 212–3 (still unpublished), prescribes, according to the standard tradition, the reading of the Heptateuch, Jeremiah, and Lamentations for Septuagesima; the second, preserved as part of Ælfric's *Letter to the Monks at Eynsham* in MS CCCC 265 fols. 265–7 (ed. Mary Bateson, Appendix 7, *Compotus Rolls of the Obedientiaries of St. Swithun's Priory, Winchester*, ed. G. W. Kitchin [London, 1892], 194–6), provides for the reading of apparently all of Genesis, Exodus, and Jeremiah, and selections from Lamentations, Augustine's commentary on the Psalms, 1 Corinthians, and Hebrews. See my paper on Ælfric's *Letter*, cited in note 14 [and Jones's new edition of

Ælfric's *Letter*, cited in n. 14, pp. 144–45, 217–20].

19. "The Origin of the Old Testament Plays," *Modern Philology* 10 (1912–13), 482. Craig goes on to discuss the formation of cycle drama in a liturgical context, but he clearly recognizes that salvation history itself is not necessarily liturgical. [I should not have written later here that Craig "fails to develop the point" but "does not develop the point": Craig's central concern is not Junius 11 but Corpus Christi cycle drama, and "fails" is not a fair term to use in the context.]

20. *The Guest-Hall of Eden* (New Haven, 1972), 16.

21. So Thorpe and Bouterwek in their editions (see note 5). The attribution of the poems to Cædmon did not go undisputed. For a detailed summary of the authorship question from the time of Junius to the late nineteenth century, see Richard P. Wülker, *Grundriss zur Geschichte der angelsächsischen Literatur* (Leipzig, 1885), 111–43. The passage from Bede is quoted later.

22. See, e.g., Kennedy, xiii; Krapp, *The Junius Manuscript*, ix; and Edward B. Irving, Jr., ed., *The Old English* Exodus (New Haven, 1953), 27.

23. *Historia ecclesiastica* 4.24; the edition used is *Bede's Ecclesiastical History of the English People*, ed. Bertram Colgrave and trans. R. A. B. Mynors (Oxford, 1969), 418.

24. "The Cædmon Poems," *Anglia* 49 (1925), 281. Under "Confession of Faith" Crawford includes Cædmon's *Hymn* and *Genesis A* (which he ascribes to Cædmon), but the inclusion of these works does not materially affect the main point that Bede's list itself belongs to the tradition of the Classification of Topics. See also Lee, 17.

25. Bede's list of Cædmon's subjects mainly differs from the contents of Junius 11 in three ways: in Cædmon's paraphrase of the whole of Genesis (cf. *Genesis A*), in his treatment of several episodes from the Exodus to the time of Christ (cf. *Daniel*), and in his treatment of the teaching of the Apostles (which lacks a parallel in Junius 11).

26. Unlike Cædmon, Augustine concludes his consideration of the material in Genesis, as does *Genesis A*, with Abraham; moreover, Augustine's treatment of the period from the Exodus to the coming of Christ is more limited than Cædmon's, specifically including only the period of prosperity in the Promised Land (with emphasis on David's rule) and the Babylonian Captivity, each paralleled by material in Junius 11.

27. For the importance of the treatise to monastic education, see Christopher's introduction to *The First Catechetical Instruction* (Ancient Christian Writers 2; Westminister, Md., 1946), 8–9. [See also Virginia Day, "The influence of the catechetical *narratio* on Old English and some other medieval literature," *ASE* 3 (1974), 51–61.] The edition of the treatise

used below is *CCSL* 46.121–78 (also edited in *PL* 40, 309–48); for a translation, see Christopher. Augustine's work is divided into two parts. The first (ch. 1–15) is a manual for the catechist; the second (ch. 16–27) contains two addresses, the latter an abridgement of the first, which are to serve as alternate models in the actual teaching of a would-be Christian. It is the long address (ch. 16–25) which receives attention in this study. Hereafter in the notes the treatise is referred to as *DCR*.

28. Crawford, 281–3, speculates that a treatise known as *De Catholica fide*, formerly attributed to Boethius, is at the basis of Cædmon's subjects. In fact, the poet's subjects are in some ways closer to Augustine's outline, and *De Catholica fide* itself belongs to the tradition of sacred history in *DCR*. [See also Day, cited in note 27, pp. 53–54.]

29. This is the conclusion of Dorothy Bethurum, ed., *The Homilies of Wulfstan* (Oxford, 1957), 294. All citation of Sermo 6 is from this edition.

30. Bethurum 293 says that Wulfstan's major immediate sources, other than the Bible, are Ælfric's "De initio creaturae" and a tract by St. Pirmin. She adds, however, that the type of homily of which Sermo 6 is an example dates back at least to Augustine's *De Gen. ad. litt.* In fact, Sermo 6 is much closer in intent and content to *DCR*. [See also Day, cite in note 27, pp. 56–57.]

31. For the distinction between *historia* and *theoria* in *DCR*, see Herbert Musurillo, "Symbolism and Kerygmatic Theology," *Thought* 36 (1961), 60.

32. Both Augustine and Wulfstan acknowledge that a treatment of salvation history of their type necessitates omitting consideration of much biblical material. See *DCR* 3.5.2; and Sermo 6.22–4.

33. Because of the loss of probably three leaves between pp. 8 and 9, *Genesis A* now contains a full account of only the first two and a half days of Creation. The narrative begins again with the creation of Eve. For a discussion of the loss, see David M. Wells, "A Critical Edition of the Old English *Genesis A* with a Translation," (diss. University of North Carolina at Chapel Hill 1969), l–li.

34. That the Fall of Lucifer is twice told may have seemed no more surprising to a medieval reader than that the Book of Genesis contains two accounts of Creation. In a different context, Bernhard ten Brink notes that "in other mediæval renderings of *Genesis*, the revolt of the angels is twice related." See *Early English Literature*, trans. Horace M. Kennedy (New York, 1883), 41 n. 2.

35. Augustine refers to the Creation in six days not here but in an earlier part of his address, 17.28.6–9.

36. On the poet's use of the two genealogies to suggest the City of God and

the City of Man, see Bernard F. Huppé, *Doctrine and Poetry* (New York, 1959), 158–68.

37. According to ancient traditions (originating in Jewish commentary), Ham was regarded as the first idolater and the Tower was constructed as a place where idols could be set up and adored. See Louis Ginzberg, *The Legends of the Jews*, trans. Henrietta Szold (Philadelphia, 1909–28; rpt. Philadelphia 1955), 1.179–80 and 5.200–1; Angelo S. Rappoport, *Myth and Legend in Ancient Israel* (London, 1928), 1. 236–7; and Oliver F. Emerson, "Legends of Cain," *PMLA* 21 (1906), 929. Though Augustine does not directly mention the Tower of Babel in *DCR*, he includes it in the briefer outline of salvation history in *De Gen. con. Manich.* 1.23.36 (*PL* 34, 190–1).

38. *The Guest-Hall of Eden*, 41.

39. This point of agreement among Augustine, Wulfstan, and the poet is a principal difference between their treatment of sacred history and that of Bede's list, the lectionary of the Anglo-Saxon Church, and the *Liber Responsalis*.

40. In relating Abraham to Shem, an involved genealogy is used in Gen. 11.10–26. Wulfstan and the poet simplify this line of descent so that Abraham's relationship to Shem is more pronounced.

41. As Robert T. Farrell says, "This final speech includes yet another mention of the promised land, with reference to the fulfillment of the covenant made to Abraham which has been stressed so often in the poem." See "A Reading of OE. *Exodus*," *Review of English Studies* n.s. 20 (1969), 415.

42. See James W. Earl, "Christian Traditions in the Old English *Exodus*," *Neuphilologische Mitteilungen* 71 (1970), 563 [reprinted in the present volume]. Shippey 137 cites this passage from Augustine as a partial justification for the poet's "sudden and undramatic leaps in time."

43. " 'Exodus' and the Battle in the Sea," *Traditio* 28 (1972), 119–40.

44. First, however, Augustine devotes a few sentences to the Paschal Lamb (20.34.4), a subject not found in *Exodus*; but other aspects of the episode of the tenth plague are treated by the poet, lines 33–53.

45. As Irving points out in his edition (98), the unlocking of Scripture here must refer to "allegorical or symbolical" interpretation.

46. See Earl 544–59. Earl points out that the crossing of the Red Sea in the poem is, in one sense, to be taken as entry into the Promised land itself. He also connects the first seven lines of the poem, on the laws of Moses and man's spiritual journey, to the present passage (516–48). See also

Neil D. Isaacs, *Structural Principles in Old English Poetry* (Knoxville, 1968), 154–5.

47. This figural dimension of the passage was first pointed out by Earl, 564–5; see also my paper "The Building of the Temple in *Exodus*: Design for Typology," [*Neophil* 59 (1975), 616–21].

48. The Junius editor had nothing to do, of course, with the poet's introduction of Solomon and the temple. But just such a treatment would eliminate any necessity the editor may otherwise have felt for including a separate poem on the time of David. One reason that *Exodus* was an excellent choice for the manuscript is precisely because the work provides considerations of other periods of sacred history, including the treatment of the temple as well as the sacrifice of Isaac. Cf. note 49, on the editor's choice of *Daniel*.

49. This passage connects so well with the conclusion of *Exodus* that certain scholars have speculated that the *Daniel* poet or a scribe wrote the passage for that very purpose. See John J. Conybeare, *Illustrations of Anglo-Saxon Poetry*, ed. William D. Conybeare (London, 1826; rpt. New York, 1964), 189; Blackburn, 107; Kennedy, lxi; and cf. ten Brink, 46, n. 1. The idea is rejected, rightly I think, by Gollancz, lxxxv; and by Francis C. Brennan, "The Old English *Daniel*, Edited with Introduction, Notes, and Glossary" (diss. University of North Carolina at Chapel Hill 1966), 70–1. The close connection does suggest that the editor chose his poems with extreme care. [I am now more willing than earlier to consider that a scribe or editor may have altered the beginning of *Daniel* to join it more forcefully to the end of *Exodus*. For evidence of such scribal intervention elsewhere, see R. M. Liuzza, "The Old English *Christ* and *Guthlac*: Texts, Manuscripts, and Critics,' *RES* 41 (1990), 1–11.]

50. In the outline of salvation history in *De Gen. con. Manich.* 1.23.38–9 (*PL* 34, 191–2), however, Augustine gives a literal interpretation of the fall of Israel which much resembles Wulfstan's and the *Daniel* poet's.

51. From here Augustine goes on to speak of David, a subject considered above in connection with Solomon in *Exodus*. The period of prosperity described at the beginning of *Daniel* historically includes the time of David's and Solomon's reigns. In *De Gen. con. Manich.* 1.23.38 (*PL* 34, 191), in fact, Augustine's characterization of David's reign is comparable to the *Daniel* poet's description of Israel's prosperity.

52. *The Guest-Hall of Eden*, 53–4.

53. See Gollancz, lxxxv; Krapp, *Junius Manuscript*, xxxi; and Brennan, xxxvi.

54. See the note to line 12 in the *CCSL* edition, 161; Christopher, 134, n. 235;

and Gustav Krüger, ed., *De catechizandis rudibus* (3rd ed.; Tübingen, 1934), 43, n. to line 8.

55. "The Old English *Daniel*," xxxiv–xxxv.

56. It may seem strange that Augustine, who gives more consideration to Moses and his time than to David and his, omits the former from his outline of the ages but includes the latter. The reason is that Augustine wishes both to limit the number of ages to six, in accord with the six days of Creation (see 17.28.7–8), and also to follow the Gospel account (Matt. 1:17) for the three of them immediately before the coming of Christ (see 22.39.2). But other medieval writers not concerned with limiting the ages to six amend Augustine's system to include Moses: e.g., the author or an editor of *Historia Brittonum* (Harleian recension), the author of the *Saltaire na Rann*, and Honorius Augustodunensis. See H. Zimmer, *Nennius Vindicatus* (Berlin, 1893), 15; Max Förster, "Die Weltzeitalter bei den Angelsachsen," *Neusprachliche Studien: Festgabe Karl Luick, Die neuren Sprachen* 6 (Marburg, 1925), 190, 201; and Roderich Schmidt, "Aetates mundi: Die Weltalter als Gliederungsprinzip des Geschichte," *Zeitschrift für Kirchengeschichte* 67 (1955–56), 310–11, 316. It is also noteworthy that in a related version of the ages of the world—found in the chronicle of Gervasius Ricobaldus, and implicit in the Vatican recension of the *Historia Brittonum* and the Book of Ballymote—Solomon (the building of the temple) is substituted for David, thus yielding an outline of history approximating the material in Junius 11: Adam, Noah, Abraham, Moses, Solomon, the Captivity, Christ. See Zimmer, 15; Förster, 201–2; and Schmidt, 311.

57. In *De Gen. con. Manich.* 1.23.39 (*PL* 34, 191–2), Augustine characterizes the period from the Babylonian Exile to the coming of Christ as man's decline into moral degeneracy. Because the return to Israel had, apparently, no spiritually uplifting effect on the chosen people, Augustine does not even mention the event.

58. Probably because of the special audience for which his catechetical address is intended, Augustine is concerned here exclusively with the moral aspect of the redemption. Elsewhere he presents a more complex view. For a review of his teachings, see, e.g. Jean Rivière, *The Doctrine of the Atonement*, trans. Luigi Cappadelta (St. Louis, 1909), 1.288–303.

59. This consequence of the Fall of Man is emphasized in *Genesis B* (397b–408, 425b–32a, 486–89a, 529b–31a, 717b–40a, 750b–58a, 791–99a).

60. For the second part of this point, see Jean I. Young, "Two Notes on the

Later Genesis," The Anglo-Saxons, ed. Peter Clemoes (London, 1959), 205–6.

61. See lines 109b–13, 261b–71 in the poem; and for a consideration of them, Isaacs, 134–5, 138.

62. The Lament serves an important role in the manuscript, but as an "event" the material lacks a parallel in the two homilists' commentary on this portion of sacred history. In treating of the coming of Christ neither Augustine nor Wulfstan refers to Lucifer's crime and punishment. The *themes* of the Lament, however, have close parallels in the final admonitions of the homilists. This question is dealt with below.

63. That the Temptation has this meaning in the poem has been demonstrated by Robert E. Finnegan, Jr., "MS Junius XI *Christ and Satan* and the Latin and Vernacular Prose Homiletic Traditions" (diss. University of Notre Dame 1969), 141–57. See also Huppé, 230–1; and Stanley B. Greenfield, *A Critical History of Old English Literature* (New York, 1965), 142–3.

64. On the importance for salvation history of Christ's conquest over the third temptation, see Shepherd, 35. The three temptations were understood by medieval commentators to encompass all sins; in this sense, Christ's conquest over the temptations was the moral high point in His life. Milton so used the episode in *Paradise Regained.* See Donald R. Howard, *The Three Temptations* (Princeton, 1966), 3, 43–75. (The second temptation is not found in *Christ and Satan,* however, owing to faulty transmission).

65. Augustine and the poet differ in where they place emphasis, however. In accord with his catechetical intentions, Augustine stresses Pentecost and the conversions which followed; in line with his Christocentric theme, the poet emphasizes the Resurrection and Ascension, and alludes to Pentecost and its conversions (568b–78). For a consideration of Pentecost in the poem, see James W. Bright, "Jottings on the Cædmonian *Christ and Satan,*" *Modern Language Notes* 18 (1903), 130–1.

66. See R. A. Markus, *Sæculum: History and Society in the Theology of St. Augustine* (Cambridge, 1970), 63. Markus contrasts the Church history in *DCR* with the lack of it in *De civ. Dei.*

67. See Cornelius Bouman, "He Descended Into Hell," *Worship* 33 (1958–59), 194. For a comparison between the second section of the poem and the Creed, see Charles W. Kennedy, *Early English Christian Poetry* (New York, 1952), 23. Augustine, of course, subscribed to the doc-

trine of the Descent into Hell; for a review of his ideas, see John A. Mac-Culloch, *The Harrowing of Hell* (Edinburgh, 1930), 122–4.

68. This point is convincingly made by Finnegan; for summary statements, see iii, 68, 150.

69. An excellent analogue to the poet's arrangement is found in an Easter sermon (formerly ascribed to Athanasius) by Basil of Seleucia (*PG* 28, 1081–92). Like the Old English poet, Basil treats the Second Coming, Harrowing, and Resurrection, and closes his homily with an account of the Temptation.

70. For a study of the Lament in its relation to vernacular and Latin homiletic traditions, see Finnegan's first two chapters.

"The Old English Epic of Redemption": Twenty-Five-Year Retrospective

J. R. HALL*

I welcome the opportunity to answer two kinds of criticism lodged in direct response to my argument. First, three scholars have resuscitated the idea that the Easter liturgy makes a more plausible organizing principle for the Junius 11 poems than does the tradition of salvation history in Augustine's *De catechizandis rudibus* and Wulfstan's Sermo 6. Second, two scholars have asserted that *Christ and Satan* was not part of the editor's original design for the volume.

The first scholar to contend in favor of the Easter liturgy is Marjorie Sue Allen in her 1976 Princeton dissertation, "The Interior Journey: Monastic Spirituality as Theme and Structure in the Junius MS."[1] Although conceding that "Unlike theories based upon liturgical practice, Hall's discussion does account for a significant number of events in the Junius 11 Manuscript" (43–44), Allen asserts that my argument "failed ultimately to satisfy three criteria which any theory proposed as the structure for Junius 11 must." She takes up each point in turn.

> First, it ignored previously noted portions of the liturgy which unquestionably link the cited historical events with preparation for the Easter season. Hall did not emphasize that Augustine's Catechetical Instructions were planned to educate those who would be baptized on Holy Saturday and enter the Church on Easter day, for example. Why is it not possible that these events were selected for instruction not merely because they are a part of salvation history but because they have a special meaning during the Lenten and Easter season? What, precisely, is the relationship between a rehearsal of Old Testament history and the commemoration of the *triduum*—the Passion, Harrowing and Resurrection of Christ—celebrated at Easter?" (pp. 45–46)

I do not ignore previous attempts to account for the contents of the Junius Manuscript by reference to the Easter liturgy; I find the attempts inadequate. I observe that Augustine's *De catechizandis rudibus* is directed to instructing catechumens but do not stress the point because Augustine's treatise is not itself part of the liturgy, nor, as Allen elsewhere acknowledges, is a survey of salvation history necessarily liturgical.[2] For example, in outlining the series of events of sacred history Cædmon treated—a series comparable to Augustine's—Bede nowhere mentions the Easter liturgy. The Easter liturgy embodies sacred history in a special way; that does not mean that every tradition of sacred history is modeled on the Easter liturgy or that the Junius Manuscript as a whole is best explained by reference to it. Later I evaluate precisely how Allen proposes to explain the organization of the codex by the liturgy.

"Second," Allen says,

> Hall did not account for the biases of the manuscript—its emphases upon temptation and obedience, exaggerated us[e] of the exile and return motif, the consistent use of martial metaphor where such might appear inappropriate, the setting of the wilderness in all four poems, and the typological suggestion within all the Old Testament poems of Christ's Passion. (p. 46)

The themes Allen mentions—temptation, exile, warfare, and wilderness—often occur in Old English poems apart from those in Junius 11 and can be explained by the general poetic tradition in conjunction with the biblical material the Junius poets treat. I discuss the thematic and typological unity of the volume in the third part of my dissertation, "The Theo-Poetic Unity of MS. Junius 11" (99–238), in which I explore enough figural readings to sate a medieval monastery. The discussion shows that there is a strong continuity of imagery, theme, and typology among the poems to invite a reading of Junius 11 as a coherent book assembled to be read as a whole. However, an argument on the organizing *principle* of the Junius Manuscript—in which the poems, composed by different authors, were brought together by an editor without an infinity of choices—does not have to account for everything and should be held suspect if it tries.

Allen continues:

> Finally, Hall, while consciously associating "theme" and "image" with the notion of Salvation History, and especially with topics in Augustine's

> *De Catechizandis Rudibus,* failed to uncover the pattern implicit within
> the Manuscript itself: the relationship between the three Old Testament
> poems and the three parts of the *Christ and Satan* poem. (p. 46)

Briefly, Allen contends at length that the tradition informing the manu-
script is monastic spirituality and that each of the three main parts of
Christ and Satan corresponds to one of the Old Testament poems: "Both
the subject matter and the spiritual lesson link the *Genesis* with the
Lament, the *Exodus* with the *Harrowing,* and the *Daniel* with the *Temp-
tation*" (p. 153). Allen's argument is inventive but unconvincing. If it
were a fact that the *Christ and Satan* poet consciously composed with
the Old Testament poems in mind, one might argue that he ordered each
third of his work respectively toward a different Old Testament poem.
But it is not a fact that the *Christ and Satan* poet, whose work much dif-
fers from that of the Old Testament poets, so much as knew the Old Tes-
tament poems. Further, the links Allen attempts to forge between the
three Old Testament poems and the three parts of *Christ and Satan* are
hardly ironclad. Rather than couple the Harrowing with *Exodus* and the
Temptation with *Daniel,* one might with equal justice yoke the Harrow-
ing with *Daniel,* in which the three young men are delivered from the
fiery furnace much as the souls of the just are delivered from hell, and
the Temptation with *Exodus,* in which the Israelites are tempted in the
wilderness as is Christ. The association of *Daniel* with the Harrowing
and *Exodus* with the Temptation would disrupt Allen's sequential
arrangement of the three Old Testament poems with the three parts of
Christ and Satan.

In her "Epilogue: The Junius MS as Lenten Agon," Allen takes up
the question of the liturgy:

> Just as the interior journey of the monk and the life of Christ are inter-
> twined in the Christian Salvation History of the Junius Manuscript, and
> just as the interior journey is reflected by the historical journey of all
> mankind, so too in the Christian liturgical calender [sic] these three
> threads are intertwined. The exile and return pattern which characterizes
> this interior journey is incorporated and symbolically represented in the
> Lenten and Easter seasons. (p. 387)

Allen writes with devout learning on monastic spirituality, but her
claim that it helps to explain the specific content of the manuscript fal-

ters. Monastic spirituality is a special kind of Christian spirituality, and nothing in the manuscript reveals an orientation toward monks as distinct from other Christians: All Christians—not simply monks—toil in exile, journey in the wilderness, and wage warfare against temptation. Similarly, the Lenten and Easter liturgy is directed to all believers, not specifically to monks. If Allen is correct that the liturgy yields the best organizing principle for the Junius Manuscript, she is correct apart from her argument that the manuscript is ordered to monastic spirituality.

In seeking to relate the Junius poems to the liturgy, Allen adduces the article (cited in n. 15 of my essay) by M.-M. Larès, who maintains that the Holy Week lections in the Old Jerusalem tradition shaped the content of the manuscript. "[W]hile there is no evidence that such a rite was known in England," Allen concedes, "the correspondences between the rite and the Junius poems are the most suggestive ever made for the unity of the manuscript through the use of the liturgy" (390). Allen does not dispute my claim that two-thirds of the more than thirty readings in the Old Jerusalem tradition lack parallels in the Junius Manuscript. Aware, however, that "assigning this Jerusalem rite as a source for the Junius Manuscript would remain problematic" (390), Allen turns to the season of Septuagesima, a period that "began, according to Amalarius, on the ninth Sunday before Easter and concluded on the Saturday following" (392). Without examining any readings for the season, she speculates that the verse in the Junius Manuscript, divided as it is into sixty-seven sections, might have been read by Anglo-Saxon monks during sixty-seven days of Septuagesima (i.e., the seventy days of Septuagesima minus the three days of the Triduum).[3] Such use of Junius 11 is possible. Absent evidence, however, that the sections in the manuscript correspond specifically to material read in the Anglo-Saxon church during Septuagesima, the proposal cannot be said to explain the organizing principle of the manuscript.

Allen's complex proposal to account for the contents of Junius 11 founders because she attempts to prove too much and is content to prove too little. She attempts to prove too much in seeking to show, first, that the manuscript is informed by monastic spirituality in particular and, second, that there is an intentional correspondence between *Genesis, Exodus,* and *Daniel* and the three parts of *Christ and Satan,* respectively. She is content to prove too little in simply speculating that the Lenten and Easter liturgy specifically influenced the compilation of the manuscript.

The second attempt to revive the liturgy as the organizing principle of the manuscript is advanced by Phyllis Portnoy in " 'Remnant' and Ritual: The Place of *Daniel* and *Christ and Satan* in the Junius Epic" (*English Studies* 75.5 [1994], 408–22). Portnoy contends "that the poems of the Junius Manuscript represent the individual liturgical lections for Holy Saturday, both severally and in their entire sequence, and that Hall's very convincing assessment of the poems as a collective 'epic of redemption' can be better served by this liturgical model" (408).

Portnoy favors the liturgical model in part because she sees the same kind of "temporal compression" and "temporal disjunction" operating in both the Junius Manuscript and the Holy Saturday readings.

In the Old English *Exodus,* Abraham and Noah are "immersed" in the Red Sea along with the Israelites, with no apparent regard for narrative continuity. The same temporal compression occurs in the series of lections read from the Old Testament on Holy Saturday. Here the stories of the Creation, the Flood, and the sacrifice of Isaac collocate with those of Exodus and Daniel, and with thematically related readings from Deuteronomy and from the prophets. The liturgical representation of salvation history is very similar to the literary one. Both the poems and the lections assemble the exemplary figures of Noah, Abraham, Isaac, Moses, and Daniel into a unity: one manuscript; one vigil. The liturgical narrative unfolds with the same kind of temporal disjunction that has perplexed critics of the Junian 'epic.' . . . [T]he liturgy offers a precedent and perhaps even a source for the problem of narrative sequence in the Junius poems. (p. 408)

Portnoy conflates two different questions of unity. She begins by alluding to the unity of *Exodus* ("In the Old English *Exodus*"), then merges this question with the question of the unity of the entire Junius Manuscript ("Both the poems and the lections"). What may explain the unity of the poem, however, need not explain the unity of the manuscript. The two questions should be kept separate.

Years ago James W. Bright cited a tradition of Holy Saturday readings to elucidate lines 362–446 in *Exodus,* in which the poet digresses from describing the Israelites' Red Sea crossing to narrate the episodes of Noah's flood and Abraham's sacrifice of Isaac.[4] In the particular Holy Saturday tradition cited by Bright, readings 2, 3, and 4 focus, respectively, on Noah's flood, Abraham's sacrifice, and the Red Sea crossing. Bright may or may not be correct that the Holy Saturday readings are the direct source for the poet's use of the material, but Portnoy is not correct in asserting that in *Exodus* "Abraham and Noah are 'immersed' in the Red Sea along with the Israelites, with no apparent regard for narrative continuity." The poet takes pains to insure narrative continuity. As Bright himself remarks, the Noah episode "is not introduced abruptly by *niwe flōdas* (362), but after the mind has been led to reflect on the origin of the *Israela cyn*" (99). In other words, when the poet is describing the Israelites' passage through the Red Sea, he pauses to ponder their origin as a people. This leads him to consider their ancestor who also ventured his life amid water, Noah. From here the poet proceeds by genealogy to another great ancestor of the Israelites, Abraham, who, like Noah, placed his faith in God, even to the point of sacrificing his own son, and received the promise that a great race would spring from him. Unlike in the Holy Saturday readings, in which lections on Noah, Abraham, and the Israelites crossing the sea are simply juxtaposed in a series, in *Exodus* the episodes on Noah and Abraham are linked to each other and to the Red Sea crossing by explicit reference to genealogy, and the two episodes are integrated inside a single work. Portnoy may characterize the occurrence of the Noah and Abraham episodes in *Exodus* as a "temporal disjunction," but it is not the same kind found in the liturgy.

But perhaps the same kind of "temporal disjunction" found in the liturgy is also found in the Junius Manuscript as a whole? The tradition of Holy Saturday readings Portnoy cites is as follows:

1. Gen. 1:1–2:2: creation

2. Gen. 5:31–8:21 (abridged): Noah's flood

3. Gen. 22:1–19: sacrifice of Isaac

4. Exod. 14:24–15:1: crossing the Red Sea

5. Isa. 54:17–55:11: "Come to the waters" (turn to and trust in the Lord for personal and national fulfillment)

6. Bar. 3:9–38: "Hear, O Israel" (a paean to divine wisdom)

7. Ezek. 37:1–14: vision of dry bones

8. Isa. 4:1–6: God's protection of Israel

9. Exod. 12:1–11: Passover

10. Jonah 3:1–10: conversion of Nineveh

11. Deut. 31:22–30, 32:1–4: an address by Moses predicting that the Israelites will disobey the Lord and suffer evil; "Attend, O heaven" (let all hear the words of salvation)

12. Dan. 3:1–24: the fiery furnace

As Portnoy says, the Holy Saturday readings show temporal disjunction. The readings are a series of high points in salvation history with no explicit connections between them. Indeed, as Portnoy acknowledges (418–19), two of the readings disrupt the general chronological flow of the arrangement: Historically, reading 9, on the Passover, belongs before reading 4, on crossing the Red Sea, and reading 11, from Deuteronomy, belongs immediately after reading 4.

The Old Testament material in Junius 11 much differs from the liturgical lections. The material on creation, Noah's flood, and Abraham's sacrifice of Isaac is not given in three discrete passages, as in the liturgy, but as part of a continuous narrative in *Genesis*. Further, the continuous narrative in *Genesis* includes the fall of Lucifer, the fall of man, Cain's murder of Abel, and the resumption of sin after the flood— episodes found in Augustine and Wulfstan but not in the liturgy. Chronological compression occurs between the end of *Genesis*, which closes with Abraham's sacrifice of Isaac, and the beginning of *Exodus*, which opens with Moses. A connection soon becomes evident between the two poems, however, when the *Exodus* poet refers to Moses as winning a homeland for "Abraham's sons" (18b). No such connection is explicit between readings 3 and 4 in the Holy Saturday series but does occur in Augustine and Wulfstan. Further, the link between *Genesis* and *Exodus* is reinforced by the *Exodus* poet's later narrating the sacrifice of Isaac as the Israelites cross the sea.

Exodus concludes with Moses telling the Israelites that God has given them the land of Canaan and will make them a great people, as he swore to their fathers, if they will obey the divine commands. The Israelites rejoice on the shore. *Daniel* begins with the poet's saying that the Hebrews lived happily in Jerusalem after Moses led them out of

Egypt until they disregarded God's commands, whereupon he led the
Babylonians to conquer Jerusalem and carry off the Israelites as cap-
tives. A similar connection between the Israelites of the exodus and
those living in the Promised Land is made by Augustine and Wulfstan.
However, in the Holy Saturday readings, seven lections drawn from var-
ious books of Scripture intervene between reading 4, on crossing the
Red Sea, and reading 12, on the three young men in the fiery furnace.
These readings make a poor match to the ending of *Exodus* and begin-
ning of *Daniel* in the Junius Manuscript.

    Portnoy objects to my objection:

> Hall's criticism of all liturgical approaches is misleading, in that his
> assessment of their failure is based upon the imperfect correspondence
> between the number and ordering of the poems and the number and order-
> ing of the lections. This criterion disregards the symbolic relationship
> between the historical events. In the sacred history rehearsed in both the
> poems and the lections, each event features a central figure, a "holy rem-
> nant" delivered from destruction through faith and grace. The "remnant,"
> variously saved from Deluge, Pasch, Passion, and Judgement, is the rep-
> resentative residue of and for all life: Noah from the Deluge, Isaac from
> the sacrifice, Moses from the Red Sea, Christ from Hell, and "in Baptism,
> the Christian by conformation with Christ." (p. 409)

The theme of a "holy remnant" may help explain the Holy Saturday
readings; it does little to explain the contents of Junius 11. As I have
elsewhere observed,[5] the theme is so broad that it appears in nearly
every book in the Old Testament and, unlike the tradition of salvation
history used by Augustine and Wulfstan, does not offer a real principle
of exclusion. If, for example, the Old English *Judith* were part of the
Junius Manuscript, the presence of the poem would invalidate my
argument but not Portnoy's. She could argue that *Judith* is yet another
example of a "holy remnant" and claim that the presence of the poem
in Junius 11 is consistent with the "holy remnant" theme of the Holy
Saturday lections. Conversely, if a lection from Judith occurred among
the Holy Saturday readings and I objected that no such material occurs
in the Junius manuscript, Portnoy could argue that the lection features
a "holy remnant" consonant with the Junius poems. An argument so
inclusive as to explain nearly everything is too inclusive to explain
hardly anything.

Equally fluid is Portnoy's argument that my objection to the Holy Saturday readings "disregards the symbolic relationship between the historical events." Her application of "symbolic relationship" is so general as to encompass whichever liturgical lections need a home. Reproduced next is the section of her chart showing liturgical parallels for *Exodus* and *Daniel* (p. 422).

Sacred Event	*Lection*	*Poem*	*"Remnant"*
Transitus	4, 9, 11	*Exodus*	Moses, Israelites
Captivity	5, 6, 7, 8, 10, 11, 12	*Daniel* 1–56	Daniel, Israelites
Fiery Furnace	12	*Daniel*	Three Children

Portnoy lists not only lection 4, crossing the Red Sea, as parallel to *Exodus,* but also lection 9, the Passover, and lection 11, the address of Moses in Deut. 31. An account of the Passover is not found in *Exodus,* however, and the address of Moses in Deut. 31 is only partly parallel to his address near the end of *Exodus:* In Deut. 31 Moses predicts that the Israelites will disobey the Lord and suffer disaster; in *Exodus* he stresses the success they will enjoy if they obey the Lord.

The address of Moses in Deut. 31 is more appropriate to the beginning of *Daniel,* and it is not surprising that Portnoy lists the passage again when giving Holy Saturday parallels for *Daniel* 1–56. As also parallel to the opening of *Daniel,* however, she lists six other Holy Saturday readings: lection 5, Isa. 54:17–55:11, "Come to the waters"; lection 6, Bar. 3:9–38, "Hear, O Israel"; lection 7, Ezek. 37:1–14, the vision of dry bones; lection 8, Isa. 4:1–6, God's protection of Israel; lection 10, Jonah 3:1–10, conversion of Nineveh; and lection 12, Dan. 3:1–24, the fiery furnace. Not one of these passages has been adduced by *Daniel* scholars as a source of the lines in *Daniel.*[6] Further, it is difficult to believe that the editor of the Junius Manuscript (or his predecessor) had in mind, for example, the vision of dry bones or the conversion of Nineveh when he compiled the poems. Yet Portnoy, invoking "the symbolic relationship between the historical events," calls lections 5, 6, 7, and 8 "prophetic readings" and lections 10 and 12 "historical/prophetic readings" (422), all six lections pointing to the opening lines of *Daniel.*

Portnoy's complex proposal to account for the content of Junius 11 through the liturgy entails lax premises and strained applications. It is to her credit, however, that she directly grapples with the major differences between the Holy Saturday readings and the material in the Junius Manuscript.

The third attempt to revive the liturgy as the organizing principle of the Junius 11 is made by Paul G. Remley in *Old English Biblical Verse: Studies in "Genesis," "Exodus" and "Daniel"* (Cambridge Studies in Anglo-Saxon England 16; Cambridge, 1996). Referring to the twelve-lection Holy Saturday system, Remley remarks:

> J. R. Hall has maintained that numerical considerations—specifically the fact that the Junius poems account for only three out of the twelve lections in question—argue against the probability on liturgical influence of the collection. This objection, however, can be overruled. Apart from the fact that the proportion is three lections out of six in some forms of the older Roman lectionary system, including the Alcuinian, a pivotal triad of readings from Genesis, Exodus and Daniel has been shown by biblical scholars to inform the very structure of the Easter Vigil recitation. In most cases, the triad in question comprises readings from Gen. I.1–II.2, Ex. XIV.24–XV.1a and Dan. III.1–24, often in conjunction with adjoining canticles. All three of these passages give rise to notably amplified treatments in the verse of Junius 11. The general notion that the content of the Holy Saturday service exerted an influence on the assortment of texts preserved in Junius 11 may thus seem quite reasonable—unless we assume that the compilation was undertaken after *c.* 950. (pp. 86–87)

I contend that the twelve-lection system does not convincingly account for the contents of the Junius Manuscript because only five (not three, as Remley has it) of the lections correspond to Junius material. Remley replies that in some versions of the older Roman system the correspondence is higher, three of six, but he brings forward no evidence that the six-lection system was known in Anglo-Saxon England and does not pursue the point. Remley reports that, according to biblical scholars, lections from Genesis, Exodus, and Daniel "inform the very structure of the Easter Vigil recitation." What Remley does not observe is that modern scholars have far more versions of Holy Saturday readings available and from a much wider range of locations and dates than did medieval liturgists and that the conclusion of modern scholars has practical importance to the Junius Manuscript only if he shows—which he does not—that the Anglo-Saxons regarded the triad as fundamental to the structure of the Holy Saturday readings. Remley claims that Gen.1–2:2, Exod. 14:24–15:1, and Dan. 3:1–24 "give rise to notably amplified treatments in the verse of Junius 11." This would be a significant finding if Remley could demonstrate it; as it is, his claim begs the question. And on the face of it, the claim is improbable since *Genesis* encompasses the first twenty-two chapters of Genesis, not simply Gen. 1–2:2, *Exodus* encompasses (often allusively) various episodes of Exod. 11–15, not simply Exod. 14:24–15:1, and *Daniel* encompasses the first five chapters of Daniel, not simply Dan. 3:1–24.[7] Finally, Remley concedes that the argument for liturgical influence on Junius Manuscript grows more doubtful if the manuscript tradition had its beginning in the second half of the tenth century. His own research independently confirms my conclusion (n. 14 in my essay) that the standard set of Holy Saturday lections in the late tenth and early eleventh centuries in England was the Gregorian, which has but four readings and does not include a reading from Daniel.[8]

The urge to explain the organizing principle of Junius 11 through the Holy Saturday readings is understandable. The facts that the Holy Saturday liturgy was enacted annually and that it contains a version of salvation history make the set of Vigil readings a natural possibility for explaining the content of the Junius Manuscript. Even if it be supposed, however, that the compiler of Junius 11 was intimately acquainted with the twelve-lection set of Holy Saturday readings, it does not follow that he would have thought of the liturgy in assembling the Junius poems. The Holy Saturday Vigil is oriented toward baptism. It is reasonable to believe that the compiler would have considered such readings as Isa. 54:17–55:11, "Come to the waters," and Ezek. 37:1–14, the vision of dry bones brought to life, at least as important to the version of salvation history embodied in the liturgy as the reading from Daniel. By what license of logic can we say that the Junius Manuscript lacks real counterparts for half of the Holy Saturday readings yet is modeled on them? Further, the twelve-lection set of readings does not well match the Junius Manuscript in organization or chronology. In contrast, the proposal to account for the contents of Junius 11 through the tradition of salvation history in *De catechizandis rudibus* and Wulfstan's Sermo 6 does not require such convoluted argumentation.

I turn now to scholars who have argued that *Christ and Satan* was not part of the editor's original design for the volume. Although the notion that *Christ and Satan* was added to the manuscript as an afterthought is common, only two scholars have advanced reasons in direct response to my essay. The first is Peter J. Lucas in "On the Incomplete Ending of *Daniel* and the Addition of *Christ and Satan* to MS Junius 11" (*Anglia* 97 [1979], 46–59). On the basis of the pricking and ruling of the manuscript's final quire, pp. 212–30, Lucas contends that the folios containing most of *Christ and Satan*, pp. 213–28, originally constituted an independent folded booklet—"the only folded booklet so far discovered which contains Old English poetry" (51)—and that the booklet was inserted into the outer full sheet of the gathering.[9] "[F]rom the present evidence," Lucas concludes, "it *is* certain that the volume was not intended to take its present form at the outset" (59); that is, the editor who assembled the three Old Testament poems did not intend *Christ and Satan* as part of the manuscript.

A few years later, Barbara C. Raw in "The construction of Oxford, Bodleian Library, Junius 11" (*Anglo-Saxon England* 13 [1984], 187–207) disproved Lucas's analysis of the quire. Raw's study of the pricking and ruling reveals that the folios on which pp. 213–14, 215–16, 225–26, and 227–28 of *Christ and Satan* are written were prepared by the scribe who copied the Old Testament poems and were not part of an independent manuscript. Further, "Evidence that space was provided for at least four and probably six full-page illustrations in this poem shows that it was intended to resemble the other poems in the manuscript in decorative appearance; this too supports the view that it was copied into the manuscript as a continuation of the three Old Testament poems rather than being bound in after a separate existence" (196).

Nonetheless, Raw supports the usual view that *Christ and Satan* was added to the manuscript as an afterthought. Her conclusion is based on the occurrence of two sketches in the gathering, the first on the lower half of p. 225 (a rosette design), the second on p. 230 (two oval loops). Raw is certain that the design of p. 225 was present before the text above it was written because "the double line marking the bottom of the text was ruled above the sketch instead of at the bottom of the page" (203), the assumption being that if the design were not present before the text was written the scribe would have used the entire page for script and made the double line at page bottom. For Raw the presence of the designs before *Christ and Satan* was copied into the quire has critical implications for the content of the manuscript as originally conceived:

> Their position in the gathering, especially that of the first at the centre of the original gathering [that is, the part of the gathering prepared by the Old Testament copyist], shows that at the time they were done there was no intention of continuing the text after the end of *Daniel*. *Christ and Satan* was an afterthought, therefore, but a fairly early afterthought, as is shown not only by its script but by the fact that it was added before the manuscript as a whole had been sewn. (p. 203)

In "On the Bibliographic Unity of Bodleian MS Junius 11" (*American Notes and Queries* 24.7-8 [1986], 104–7), I argue that the sketch on p. 225 was not present when the text on the top half of the page was copied and that Raw's sole reason for believing that *Christ and Satan* was added as an afterthought cannot stand. First, I note that the final word on the page marks the end of the tenth section of *Christ and Satan*. It seems more likely that the scribe estimated the amount of space needed to complete the section and made the double line at midpage to indicate that no text was to be written on the lower half of the page than that it was a pure coincidence that the end of section ten should come immediately before a sketch already present. (Indeed, if the sketch were already present when the scribe began writing on the page, there would have been no need for a double line marking the place where the text should end.) Second, I note that Raw's finding that the sketch preceded the text on p. 225 is inconsistent with her conclusion that a series of illustrations was planned for *Christ and Satan* comparable to that planned for the Old Testament poetry. Scribes concerned with the illustration of their poem would not have chosen to use a folio with an irrelevant sketch on it. Third, I note that one of the provisions made for illustrating the Old Testament poetry was to leave half pages blank for illustration. This fact suggests that scribes wanting *Christ and Satan* to resemble the Old Testament part pictorially would have left a half page blank somewhere as well. By leaving blank the lower half of p. 225, the scribes gave an artist the opportunity of illustrating the Crucifixion, described earlier on the page. Fourth, I note that, according to

Raw and others, the same artist who did the sketch on p. 225 also did the sketch on p. 230. If p. 225 were blank when the artist drew the rosette sketch, it seems odd that he should have turned to p. 230 to draw the oval loops when (with rearrangement) both sketches could have fit on p. 225. A different sequence seems more likely: The artist used the blank lower half of p. 225 for the rosette design, the top half of the page being occupied by script, then turned to p. 230, where he found ample space for the loops. In short, what was added as an afterthought to the final gathering of Junius 11 was not *Christ and Satan* but the incomplete sketches on pp. 225 and 230.

To date no one has challenged my answer to Raw's analysis, nor has anyone attempted to refute the argument made in my dissertation (16–22) that all the poems in Junius 11 were copied from the same exemplar. Still, perhaps because of the change of scribes from the Old Testament poems to the New Testament poem, the conviction remains common that *Christ and Satan* was not part of the editor's original plan for the volume.

For those who hold this conviction, I would like to suggest a scenario reconciling the view that *Christ and Satan* was copied into the manuscript as an afterthought with the view that the manuscript was planned from the outset as a book of salvation history. Suppose that an editor wanted to assemble a book of salvation history, from Creation to the Last Judgment, and had managed to collect only *Genesis, Exodus,* and *Daniel.* He would have the three poems copied but could not complete the project until he found an appropriate New Testament poem. Some time later (two months? two years?), he read *Christ and Satan,* saw that the poem would serve his purpose, and arranged to have scribes copy it into the last quire of the manuscript, allowing spaces for illustrations like those in the Old Testament part of the volume. Using folios the Old Testament scribe had prepared and adding new ones of their own, the scribes copied the poem. Its contents now complete, the manuscript was bound. In this hypothetical reconstruction, *Christ and Satan* specifically was not in the mind of the editor when he planned the volume, but a New Testament poem was part of his design. In a literal sense *Christ and Satan* was an afterthought, but in another sense it was a forethought—the final piece needed to complete Junius 11, the manuscript as a whole comprising "The Old English Epic of Redemption."

NOTES

*I dedicate this and the reprint of the original essay to Professor James F. Doubleday (now of the University of Rio Grande), who served as my dissertation director and has given me the boon of his friendship and benefit of his counsel for decades.

1. Allen does not directly respond to my essay, published in *Traditio* in the same year in which she completed her dissertation, but to my dissertation itself.

2. Allen is well aware that Augustine's tradition of salvation history in *De catechizandis rudibus* is not necessarily liturgical. She points out, pp. 44–45, that Augustine uses a similar tradition in Book II of *De trinitate*, which has nothing to do with the Holy Saturday vigil. It is also relevant to note that Day, pp. 59–61 (n. 27 in my essay), argues that Corpus Christ cycle drama did not develop from the liturgy but from "catechetical *narratio*" like that in Augustine's *De catechizandis rudibus*.

3. The scheme is not as neat as Allen implies. On Easter Monday the monks would still be reading the lament of the fallen angels in *Christ and Satan*. A similar suggestion is made by Raw, *Art and Background,* p. 1 (n. 16 in my essay). Speaking of *Genesis, Exodus,* and *Daniel,* she says, "The poems are divided into fifty-six [*recte* fifty-five] numbered sections, and if one section were read each day the material would last either from Septuagesima to the day before Palm Sunday or from Sexagesima to Holy Saturday."

4. James W. Bright, "The Relation of the Cædmonian *Exodus* to the Liturgy," *MLN* 27 (1912), 97–103.

5. "The Year's Work in Old English Studies 1994," *Old English Newsletter* 29.2 (1996), 41.

6. See Remley (cited later), 255–73, for a thorough discussion of sources for the opening of *Daniel*.

7. The correspondence between *Daniel* and the reading from Daniel in the six-lection set (including the Alcuinian) found in some older Roman systems is even weaker. In the six-lection set the Daniel reading consists only of three verses, 3:49–51, followed by a canticle from 3:52–55 (Remley, 84).

8. The evidence has become more complicated, however, with the recent publication of the Winchcombe Sacramentary (n. 14 in my essay), which shows that the twelve-lection set of Holy Saturday readings was used in at least one Anglo-Saxon monastery in last quarter of the tenth century. However, my finding in "Some Liturgical Notes" (n. 14 in my essay)—that the standard set of Holy Saturday readings in late tenth-century England was

the Gregorian, the system specified in the *Regularis Concordia* itself—
remains accurate.

9. However, the last lines of *Christ and Satan,* 710–29, are written on the
recto (p. 229) of the bottom outer leaf of the gathering, not on the verso of
the last inner leaf (p. 228, part of Lucas's original folded booklet). Lucas,
pp. 51–52, would explain the fact by arguing that original last leaf of the
folded booklet was simply discarded and the lines on that leaf were copied
on to p. 229, part of the original quire.

Some Uses of Paronomasia in Old English Scriptural Verse

ROBERTA FRANK

This essay first appeared in *Speculum* 47 (1972), 207–26.

It is remarkable how many episodes from the annals of early British history owe their preservation in popular tradition to the wit and playfulness of the words in which they were recorded. Thanks to a quip uttered by a post-Conquest wag on discrepancies between a royal name and royal deeds, posterity was made permanently aware of the disastrous reign of Ethelred the Unready.[1] And everyone knows what happened when Gregory the Great saw some English boys in the marketplace and started to meditate on Angles and angels.[2] Like Gregory, the Old English poet was adept at putting similar-sounding words together. Like Gregory too, he could have serious reasons for such an exercise: "In meeting magic with a higher magic, in promoting a superior and more comprehensive rationality, the chief instrument of Christian champions was the art of words."[3] In the Old English prose dialogue of *Solomon and Saturn*, Solomon vanquishes his pagan opponent by means of this higher magic. Saturn demands: "Saga me for hwylcum þingum heofon sy gehaten heofon" [Tell me why heaven is called heaven]. Solomon replies: "Forðon he behelað eal þæt him be ufan bið" [Because it hides everything that is above it].[4] Solomon wins the round: Not only has he managed to recapture the sounds of *heofon* in his etymological explanation (*he behelað . . . ufan*), but he has approximated in Old English the newest and most deliberately Christian of the several Latin etymologies for *caelum*: *caelum a celando superiora* (heaven, from hiding what is above it).[5] He wins because he has shown Saturn how Christian learning—operating through God-given words—can fathom the secret significances of things.

In the past few years, there has been a resurgence of scholarly efforts to discover more about medieval habits of thought. Patristics, typology, and numerological composition, for instance, have all contributed of late to our understanding of Old English literature and the culture which produced it. Recently, the prevalence of literary name etymologizing among the Anglo-Saxons has been persuasively demonstrated by Fred C. Robinson.[6] The present study takes up a related topic: the importance and meaning of etymological or pseudo-etymological wordplay (paronomasia) in Old English scriptural verse.[7] This aspect of the Old English poetic imagination has received little scholarly attention, despite official recognition of its existence from Bede at the beginning of the Old English literary period and from Byrhtferth at the end.[8] To counter this neglect, I have assembled a number of passages from Old English biblical poetry in which the authors seem to be deliberately playing with the sounds of key words; this evidence is intended to be representative and suggestive, not inclusive. Most of the examples that will be cited here seem to have passed unnoticed by editors and commentators, perhaps at least partly because the style of verbal wit favored by the Old English poets is one that is no longer immediately apparent or appealing to us. "I do not like *lucus a non lucendo*," proclaimed a scholar upset by the excesses of patristic-exegetical trends in Old English scholarship.[9] Yet, whether we like it or not, such etymologies were an undeniable aspect of the medieval verbal imagination. And sometimes—as in the linkage through sound association of *lucus* and *luceo*— the medieval imagination was right.[10]

There was nothing exclusively Latin or Christian about the basic rhetorical device used by Solomon in his etymologizing of "heaven": the fitting together of alliterative and assonant words to prove the mutual relevance of name and essence. It was more a matter of beating Saturn at his own game, of converting a style associated with pagan sympathetic magic into a highly effective and sophisticated weapon of Christian supernaturalism. Primitive magic operates on the principle *similia similibus*, "like produces like"—so when an Anglo-Saxon poetic charm wants bees to settle (*sigan*) to earth, it addresses them as *sigewif*, "women of victory"; another charm tells of an herb called *stune* which grows on *stane*, "stone," and can be used to *stunun*, "repel," pain.[11] Ælfric has a homily in which he exhorts his countrymen not to mutter such charms over herbs, but to recite Christian prayers instead. He puts it this way: "Ne sceal nan man mid galdre wyrte besingan, ac mid Godes wordum hi gebletsian" [No one shall enchant herbs with a charm, but shall bless them with God's words].[12] Ælfric's sentence with its balanced alliterative phrases (the doubled *m-g-w-b* sequences) and the homophonic attraction of *wordum* and *wyrte* seems to imitate the rhetoric of pagan incantations only to disprove their efficacy: By the principle of *similia similibus*, *wyrte* are shown to be more susceptible to "Godes wordum" than to a heathen *galdre*.[13] Such associative rhetoric pervades much early sacral poetry.[14] We find it used in a magico-religious verse from the Veda to focus attention on a desired link between a "sacrificial post" and "heaven" (*yasmai miyante svaravah svarvide*, "for whom, the heaven-finder, sacrificial posts are set up").[15] Cynewulf discovered an analogous relationship in Old English between *rod*, "the rood, cross," and *rodor*, "the heavens," and proceeded to invoke this paronomastic incantation fifteen times:

Elene	147	rice under *rodorum*, þurh his *rode* treo
	206	on *rode* treo *rodora* waldend
	482	of *rode* ahæfen *rodora* wealdend
	624	hwær seo *rod* wunige *rador*cyninges
	631	rice under *roderum*, ge he ða *rode* ne tæhte
	855	on *rode* treo. *Rodor* eal geswearc
	886	*rod* aræred, *rodor*cyninges beam
	918	ræd under *roderum*. Ic þa *rode* ne þearf
	1022	reord of *roderum*. Heo þa *rode* heht
	1066	mid þam on *rode* was *rodera* wealdend
	1074	*rode rodera* cininges ryhte getæhtesð
	1254	*rode* under *roderum*, þa se ricesta
Jul.	305	on *rode* aheng *rodera* waldend
	447	*rodor*cyninges giefe, se þe on *rode* treo
Chr.	727	*rodor*cyninges ræs, þa he on *rode* astag

Cynewulf's wordplay, however, was not employed in the straightforward, directive manner of pagan magic merely to speed a "post" to its goal, "heaven." Over and above such a signification, he used this phonological coincidence to outline a basic Christian paradox: the lowest thing (*rod*) juxtaposed with the highest (*rodera wealdend, rodorcyning,* "lord of the heavens"), the mystery of Divinity's historical impact on mankind. It is an ironic and startling collocation of sound and sense, yet this repeated formula succeeds as persuasive rhetoric by implying that the convergence of heaven (*rodor*) and earth (*rod*) was predestined by God from the beginning, the link foreshadowed and made manifest in these two English words.[16]

"Ðæt Englisc hæfst his agene wisan," "English has its own style, its own way," reflected Ælfric in his *Preface to Genesis.*[17] It was only by submitting to this "wise," to this innate "melody" of a language, that a translator could master his medium. *Caro verbum factum est,* "the Word was made flesh" (John 1:14), became Ælfric's "*Word* wæs ge*word*en flæsc," an unavoidable paronomastic locution whose very naturalness in Old English seemed to embody the cyclic inevitability of the Christian doctrine it probed, the verbal self-realization and fulfillment in time of the "*Word* þæt ge*word*en is."[18] The practitioners of Anglo-Saxon biblical poetry often appear similarly intent not just on recapitulating the contents of a given text but on re-creating, rediscovering in English terms, some of the traditional theological assumptions underlying the Scriptures. In the case of a poem dealing with Old Testament history, such repeated paronomasia can function as a kind of typological "punctuation," quietly pinpointing the moments at which pre-Christian history was a shadow, a figure, of events to come.

It is not particularly unusual for an early Christian writer to begin his work with a multiple pun on "word." Jerome, for example, begins his first *Epistola* with the hope that "neque eum posse *verba* deficere, qui credidisset in *Verbo*," "words cannot fail him who places his trust in the Word."[19] The Old English *Genesis* poet opens his work not with the first verse of the Book of Genesis but with a threefold play on "word":

Us is riht micel   þæt we rodera *weard,*
wereda wuldorcining,   *wordum* herigen   (*Gen.* 1–2)
[It is our great duty to praise in words the Guardian of Heaven,
the Glorious King of Hosts.]

His triple paronomasia seems to be trying to persuade us that the poet's literary and Christian purposes are one, that nothing could be more natural or right in English than that the *weard*, king of *weroda*, should be praised in *wordum*. Moreover, this English sound correspondence would have seemed to the poet to reflect a theological reality, the mysterious identity of *Deus* and *Logos*, *weard* and *word*, as formulated in John 1:1: *In principio erat verbum, et verbum erat apud Deum, et Deus erat verbum*. The Anglo-Saxons followed the patristic practice of conflating the first verse of Genesis (*In principio creavit Deus coelum et terram*) with this first verse of John (and John 8:25—*Ego sum principium, qui et loquor vobis*) to prove that God first created the universe in his son.[20] The active presence of the Word at the moment of creation is suggested in the English poem by paronomastic constructions such as "oðþæt þeos *woruld*gesceaft / þurh *word gewearð wuldor*cyninges," "until this world-creation came about through the Word of the King of Glory" (110–111), a construction which the poet uses to preface his paraphrase of Gen 1·1 Thus the first 111 lines of the Old English *Genesis*, comprising the poet's original introduction to his scriptural text, begin and end with plays on "word." And when at v. 112 the poet finally starts to paraphrase the first chapter of Genesis, each time he comes across the words *Dixitque Deus*, "And God said," he translates them in such a way as to emphasize once more that God (the *weard*, 144, 163) first brought things into being "þurh his agen *word*," "through his own word" (130, 149, 155). This is precisely the same emphasis that the Church Fathers insisted upon in their exegesis of Gen. 1:3, *Et dixit Deus:* "Fit autem Filii commemoratio, quia Verbum est, in eo quod scriptum est, *dixit Deus* . . ." [There is, moreover, mention made of the Son, because He is the Word, in what was written: "God spoke"].[21] The biblical exegete states this doctrine directly; the Old English poet prefers to suggest it through artful and subtle sound congruences. We should probably recognize in the Genesis poet's recurrent plays on "word" a deliberate and specifically Christian attempt to show the same Word of God at work, shaping the course of history, from the very beginning of time.

The wordplay observed in the opening lines of Genesis appears in two subsequent sections of the poem, each telling of a covenant granted by God to man. Noah, the first beneficiary, enters the ark—

    swa him ælmihtig
weroda drihten   þurh his *word* abead.
Him on hoh beleac   heofonrices *weard*
merehuses muð   (1361–64)
[as the Almighty Lord of Hosts commanded him through His Word. The
Guardian of the Kingdom of Heaven closed behind him the door of the
sea-house]

The ark is guided by God's word:

    Gelædde þa wigend   *weroda* drihten
    worde ofer widland.   (1411–12)
    [The Lord of Hosts led the warriors by His Word over the world.]

The poet has suddenly revived these homophonic sound sequences to
describe two details: God's sealing of the vessel, and his leading it through
the world by means of his Word. An Old English audience, sensitive to
changes in the poet's style, would be left wondering why such wordplay
chose this moment to intrude again upon human history: What has Noah
to do with God's *word*, and why emphasize that the *scyppend*, "Creator,"
enclosed the *scip*, "ship" (1391)? Earlier, the poet's paronomastic criss-
crossing of sounds seemed to foreshadow a complexity in the Christian
order of things. It would here too if, like Ælfric, the poet's audience
approached the Old Testament story "æfter gastlicum andgite," "according
to spiritual understanding," recalling "þæt se swymmenda arc getacnode
Godes gelaðunge, and þæt se rihtwisa Noe getacnode Crist" [that the
floating ark is a type of God's Church, and that the righteous Noah is a
type of Christ].[22] God establishes and seals the Ship of the Church but
Christ, the *Logos*, is helmsman and leads it.[23] The poet states none of this.
His paronomastic rhetoric merely "points" the poetic text and has, per-
haps, the same impact on the meaning of a verse as has the pair of quota-
tion marks just inserted in this sentence: a hint, a slight emphasis, that the
words so enclosed may have other than a strictly literal significance.
    Like Noah, Abraham, on whom the second and final pre-Mosaic
covenant was bestowed, always did "swa him sigora *weard*, / waldend
usser, þurh his *word* abead," "as the Guardian of Victories, our Lord,
commanded him through His Word" (1770–71); he always remembered
the "heofon*weardes* gehat, þa him þurh halig *word* . . . gecyðde," "the
promise of the Guardian of Heaven which He made known to him

through the Holy Word" (1796–97). But a new dimension is revealed in and by the poet's wordplay when God announces that Sarah will bear a son: "soð forð gan / *wyrd* æfter þissum *word*gemearcum," "truth shall come to pass, fate according to these terms" (2356–57). When Isidore derived *fatum*, "fate," from *fari*, "to speak" (*A fando igitur fatum dicunt, id est a loquendo*), he also provided a Christian meaning for this etymology based on Psalm 61:12: *Semel locutus est Deus*, "God has spoken once" (*Etymologiae*, VIII, xi, 90–91). The *Genesis* poet initiates in English a parallel sound and sense correspondence between *word* and *wyrd*, yet confines their paronomastic juxtaposition to those verses in his text which prophesy the birth of Isaac,[24] as when God answers Sarah's disbelieving laugh:

> Ne wile Sarran   soð gelyfan
> *wordum* minum.   Sceal seo *wyrd* swa þeah
> forð steallian   swa ic þe æt frymðe gehet.   (2390–92)
> [Sarah does not want to believe the truth in My words. Nevertheless, that destiny must take place which I promised you in the beginning.]

When Ælfric wrote of the incarnation *Word wæs geworden flæsc*, he, too, was associating *word* and *wyrd* (< *geweorðan*) in the way proposed by Isidore. *Wyrd*, the working out in time of God's *word æt frymðe*, in *Genesis* attends on Isaac alone; it is through him that God's Word is to be fulfilled. Earlier in the poem, God's pronouncement that the aged Sarah would bear a son—"bearn of *bryde* þurh *gebyrd* cumen," "a child come from the bride through birth" (2198)—was couched in the same paronomastic terms used to describe Mary in *Christ I*;[25] later, only Abraham of all mankind is distinguished through punning association with God the Father: "He is *god* and gleaw, mæg self wið *God* sprecan," "he is good and wise, he can himself speak with God" (2658). Such wordplay could not help but reinforce the traditional theological paradigm which made the birth and offering of Isaac a figure of the incarnation and passion of God's son, the *Verbum in principio*:

> We sceolon understandan on Abrahame þone Ælmihtigan Fæder, and on Isaace his leofan sunu, urne Hælend Crist. And we sceolon tocnawan on Isaaces offrunge Drihtnes ðrowunge, be ðam cwæð se apostol Paulus, þæt "God Fæder ne sparode his agenum Bearne, ac for us eallum hine to deaðe sealde."

[We must perceive in Abraham the Almighty Father, and in his beloved
son Isaac our Saviour Christ. And we must recognize in the sacrifice of
Isaac the passion of the Lord, about which the apostle Paul spoke: "God
the Father did not spare His own Son, but for us all gave Him unto
death."][26]

There is no doubt that the main concern of the *Genesis* poet was to nar-
rate the historical truth of Old Testament events; yet, as a Christian poet,
he was compelled at the same time to perceive and intimate how these
events were foreshadowings of things yet to come. To do this, to pre-
serve the delicate balance between literal paraphrase and typological
translation, he highlighted potentially Christological episodes in his
poem with multiple plays on "word" as if striving to make the Old Eng-
lish *word* more like the *Logos* in which all meanings were enclosed.
Because such wordplay meant more than it said, the poet was able to
hint at a correspondence between Noah, Abraham, Isaac, and Christ
without ever leaving the literal level of narrative; he could outline a par-
adigm, effect a congruence, without ever forging an overt theological
equation. The poet's paronomastic style in *Genesis* also had peculiar
power to express a mood of cyclic inevitability and timelessness.[27]
Phonological recurrence, the repetition of similar words linking related
things, imparts a ritualistic, almost litany-like quality to the Old Testa-
ment events described and, like the invariable return through alliteration
of the second half line to the first in an Old English verse, manages to
convey the sense of an underlying order and purpose in the flux of divine
history.

The Old English poet sometimes took advantage of this metrical
balance, the readiness with which the two major alliterative lifts on
either side of the caesura seemed to assume a paronomastic function, to
suggest a relationship between scriptural names and their bearers'
behavior. One quickly discovers that vernacular sound associations rein-
force Sarah's propensity to be sad ("þa wæs *Sarran sar* on mode," *Gen.*
2216), Pharaoh's to be *fah*, "guilty" (*Gen.* 1860), Eve's to behave *yfele*,
"badly" ("Hwæt, þu *Eve*, hæfst *yfele* gemearcod," *Gen.* 790), and Nero's
to cause *nearu*, "distress, anguish" (*Fts. Ap.* 13, *Jul.* 302).[28] This ten-
dency to equate two similar phonemic sequences metrically balanced is
exploited by the poet, even when the sound correspondence between a
name and its alliterative partner is not striking. If, for example, the poet

wants to show the etymological connection between a Latin or Hebrew name and its English translation, he can, by repeated linkages of that name with its interpretive epithet, gradually suggest a paronomastic relationship. The *Daniel* poet, wanting his hearers to recognize that the prophet bore a symbolic name (Heb. *Dan-el*, "God has judged", Jerome's *iudicium dei*, "the judgment of God," OE *drihtnes dom*),[29] transformed its Hebrew meaning into a descriptive leitmotiv which accompanies Daniel on each of his public appearances.

149–150 Daniel comes to interpret Nebuchadnezzar's first dream:

oðþæt witga cwom,
Daniel to *dome*,   se wæs *drihtne* gecoren . . .
[until the prophet Daniel came to judgment; he was chosen by God . . .]

531–532 Daniel comes to interpret Nebuchadnezzar's second dream:

Ða wæs to ðam *dome*   *Daniel* haten,
godes spelboda.
[Then Daniel was called to that judgment, God's prophet.]

735–744 Daniel comes to interpret the handwriting on the wall:

oðþæt *Daniel* com,   drihtne gecoren,
. . .
drihtnes domas . . .
[Until Daniel came, chosen by God, [to pronounce] God's judgments . . .]

Nomen est omen: Daniel can read *drihtnes dom*, "the judgment of God," and proves to the Chaldean soothsayers that his magic is stronger than theirs; at the same time, the poet shows how the prophet's name foreshadowed his historical function, how events did but recapitulate sacred etymology.[30] That Daniel's name and its Hebrew interpretation converged so gracefully in Old English verse—with an alliterative inevitability missing in the Latin translation—might have seemed to the poet to confirm the fitness of his native tongue to transmit biblical truths.

That Adam's name and its etymology (Heb. *'adamah* "earth," Jerome's *terrenus, terrigena*, Alcuin's *aequivocus terrae*, OE *eorðe*) also alliterated in Old English verse must have seemed significant to the poet of *Genesis B*, for the name:etymon pair of Adam: *Eorðe* occurs repeatedly in the first half of his poem (365, 419, 454, 522). The poet shows Adam's origin and his *originatio*, "etymology," to have been identical by describing him as one þe *wæs of eorðan geworht*, "who was created out of earth" (365). However, after Adam has eaten the apple, this alliterative equation never occurs again. Instead, Adam's postlapsarian world is called *land* (784, 787, 795, 805), the word previously used by the fallen angels to describe their new habitation (332, 376, 487, 737). The omission, if it is deliberate, seems intended to imitate Adam's sudden alienation from his own being (*eorðe*), man's painful separation from his matrix. Moral disintegration is thus paralleled by the linguistic dissociation, the lack of phonological and semantic correspondences, which sets in as soon as Satan's emissary manages to "words, actions all infect."[31]

When the Old English form of a scriptural name suggested the original Hebrew meaning of that name, paronomastic constructions were inevitable.[32] The name Sion (Jerome's *specula*, "look-out, watchtower," *speculator*, "observer") was glossed in Old English as *Sceawungstow*, "place of observation," and *Wlitesceawung*, "observation of beauty, of splendor."[33] The close semantic and phonological parallelism between Heb. *Sion* and OE *seon*, "to see, view," was not allowed to pass unremarked: "on *Sione* beorh . . . wuldor *gesawon*," "on the hill of Sion they saw splendor" (*Exod.* 386–387); "þær wæs miht *gesawen* / on *Sion*beorge soðes drihtnes," "there was the power of the true Lord seen on the hill of Sion" (*Psalm* 83:6). The author of *Christ III*, through a complex interlacing of sound and sense, constructs a powerful description of Christ's appearance at Sion on Judgment Day (899–924). A slow and solemn accumulation of synonyms and near homonyms (e.g., on *Syne, onsyn, sunne, synnig, geseon, scyne, on gesihðe*) culminates in etymological translation when, on Sion, the righteous before Christ are permitted *to sceawianne þone scynan wlite*, "to look upon that shining beauty" (914). The name of Sion and its Christian significance are shown to be one, and the Old English poet leaves us with an impression of complete linguistic and theological harmony.

Sometimes the paronomasia in Old English scriptural poetry has a kind of onomatopoeic function, the patterning of the sound in successive words in apparent imitation of the very action they denote. The *Genesis* poet suggests the envelopment of land by seas in the beginning of creation by two mirror-image terms, one hemisphere enfolding the other in a kind of cosmic metathesis:

> ac stod bewrigen fæste
> *folde* mid *flode*.   (156–57)
> [but the earth remained firmly enfolded by water.]

The initial *entrelacement* of the two elements, earth and water, is thus reenacted in the homophonic attraction of their names. Through parallel sound sequences, the *Genesis* poet could also underline the paradoxical nature of an experience. In his depiction of hell, the poet uses paronomasia to evoke the ambiguous quality of that habitation—the fire which lacks light, the continual interchange of heat and cold:

> geondfolen *fyre*   and *fær*cyle,
> rece and *reade* lege.   Heht þa geond þæt *ræd*lease hof
> weaxan witebrogan.   Hæfdon hie wrohtgeteme
> *grimme* wiþ god gesomnad· him þæs *grim* lean becom.   (43–46)
> [wrapped in fire and intense chill, in smoke and red flame. He then com
> manded torture-terror to increase throughout that wretched dwelling.
> They had cruelly gathered together a series of crimes against God; for that
> a grim reward came upon them.]

Wordplay sets up the ironic contrasts: Hell is both *read* and *rædleas*; the devils wanted a *rice*, "kingdom," (47) but were surrounded by *rece*; they wanted a *lean*, "reward" (46), but "him seo wen *geleah*," "hope deceived them" (49); their compensation was *grim* for they had acted *grimme* against God. Because the poet made the initial sounds of the hot and cold blasts seem almost interchangeable, their reciprocity and reversibility in Hell appear at once more comprehensible and terrifying.

Dante in the Paolo and Francesca episode of the *Inferno* used paronomasia to render the reciprocity inherent in love:

> *Amor* ch' a nullo *amato amar* perdona[34]
> [Love which absolves no loved one from loving]

The *Daniel* poet used such paronomasia to illustrate in onomatopoeic fashion the circularity of hate, the revolution of a torment which lashes back at its perpetrators:

ne se bryne *beot* mæcgum   þe in þam *beote* wæron,
ac þæt *fyr fyr scyde*   to ðam þe ða *scylde* worhton . . .   (264–265)
[nor did the fire injure the men who were in that danger, but the fire
passed further on to those who did that crime . . .]

Verbal pyrotechnics sparkle again and again in imitation of the fire,
which boomerangs upon the sinners:

fyr on feondas   for *fyren*dædum   (344)
[fire on the enemies for their wicked deeds]

Much of this wordplay seems to reflect the *Daniel* poet's eschatological
concerns.[35] As collocations of the type *fyr:fyr, fyr:fyren* pave the way to
the flames of Doomsday, paronomastic constructions of finality and ful-
fillment such as *wyrd wæs geworden*, "fate came to pass" (652), and *dom
gedemed*, "judgment judged" (654), provide a series of sombre bass
chords. A similar and favorite construction of the *Daniel* poet is the com-
bination in one half line of a noun and a past participle, so that the sound
of the first word appears to be echoed and enclosed in the latter: e.g.,
"*mane* ge*men*ged," "mingled with sin" (184), "*foldan* be*fol*en," "entrusted
to the earth" (559), "*lige* be*leg*de," "surrounded by flame" (295). These
past participles that contain within them the sound of an adjacent key noun
must have seemed to the poet to epitomize the inevitable completion of
God's plan, the working out of structures imbedded in language from the
very beginning. At times, the poet appears to be testing the limits of
paronomasia, as when he plays upon the sounds of *gyld*, "idol," *gold*,
"gold," and *God*, "God." The idolatrous statue in question is a "*gyld* of
golde" (175). Although the heathen blindly pay homage "to þam *gyldnan
gylde*, þe he him to *gode* geteode," "to that golden idol which he [the king]
set up as his God" (204), Daniel and the three Hebrew youths see the
phonological and theological incongruity in that second half line which
identifies *gold* and *God*. "Hie him þæt *gold* to *gode* noldon," "they would
not have that gold as God" (197), and they refuse to bow "to þam *golde*,
þe he him to *gode* teode," "to that gold which he set up as his God" (216).
The heathen believe that gold and God are associated; the *Daniel* poet
knows they are not, yet continues to link them. Since this particular
phonological association was for him nonetymological in conception, its
rhetorical value must have resided in its shock potential, in its contradict-
ing in meaning the very verbal ties its sounds seemed initially to propose.

Augustine uses such dissociative paronomasia in his sermons: Man prospers "honorando martyrum *passiones,* non amando *potiones,*" "by honoring the passions of martyrs, not by loving drinks."[36] His faintly humorous collocation of two nonetymological, accidental homonyms is easily recognizable as wordplay. That *Daniel* was among the first Old English poems to arouse the curiosity of recent scholarship as to the likelihood of deliberate Old English punning is a tribute to the equally high visibility of some of its wordplay.[37] It is possible for us to pass over etymological constructions such as *Daniel . . . drihtnes dom, wyrd geworden,* or *dom gedemed,* but difficult indeed to miss insistent sound effects such as "guman to þam *gyldnan gylde,* þe he him to *gode geteode.*" Christine Mohrmann has demonstrated that Augustine employed two very different styles of paronomasia in his writings, his rhetorically correct, etymological wordplay in the *Civitas Dei* being quite distinct in its subtlety from the humorous puns, rhymes, and nonetymological homonyms of the *Sermones* (such as *passiones* and *potiones* already mentioned).[38] The *Daniel* poet's wordplay exhibits a similar dichotomy. His first paronomastic style (consisting of etymological, solemn, and congruous pairings) seems characteristic of the Old English charms, maxims, and scriptural poems; the *Daniel* poet's second style (nonetymological, incongruous pairings, with a tendency toward rhyme) is more characteristic of the Old English poetic homily or saint's life, and seems to use wordplay primarily as a teaching device to test our conditioned verbal responses.[39]

Unlike *God* and *gold* in *Daniel,* most objects in the Old English scriptural poems that are linked by single-line paronomasia really do appear to belong together. The individual poets seem to have had favorites among their paronomastic collocations. These often represent a social norm, a basis for stability and order in this world. The coupling of God and good is approved by the *Genesis B* poet:[40]

291   *gode* æfter *gode* ænegum

657   *godes* engel *god*

740   *god*lice geardas.   Unc wearð *god* yrre

779   *godne* gretton and *god* nemdon

816–817 nu me mæg hreowan   þæt ic bæd heofnes *god,*
         waldend þone *godan*

849–850   þæt hie ne forgeate   *god* ælmihtig,
                 and him gewisade   waldend se *goda*

In *Genesis*, as in *Exodus*, a *maga*, "man," belongs with his *mægð*, "tribe, people":

Gen.	1082	swylce on ðære *mægðe* *maga* wæs haten
	1123	*mægðum* and mæcgum *mæg*burg sine
	1172–73	Se *maga* wæs on his *mægðe*
	1624	se *mago*ræswa *mægðe* sinre
Exod.	17	modgum *mago*ræswan, his *maga* feorh
	55	modig *mago*ræswa, *mæg*burh heora

The noble man always remains attached to his native land[41]:

Gen.	1634	ærest *æðelinga*; *eðelð*rym onhof
	1735–37	of þære *eðel*tyrf . . . *æðelinga* bearn
	2131	eft on *eðel* *æðelinga* bearn
Dan.	637	eard and *eðel* æfter þam *æðelinge*

Through associative paronomasia, the poets can also suggest how man has within him the potential for both sin and holiness; the homophonic attraction of *mann*, "man," to *man*, "sin," is as real as that of *hæleð*, "man," to *halig*, "holy"[42]:

Gen.	297–299	Swa deð *monna* gehwylc
		þe wið his waldend winnan ongynneð
		mid *mane* . . .
	451	mid *man*dædum *men* beswican
	1271	hwæt wæs *monna* *manes* on eorðan
Psalms	63.8	sceal him *manna* gehwylc *man* ondrædan

	61.3	ðonne ge mid *mane* *men* ongunnon
	61.9	hwæðere ge, *manna* bearn, *manes* unlyt
	139.4	and fram þam *mannum* þe *man* fremmen
Sol. Sat.	327	Wa bið ðonne ðissum modgum *monnum*, ðam ðe her nu mid *mane* lengest
Christ	1600	*men* on mode, þonne *man* fremmað
Exod.	388	*halige* heahtreowe, swa *hæleð* gefrunon
	394	heahst and *haligost*, *hæleðum* gefrægost
Christ	461	*hæleð* mid hlaford, to þære *halgan* byrg
	534	*hæleð* hygerofe, in þa *halgan* byrg
Judith	203	*hæleð* under helmum of þære *haligan* byrig

An Old English scriptural poet could, when he wished, imitate directly the paronomasia he found in the Old Testament text before him: *wæter of wætrum* (*Gen.* 152; from *aquas ab aquis*); *drihtna drihten* (*Gen.* 638, 2255, *Ps.* 135.3; *dominus dominorum*); *on worulda woruld* (*Ps.* 84.5, *Christ* 778; *in saecula saeculorum*); *of mægene on mægen* (*Ps.* 83.6; *de virtute in virtutem*); *of cynne on cynn* (*Ps.* 84.5, 121.4; *a generatione in generationem*); *gehat gehet* (*Ps.* 131.2; *votum vovit*)[43]; or he could create etymological figures of his own: "*dwæl on gedwilde*," "erred in error" (*Gen.* 23), "his *boda beodan*," "his messenger to announce" (*Gen.* 558), "on þinne *wlite wlitan*," "on your beauty to gaze" (*Gen.* 1825), "be *naman nemnan*," "to name by name" (*Jud.* 81).[44] This etymological style would probably have had meaning for an Old English poet above and beyond its function as conveyor of a lofty and oracular message. Old Testament paronomasia, such as God's warning to Adam—*morte morieris*, "thou shalt die the death" (Gen. 2:17)—was received and analyzed with seriousness by the Anglo-Saxon exegetes who discovered within it hidden theological messages: *morte morieris*, an apparent tautology, becomes in their hands an allusion to man's twofold death (soul and body).[45] That Satan falling "*dwæl on gedwilde*," "erred in error" (*Gen.* 23), while the fallen Eve was blamed by God only for *dæda gedwild*, "the error of deeds" (*Gen.* 922), might have signaled to an enthusiastic exegete that the devil's crime, being paronomastic, was twice as serious: "Forþon þe se heaengel þe nu is heatol deofol himself his synne afunde, ond se man wæs beswicen. And eac swa myclum swa þæs engles gecynd mare wæs on wuldre, swa hit wæs mare on forwyrde" [Because the archangel who is now called the devil discovered his sin for himself, and man was deceived. And as much as the nature of that angel was greater in glory, so it was greater in fall].[46] In early England—as elsewhere—the world of the divine was imagined to require a separate, more sacred language than that used by men.[47] As far as Chaucer was concerned, "goddes speken in amphibologies"[48]; in the Old English scriptural poems, the voice of divinity is more often heard through paronomasia.

The objection could be raised that the Anglo-Saxon scriptural poets would not have treated their own vernacular paronomasia as seriously as they would wordplay in Latin, which was—along with Greek and Hebrew—one of the three *linguae sacrae*, "holy languages."[49] Yet from Bede on, the Anglo-Saxons displayed a remarkably revolutionary attitude in this area of linguistic theology. Bede, for instance, was the first to break away from the Augustine-to-Isidore tradition of distinguishing only three sacred languages.[50] He reasoned that all the languages of Babel were God-given and, therefore, all were to be considered equally holy and fit for discovering and transmitting biblical truths.[51] Hebrew could be regarded as the oldest tongue without concluding that all other languages were merely corrupt and confused offshoots. This may account for some of the pleasure the Anglo-Saxons seem to have derived from their etymological translations of Hebrew names, in their proving that *drihtnes dom* was closer to Daniel in sound than *iudicium dei*, that Seth was closer to *sæd* than to *gramen* or *semen*, that Sion was more like *seon* than *specula*. And in their competition with Latin, the Old English writers could point with pride to the fact that *caelum a celando superiora* was given new life in *heofon . . . behelað ufan,* and that *fatum:a fando* was more than matched by *wyrd:word*. Three centuries after Bede, another Englishman—this time, Ælfric—seems to have been first to state in practical terms the notion of a universal grammar: There was just one deep structure, the same divinely ordained framework ordered all sublunary tongues.[52] Attitudes such as these would have encouraged Anglo-Saxon England to devote the same meticulous attention and analysis to its own language, its own scriptural poetry, as had previously been given to Latin, Greek, or Hebrew.

The tentative and speculative nature of the present subject probably needs no underlining. Much remains to he discovered about the function of etymological and pseudo-etymological wordplay in Old English poetry as a whole. In the Exeter Book *Maxims*, in lines like "*treo* sceolon brædan ond *treow* weaxan," "trees must grow and truth increase" (159), one senses that the Old English poet is envisioning his language as a divining rod, meditating upon words in a prophetic fashion in order to seek out as yet hidden streams of thought.[53] However, in *Beowulf*, in the description of the *heorot*, "hart," who would rather die than set foot in the haunted *mere*, the poet's concluding aside with its paronomastic echo of heorot in *heoru*—"nis þæt *heoru* stow," "that is not a pleasant place" (1372)—seems wry and detached rather than awe-inspiring.[54] There is a danger, of course, in single-minded concentration upon a poet's etymological wordplay: "Wer immer nach Gründen geht, geht zu grunde." This warning applies, one would think, particularly to the paronomasia of a dead language like Old English, where uncertainty as to the actual sounds of the words, their expressive values, and even their lexicographical meanings might lead us to discover wordplay where none existed. Yet because of the notable subtlety and indirectness of most Old English paronomasia, the real danger at the moment seems to lie in another direction. There is probably a much greater chance that our untrained ears will miss the paronomastic expression of praise in the final line of *Genesis* for all things that the "*gifena* drihten for*gifen* hæfde," "Lord of gifts had granted" (2936), than that our eyes will over-look the pun in the superficially similar sentiment expressed by one of Laud's enemies in Charles I's court: "Great praise be to God and little *Laud* to the devil." To appreciate the difference between these two modes of wordplay is the first step in increasing our sensitivity to an important aspect of the Old English poetic imagination.

There do seem to be various ways in which Old English paronoma-sia might profitably be studied. One possible approach would be to examine its use in the poetry as an ornamental or framing device. Just as the Anglo-Saxon illuminator adorned the initial capitals of a poem and the capitals of each major structural division within the work, so the Old English scriptural poet seems to have concentrated his most elaborate paronomastic constructions within prologues and epilogues, as well as arranging them so as to frame in a kind of envelope pattern particularly dramatic or elevated passages in the body of his work.[55] It was earlier

noted that *Genesis* opens with a series of plays on *word*; *Exodus* opens
with a highly significant play on *lif and lifigend* (5–6), and *Daniel* with
verses like "*cyning*dom habban, swa him *gecynde* wæs" (3) and "wearð
wig gifen *wigena* mænieo" (5). The *Daniel* poet also employs parono-
masia to frame with elegance the two lyrical outbursts within his narra-
tive ("Prayer of Azariah," 283–332, and "Song of the Three Children,"
362–408), while the *Genesis B* poet tends to save his trains of sound
associations to round off a verse paragraph—

> fylde *helle*
> mid þam andsacum.   *Healdon* englas forð
> heofonrices hehðe,   þe ær godes *hyldo* gelæston.   (319–321)
> [God] filled Hell with those adversaries. The angels who had kept faith
> with God inhabited still the summit of the heavenly kingdom.]

—or an entire section, as in his final lines:

> ac hie on *gebed* feollon   bu tu ætsomne
> morgena gehwilce,   *bædon mihtigne*
> þæt hie ne forgeate   *god ælmihtig*,
> and him gewisade   waldend se *goda*,
> hu hie on þam leohte forð   libban sceoldon.   (847–851)
> [and they bowed, both together, in prayer each morning; they entreated
> the Mighty One that He, God Almighty, might not forget them, and that
> the good Lord would show them how they must henceforth live in the
> world.]

Such wordplay, extending beyond the metrical boundaries of the long
line and depending in large part on words not required by the allitera-
tion, suggests that here the rhetorical framework is dominant in the
poet's mind, the verse unit secondary. The paronomasia of the Old Eng-
lish scriptural poet can thus serve to bring into sharper focus the formal
structures and balances of his narrative.

The Old English poet's use of paronomasia as a characterizing
device might also be studied. In *Genesis B*, for example, Lucifer shows
his hand in his very first speech when he announces his intention not to
look "*gode* æfter *gode* ænegum," "to God for any good" (291). The
rebellious angel consistently inverts and denies apparent etymological
ties, such as the link between God and good insisted upon by the poet,

preferring instead to twist language to fit his own view of things. Man (*hæleð*) is not holy (*halig*) but, declares the devil with false etymological wit, "mid *hæleða* forlore . . . is min mod *gehæled*," "with the damnation of men . . . is my heart healed" (757–758). It is this insensitivity to the ways of words, this forging of perverse puns, which seems to distinguish him at the outset from the other angels and start him on his downward path.[56]

Still another approach to Old English paronomasia might be to examine how the originality of the poet makes itself known through his flashes of verbal insight and wit, through that linguistic agility which allows him to associate formulaic half lines in effective ways.[57] The subjects, sources, meter, formulaic diction, and structural procedures of Cynewulf's poems may all be inherited and highly traditional, but that poet's evocative paronomastic plays on *rod . . . rodor* serve to sign his work as uniquely and irrevocably his, just as do the runic letters with which he closes.[58] So too, in the Old English *Genesis*, we saw that much of the poet's originality derived from his skill in manipulating paronomastic language so as to project his inner vision of the moving force behind Old Testament history. Such wordplay seems to represent the innovative, untypical aspects of a poetic tradition more often cited and revered for its conventional nature.

NOTES

1. Dorothy Whitelock, ed., *English Historical Documents c. 500–1042* (London, 1955), 49, notes that Ethelred's punning nickname (*Æðelræd*, "Noble Counsel," is *unræd*, "bad, foolish counsel") is not recorded before the thirteenth century. The first element of that king's name was played upon in *The Battle of Maldon*: "*eðel* þysne / *Æðel*redes eard," "this native land, land of Ethelred" (52–53); "þurh þone *æðelan Æðel*redes þegen," "through that noble thane of Ethelred" (151). All quotations from OE poetry are taken from *The Anglo-Saxon Poetic Records* (= *ASPR*), ed. George P. Krapp and Elliott V. K. Dobbie, 6 vols. (New York, 1931–1953). Words involved in paronomastic constructions are silently italicized, as here.

2. Bede, *Historia ecclesiastica* 2.1, relates how Gregory the Great foretold the conversion of the Anglo-Saxons by punning on the names *Angle*, *Ælle*, and *Deira*. Another account of the legend with even more elaborate wordplay is found in the Whitby Life of Gregory; see *The Earliest Life of*

Gregory the Great, ed. Bertram Colgrave (University of Kansas Press, 1968), 90–91.

3. Geoffrey Shepherd, "Scriptural Poetry," in *Continuations and Beginnings: Studies in Old English Literature*, ed. Eric G. Stanley (London, 1966), 7.

4. John M. Kemble, ed., *The Dialogue of Salomon and Saturnus* (London, 1848), 7.

5. Kemble, 193, recognized that Solomon was forging an etymology along Latin lines: "that is, *caelum*, from *celare*, an etymology worthy of Isidore or Hierome." However, the particular form of the etymology used by Solomon first appears in Cassiodorus (*caelam . . . quod intra se celet universa*), *Expositio psalmorum*, *CCSL* 98 (Turnhout, 1958), 1035, 298ff. It is repeated in several MSS of Isidore (*caelam a celando superiora*), *Etymologiarum sive originum libri XX*, ed. W. M. Lindsay, 2 vols. (Oxford, 1911) (hereafter cited as *Etymologiae*), XIII, iv, 1–2, and in Bede, *De orthographia*, *PL* 90, 130A. For discussion of this version of the etymology as a Christian modification of the earlier *caelum dictum . . . contrario nomine celatum, quod apertum est* (Varro, *De lingua latina*, V, 18) see Ilona Opelt, "Christianisierung heidnischer Etymologien," *Jahrbuch für Antike und Christentum*, II (1959), 80ff., and Roswitha Klinck, *Die lateinische Etymologie des Mittelalters* (Medium Aevum, Philologische Studien, 17, Munich, 1970), 85–89.

6. "The Significance of Names in Old English Literature," *Anglia* 86 (1968), 14–58. Related articles by the same author include "Some Uses of Name-Meanings in Old English Poetry," *Neuphilologische Mitteilungen* 69 (1988), 161–171, and "Lexicography and Literary Criticism: A Caveat," in *Philological Essays in Honor of Herbert Dean Meritt*, ed. James L. Rosier (Mouton, The Hague, 1970), 99–110 (pp. 107–109 for wordplay in OE poetry).

7. Since wordplay itself operates by breaking down conventional verbal boundaries, it is not surprising that the terminology devised by rhetoricians to differentiate its various forms (*paronomasia, annominatio, traductio, figura etymologica*, et al.) is equally slippery and inconsistent. Hans Holst discusses the historical confusion of terms for wordplay in *Die Wortspiele in Ciceros Reden*, Symbolae Osloenses, fasc. supplet. 1 (Oslo, 1925). For the purposes of the present study, only two basic forms of OE poetic wordplay need be distinguished: *paronomasia*, referring to the establishing of an etymological or pseudo-etymological relationship between two or more words, and the *ambiguum*, referring to the establishment of such a connection between two meanings contained in one word. The most convincing evidence so far for the presence of the *ambiguum* in

Old English poetry comes from *The Riddles of the Exeter Book*, ed. Frederick Tupper, Jr. (Boston, 1910), notes to 32:14, 38:7, and 73:22. A recent attempt to uncover *ambigua* in *Beowulf* is J. Edwin Whitesell's "Intentional Ambiguities in *Beowulf*," *Texas Studies in Literature* 11 (1966), 145–149. Bernard F. Huppé, *The Web of Words* (Albany, 1970), pp.10, 18, 50, 80, 86, 102, 167, 169, finds deliberate ambiguity in four other OE poems. Only *Exodus* among the OE scriptural poems appears to use the *ambiguum* to any extent.

8. *Bedae venerabilis de schematibus et tropis liber*, in Karl F. Halm, ed., *Rhetores latini minores* (Leipzig, 1863), 609, l. 29; trans. Gussie H. Tanenhaus, "Bede's *De Schematibus et Tropis*: A Translation," *Quarterly Journal of Speech* 48 (1962), 242. Samuel J. Crawford, ed., *Byrhtferth's Manual*, EETS 177 (1929; repr. 1966), 176. Both Bede and Byrhtferth used scriptural paronomasia as their model. William M. Ryan, "Word-Play in Some Old English Homilies and a Late Middle English Poem," *Studies in Language, Literature and Culture of the Middle Ages and Later*, ed. E. Bagby Atwood and Archibald A. Hill (Austin, 1969), 265–278, looked at paronomasia in the OE homilies, as did James Waddell Tupper, *Tropes and Figures in Anglo-Saxon Prose* (Baltimore, 1897). Dorothy Bethurum, ed., *The Homilies of Wulfstan* (Oxford, 1957), 92, and John C. Pope. ed., *Homilies of Ælfric: A Supplementary Collection*, EETS 259–260 (1967–68), 1:109–110, 131–132. The first scholar to treat systematically the figures of rhetoric in OE poetry, Gottfried Jansen, *Beiträge zur Synonymik und Poetik der allgemien als ächt anerkannten Dichtungen Cynewulfs* (Münster, 1883), concluded with reference to paronomasia that "die Verwendung dieser Klangfigur ist sehr selten" (73). He was followed by Samuel Shellabarger, "A Thesaurus of the Figures of Speech in Anglo-Saxon and the Edda" (unpubl. diss. Harvard 1917), who systematically ignored wordplay. Heinrich Ziegler, *Der poetische Sprachgebrauch in den sogen. Cædmonischen Dichtungen* (Münster, 1883), did not mention paronomasia but included some examples under the headings "Parallelismus" and "Die Zergliederung" (63–70). Richard M. Meyer, *Die altgermanische Poesie nach ihren formelhaften Elementen beschreiben* (Berlin, 1889), 296–302, listed numerous cases of paronomasia in OE verse; Adeline C. Bartlett, *The Larger Rhetorical Patterns in Anglo-Saxon Poetry* (New York, 1935), 36, 41, 66, also acknowledged its importance.

9. Kenneth Sisam, *The Structure of Beowulf* (Oxford, 1965), 20.

10. Modern etymological science confirms that *lucus*, "sacred grove," and *luceo*, "to be bright, shine," are cognates; the original "shining" or "open place" in the woods was later taken to signify the grove itself. See

Dictionnaire étymologique de la langue latine, by A. Ernout and A. Meillet, quatrième édition (Paris, 1959), s.v. *lucus*.

11. *ASPR* 6 (1942), p. 125: "For a Swarm of Bees," 9; p. 119: "The Nine Herbs Charm," 14–15. The verbal homeopathic magic of "sitte ge, *sige*wif, *sigað* to eorðan," is reinforced by the speaker's imitative casting of sand over the swarm: as the grains settle, so shall the bees.

12. *The Homilies of the Anglo-Saxon Church*, ed. Benjamin Thorpe, 2 vols. (London, 1844–46), 1:476 (hereafter cited as *Thorpe*). Similar instructions are given in a tenth-century OE version of a ninth-century Latin penitential: Josef Raith, ed., *Die altenglische Version des Halitgar'schen Bussbuches* (*sog. Poenitentiale Pseudo-Ecgberti*), Bibliothek der angelsächsischen Prosa 13 (Hamburg, 1933; 2nd ed. Darmstadt, 1964), 30.

13. The power of Christian verbal magic is at issue in Bede's story (*Historia ecclesiastica*, 4.22) of Imma, the captive whose bonds were loosened each time masses were said for him: Charles Plummer, ed., *Vitae Sanctorum Hiberniae* (Oxford, 1910), 1:clxvii–clxxix, presents the evidence for Irish saints gaining power over heathen magicians by chanting psalms and hymns.

14. The employment of this technique in contemporary Eskimo and Australian aboriginal poetry is examined by C. Maurice Bowra, *Primitive Song* (New York, 1963), 85–87. Johan Huizinga, *Homo ludens: A Study of the Play-Element in Culture*, trans. from 1944 Gm. ed. by R. F. C. Hull (London, 1949), 122, describes an extreme form of associative composition practiced by the inhabitants of Buru in the East Indian archipelago.

15. J. Gonda, *Stylistic Repetition in the Veda*, Verhandelingen der Koninklijka Nederlandse Akademie van Wetenschappen, afd. Letterkunde, 65, no. 3 (Amsterdam, 1959), 259. In the oldest preserved Slavic MS, the tenth-century Kiev Leaflets (Old Church Slavonic translation of the Latin Mass formulary), paronomasia is similarly used to focus attention on a desired link between Lord and sacrifice: "*Priimi gi prosimə tę prinosə sə prineseny tebě*" (Lord, we ask you, accept this sacrifice offered to you). See Ladislav Matejka, "Systematic Sound Repetition in the Kiev Leaflets," *The Slavic and East European Journal* 6 (1962), 337.

16. Cf. John 12:32 on the predestined convergence of heaven and earth: *si exaltatus fuero a terra, omnia traham.*

17. "Ælfric's Preface to Genesis," line 100, in *The Old English Version of The Heptateuch, Ælfric's Treatise on the Old and New Testament and his Preface to Genesis*, ed. Samuel J. Crawford, EETS 160 (London, 1922; repr. with addendum by N. R. Ker, 1968).

18. Ælfric in Thorpe, 1:40. The two forms were associated in the earliest

Anglo-Saxon word lists. Adjacent entries in Laurence Nowell's *Vocabu-larium saxonicum* (ca. 1567), ed. Albert H. Marckwardt (Michigan, 1952), read:

Word—a word, verbum

Wordcwedene

ge*Worden* wæs—Res gesta. A thing which was indeede [sic]

See also William Somner, *Dictionarium Saxonico-Latino-Anglicum* (1659), Scolar Press Facsimile (Menston, Eng., 1970), s.v. *word*.

19. *The Letters of St. Jerome*, ed. and trans. Charles C. Mierow, notes by T. C. Lawler, Ancient Christian Writers 33 (London, 1963), 21. Others who indulged in initial plays on *word* include Dante, who began the *De vulgari eloquentia* by invoking Christ as the Word (*Verbo aspirante de coelis*), and Otfrid, who, in the prologue to his *Evangelienbuch*, used such wordplay to explore the interrelation of his literary and theological endeavors. See Peter von Polenz, "Otfrids Wortspiel mit Versbegriffen als literarisches Bekenntnis," in *Festschrift für Ludwig Wolff zum 70 Geburtstag*, ed. Werner Schröder (Neumünster, 1962), 121–134. The Anglo-Saxons justified the sanctity of poetic creation by reference to the concept of the *Logos*: The Christian poet was to derive each word from the Word. Examples in Geoffrey Shepherd, "The Prophetic Cædmon," *RES* 5 (1954), 113–122; also G. J. M. Bartelink, "Jeux de mots autour de ΛΟΓΟΣ, de ses composés et dérivés chez les auteurs chrétiens," in *Mélanges offerts à Mademoiselle Christine Mohrmann* (Utrecht, 1963), 23–37.

20. For Bede's synthesis, see his commentary to Gen. 1:1 in *Bedae venera-bilis opera, CCSL* 118A, Pars ii, 1, *Opera exegetica: libri quatuor in prin-cipium Genesis usque ad nativitatem Isaac et ejectionem Ismahelis adnotationum*, ed. Charles W. Jones (Turnhout, 1967), 3, 25. Also Pseudo-Bede, *Expositio in primum librum Mosis, PL* 91, 190D. The Lind-isfarne Gospels gloss to John 1:1 reads "Word, þæt is godes sunu." The full equation is restated by Alcuin, *De fide sanctae et individuae Trinitatis* II, 14 (*PL* 101, 32B-D): "*In principio* fecit *Deus coelum et terram* (Gen. 1:1), id est, in Christo fecit Deus, qui est Filius Dei, qui est Verbum Dei . . ." Ælfric provides an English summary of the synthesis in *Exam-eron Anglice*, ed. Samuel J. Crawford, Bibliothek der angelsächsischen Prosa 10 (Hamburg, 1921; Darmstadt, 1968), 37, lines 47–51. For an allu-sion to Christ as the Word in OE poetry, see Thomas D. Hill, " 'Byrht Word' and 'Hælendes Heafod': Christological Allusion in the Old English

Christ and Satan," *ELN* 8 (1970), 6–9. For background on the *Deus-Logos-Verbum* relation, see H. Paissac, *Théologie du verbe; Saint Augustin et Saint Thomas* (Paris, 1951).

21. Pseudo-Bede, *Expositio in primum librum Mosis*, *PL* 91, 191A. Also Bede on Gen. 1:3 in *Libri quatuor in principium Genesis*, *CCSL* 118A, 8, 170-172: ". . . sed altius intelligendum dixisse Deum ut fieret creatura, quia per Verbum suum omnia, id est, per unigenitum Filium fecit."

22. Thorpe, 2:60. The meaning of God's sealing the ark is outlined in Pseudo-Bede, *Expositio in primum librum Mosis*, *PL* 91, 225D: "Quodque dixit, *Inclusit illum Dominus*, ostendit Christum suam custodire Ecclesiam a persequentibus." Also Bede, *Libri quatuor in principium Genesis*, *CCSL*, 118A, 117, 1589–1594. Fred C. Robinson, "The Significance of Names in Old English Literature," 33, points out that at line 1304 the *Genesis* poet alludes to the meaning of Noah's name as interpreted in the commentaries: Noah = *requies* = rest; this name meaning reinforced the typological equation of Noah with Christ.

23. Clement of Alexandria has a classic statement to this effect in his *Protrepticus*: *Clemens Alexandrinus, Protrepticus und Paedagogue*, ed. Otto Stählin in *Die griechischen christlichen Schriftsteller der ersten drei Jahrhunderte* (Leipzig, 1905), 1:72. Also K. Goldammer, "Das Schiff der Kirche," *Theologische Zeitschrift* 6 (1950), 232–237; Per Beskow, *Rex Gloriae: The Kingship of Christ in the Early Church* (Uppsala, 1962), 206–208.

24. A doubtful case of wordplay on *word* and *wyrd* occurs in vv. 2567–74 (Lot's wife, having disobeyed God's *words*, is handed her *fate*) and in vv. 2775–79 (the narrator, having recalled God's *word* regarding the birth of Isaac, shows Sarah sealing Ismael's *fate*). In both these episodes, *word* and *wyrd* are separated by several half-lines. The *wyrd gewearð* play in the latter passage is noted by Ladislav Mittner, *Wurd: Das Sakrale in der altgermanische Epik*, Bibliotheca Germanica, 6 (Bern, 1955), 89–91: "Bei *þa se wyrd gewearð* (Gen. 2777) handelt es sich nicht am blosse 'etymologische Spielerei' (Brandl, p. 84), sondern um das richtige Gefühl dafür, dass man die Function der Wurd nur durch ihre Selbstaussage bestimmen könne, indem man der Wesen ihrem Wirken gleich setzte" (91).

25. *Christ* 38: "þæt þurh bearnes *gebyrd bryd* eacen wearð."

26. Ælfric in Thorpe, 1:62. For background on the typology of Isaac's sacrifice, see Jean Daniélou, *Sacramentum futuri; études sur les origines de la typologie biblique* (Paris, 1950), 97–128; trans. Dom Wulstan Hibberd, *From Shadows to Reality: Studies in the Biblical Typology of the Fathers*

(London, 1960), 115–131. Patristic exegesis found in Genesis a specifically Christian pattern of creation, fall, *and* ultimate redemption; the commentators assumed that this was Moses's primary intention: "Intentio quippe Moysis est restaurationem humani generis per Christum figuraliter narrare, quam intentionem omnimode satagit suae materiae adaptare" (Honorius of Autun, *Hexaemeron, PL* 172, 253B). Bede structures his four-part commentary on Genesis (see n. 20) to conclude with the joyful advent of Isaac, just as the OE poet ends triumphantly with Isaac's (averted) sacrifice. Each of Bede's four books on Genesis finishes on a high note (Creation, Noah, Abraham, and Ismael-Isaac). These are the same four Old Testament episodes which the OE poet attempts to underscore with his paronomastic plays on *word*.

27. There is a similar sense of fleetingness in the *Gawain* poet's paronomastic verse—"A ȝere ȝernes ful ȝerne, and ȝeldez neuer lyke," "a year runs by very swiftly, and never brings back the same things" (498)—which is hard to imitate in modern English (MnE). Cf. the evocative etymological plays in the *Ancrene Wisse* on the theme of transience: "Ha beoð her *hweolinde*, ase *hweoles* ouerturneð sone ne leasteð nane *hwile*," "they are here revolving [play on *hwilende*, "transitory"], as wheels turn over quickly and do not stop [*or* remain in one place] for a moment." Geoffrey Shepherd, ed., *Ancrene Wisse, Parts Six and Seven* (London, 1959), 6, lines 35–36.

28. Adam's observation that *Eve* did *yfele* is echoed in Milton's pun: "O *Eve*, in *evil* hour . . ." (*Paradise Lost*, 9:1067). Ælfric seems to make an effort to associate Pharaoh with *faran*: he translates Exodus 3:10 (*sed veni, et mittam te ad Pharaonem, ut educas populum meum . . . de Aegipto*) as "*Far* to ðam cyninge *Pharao*, and bend him þæt he min folc forlæte of his leode *faran*" (Thorpe, 2:192).

29. Jerome, *Liber interpretationis hebraicorum nominum, CCSL* 72, Pars I, 1 (Turnhout, 1959), 135, 11. Aldhelm's prose *De virginitate* in *Opera omnia*, ed. Rudolf Ehwald, Monumenta Germaniae historica, Auctores antiquissimi (Berlin, 1919), xv, 250, makes literary use of this same etymology: "Daniel vera, praesago nominis vocabulo *iudicium Dei* . . ." Interest in the first element of Daniel's name can be traced from the biblical paronomasia of Gen. 49:16—"*Dan* shall *judge* his people"—to the etymological allusion in Shakespeare's *Merchant of Venice*, 4.1.220—"A Daniel come to judgement." The *Daniel* poet in vv. 163, 547, 654, and 661 similarly associates Daniel with "judgment" alone.

30. The *Daniel* poet turns the name into a descriptive phrase through morphemic division (*Dan* "judgment" + *el* "God") or *tmesis*, the "cutting" or

separation of the parts of a compound word by an intervening word or words. For a discussion of this rhetorical device in medieval Latin, see Dag Norberg, *Introduction à l'étude de la versification latine médiévale*, Acta Universitatis Stockholmiensis, 5 (Uppsala, 1958), 58ff. Bede, *De schematibus et tropis liber*, 614, line 23, gives as an example of *tmesis* the verse: "*Hiero* quem genuit *solymis* Davidica proles," "whom the descendant of David has brought forth from Jerusalem." Comparable, perhaps, is the OE presentation of the etymology for Jerusalem (*sibbe gesihþ*, "vision of peace") as *sibbe ond gesihþ*, "peace and sight" (*Guthlac* 816).

31. *Paradise Lost*, 10:608. Arnold S. Stein, *Answerable Style: Essays on Paradise Lost* (Minneapolis, 1953), 66–67, noted that the word "error" was employed in its full etymological significance of "right wandering" in Milton's prelapsarian garden; after the Fall, however, Milton uses the word only in its modern pejorative sense of "wrong wandering, a deviation."

32. Fred C. Robinson, "The Significance of Names in Old English Literature," 29–32, notes that Seth's name (Heb. "seed," Jerome's *vel gramen aut semen seu resurrectio*) and its nearly homophonic meaning in OE—*sæd*, "seed"—are linked in *Genesis* 1145: "*Sæd*berendes *Sethes* lice," "the body of seed-bearing Seth."

33. Herbert D. Meritt, *Fact and Lore About Old English Words* (Stanford, 1954), 207.

34. V, 103. See Leo Spitzer, "Speech and Language in *Inferno* XIII," *Italica* 19 (1942), 98.

35. Some of the most exuberant wordplay in *Daniel* is employed to mark the deliverance of Shadrach, Meschach, and Abednego from the furnace, a scriptural episode that was almost invariably the last reading in the liturgy for Holy Saturday; it was also a popular subject in the frescoes of the catacombs as a paradigm of the eschatological death and resurrection of Christian martyrs. See Abbé Martimort, "L'Iconographie des catacombs et la catéchèse antique," *Rivista di archeologia cristiana* 25 (1949), 1–10.

36. *Passiones* and *potiones* were near homonyms in early medieval Latin. This example comes from Christine Mohrmann, "Woordspeling in de brieven van Sint Cyprianus," *Tijdschrift voor Nederlandsche taal en latteren* (1939), 172; trans. as "Wordplay in the Letters of St. Cyprian," in *Etudes sur le latin des chrétiens* (Rome, 1958), 1:296.

37. The lavish wordplay of *Daniel* has been noted by, among others, Robert T. Farrell, "The Unity of the Old English *Daniel*," *RES* 18 (1967), 128; Bernard F. Huppé, *Doctrine and Poetry: Augustine's Influence on Old English Poetry* (New York, 1959), 225; George P. Krapp, ed., *The Junius*

Manuscript, ASPR 1, 222 (v. 194); and Geoffrey Shepherd, "Scriptural Poetry," in *Continuations and Beginnings*, 32.

38. "Das Wortspiel in den augustinischen *Sermones*," *Mnemosyne* 3 (1936), 33–61; repr. in *Etudes sur le latin des chrétiens*, 1:323–349 (esp. pp. 344–349).

39. The sporadic presence of this second style in two OE scriptural paraphrases, *Daniel* and *Judith*, is probably related to the Anglo-Saxons' attitude towards these Old Testament books; they seem to have been regarded as exemplary histories, as Hebrew saints' lives, and not, like Genesis and Exodus, as the words of God set down by Moses. See B. J. Timmer, ed., *Judith* (London, 1952), 7. For Ælfric's exegetical approach to Judith, see his *Treatise on the Old and New Testament*, 48, and "Ælfric's Homilie über das Buch Judith," ed. Bruno Assmann, in *Angelsächsische Homilien und Heiligenleben*, Bibliothek der angelsächsischen Prosa 3 (1889; repr. with introd. by P. Clemoes, Darmstadt, 1964), 102–116 (esp. lines 412–417, pp. 114–115).

40. Plays on God and good are frequent in OE poetry and prose. They range from the rather general statement of the *Exeter Maxims*—"*god* bið genge, and wið god lenge," "good is prevailing and belongs to God" (120)—to Ælfric's more specific "*good* is þæs lichaman wæcce, þe for *Gode* bið gefremod," "good is the vigil of the body which is done for God" *(Homilies of Ælfric: A Supplementary Collection*, 1:132).

41. The same pun occurs in *Andreas* 642, *Death of Edward* 24, and the macaronic tribute *Aldhelm*: "Ealdelm, æpele sceop, etiam fuit / ipselos on æpele Anglosexna" (3–4). See note 1.

42. *Man ... mann* paronomasia also occurs in *Christ* 1416, 1094, *Guthlac* 909, *Elene* 626, *Juliana* 459, *Beowulf* 110, 712, *Meters of Boethius* 4.48. For more *hæleð ... halig* collocations, see *Guthlac* 683, 890, *Andreas* 885, 996, 1054, 1607, *Elene* 1203.

43. Old Testament paronomasia is analyzed in Immanuel M. Casanowicz, *Paronomasia in the Old Testament* (Boston, 1894); H. Reckendorf, *Über Paronomasie in den semitischen Sprachen* (Giessen, 1909); Gustav Boström, *Paronomasi í den äldre hebreiska maschallitteraturen med särskild hänsyn till Proverbia*, Lunds Universitets Årsskrift, N. F., Avd. 1, Bd. 23 (1927); A. Guillaume, "*Paronomasia* in the Old Testament," *Journal of Semitic Studies* 9 (1964), 282–290. For a recent treatment of the *figura etymologica* (*in saecula saeculorum*, etc.) in the vernacular, see Albert Wifstrand, "Kvällarnas kväll" in *Septentrionalia et orientalia*, ed. Bernhard Karlgren, Kungliga vitterhets, historia, och antikvitets akademins *Handlingar*, 91 (Stockholm, 1959). The *on*

worulda woruld construction occurs 21 times in OE poetry, 14 of these in the *Psalms*.

44. This latter practice is also very common in OE prose translations from Latin. The author of the OE *Apollonius* translates "gaude, gaude, Apolloni; quod filia mea te cupit, et meum votum est. Nichil enim in huius rei . . . negotio sine deo agi potest" as "blissa, blissa, Apolloni, for ðam ðe min dohtor *gewilnað* þæs þe min *willa* is. Ne mæg soðlice on þillicon þingon nan þinc gewurðan buton Godes *willan*." *The Old English Apollonius of Tyre*, ed. Peter Goolden (London, 1958), 34, 4–7. The OE translator of Orosius adapts Lat. "regnum avi, muros fratris, templum soceri *sanguine dedicavit*" as "ðuss *gebletsade* Romulus Romana rice on fruman: mid his broðor *blode* ðone weall and mid ðara sweora *blode* ða ciricean, and mid his eames *blode* ðæt rice," playing on the etymological connection between *bletsian*, "to bless, consecrate," and *blod*, "blood." *King Alfred's Orosius*, ed. Henry Sweet, EETS 79 (London, 1883; repr. 1959), 65–66. Mattias Tveitane, *Den lærde Stil: Oversetterprosa í den norrøne versjonen av Vitae Patrum*, Årbok for Universitet í Bergen, Humanistisk Serie, 2 (1967), 86–88, notes a similar tendency in certain Old Norse (ON) prose translations from Latin.

45. George E. Maclean, ed., "Ælfric's Version of *Alcuini Interrogationes Sigeuulfi in Genesin*," *Anglia* 7 (1884), 22, #31: "Se twyfealda deað wæs mid þam getacnad, þære sawle 7 þæs lichoman."

46. *Alcuini Interrogationes Sigeuulfi*, 4, #4.

47. Thus Homer, *Odyssey*, 10:35, gives a "divine" word as well as a human word for the same thing, and the ON *Alvíssmál* lists the different names for objects among different classes of beings in each world. In early England and Ireland, the patristic tradition that the inhabitants of heaven spoke Hebrew was widespread. See *Auraicep na n'Éces*, ed. George Calder (Edinburgh, 1917), 17; C. H. Talbot, *Analecta monastica. Textes et études sur la vie des moines au moyen-âge*, troisième série, Studia Anselmiana, 37 (Rome, 1955), 4:115. In the Irish text *In Tenga Bithnua*, "The Evernew Tongue," ed. Whitley Stokes, *Ériu* 2 (1905), 96–162, a voice from heaven speaks an unintelligible language which purports to be either Hebrew or the tongue of Paradise. See references in Proinsias MacCana, "On the Use of the Term *Retoiric*," *Celtica* 7 (1966), 86.

48. *Troilus and Criseyde*, 4:1406.

49. For background on this tradition, see Arno Borst, *Der Turmbau von Babel: Geschichte der Meinungen über Ursprung und Vielfalt der Sprachen und Völker* (Stuttgart, 1957–63), 2.1:396, 454, 468; 2.2:634. Also Robert E. McNally, S. J., "The *tres linguae sacrae* in Early Irish Biblical Exegesis," *Theological Studies* 19 (1958), 395–403.

50. *Der Turmbau von Babel*, 2.1:477–483.
51. King Alfred bases his case for OE translation on a similar argument: *King Alfred's West-Saxon Version of Gregory's Pastoral Care*, ed. Henry Sweet, EETS 45 (1871; repr. 1958), 5–6.
52. See Robert H. Robins, *Ancient and Medieval Grammatical Theory in Europe with Particular Reference to Modern Linguistic Doctrine* (London, 1951), 71–74.
53. The Hebrew prophets could meditate in this way upon an object, discovering in its name one or more homonyms relevant to their message: The vision of a "summer" fruit (Heb. *kayits*) prompted from Amos (8:1–2) an oracle on the prophesied "end" (Heb. *kayts*) of the kingdom. See other examples in Abraham Avni, "Inspiration in Plato and the Hebrew Prophets," *Comparative Literature* 20 (1968), 60. In the OE *Maxims*, the poet sometimes seems to be annexing one gnomic idea to the next through this kind of prophetic sound-association. In lines 185–187 of the *Exeter Maxims*, for example, a description of rowing against the wind appears to lead abruptly into comments on fraud and corruption. The apparent break comes with the half line "drugað his *ar* on borde," "his oar dries up on board" (188). Yet since a common homonym of *ar*, "oar," is *ar*, "honor," and dried-up honor leads to corruption, the poet's swift transition from the nautical to the moral sphere seems more to be due to a chain reaction of sound-associations than to a dropped or broken narrative thread. For a different view, see R. MacGregor Dawson, "The Structure of the Old English Gnomic Poems," *JEGP* 61 (1962), 20.
54. The *Beowulf* poet's associative habit of mind has been noted in several important studies, chief among which are John O. Beaty, "The Echo-Word in *Beowulf* with a Note on the Finnsburg Fragment," *PMLA* 49 (1934), 365–373; James L. Rosier, "The Uses of Association: Hands and Feasts in *Beowulf*," *PMLA* 78 (1963), 8–14; and Eric G. Stanley, "*Beowulf*," in *Continuations and Beginnings*, 104–141.
55. For this envelope pattern in OE, see Bartlett, *The Larger Rhetorical Patterns in Anglo-Saxon Poetry*, 9–29.
56. As Landor commented, with reference to Milton's devil: "It appears then on record that the first overt crime of the refractory angels was *punning*; they fell rapidly after that." *The Complete Works of Walter Savage Landor*, ed. T. Earle Welby (London, 1927–36), 5:258. In *Genesis B*, the devil uses paronomasia to prove to Adam and Eve that God must have meant the apple for eating: "Het þæt þu þisses of*ætes æte*," "He commanded that you eat of this fruit" (500, 564, 599), says the devil, *nomen est omen*. The devil's paronomastic address to Eve similarly prophesies her eventual capitulation: "Gif þu . . . *wilt*, / wif *willende*," "if you . . . will, willing woman" (559–560).

57. Randolph Quirk, "Poetic Language and Old English Metre," in *Early English and Norse Studies Presented to Hugh Smith*, ed. Arthur Brown and Peter Foote (London, 1963), 150–71, has demonstrated how the OE poet created striking and original formulations by playing upon his audience's expectation of congruity at specific points, how "the sophisticated poet, well learned in the conventions, could 'shade and knit anew the patch of words.'"

58. In OE poetry other than Cynewulf's, this *rod . . . rodor* play occurs only in Riddle 55: "ond *rode* tacn, þæs us to *roderum* up . . ." (5).

Tempter as Rhetoric Teacher: The Fall of Language in the Old English *Genesis B*

ERIC JAGER

This essay first appeared in Neophilologus *72 (1988), 434–48. Translations of Old English passages have been supplied by the editor in square brackets.*

Critics of *Genesis B* have increasingly focused on the rhetoric and logic of the Tempter's speeches.[1] But apart from brief comments to the effect that Eve is the Tempter's "instrument," or that her tempting of Adam "mirrors" or "parallels" her own by the Tempter,[2] little attention has been paid to the Tempter's rhetorical instruction of Eve. And no systematic study has been given to the question of to what extent Eve's discourse actually resembles the Tempter's, and what such resemblance might signify. Judging from Eve's studious fulfillment of his rhetorical advice and the similarities between his speeches to her and hers to Adam, it would appear that she learns[3] a great deal from the Tempter. The present article will investigate this diabolical *translatio studii* in three parts: (1) by analyzing the Tempter's specifically rhetorical advice to Eve; (2) by comparing their speeches to determine the amount of implied influence; and (3) by examining the narrative's accompanying psychology of persuasion.

In his first speech to Eve (551–87),[4] the Tempter plants the idea that she should persuade Adam and begins to specify how this is to be done:

"Gif þu þeah minum wilt,
wif willende,   wordum hyran,
þu meaht his þonne rume   ræd geþencan.

> Gehyge on þinum breostum   þæt þu inc bam twam meaht
> wite bewarigan,   swa ic þe wisie."   (559–63)
> [If you, willing woman, will obey my words, you might think more
> openly about a remedy for it. Consider in your heart that you can avert
> punishment for both of you, just as I will show you.]

The formula *ræd geþen(c)an,* "devise a plan,"[5] has last been used by
Satan (286), who urges the devils to think of a strategy for seducing the
humans. Now used by the Tempter to similarly urge Eve with respect to
persuading Adam, the repeated phrase ominously implies that she
(though unknowingly) carries on a diabolical tradition. *Gehyge on
þinum breostum* also suggests that Eve is to devise a plan and introduces
the theme of her "breost" as the Tempter's instrument. The Tempter
alludes to his own verbal persuasion of Eve in the phrase
minum . . . wordum and in *swa ic þe wisie,* " 'as I show (or guide) you,"
claims the role of Eve's advisor, preparing for the explicitly rhetorical
instruction that follows.

A few lines later, the Tempter changes the focus from his own
words to Eve's and begins to outline a program for her persuasion of
Adam:

> "Meaht þu Adame   eft gestyran,
> gif þu his willan hæfst   and he þinum wordum getrywð."   (568–69)
> [you might be able to move Adam if you have his desire and he trusts your
> words]

The Tempter's promise that Eve will "rule"[6] Adam is predicated on the
vision he promises her (564–67), but the specified means of her influ-
ence over him is clearly verbal—"þinum wordum." The echo of
"minum . . . wordum" reinforces the idea of verbal persuasion at the
same time that it signals the Tempter's shift of emphasis from verbally
persuading Eve (" 'Gif þu þeah minum . . . wordum hyran' ") to simi-
larly persuading Adam (" 'gif . . . he þinum wordum getrywð' "). This
pattern of repetition and variation emphasizes that in persuading Adam
just as she herself has been persuaded, Eve will be imitating the
Tempter's verbal model.

The Tempter next specifies how Eve's verbal persuasion of Adam
will operate:

"Gif þu him to soðe sægst   hwylce þu selfa hæfst
bisne on breostum,   þæs þu gebod godes
lare læstes,   he þone laðan strið,
yfel andwyrde   an forlæteð
on breostcofan,   swa wit him [butu]
an sped sprecað."   (570–75)
[If you will tell him truly what examplary command you hold in your
heart by which you keep God's precepts and teaching, he will abandon in
his heart this hostile strife and evil reply, if we two both talk to him for his
own good.]

This passage encapsulates the Tempter's plan to substitute Eve's voice
for his own in persuading Adam. Having the "command" in her mind
("bisne on breostum"), Eve is now to enunciate it faithfully ("to soðe
sægst") to Adam. The distinction between reception and performance of
a speech act emphasizes Eve's intermediary role as one who receives,
holds, and in turn transmits the "command." Moreover, the term *breost*,
because it suggests both psychological and physical aspects of speech,
underscores the centrality of Eve's verbal activity. In the sense "mind" or
"heart," *breost* is associated with the faculty of understanding and
remembering speech; and in the sense "chest," it is associated with the
physical production of speech.[7] In both senses, Eve's "breost" is to be
the Tempter's instrument for persuading Adam.

Adam's described response is centered in his "breostcofa," the
physical and psychological counterpart to Eve's "breost."[8] Eve's speech
is to cause Adam to relinquish ("forlætan") his words of refusal, with the
implication that the command now in her "breost" will likewise be
lodged in his "breostcofa." The scenario of the mimetically repeated
"command," mimetically received into the "breost," discloses the
Tempter's design to use Eve as his verbal instrument.

Although *wit*, "we two,"[9] and *butu*, "both," imply Eve's equal part-
nership with the Tempter in persuading Adam, these terms are instead a
covert expression for his use of her voice. The Tempter's entire proposi-
tion, framed by the theme of speech, moves significantly from the idea of
Eve herself speaking to Adam (" 'Gif þu him . . . sægst' ") to the idea of
their speaking to him together (" 'swa wit him [butu] . . . sprecað' ")—a
transition suggesting the Tempter's appropriation of Eve's voice.

Increasingly specific about his plan, the Tempter next counsels Eve

as to the manner of her persuasion—" 'Span þu hine georne' " (575)—
and states explicitly that her performance is supposed to move Adam to
comply—" 'þæt he þine lare læste' " (576)—lest they incur God's
wrath. OE *spanan* commonly translates a range of Latin verbs denoting
persuasive speech—e.g.,[10] *provocare, suadere, persuadere, exhortare,*
and *perurgere*—and though it (and OS *spanan*) denotes other than just
verbal persuasion, the context of the Tempter's directly preceding
advice, with its wealth of specifically verbal terms—*sægst, gebod, lare,
andwyrde, sprecað*—suggests a specifically verbal sense of the word
here. *Georne*, in reference to speech, or discourse generally, has the
attested senses "eagerly, earnestly," and, in addition, "[*Suppl.* (4)] where
there is a strong desire to attain an end or to produce an effect, *earnestly,
pressingly* (of a request, inquiry, injunction, &c.)."[11] In combination with
the imperative *span, georne* suggests that Eve is to undertake a very
strong line of persuasion. Her remark to Adam that she gives him the
apple, *georne* (679), suggesting her self-conscious adoption of the
Tempter's rhetorical program, is discussed in this connection later.

The proposed aim of Eve's persuasion, " 'þæt he [Adam] þine lare
læste,' " actually invokes two rhetorical functions: (1) to teach, and (2)
to move.[12] Ehrhart observes that the Tempter's attribution of his *lar* to
Eve ("þine lare") elevates her to a teacherly role with respect to Adam, at
the same time reminding the audience that the Tempter is falsifying
God's true *lar.*[13] The transfer of diabolical teaching to Eve under the
name of God's *lar*, like the earlier shift from *minum* to *þinum*, empha-
sizes Eve's role as a verbal conduit. In addition to urging that Eve
"teach" Adam, the Tempter instructs that she move Adam to obey her.
The conjunction *þæt* has causative force, providing the imperative
phrase *span þu hine* with a specific rhetorical end—persuading Adam to
obey (*læste*) Eve's teaching. The twin rhetorical goals which the
Tempter urges upon Eve are precisely those which he has already
assumed toward her. The phrase *þæt he þine lare læste* echoes the
Tempter's wording a few lines before, *þæs þu gebod godes lare læstes,*
which describes Eve (*þu*) as the one being taught and moved to obey.
Insofar as she recognizes her role as the Tempter's persuadee, Eve will
better understand her reciprocal role as Adam's persuader.

To ensure Eve's performance of this role, the Tempter offers not to
tell God about Adam's previous refusal to obey him. The promise is
explicitly conditional: The Tempter will keep silent, " '*Gif þu þæt angin*

fremest' " (578). *Angin* (*ongin*) is attested in verbal—though specifically literary—applications, and *fremman* in reference to speech.[14] The description in *Genesis A* of the angel "þe þone unræd ongan ærest fremman [who first began to frame that evil counsel]" (30) is suggestive for the sense of *fremman* here.[15] " 'Gif þu . . . fremest,' " after the Tempter's intense rhetorical coaching, may have the sense, " 'If you speak (perform in words, frame (such) counsel).' " But even if it has a nonverbal sense here, it clearly expresses the Tempter's wish that Eve "perform" or "carry out" his project as described. And this again implies Eve's rhetorical subservience.

In his second speech to Eve (611–22), the Tempter advises her principally on the content of her persuasion. By now Eve has been swayed by the Tempter's words (588–92) and the "vision" he has allowed her (600–09). Having convinced her to undertake the project, the Tempter can pass from the preliminary concerns of why and how Eve should persuade Adam to what she should actually say. Referring to the vision, the Tempter prompts her to tell Adam what she has seen. But this broadly rhetorical advice is accompanied by numerous practical suggestions in the form of descriptive details which preempt Eve's own experience:

"þu meaht nu þe self geseon, swa ic hit þe secgan ne þearf,
Eue seo gode, þæt þe is ungelic
wlite and wæstmas, siððan þu minum wordum getruwodest,
læstes mine lare. Nu scineð þe leoht fore
glædlic ongean þæt ic from gode brohte
hwit of heofonum; nu þu his hrinan meaht.
Sæge Adame hwilce þu gesihðe hæfst
þurh minne cime cræfta. Gif giet þurh cuscne siodo
læst mina lara, þonne gife ic him þæs leohtes genog
þæs ic þe swa godes gegired hæbbe.
Ne wite ic him þa womcwidas, þeah he his wyrðe ne sie
to alætanne; þæs fela he me laðes spræc." (611–22; emphasis added)
[Now you can see for yourself, and I need not tell you, good Eve, that your beauty and form have changed since you have trusted my words and done my bidding. Now a gleaming light shines around you, which I have brought forth from God in heaven: now you can touch it. Tell Adam what vision you have through the power of my coming. If he will yet do my bidding in a humble fashion, I will give him abundantly of this light with which I have adorned you, so fair. I will not punish him for his harsh

words, though he be not worthy of reprieve, since he spoke so much evil
against me.]

Rather than allowing Eve to say for herself what she has seen, the
Tempter prompts and cues her perceptual reporting by interpolating his
own agenda. Wanting Eve to articulate her vision to Adam in such a way
that—simply by being reported—it will convince him too, the Tempter
literally provides the basic material for her speech.

The influence of the Tempter's rhetorical instruction upon Eve's
speech to Adam may be observed first of all in the large number of the-
matic parallels between them. Simply in terms of content and argument
there are striking similarities, as the following tabulation summarizes:

Themes	T:E (2)	E:A[16]
Validation by Sight	þu meaht nu þe self geseon, swa ic hit þe secgan ne þearf (611)	ic on his gearwan geseo (657) Ic mæg heonon geseon hwær he sylf siteð (666–67) mæg ic . . . swa wide geseon (673–4)
Bestowal of Light	Nu scineð þe leoht fore glædlice ongean (614–15) gife ic him þæs leohtes genog þæs ic þe swa godes gegired hæbbe (619–20)	Wearð me on hige leohte utan and innan (676–77)
Tempter as God's Messenger	þæt ic from gode brohte hwit of heofonum (615–16)	boda sciene, godes engel god (656–57) ærendsecg uncres hearran (658) þines hearran bodan (664) þes ar (682)
Tempter's Verbal Reliability	siððan þu minum wordum getruwodest, læstes mine lar (613–14)	me þe boda sægde wærum wordum (680–81) swa þes ar sægeð (682)
Adam's Evil Speech to Be Forgiven	Ne wite ic him þa womcwidas . . . þæs fela he me laðes spræc (621–22)	Gif þu him heodæg wuht hearmes gespræce, he forgifð hit þeah (661–62)
Obedience as Condition	Gif giet þurh cuscne siodo læst mina lara (618–19)	gif wit him geongordom læstan willað (662–3)

More than twice as long as T:E (2), E:A elaborates considerably upon the material suggested by the Tempter, especially the themes of messenger and eyesight. Some similarities include carryover from T:E (1), where, for instance, the theme of message and messenger is heavily reiterated. Thus Eve's *ærendsecg* appears to be formed on the repeated *ærende* in T:E (1), as discussed in more detail later. But Eve also omits provided material, as for instance the Tempter's parenthetical complaint that Adam does not really deserve to be forgiven (621–22). Taken together, the thematic parallels, amplifications, and omissions suggest that Eve has taken to heart the Tempter's advice about both substance and method. A loving (or cunning) expression of her instructor's agenda, Eve's speech combines an inculcated rhetoric with a natural knowledge of her audience, showing a genuine attempt to persuade Adam "georne."

Beyond the thematic parallels, one may point to the influence of the Tempter's discourse upon Eve's in terms of phrasing and vocabulary. By "influence" is meant the poet's transfer of verbal features from one speaker to the other, thus making the Tempter's style appear to influence Eve's. The features common to T:E and E:A, and exclusive to them alone, argue strongly for influence, while other features shared by them, though nonexclusive, are also significant in ways that will be shown. It will be seen that both categories of implied influence escape Vickrey's overly broad generalization that excessive repetition in the poem obscures significant patterns of repetition.[17] The Tempter's two speeches to Eve are considered together as one verbal "source," since both exhort Eve to persuade Adam and both offer suggestions for the strategy and material of her speech. And although the poet implies that Eve said more to Adam than we are told ("Hio spræc him þicce to and speon hine ealne dæg" [684: she talked to him repeatedly and coaxed him all day]), it is assumed that he shows in direct discourse whatever he intends to show of the Tempter's influence as a rhetorical model. For the audience, Eve's echoes of the Tempter's vocabulary and phrasing would have been as ominous as the more general thematic repetitions in her speech, and all of these mimetic features together would have emphasized Eve's adherence to the Tempter's advice and example.

Phrases (apart from lexical *items*) found exclusively in T:E and E:A are limited to the formulaic *laðan strið / laðlic strið* (572, 663) and *hearmes . . . gespræc(e)* (579–80, 661).[18] Both are used in reference to Adam's retort to the Tempter. Eve adopts the Tempter's phraseology but softens his accusations into a conditional statement (" 'Gif þu him heodæg wuht *hearmes gespræce*' ") and a rhetorical question (" 'Hwæt scal þe swa *laðlic strið wið* þines hearran bodan?' "). Since Eve depends entirely upon the Tempter for knowledge of Adam's reply, credulously accepting his exaggerated report of Adam's behavior, she has no terms other than the Tempter's by which to understand the matter (as is not the case with, say, her knowledge of God's command, the vision, and other matters directly experienced by her). Eve's acceptance of the Tempter's terms, but her diplomatic rephrasing of these to Adam, show her to be doubly under his tutelage—taking the facts as given, and framing them in the most persuasive way.

A syntactical item not limited to T:E and E:A but dramatically frequent in these speeches is the conditional phrase beginning with *gif*. The term first appears repeatedly and obsessively in Satan's speeches, sometimes in rather close succession (398, 400, 409, 413, 427, 430, 434), as he twists and turns in his world of straitened possibilities. The Tempter employs it with equal obsessiveness in his speeches to Eve. In the first speech it always occurs in the phrase *gif þu* (559, 569, 570, 578)—setting a condition for Eve to fulfill. In the second speech it is used to frame the condition that Adam must obey (618), thus indicating the Tempter's shift of focus from Eve's decision to Adam's. With one intervening instance in the narrative ("gif hie þone wæstm an lætan wolden" [643–44: if they would let be that fruit]), a reminder of what hangs by all of these *if*'s, the term is next used no fewer than three times in E:A. Eve herself has learned how to dangle promises from the conditional:

> "*Gif* þu him heodæg wuht   hearmes gespræce,
> he forgifð hit þeah,   *gif* wit him geongordom
> læstan willað."   (661–63)
> [If you have spoken anything harmful to him today, he will still forgive you, if we will do him reverence.]

And she skillfully uses *gif* with argumentative force:

> "Hwa meahte me swelc gewit gifan,
> *gif* hit gegnunga   god ne onsende,
> heofones waldend?"   (671–73)
> [Who could give me such understanding if God, the Ruler of heaven, had not sent it directly to me?]

The next instance is the narrator's (787), with reference again to the central *if* of the poem. The final occurrences belong to Adam, who appears to have contracted his *gif* (806, 828, 834) from Eve, the Tempter (indirectly), and ultimately Satan himself. With *gif* the poet dramatically shows the progress of a verbal tic (and its correlative attitudes) through a succession of speakers. But whereas Adam's *gif* shows mainly his new-found uncertainty about his fate, Eve's shows her assimilation of a rhetorical strategy from the Tempter, for both she and the latter use it deliberately to entice and persuade another.

A lexical item exclusive to T:E and E:A is the adverb *rume*. Eve tells Adam that she can hear *rume*, "spaciously, amply" (673), thus seeming to echo the Tempter's exhortation that she think or consider *rume* (561). These are the only instances of this adverb; the related adjective, *rum*, occurs only in T:A (519), and its cognate *gerume* only in T:S (759), clearly confining this set of terms to devilish discourse and its derivative in Eve's.

A number of lexical items occurring in T:E and E:A, though not exclusively there, are significant for various reasons, usually because of frequency or modified use in other contexts.[19] Each requires individual consideration.

1. *Boda*, "messenger," is introduced by the narrative in a pejorative sense, "dyrne deofles boda" (490), and accumulates further negative connotations when the Tempter uses the term as a disguise in which to introduce himself to Adam (510). Adam's doubt that the Tempter really is God's *boda* (533) clearly allows that the term may be used *in sensu bono*. But when the Tempter subsequently identifies himself to Eve by the same title (558), and Eve persists in thus identifying the Tempter to Adam (656, 664, 680), the term implicates her in devilish speech. Indeed, Adam's refusal to let the Tempter bear the name of *boda* underscores Eve's credulous assimilation of the Tempter's language. Eve goes so far as to endearingly qualify the term, producing "þes boda sciene" and "þines hearran bodan" (first two instances). The narrative's commentary on Eve's grave terminological error is clear: Rather than omitting to use *boda*, the narrative qualifies the term negatively to condemn its diabolical misappropriation, "wraða boda" (686),

"laðan bodan" (711), "boda bitre gehugod," (725), and "boda bitresta" (763), thus continuing its original pejoration. Between the narrator's introduction of the term and this final and emphatic condemnation, the term is used only by the speakers in the drama, where it undergoes its various contextual modifications. The main point with respect to Eve's rhetorical schooling is that, whereas Adam clearly attempts to save the term for legitimate use, Eve falls for the Tempter's deceptive abuse of it and, under a misprision that even leads her to embellish the term, unknowingly continues its abuse.

2. Eve similarly echoes the Tempter's use of the adjective *god* as an honorific. Though a very common word in OE, its use with other terms as a *captatio benevolentiae* provides a significant group of instances in the poem. T:E has "Eue seo gode" (612), and E:A "godes engel god" (657) and "herra se goda" (678). The only other instances are the narrative's honorifics applied to God (302, 850), and a single instance employed by the fallen Adam in reference to God (817), though not in direct address since it occurs in conversation with Eve. As a flattering epithet used as a *captatio benevolentiae*, the term appears only in T:E and E:A.

3. *Ærende* and its cognates also demonstrate the Tempter's lexical influence upon Eve. In T:A the term occurs once (497); Adam does not use it in return. In T:E it occurs twice, emphatically, in a very short space (555, 557). Eve studiously repeats the root word in a compound noun and a cognate verb, referring to the messenger as an *ærendsecg* (658) who will *ærendian*, "represent," them to God (665). The reappearance of *ærend* in these related forms strongly suggests that Eve not only assimilates the Tempter's vocabulary but also builds advantageously upon it. *Ærende* and *ærendian* are common in OE, and *ærendsecg* unique.[20] The unusualness of the latter term would have emphasized to the audience that Eve is repeating, in compounded form, a term in the poem that is peculiar to the Tempter's discourse.

4. Perhaps the most striking of Eve's acquisitions is the adverb *georne*, "eagerly, earnestly." Again, contrast with Adam's speech is useful. Adam hears the term from the Tempter, who

urges him to obey him "georne" (517), but Adam himself does not use the word. To Eve the Tempter says not only " 'Span þu hine *georne*,' " but within a few lines also repeats the rather sonorous first syllable of this word in the related adjective *georn* (581) and the adverb *geornlice* (585), thus producing an emphatic reverberation. As to the idea conveyed by *georne*, Eve in repeating the term seems to be following the Tempter's advice literally, and quite self-consciously, when she says to Adam, " 'gife ic hit [the apple] þe *georne*' " (679). Although her own inflection of the word may be "willingly," "gladly," or any one of a number of emotional shadings, the import of its enunciation here—just as she proffers the apple—is to fulfill the Tempter's specific advice that she persuade Adam "georne."

5. One item exclusive to Eve's vocabulary alone deserves notice since it is so crucial to her entire rhetorical performance. As though the verbal traits acquired from her teacher were not enough to demonstrate Eve's enhanced art of persuasion, the poet gives her a verbal tic that is all her own. *Gegnunga*, meaning "certainly, assuredly," appears twice, at strategic points in E:A, and there only in the poem.[21] Eve asks who, if not God himself, could send such knowledge as she has received from the Tempter: " 'Hwa meahte me swelc gewit gifan, gif hit *gegnunga* god ne onsende, heofones waldend?' " (671–73). And she reassures Adam that the apple (with its associated knowledge) must certainly come from God: " 'Hit nis wuhte gelic elles on eorðan, butan swa þes ar sægeð, þæt hit *gegnunga* from gode come' " (681–83). The second instance occurs in the last line of Eve's speech, where it underscores her credulity, the false sense of certainty, instilled in her by the Tempter. Both instances of *gegnunga* accompany Eve's reassurances that doubtful things—the Tempter's credentials, the new "command"—are certain, reliable. With *gegnunga*, Eve supplements the Tempter's own overly protesting assurances,[22] thereby extending his rhetorical principle and practice.

As a whole, Eve's performance is an impressive fulfillment of the Tempter's proposal that she persuade Adam in his stead. Her elaborations and repetitions of thematic material, her careful omissions, her politic rephrasing of received ideas, and her borrowing and adaptations of terms and phrases all suggest that she is heavily influenced by the Tempter's rhetorical guidance and example, committed to his program of persuasion, even as she exercises her innate intelligence and rhetorical craft.

The narrative description that follows E:A emphasizes Eve's rhetorical subservience to the Tempter in several ways. Directly after Eve's speech, the poet indicates her persistence in persuading Adam:

> Hio spræc him þicce to   and speon hine ealne dæg
> on þa dimman dæd   þæt hie drihtnes heora
> willan bræcon.   (684–86)
> [She talked to him repeatedly and coaxed him all day toward the dark
> deed that they should violate their Lord's will.]

Here *speon* seems to confirm that Eve follows the Tempter's advice, " 'span þu hine' "; and *þicce,* with its echo a few lines later in *þiclice* (705), implies an "incessant persuasion"[23] in keeping with the advice that Eve persuade Adam "georne."

The Tempter's described behavior during Eve's speech to Adam— "legde him lustas on and mid listum speon" (687)—evokes Finnegan's remark that the Tempter "choreographs" the temptation for his "instrument" Eve.[24] Woolf emphasizes that during Eve's "long and fluent speech" the Tempter "all the while stands silently by."[25] There may be in *listum speon*, "urged them with cunning,"[26] a suggestion that he adds persuading words to hers; simultaneous or alternating speech could be the intended meaning of the Tempter's previous remark that he and Eve shall *both* ("wit . . . [butu]") speak to Adam. However, it is clear that the Tempter schools Eve in the persuasion of Adam precisely because Adam has rejected his own persuasions. Therefore, the idea that the Tempter and Eve persuade Adam by speaking to him together, either in unison or antiphonally, does not seem exactly consistent with the poet's emphatic depiction of Eve as the Tempter's verbal extension.

Moreover, there is yet another strong narrative indication that Eve acts in the Tempter's stead as his rhetorical instrument. This appears in the poet's comment that the Tempter mistaught Eve with the result that she in turn misteaches Adam:

> he *forlærde*   mid ligenwordum
> to þam unræde   idese sciene,
> wifa wlitegost,   þæt heo on his willan spræc,
> wæs him on helpe   handweorc godes
> to *forlæranne*. (699–703)

[he misguided that lovely woman, most beautiful of wives, with lying words to that evil counsel, so that she spoke as he desired, and became a help to him in misguiding God's handiwork.]

But the emphatic repetition of *forlæran* implies more than a parallel miseducation.[27] It implies also that Eve, having been mistaught, now imitates the Tempter in misteaching Adam. Besides this grammatical echo, the intervening clauses *heo on his willan spræc* and [*heo*] *wæs him on helpe* reinforce the idea of rhetorical modeling: Eve speaks "as he (the devil) willed,"[28] and as an instrument ("on helpe") for the persuasion of Adam.

In thus speaking for the Tempter, Eve becomes virtually his mouthpiece—a role very different from that of the Tempter, who knowingly acts as Satan's spokesman.[29] The phrase *heo on his willan spræc* suggests the sort of "ventriloquism" cited by Scriptural commentators to explain how Satan caused the Serpent to persuade Eve, and Eve to persuade Adam. Augustine, in an influential passage followed by later commentators, distinguishes between two ways in which Satan used another to speak for him:

> in serpente ipse [diabolus] locutus est, utens eo velut organo, movensque ejus naturam eo modo quo movere ille, et moveri illa potuit, ad exprimendos verborum sonos et signa corporalia, per quae mulier suadentis intelligeret voluntatem. In ipsa vero muliere, quia illa rationalis creatura erat, quae motu suo posset uti ad verba facienda, non ipse locutus est, sed ejus operatio atque persuasio; quamvis occulto instinctu adjuvaret interius, quod exterius egerat per serpentem.
>
> [In the serpent it was the Devil who spoke, using that creature as an instrument, moving it as he was able to move it and as it was capable of being moved, to produce the sounds of words and the bodily signs by which the woman would understand the will of the tempter. But in the woman, who was a rational creature and able by her own powers to speak, it was not the Devil who spoke, but it was the woman herself who uttered words and persuaded the man, although the Devil in a hidden way interi-

orly prompted within her what he had exteriorly accomplished when he used the serpent as an instrument.][30]

If Eve is the Tempter's "instrument," it is in the second sense distinguished here; "able by her own powers to speak," she also speaks at the external prompting of the Tempter—and possibly at his internal prompting too, as "legde him lustas on and mid listum speon" and "heo on his willan spræc" may also be interpreted to mean. Eve's extensive assimilation of the Tempter's discourse complements these suggestions in the narrative that the Tempter uses Eve as a rhetórical extension of himself.

In three major ways *Genesis B* represents Eve as the Tempter's student in the art of rhetoric. Before Eve persuades Adam, the Tempter offers her explicit rhetorical advice; in her speech to Adam, Eve adopts the Tempter's agenda of persuasion and echoes his words and style; and, after Eve's speech, the narrative emphasizes her verbal subordination to her instructor. On the one hand, all of this may merely reinforce the poet's repeated remarks about Eve's comparatively weaker mind (590, 649); more impressionable than Adam (as her tropological significance requires),[31] she more easily comes under the Tempter's sway. But on the other hand, the poet may be suggesting that a corruption of language passes from the Tempter to Eve on its way from Satan to Adam.

The described psychological effect of the Tempter's first speech to Eve emphasizes that his teaching or discourse enters her mind and continues there as an active presence: The Tempter is said to speak to her "oðþæt hire on innan ongan weallan wyrmes geþeaht" (589–90) [until the serpent's thought began to well within her]. The verb *weallan*, with its connotations of springs, wells, or "sources" in general, occurs elsewhere only in reference to Satan's thoughts (353); with the genitive, *wyrmes*, it implies that Eve is thinking not her own but another's thoughts. The Tempter's use of Eve's "breost" likewise suggests a discourse passing from him through her to Adam. The narrative reinforces this idea by stating that Eve took the Tempter's command *into* her mind, "þæs heo *on mod* genam" (710), causing in turn a change *within* Adam,

oðþæt Adame *innan breostum*
his hyge hwyrfde   and his heorte ongann
wendan to hire willan.   (715–17)

[until Adam's mind changed within his breast, and his heart began to bend to her will.]

Similarly the apple is said to go *into* Adam and affect his heart: "hit him on innan com, hran æt heortan" (723–24). And the humans are said to consume—"hie to mete dædon" (722)—the various evils represented by the apple, including the Devil's persuasion, "deofles gespon" (720).[32] The interior effects of the false teaching thus foreshadow, as a kind of *figura*, the interior effects of the forbidden fruit. By taking in and assimilating the Tempter's word, the humans figuratively swallow the apple itself.

The corruption of discourse is evident from the Tempter's usurpation of God's authority and mendacious substitution of a new teaching, or command, for the original one. But verbal corruption is evident also in Eve's erroneous descriptions of the world. The Tempter, to her eyes, is beautiful, "boda sciene," though the narrative describes him unattractively as "boda bitre gehugod." And in her first declaration to Adam, just after receiving the Tempter's instruction, Eve describes the apple as tasting "swa swete" (655), flatly contradicting[33] its attributed bitterness (479, 645). Eve's skewed perceptions—she finds sweetness and light in what is bitter and dark—dramatize the Tempter's comment that, as a result of *following his word*, all things look different to her:

> þe is ungelic
> wlite and wæstmas,   siððan þu minum wordum getruwodest,
> læstes mine lare.   (612–14)
> [your beauty and form have changed since you have trusted my words and done my bidding.]

Though doubtless an allusion to Eve's diabolically inspired "vision," this remark also hints at a change in Eve's moral perception. Eve sees differently because of verbal influence (*wordum, lare*) rather because of eating the apple *per se*. Eve's changed perceptions result from her changed terms of reference for understanding the world of her experience. She has exchanged God's terms for the Tempter's. The outright crisis of signification in which Eve's discourse perverts—by putting bitter for sweet, dark for light—the established order of words and things in God's world is the plainest clue that something has gone wrong with discourse in the Garden. The poet of *Genesis B* seems to be suggesting that the Fall of Man is correlative with an equally disastrous fall of language.

NOTES

1. Influential remarks on the Tempter's speeches appear in Rosemary Woolf, "The Fall of Man in *Genesis B* and The *Mystère d'Adam*," in *Studies in Old English Literature in Honor of Arthur G. Brodeur*, ed. Stanley B. Greenfield (Eugene, OR, 1963), 187–99. See also Alain Renoir, "The Self-Deception of Temptation: Boethian Psychology in *Genesis B*," in *Old English Poetry: Fifteen Essays*, ed. Robert P. Creed (Providence, 1967), 47–67, esp. 55–61. Michael D. Cherniss remarks briefly on the Tempter's logic in "Heroic Ideals and the Moral Climate of *Genesis B*," *MLQ* 30 (1969), 479–97; see 490–92. Michael Benskin and Brian Murdoch point out the importance of the Tempter's flattery, "The Literary Tradition of Genesis: Some Comments on J. M. Evans' Paradise Lost *and the Genesis Tradition* (Oxford UP, 1968)," *NM* 76 (1975), 389–403; see 397. The most thorough discussion to date of the Tempter's discourse is to be found in two articles by Robert Emmett Finnegan, "Eve and 'Vincible Ignorance' in *Genesis B*," *Texas Studies in Literature and Language* 18 (1976), 329–39, and "God's *Handmaegen* Versus the Devil's *Cræft* in *Genesis B*," *English Studies in Canada* 7 (1981), 1–14.

2. Finnegan (1981): "We see Eve in her long speech (655–83) exercising her newly discovered skill in deception, and mirroring in tempting Adam her own temptation" (9); Eve is the Tempter's "instrument" for persuading Adam, and the Tempter "her source of *cræft*" (9), where *cræft* means, *inter alia*, "perverted rhetorical skill" (2). J. R. Hall: "Eve's use of *þu* and *wit* parallels the demon's earlier manipulation of *þu* and *git*," "Duality and the Dual Pronoun in *Genesis B*," *Papers on Language and Literature* 17 (1981), 139–45; see 143.

3. Instructional vocabulary (*lar, læran, forlæran*, etc.) in *Genesis B* has been analyzed by Margaret J. Ehrhart, "Tempter as Teacher: Some Observations on the Vocabulary of the Old English *Genesis B*," *Neophilologus* 59 (1975), 435–46. Though Ehrhart emphasizes the poet's ironic contrast of God's "true teaching" and the "false teaching" of Satan and does not address the specifically rhetorical matters discussed here, her demonstration of the Tempter's role as "teacher" is fundamental to my thesis. The instructional theme in accounts of the Fall has been relatively ignored. In regard to the prominence of this theme in *Genesis B*, it is worth remarking that the *Poematum de Mosaicae Historiae Gestis Libri quinque* of Avitus, often cited as a "source"—for a review of the literature, see B. J. Timmer, *The Later Genesis* (Oxford, 1948) 45–48; also J. M. Evans, "*Genesis B* and Its Background," *RES* n.s. 14 (1963), 1–16, 113–23, esp. 12–15—presents the humans' transactions with God and the Serpent through numerous

instructional (and rhetorical) terms: *docere* (2.184, 3.103), *doctus* (2.181, 245), *doctor* (1.314), *magister* (2.183, 421), *instructos* (1.324), *suadere* (2.170), *persuadere* (3.101); for *Poematum*, ed. Rudolf Peiper, *Monumenta Germaniae Historica* 6, pt. 2 (Berlin, 1883).

4. The edition used is *The Junius Manuscript*, ed. George Philip Krapp, *ASPR* 1 (New York, 1931). Emendations are placed in brackets.

5. Timmer, line note [560] 109.

6. Joseph Bosworth and T. Northcote Toller, *An Anglo-Saxon Dictionary* (Oxford, 1898), s.v. *gestyran*. Under the sense "to restrain" the verb is attested as meaning to influence verbally; and another attested sense, "to reprove, rebuke," is implicitly verbal, *Supplement* (Oxford, 1921), s.v. *gestiran*. Thus the initial idea of Eve's guiding or controlling Adam may already be flavored with connotations of verbal persuasion. See also Timmer's line note [560] 109.

7. Concerning the breast as the seat of reason, see Thomas D. Hill, "The Fall of Angels and Man in the Old English *Genesis B*," in *Anglo-Saxon Poetry: Essays in Appreciation for John C. McGalliard*, ed. Lewis E. Nicholson and Dolores Warwick Frese (Notre Dame, 1975), 279–90, esp. 284–85. Also compare the Tempter's remark that Eve is to "Gehyge on þinum breostum" (562). For a similar instance of *breost* as the origin of speech, see *Beowulf* 2791–92, ed. Fr. Klaeber, 3rd ed. (Lexington, MA, 1950).

8. The *Concordance*, s.v. *breostcofa*, lists five instances besides the present one, two of which have a physical and three a psychological sense.

9. On duals and "duality" in the poem, see the article by Hall cited in note 2.

10. Bosworth-Toller, s.v. *spanan*, distinguishes a "good" from a "bad" sense of the term, the latter being frequently applied to the urgings of the devil. OS *spanan* is not specifically verbal, denoting "antreiben, veranlassen, locken [i.e.. drive, incite; instigate; tempt, entice]"; Edward H. Sehrt, *Vollständiges Wörterbuch zum Heliand und zur Altsächsischen Genesis* (Göttingen, 1925).

11. Bosworth-Toller, and *Suppl.* s.v. *georne*. See also glossaries in Timmer and John Frederick Vickrey, Jr., "*Genesis B*: A New Analysis and Edition" (Diss., U Indiana, 1961). OS *gerno* is attested frequently with verbs of speech, especially with *biddian* (OE *biddan*), Sehrt. In conjunction with OE *biddan*, *georne* renders Latin *compellere*, as in *Genesis* 2442 (Gen. 19:3); cited in Bosworth-Toller, *Suppl.*, s.v. *georne* (4). With the even more hortatory *spanan*, *georne* suggests very strong urging indeed.

12. As Augustine (paraphrasing Cicero) defines the agenda of rhetoric, one should speak "Ut doceat, ut delectet, ut flectat," *De doctrina Christiana* 4.12.27 (*CCSL* 32, 135). Augustine's substitution of *docere* for Cicero's *probare* (*Orator* 21.69), representing a significant shift away from legal to

doctrinal purposes, puts teaching at the forefront of the rhetorical agenda. OE *lar* and *læran* commonly render Latin *doctrina* and *docere*, respectively; Bosworth-Toller, s.v. *lar*, *læran*.

13. Ehrhart, 440–41.

14. Bosworth-Toller, s.v. *fremman*, II (quots. Elen. Kmbl. 942; 1046); and *Suppl.*, s.v. *angin*, II (quot. Guth.), IIIa (quots. Gr. D.).

15. Ed. Krapp. Bosworth-Toller, s.v. *fremman*. But, s.v. *angin*, line 578, is rendered, "if thou perfect that attempt," omitting mention of language specifically.

16. For convenience of reference, the following abbreviations for the speeches are used: T:A = Tempter to Adam, A:T = Adam to Tempter, T:E = Tempter to Eve (with [1] and [2] distinguishing the speeches), E:A = Eve to Adam (655–83 only; does not include 824–26), A:E = Adam to Eve, T:S = Tempter to Satan.

17. Vickrey, 145.

18. Some echoes in phrasing are too uncertain to classify as influence; e.g., T:E "*þæt ic from gode brohte*" (615), and E:A "*þæt hit from gode come, broht* from his bysene" (679–80).

19. Besides the items discussed, others occurring (but not exclusively) in both T:E and E:A include *læstan* (554, 572, 576, 614, 619/663), *geseon* (566, 611/657, 666, 669, 674), *leoht* (564, 619/676), *engel* (582, 583/657, 669), *breost* (562, 571, 574 [compounded with -*cofa*]/656), *hyldo* (567, 625 [disputed passage]/659, 664).

20. Concordance, s.v. *ærend*, -*a*, -*an*, -*e*, -*es*, -*o*, -*u*, -*um*; *ærendan*, -*að*, -*ian*, -*ige*, -*igean*, -*ode*, -*odan*, -*unge*; *ærendsecg*.

21. The *Concordance* lists two other instances, s.v. *gegninga*, *gegnunga*.

22. Renoir comments that the Tempter "protest[s] far too much" to Eve (58).

23. Woolf, 197. Vickrey, line note, gives *þicce* the sense " 'with many rapid words,' i.e., 'pressingly, urgently' " (245–46). Anne L. Klinck remarks that *þicce*, with *þiclice* (705), implies "the energy and volubility" of Eve's appeals, "Female Characterisation in Old English Poetry and the Growth of Psychological Realism: *Genesis B* and *Christ I*," *Neophilologus* 63 (1979), 597–610; 600. Regarding *þicce*, Benskin and Murdoch maintain (*contra* Evans [1968]) that Adam "did not eat 'because he had been given the proof he [had] demawnded' (p. 181), but gradually succumbed to Eve's persistence" (397).

24. See reference to Finnegan (1981) in note 2. Compare *instrumentum* in Augustine's description of how Satan spoke through the Serpent, as cited in note 30.

25. Woolf, 197.

26. Trans. R. K. Gordon, *Anglo-Saxon Poetry* (London, 1926), 119.

27. See Ehrhart on the instructional overtones of *forlæran*, 438–39, and the pattern of its repetition, 442.

28. Vickrey, 247.

29. Not only does the Tempter act in response to Satan's plea that someone deceive the humans (" 'Hycgað his ealle, hu ge hi beswicen!' " [432–33]), but the sketch of the Tempter's character mentions deceit ("hæfde fæcne hyge" [443]) and specifically verbal competence ("wiste him spræca fela, wora [glossed: wraþra] worda" [445–6]) as being among his qualifications. By contrast, though Eve does everything she can to per-suade Adam, there is no hint of deception on her part. As has been noted by numerous critics, she does all "þurh holdne [*not* "fæcne"] hyge" (708); moreover, she believes that the emissary too acts with "holdne hyge" (654), and that he speaks "wærum wordum" (681).

30. *De Genesi ad litteram* 11.27.34 (*PL* 34, 443); trans. John Hammond Tay-lor, *The Literal Meaning of Genesis*, Ancient Christian Writers, vols. 41–2 (New York, 1982). 2:159. See also *The City of God* 14.11: "tamquam instrumento abutens fallacia sermocinatus est feminae" (Loeb ed. 4:328). In classical rhetoric, *instrumentum* denotes variously the orator's store of knowledge (Cicero, *De oratore* 1.36.165), his stock of cases and types (2.34.146), and his "natural" equipment (*Brutus* 77.268). Augustine may be using the term here with such associations in mind. Compare Augus-tine's extension of Satan's ventriloquism in *Confessions* 6.12: "per me ipsi quoque Alypio loquebatur serpens et innectebat atque spargebat per linguam meam dulces laqueos in via eius . . . [it was by means of me that the serpent began to speak to Alypius himself. My tongue was used to weave sweet snares and scatter them in his path . . .]"; ed. P. Knöll (Leipzig, 1926), trans. Rex Warner, *The Confessions of St. Augustine* (New York, 1963), 130. Pseudo-Bede: "Serpens per se loqui non poterat, nec quia hoc a Creatore acceperat assumpsit, nisi nimirum illum diabolus utens, et velut organum per quod articulatum sonum emitteret: per illum nempe verba faciebat, et tamen hoc etiam ille nesciebat," *Quaestiones super Genesim* (*PL* 93, 276C). See also Bede, *Libri quatuor in principium Genesis* 3.1 (*CCSL* 118A, 59-60 [1.1874–1920]). Alcuin: "Utebatur enim serpente diabolus quasi organo ad perpetrandam calliditatis suae mali-tiam," *Interrogationes et responsiones in Genesin* 60 (*PL* 100, 522); also, "sicut daemoniacus et mente captus loquitur quae nescit, ita serpens verba edebat quae non intelligebat," 62 (col. 523). Rabanus Maurus: "serpens irrationalis, quod decipiendum hominem velut organo suo usus est diabo-lus," *Commentaria in Genesim* 1.18 (*PL* 107, 495C).

31. The most complete discussion of the poem's tropology is Hill, cited in note 7.

32. Thus Charles W. Kennedy, trans. *The Cædmon Poems* (1916; rpt. Gloucester, MA, 1965): "these [forenamed ills] were the fatal fruit whereon they feasted" (30). But Timmer, emending Krapp's punctuation at 722b, reads *ofet unfæle* (723) as the object of the verb phrase *to mete dædon*, line note [722] 110.

33. Contradictions and other logical flaws in the Tempter's speeches have been noted and discussed by several critics: see Woolf, 193–4, Renoir, 58–61, Cherniss, 491–2, and Finnegan (1976), 331–3. However, to my knowledge no critic has yet pointed out this fairly obvious flaw in Eve's speech.

Conspicuous Heroism:
Abraham, Prudentius,
and the Old English Verse *Genesis*

ANDREW ORCHARD

This essay first appeared in Heroes and Heroines in Medieval English Literature: A Festschrift Presented to Andre Crépin on the Occasion of the Sixty-Fifth Birthday, *ed. Leo Carruthers (Woodbridge, 1994), 45–58.*

In the poetry of *Cædmon's Hymn* we can already recognize the typically Anglo-Saxon tendency to harmonize traditions, to call the Christian God by the lordly titles of their secular past.[1] It is the same impulse which brings together boar and cross on the Benty Grange helmet, or Wayland and the Magi on the Franks Casket. This cunning combination of Christian and secular, of biblical and heroic—which (according to Bede) Cædmon made so popular—is also clear in the verse manuscript Oxford, Bodley Library Junius XI, which once bore his name.[2] The poems contained in that manuscript (*Genesis*, *Exodus*, *Daniel*, and *Christ and Satan*) give a majestic survey of biblical history, and the Old Testament accounts in particular fully exploit the epic potential of their source, offering a succession of heroes such as Noah, Abraham, Moses, or Daniel, each of whom is described in the traditional diction, at once martial and heroic, that distinguishes Old English verse.[3]

The version of *Genesis* which opens the Junius manuscript is often considered the least appealing of Old English biblical poems, and the most clearly dependent on its source; W. P. Ker described the work as "mere flat commonplace, interesting as giving the average literary taste and the commonplace poetical stock of a dull educated man."[4] The most recent editions have underlined the basic unfairness of such a description; the verse *Genesis* is far from slavish translation.[5] Of the biblical account (like Ælfric's, representing Genesis "oð Isaace"), comprising in this case Genesis 1:1–22:13, A. N. Doane notes almost 150 verses wholly omitted,[6] and "nearly 300 isolable additions of content which extend over more than half a line."[7] Three episodes in particular mark considerable divergence from the biblical text, of which the first two are separate accounts of the Fall of Angels, one opening the poem (ll. 1–111), and the other derived from an Old Saxon original, and usually designated *Genesis B* (ll. 235–851).[8] The third episode, which has most biblical warrant, comprises a free and vigorous rendering of Abraham's martial exploits in Genesis 14 (ll. 1960–2095). All three episodes can be considered in some sense "heroic," but here I wish to focus on the last, with its lengthy and lively account of the battle between four gentile kings and five kings allied to Sodom and Gomorrah, the capture of Lot, and his recovery by a small band of 318 warriors led by Abraham.[9]

The distinctive diction of the episode, as much as its exuberant expansion of the biblical source, effectively characterizes the difference in style and tone of this passage of the poem. The battle-scenes, in particular, offer a significant clustering of unusual, poetic, and compound diction which can scarcely be matched elsewhere in *Genesis*. We might consider, for example, the description of the battle of the kings (1982–99):

Foron þa tosomne francan wæron hlude,	
wraðe wælherigas. Sang se wanna fugel	
under deoreðsceaftum, deawigfeðera,	
hræs on wenan. Hæleð onetton	1985
on mægencorðrum, modum þryðge,	
oðþæt folcgetrume gefaren hæfdon	
sid tosomne suðan and norðan,	
helmum þeahte. Þær wæs heard plega,	
wælgara wrixl, wigcyrm micel,	1990
hlud hildesweg. Handum brugdon	
hæleð of scæðum hringmæled sweord,	
ecgum dihtig. Þær wæs eaðfynde	
eorle orlegceap, se ðe ær ne wæs	
niðes genihtsum. Norðmen wæron	1995
suðfolcum swice; wurdon Sodomware	
and Gomorre, goldes bryttan,	
æt þæm lindcrodan leofum bedrorene,	
fyrdgesteallum.	

[Then they came together; javelins were loud, the slaughter-bands violent; the dark bird sang under spear-shafts, dewy-feathered, expecting flesh. Warriors rushed on in mighty troops, brave in heart, until the nations' armies had come together widely, from south and north, protected by helmets. There was a hard struggle, an exchange of slaughterous spears, a great battle-din, the loud sound of war. With hands the heroes drew from sheaths the ring-adorned swords, keen in edge. A battle-bargain was easy to find there for a warrior who was not already satisfied with slaughter. The northmen were false to the southmen: The men of Sodom and Gomorra, distributers of gold, were deprived in that shield-press of dear battle-companions.]

We find a proliferation of compound words, the great majority of which are unattested elsewhere.[10] A number of the other words in the passage are particularly poetic and have, for example, been identified by M. S. Griffith as "constituents of the [poetic] word hoard."[11] Much of the rest of the diction is weighty and oblique, inviting interpretation; one might signal here the compound *orlegceap* ("battle-bargain," l. 1994), presumably a reference at once to the greed of the combatants and the price of that greed,[12] or the simplex *swice* (l. 1996), paradoxically applied to the northern kings, who have themselves been denied their tribute.[13] None of this passage can be matched in the Latin, but is a wholly native invention, peculiar to the verse. We might compare the rather bald account in the Old English prose Hexateuch, which has been dramatically abbreviated; indeed, in the illustrated manuscript BL Cotton Claudius B. iv the abbreviation is especially marked, since in addition to omitting the many foreign names which clutter the Latin account, a careless scribe has left out the last words of the phrase "four kings against five kings," and, as C. R. Dodwell indicates, "significantly the illustration shows only four kings instead of nine fighting in the battle and only two kings (instead of seven) taking possession of Sodom."[14] By contrast the expansive account in the verse of *Genesis* is highly conventional, recalling freely other Old English battle poetry, particularly *Beowulf*, *Maldon*, and *Brunanburh*, the closing lines of which bear a striking resemblance to the end of the episode depicted here.[15] As Barbara Raw has pointed out: "The king of Elam, like Scyld, exacts tribute from the people of Sodom and Gomorrah; the warriors are equipped with the yellow shields, javelins, and ring-patterned swords of Anglo-Saxon heroes; birds of prey tear the corpses; Abraham's friends, like Byrhtnoth's *comitatus* promise to avenge his injury or fall among the slain, and Abraham himself, like Beowulf, gives war as a pledge instead of gold."[16]

The episode comprises sections 28–29 of the Junius manuscript, and opens with a traditional formula (*þa ic . . . gefrægn*, l. 1960), which introduces the battle of the kings and provides the first taste of the heroic matter to come; the same formula is repeated verbatim (l. 2060) at the beginning of the description of Abraham's night attack which avenges the capture of Lot. An alternative (but still traditional) formula (*we þæt . . . magon / secgan*, ll. 2013b–14a) effectively seals the first part of the episode (and ends section 28), briefly summarizing the capture of Lot, and promising to describe what happens next (ll. 2013b–17):[17]

> We þæt soð magon
> secgan furður,   hwelc siððan wearð
> æfter þæm gehnæste   herewulfa sið,   2015
> þara þe læddon Loth   and leoda god,
> suðmonna sinc,   sigore gulpon.
> [We can tell the truth further, as to what was the experience of the slaughter-wolves after that conflict, of those who led off Lot and the peoples' goods, the treasure of the southerners: they boasted in victory]

The entire martial episode, then, related over two sections, is effectively divided into three scenes, considering (a) the battle between the kings and the capture of Lot (ll. 1960–2017); (b) the preparations of Abraham (ll. 2018–2059); and (c) the battle against the kings and the rescue of Lot (ll. 2060–95). The poet has entirely altered the focus of a narrative which in the biblical source consists largely of a sonorous list of names and places, which are barely represented in Old English, and chosen instead to expand dramatically what in the Latin are the barest hints of actual combat. Of the first encounter, the opening ten verses of Genesis 14 yield "inirent bellum . . . direxerunt contra eos aciem . . . terga verterunt cecideruntque ibi" [They brought war . . . they lined up a battle formation against them . . . they turned tail and there fell]; the second conflict is still more sparsely told: "Abram . . . inruit super eos nocte . . . percussitque eos et persecutus est" [Abram . . . attacked them at night . . . he struck and chased them, 14:15].[18]

In the same way that the poet of the Old English *Judith*, by reducing the eight or so characters in the Latin source to some four main speaking roles, is able to heighten the poetic contrasts and comparisons to be made between the named characters (Judith and Holofernes) on the one hand and the anonymous ones (the Jewish handmaid and the Assyrian soldier) on the other, or between the men (Assyrian) and the women (Jewish),[19] so the poet of *Genesis*, by omitting a large number of foreign names and reducing the episode to three discrete but related scenes, is able to point up the causal link between the two battles. Elsewhere in the Junius manuscript, the poet of *Daniel* tidies up the biblical narrative (and gives structure to his poem) in a similar way, highlighting the parallels to be drawn between the visions of Nebuchadnezzor and Balshazzar by introducing Daniel to each scene (his first and last appearances in the text) in substantially the same words.[20] Earlier in *Genesis* the poet has used a similar method to mark off the opening 111 lines, which concern the Fall of Angels, beginning and ending this unbiblical episode (as Roberta Frank has shown) with a series of examples of paronomasia on "*weard . . . wereda wuldor . . . word*" (ll. 1–2) and "*woruld . . . word . . . gewearð . . . wuldor*" (ll. 110–11), before translating Genesis 1·1, "*her ærest gosceop ece drihten, / helm eullwihta, heofon and eorðan*" (ll. 112–13).[21]

The same technique of employing verbal repetition to heighten thematic parallels and lend structure to the poem is further used here in *Genesis* to link the battle sequences. So in the account of the first battle we are given a stirring picture of the fate of the captive women (ll. 1969–72), which has no warrant in the biblical source, presumably to match the account of the return of the captured women at the end of the episode (ll. 2086–90), extrapolated from the single word *mulieres* in Genesis 14:16; likewise *bryda and beaga* (l. 1972) is matched by *sinc and bryda* (l. 2090). We find in each account a mention of the common Old English theme of the carrion birds of battle (ll. 1983–85 and 2088),[22] and an unusual description of the fate of the slain: *him on swaðe feollon* (l. 2001) and *on swaðe sæton* (l. 2077).[23] The description of the army of the four kings, in turns conquering and conquered, remains essentially the same: They may battle with a mighty force *þrymme micle*, l. 1965 and *miclum mægne*, l. 2095), but they are still just a band of battle-wolves (*herewulfa sið* [l. 2015] and *hildewulfas* [l. 2051]—the only occurrences of *wulf* compounds in the poem). It is interesting to note that most of the characteristics mentioned are repeated in the following section of *Genesis* (ll. 2096–172), where Abraham is met by Melchisedech at the gates of Sodom and reports on the battle. There

again we find mention of the birds of prey (ll. 2059–61) and attention
focussed on the captive women (ll. 2155–7), together with the same
unusual phrase *on swaðe sæton* (l. 2114). There is no warrant for such
additions in the biblical source, which appear to have been incorporated
largely to lend unity to the battle scenes and to align the episode con-
cerning Melchisedech with the earlier battles.

A similar motive of linking the battle scenes doubtless lies behind
the poet's quite unbiblical insistence that in each case the battle is
between north and south, with his (and our) sympathies firmly in favour
of the south; there are no less than ten occasions in this episode when
the poet stresses such geographical affiliation,[24] a north/south distinc-
tion which is once more repeated in *Genesis* in the subsequent section,
describing Abraham's meeting with Melchisedech after his victory, and
recapitulating these same two battles (ll. 2096 and 2159). Doane's sug-
gestion that the north/south axis which runs throughout these episodes
was "formulaically more available than east/west" is bizarre[25]; a glance
at *Beowulf* indicates East Danes, North Danes, West Danes, and South
Danes (always carrying the alliteration) in almost equal abundance,
with East Danes and West Danes indeed slightly more common.[26] Else-
where in *Genesis* east and west are specified four times.[27] Clearly
another explanation is required. Outside the passages already men-
tioned, there is but a single geographical indication, itself in the open-
ing section of the poem which is not drawn from a biblical source. Here
it is stated (ll. 32–34) that Satan has his seat in the north, a notion
alluded to again in *Genesis B* (ll. 274–76), where, however, the north-
west is specified. Successive studies by Paul Salmon and Thomas D.
Hill have demonstrated that patristic authorities such as Augustine and
Gregory popularized the notion (derived ultimately from Isaiah
14:12–14) that the north was to be associated with evil, and that several
Anglo-Saxons, notably Bede (in Northumbria!), adopted and transmit-
ted the idea in their own writings.[28] With such a predominant patristic
background we need not assume, like Dietrich Hofmann, that the poet's
insistence on a north/south axis necessitates a late-tenth-century com-
position and a reference to the Danes, although it may be, as Malcolm
Godden has suggested, that at the time of the manuscript's compilation
such an association was likely.[29]

The poet of *Genesis* is elsewhere clearly familiar with patristic texts. Of the many additions to the biblical source made by the Old English poet, some simply providing extra detail (such as the names of the wives of Noah and his sons, ll. 1546–49)[30] or interpretation (equating the "sons of God" of Genesis 6 with the children of Seth, ll. 1245–52),[31] many clearly derive from exegetical sources.[32] In at least one case of expansion, the description of the raven released by Noah feeding on a corpse (ll. 1438–48), a patristic and exegetical notion appears to have been combined with the traditional heroic diction and imagery of Old English verse.[33] A series of more-or-less learned onomastic and etymological puns on (for example) Adam, Eve, Sarah, and Daniel have been isolated in Old English biblical verse by Fred Robinson and Roberta Frank.[34] In other ways the Old Testament source appears implicitly supplemented by allusion to the events of the new. The closing episode of the poem, describing Abraham's offering of Isaac, has been successively interpreted by Huppé, Creed, McKill, and Frank as allegorically depicting the circumstances of the crucifixion in complementary studies which together underline the subtlety of the poet's technique.[35]

There was certainly patristic warrant for an allegorical reading of Abraham's battling heroism too, and Anglo-Saxon authors demonstrate a knowledge of a range of interpretations. In commenting on Genesis 14, Bede stresses right from the start the importance of the wider allegorical perspective: "non est autem putandum haec sacrae auctorem scripturae historici tantum studii gratia memoriae mandasse, et non intuitu potius commendandae nobis gratiae caelestis" [it should not be thought that the author of Holy Scripture has committed this to memory only for the sake of historical interest, and not rather in seeking to commend to us heavenly grace].[36] Explicitly linking this episode with the subsequent rescue mission of Abraham, Bede interprets this and the following passage as teaching the value of faith in overcoming great odds with little resources, as well as providing a stern warning of the dangers of moral laxness which the people of Sodom, though reprieved in this instance, fail to heed. As the commentary says: "docet namque nos per uictoriam Abrae, qua tantos reges cum paucis superauit, quae sit uirtus fidei qua erat munitus; quanta gratia benedictionis diuinae qua erat praeditus" [for it teaches us through Abram's victory, in which he defeated such powerful kings with a few men, what is the power of the faith with which he was fortified, and how great was the grace of divine blessing with which he was endowed].[37] Bede's words seem echoed in the closing lines of this passage of *Genesis* (ll. 2092–95):

> Næfre mon ealra
> lifigendra her   lytle werede
> þon wurðlicor   wigsið ateah,
> þara þe wið swa miclum   mægne geræsde.
> [Of all men living here never did anyone conduct with a small troop against so great a force a more worthy warfare.]

Bede repeats the same notion later in his commentary, "miraculum quidem est diuinae potentiae permaximum, quod cum cohorte tam modica tantam hostium stragem fecerit Abram" [it is a very great sign of divine power, that Abram caused so great a slaughter of enemies with so small a troop],[38] before going on to elaborate the mystical significance of the number 318, which, following Ambrose,[39] he interprets as ΤΙΗ in Greek reckoning, standing for Christ crucified: "bene ergo in trecentis decem et octo sociis uicit hostes, ac fratrem liberauit Abram, ut mystice figuraret nasciturum de suo semine eum qui per passionem crucis mundum a morte reuocaret" [therefore well did Abram conquer his enemies with 318 allies, and set his brother free, since he prefigured the one to be born from his own seed, who through suffering on the cross summoned the world from death].[40] It was on the basis of such patristic comments that Bernard Huppé considered that "Abraham's battle against the four kings 'signifies the battle of the virtues and the vices.' It is, in short, the first *psychomachia*."[41] Pointing in particular to the (unbiblical) opening words of the priest-king Melchisedech to Abraham on his return from the fray (*wæs ðu gewur ðod on wera rime,* l. 2107), Huppé noted: "Abraham is honoured in the number of men, that is, 'among men,' but also quite literally in the number, 318, of his little band, which symbolically was prophetic of the Redemption through which . . . the faithful Christian soldier everywhere triumphed."[42] Huppé's analysis, however, which apart from this single instance makes no attempt to link the passage explicitly to such an allegorical interpretation, has proved less influential than it might: Doane, for example, makes no reference to it in the notes to this passage in his edition, condemning the efforts of patristic commentators such as Isidore and Hrabanus to interpret the battle allegorically as "sporadic and non-influential."[43]

Two small pieces of further evidence, however, could perhaps be used to bolster such an allegorical view, both deriving from the same kind of onomastic ingenuity the role of which in Old English poetry has been highlighted by Robinson and Frank.[44] One of the main alterations to the biblical text made by the poet of *Genesis* is greatly to heighten the importance of the king of Elam, mentioned third of four kings in the Latin account, but here elevated to the primary role (l. 1960); Elam and the Elamites are themselves mentioned by name no less than four times in the episode.[45] If we accept that the poet wished to depict a series of battles first lost and then won primarily against the forces of Elam, it is intriguing to note that in his widely known *Liber interpretationis hebraicorum nominum* Jerome equates Elam with the forces of worldliness, and the secular world (*saeculi uel orbis*).[46] Again, one might note that the place where Abraham finally disposed of the Elamites (and from where they are driven to Damascus) is given in the Bible as Dan, a Hebrew word interpreted by Jerome as "judgment" (*iudicium*, Old English *dom*).[47] The interpretation was played upon in Anglo-Saxon literature from the earliest period, and was alluded to, for example, by Aldhelm (in Latin) and the poet of *Daniel* (in Old English).[48] In addition to meaning "judgment," of course, the Old English word *dom* carries the heroic sense "glory." Such onomastic knowledge lends some ironic depth to the poet's assertion that in fleeing to Damascus the Elamites were *dome bedrorene* ("bereft of glory" or "bereft of judgment," l. 2082).

Moreover, there were certainly available to Anglo-Saxon authors much closer models for the versified allegorical interpretation of scripture than the exegetical prose works considered hitherto; nor were these models "sporadic and non-influential." The verses of the Latin biblical narrative poets Juvencus, Cyprianus Gallus, Caelius Sedulius, and (especially) Arator were all widely read and closely studied in Anglo-Saxon England, and are steeped in a tradition of rhetorical paraphrase and amplification in which allegorical interpretation played a major part.[49] The most influential of all accounts of a *psychomachia* is, of course, the eponymous Latin poem by Prudentius, which was widely copied, studied, and imitated in Anglo-Saxon England by authors as diverse in time and temperament as Aldhelm and Byrhtferth of Ramsey.[50] There are no fewer than ten extant Anglo-Saxon manuscripts of the *Psychomachia*, while the pervasive influence of the poem on the vernacular (particularly, for example, on the *Pater Noster* battle episode in *Solomon and Saturn*) has been discussed in detail by Hermann, and Wieland has in hand a similar study of the Anglo-Latin debt.[51] Since so many Anglo-Saxon authors clearly drew their inspiration from Prudentius's work, it is intriguing to note that the entire preface to the *Psychomachia* (some sixty-eight verses) consists of a discussion of the main events in the life of Abraham, who is held up as a model both of external action and internal struggle (ll. 9–10 and 13–14): "[Abraham] pugnare nosmet cum profanis gentibus / suasit suumque suasor exemplum dedit . . . strage multa bellicosus spiritus / portenta cordis seruientis uicerit" [Abraham has persuaded us to battle against profane nations, and the persuader has offered his own example . . . the warlike spirit has conquered the monsters of the servile heart with great slaughter]. Prudentius at least was inviting his audience—to emend Huppé's much-censured words—"to see in Abraham not *only* a pagan warrior, but *also* an ideal of Christian living."[52] Prudentius considers the offering of Isaac, the blessing of Melchisedech, and the entertaining of the three angels, but concentrates mainly and specifically on the episode of Lot's abduction, and his subsequent rescue by Abraham and his followers, whose number, 318, is described as a mystical figure ("figura . . . mystica," l. 58). The vigor and martial imagery of the description of this episode are quite in keeping with Prudentius's normal practice elsewhere in the *Psychomachia*, where he borrows freely from the diction and imagery of earlier (pagan) heroic verse, particularly that of Vergil, Lucan, and Statius.[53]

Five chief features stand out in Prudentius's retelling of this episode and distinguish it from a straight versification of biblical narrative. In each case it is possible to point to parallel techniques employed by the poet of *Genesis*. Firstly, one might consider the prevalence in this passage of Prudentius of heroic poetic diction, of the sort found frequently in Latin hexameter verse, here applied in iambic trimeter. So, for example, we find reference to the extensive slaughter (*strage multa*, l. 13; *caede . . . tanta*, l. 38), to the ruthless victory (*pellit fugatos, proterit sauciatos*, l. 28), and to the pomp and splendor of the kings (*reges*

ing to note that the second illustrator of the Junius manuscript, up to the
passage in *Genesis* discussed here, has been identified with the artist of
the Vices and Virtues illustrations of MS Cambridge, Corpus Christi
College 23, the most celebrated Anglo-Saxon manuscript of Pruden-
tius's *Psychomachia*.[59] More significantly, Corpus 23 contains a number
of glosses and marginal scholia which make explicit the allegorical
interpretation to be placed on Abraham's heroism in the *Psy-
chomachia*.[60] Two of these marginal scholia are worth quoting in full:
"Antequa*m* immolaret filiu*m* / bellu*m* gessit .cu*m*. iiii*or*. regib*us*; / Sic
nos antea non possum*us* / immolare filium d*eo*.i.ani/mum quousque bel-
lum cu*m* / uitiis geramus sicut ide*m* fecit" [Before he came to sacrifice
his son he waged war against four kings; so we cannot sacrifice our son
(that is, our soul) to God until we wage war against the vices, as he did];
"Sicut abraham filiu*m* coniuga. / lem gignere no*n*potuit. Antequa*m* /
reges qui loth uinctu*m* tenebant / per*quos*&iam uitia designebant*ur* /
sup*er*ass&; ita nemo uirtute sexe/gegnere ual&. Antequa*m*uitia / sibi
repugnantia penit*us* deuicerit" [Just as Abraham could not get a son by
his wife until he had conquered the kings (by whom the vices are desig-
nated) who held Lot captive, so no one can engender virtues before he
has utterly conquered the vices battling against him].[61] It is particularly
intriguing to note that the second of the scholia quoted includes the
phrase "loth uinctum," since, as we have seen, this is simply to make
explicit the traditional interpretation of the name implicitly employed by
Prudentius in the course of the narrative.[62] Indeed, Corpus 23 has the
reading "UINC TUM" where the printed editions agree in preferring
"uictum" (l. 15), as above; the gloss ".i.superatum" found in Corpus 23
clearly refers to the favored variant.[63] It seems possible that in this
instance the patristic and allegorical tradition has influenced not only the
scholia but also the text itself.

Whether or not one regards the *Psychomachia* of Prudentius as
source or literary impetus for this heroic set piece in the Old English
Genesis, the poem provides, I suggest, a useful analogue for the way in
which a poet steeped in heroic tradition can interpret and elaborate a
promising piece of scripture. In both cases, though the rendering is far
from faithful, the sense is always full of faith. Episodes such as this from
Genesis demonstrate the remarkable success with which, after Cædmon,
the new Christian notions were accommodated within the traditional

techniques and diction of native verse; the poetry of Cædmon's contemporary, Aldhelm, and his student, Æthilwald, demonstrate that in the earlier period at least, the direction of influence was not always one way: vernacular traditions and techniques of versification could equally be assimilated into Anglo-Latin verse.[64] Such characteristically Anglo-Saxon verses, both in Latin and the vernacular, amply show (in answer to Alcuin's famous question) what Ingeld had to do with Christ. In contemplating this remarkable episode in *Genesis*, where the traditional and martial language of heroic and secular verse has been put to the service of biblical story, we might do worse than consider the words of Gregory the Great, commenting on the first Book of Kings:

> ad spiritalia bella non per saeculares litteras sed per diuinas instruimur ... fideles deum uidentes arte saecularis scientiae contra malignos spiritus nequaquam proeliantur ... quae profecto saecularium librorum erudito etsi per semetipsam ad spiritalem sanctorum conflictum non prodest, si diuinae scripturae coniungitur, eiusdem scripturae scientia subtilius erudimur.
>
> [we are prepared for spiritual battles by sacred and not by secular literature ... the faithful who see God through the skill of secular knowledge battle in vain against evil spirits ... but assuredly this knowledge of secular books, even if it does not of itself avail in the spiritual conflict of the holy, if it is joined to sacred scripture, brings us to a more profound understanding of that scripture].[65]

NOTES

1. For a detailed survey of the phenomenon, see André Crépin, *Poétique vieil-anglaise: désignations du Dieu chretien.* Thèse de doctorat-ès lettres (Université de Paris, 1969).
2. For a facsimile, see Sir Israel Gollancz, *The Cædmon Manuscript of Anglo-Saxon Biblical Poetry Junius XI in the Bodleian Library* (Oxford, 1927); for an overview of scholarship on the manuscript, see Graham D. Caie, *Bibliography of Junius 11 Manuscript, with Appendix on Cædmon's Hymn*, Anglica et Americana 6 (Copenhagen, 1979).
3. See further (for example) T. A. Shippey, *Old English Verse* (London, 1972), 134–54.
4. *The Dark Ages* (Edinburgh, 1904), 256.

5. A. N. Doane, ed., *Genesis A: A New Edition* (Wisconsin, 1978). See too Colette Stévanovitch, ed., *La "Genèse" du manuscrit Junius XI de la Bodleienne, Edition, traduction et commentaire*, Association des Médiévistes Anglicistes de l'Enseignement Supérieur, hors série 1, 2 vols. (Paris, 1992).

6. Doane, *Genesis A*, 62.

7. Ibid., 68.

8. See now A. N. Doane, ed., *The Saxon Genesis* (Madison, WI, 1991).

9. Cf. Doane, *Genesis A*, 295–300; Stévanovitch, *La "Genèse,"* 2:571–82.

10. So for example, we find the following fifteen compound nouns and adjectives: *wælherigas, deoreðsceaftum, deawigfeðera, mægencorðrum, folcgetrume, wælgara, wigcyrm, hildesweg, hringmæled, eað-fynde, orlegceap, suðfolcum, Sodomware, lindcrodan,* and *fyrdgesteallum.* Of these, no fewer than nine are signaled by Doane to be unique to *Genesis.*

11. M. S. Griffith, "Poetic Language and the Paris Psalter: The Decay of the Old English Tradition," *Anglo-Saxon England* 20 (1991), 167–86, p. 168. Griffith lists some 350 "poetic words" in an Appendix to his article at 183–5, of which a number appear in this passage, including *brytta, eorl, gar, hæleð, hild, lind, orlege,* and *plega.*

12. As Doane notes (*Genesis A*, 297): "the whole passage 1985b–2003a, satirizes the Sodomites"; cf. the other compounds *orlæggifre* (l. 2289), *orlegnið* (ll. 84 and 915), and *orlegweorc* (l. 2020), all unique to *Genesis.*

13. Cf. *ac him from swicon* (l. 1980); as Doane notes (*Genesis A*, 298), "the word play is particularly rich here."

14. C. R. Dodwell and Peter Clemoes, ed., *The Old English Illustrated Hexateuch: British Museum Cotton Claudius B.IV*, EEMF 18 (Copenhagen, 1974), 71.

15. As noted by Malcolm Godden, "Biblical Literature: the Old Testament," in Malcolm Godden & Michael Lapidge, ed., *The Cambridge Companion to Old English Literature* (Cambridge, 1991), 206–26, p. 210.

16. Barbara C. Raw, *The Art and Background of Old English Poetry* (London, 1978), 82.

17. On these traditional formulas, see further Ward Parks, "The Traditional Narrator and the 'I heard' Formulas in Old English Poetry," *Anglo-Saxon England* 16 (1987), 45–66.

18. Biblical quotations are taken from R. Weber, ed., *Biblia Sacra iuxta Vulgatam Versionem*, 2nd ed., 2 vols. (Stuttgart, 1975).

19. See further James F. Doubleday, "The Principle of Contrast in *Judith*," *Neuphilologische Mitteilungen* 72 (1971), 436–41.

20. Roberta Frank, "Some Uses of Paronomasia in Old English Scriptural Verse," *Speculum* 47 (1972), 207–26, p. 216 [reprinted in the present volume—*ed.*].

21. Ibid., 211–13.

22. See further Francis P. Magoun, "The Theme of the Beasts of Battle in Anglo-Saxon Poetry," *Neuphilologische Mitteilungen* 56 (1955), 81–90.

23. Cf. Doane, *Genesis A*, 299.

24. Ll. 1966, 1975, 1977, 1988 (twice), 1995, 1996, 2017, 2068, and 2090.

25. Doane, *Genesis A*, 296.

26. Fr. Klaeber, ed., *Beowulf and the Fight at Finnsburg*, 3rd ed. (Lexington, 1950), ll. 392, 616, and 828 (*East-Dene*); 383 and 1578 (*West-Dene*); 783 (*Norð-Dene*); 463 and 1996 (*Suð-Dene*).

27. Ll. 1052, 1794, 1802, and 1884.

28. Paul Salmon, "The Site of Lucifer's Throne," *Anglia* 81 (1963), 118–23; Thomas D. Hill, "Some Remarks on 'The Site of Lucifer's Throne'," *Anglia* 87 (1969), 303–11.

29. Dietrich Hofmann, "Untersuchungen zur altenglischen Gedichten *Genesis und Exodus*," *Anglia* 75 (1957), 1–34, pp. 16–18; Godden, "Biblical Literature," 210.

30. Doane, *Genesis A*, 276–77.

31. Ibid., 256–57.

32. Ibid., 49–58.

33. Ibid., 271; cf. Samuel Moore, "The Old English *Genesis*, ll. 1145 and 1146–48," *Modern Language Review* 6 (1911), 199–202.

34. Frank, "Some Uses of Paronomasia," 216–17; Fred C. Robinson, "The Significance of Names in Old English Literature," *Anglia* 86 (1968), 14–58. See now Fred C. Robinson, *The Tomb of Beowulf and other Essays on Old English* (Oxford, 1993), 183–235, where four articles on "Names in Old English Literature" are updated.

35. Bernard F. Huppé, *Doctrine and Poetry: Augustine's Influence on Old English Poetry* (Albany, 1959); Robert P. Creed, "The Art of the Singer: Three Old English Tellings of the Offering of Isaac," in *Old English Poetry: Fifteen Essays*, ed. Robert P. Creed (Providence, RI, 1967), 63–92; Laura N. McKill, "The Offering of Isaac and the Artistry of Old English *Genesis A*," in Jane Campbell and James Doyle, ed., *The Practical Vision: Essays in English Literature in Honour of Flora Roy* (Ontario, 1978), 1–11; Frank, "Some Uses of Paronomasia," 214–15.

36. C. W. Jones, ed., *Bedae Venerabilis Libri Quattuor in Genesim, CCSL* 118A (Turnhout, 1967), 182.

37. Ibid.

38. Ibid., 187.

39. M. L. W. Laistner, "The Library of the Venerable Bede," in A. Hamilton Thompson, ed., *Bede: His Life, Times, and Writings* (Oxford, 1935), 237–66, p. 247, argues that Bede drew his interpretation specifically from Ambrose's *De Abraham*.

40. *In Genesim*, 187.

41. Huppé, *Doctrine and Poetry*, 197.

42. Ibid., 198.

43. Doane, *Genesis A*, 295; cf. the similar skepticism of Stévanovitch, *La "Genèse,"* 2:571.

44. See note 34.

45. Lines 1960, 1980, 2004,and 2081.

46. P. de Lagarde, ed., *Liber interpretationis hebraicorum nominum, CCSL* 72 (Turnhout, 1959), 65.

47. Ibid., 64.

48. Frank, "Some Uses of Paronomasia," 216–17.

49. See further Michael Roberts, *Biblical Epic and Rhetorical Paraphrase in Late Antiquity* (Liverpool, 1985), 161–218. On the knowledge and study of Latin biblical poets, see Michael Lapidge, "The Study of Latin Texts in Late Anglo-Saxon England: [1] the Evidence of Latin Glosses," in Nicholas P. Brooks, ed., *Latin and the Vernacular Languages in Early Medieval Britain* (Leicester, 1982), 99–140; Andy Orchard, *The Poetic Art of Aldhelm*, Cambridge Studies in Anglo-Saxon England 8 (Cambridge, 1994), 161–70.

50. M. P. Cunningham, ed., *Aurelii Prudentii Clementis Psychomachia, CCSL* 126 (Turnhout, 1966), 149–81. On the knowledge of Prudentius in Anglo-Saxon England, see Gernot R. Wieland, "Prudentius," in Frederick M. Biggs, Thomas D. Hill, and Paul E. Szarmach, ed., *Sources of Anglo-Saxon Literary Culture: A Trial Version* (Binghamton, NY, 1990), 150–56; Orchard, *The Poetic Art of Aldhelm*, 171–78.

51. John P. Hermann, "The Recurrent Motif of Spiritual Warfare in Old English Poetry," *Annuale Medievale* 22 (1982), 7–35; idem, "Some Varieties of Psychomachia in Old English," *American Benedictine Review* 34 (1983), 74–86 and 188–222; idem, *Allegories of War: Language and Violence in Old English Poetry* (Ann Arbor, MI; 1989); Wieland, *Trial Version*, 150–6. On the Anglo-Saxon manuscripts of the Psychomachia, see

Gernot R. Wieland, "The Anglo-Saxon Manuscripts of Prudentius's Psy-chomachia," *Anglo-Saxon England* 16 (1987), 213–31; idem, *The Latin Glosses on Arator and Prudentius in Cambridge University Library MS Gg. 5.35* (Toronto, 1983).

52. *Doctrine and Poetry*, 197 (my italics).

53. See, for example, the detailed discussion of Macklin Smith, *Prudentius' Psychomachia: A Reexamination* (Princeton, 1976), 234–300, who argues that the overwhelming use of heroic diction and direct imitation of pagan authors by Prudentius is a deliberate attempt to purge and Christianize the hexameter form.

54. For a convenient overview, see G. Bardy, "Melchisédech dans la tradition patristique," *Revue Benédictine* 35 (1926), 496–509.

55. So, for example, we find *suasit . . . suasor* (l. 10) and *uicerit / uictum* (ll. 14–15).

56. Cf. the mention of *vinculis* (l. 21), *catenas* (l. 29), and *nexibus* (l. 32).

57. *Liber interpretationis hebraicorum nominum*, 68.

58. Macklin Smith, *Prudentius' Psychomachia*, 206–33

59. See David N. Dumville, *English Caroline Script and Monastic History: Studies in Benedictinism A.D. 950–1030* (Woodbridge, 1993), 105–6.

60. The most detailed study (including a plate of the opening passage) is that of R. I. Page, "On the Feasibility of a Corpus of Anglo-Saxon Glosses: The View from the Library," in R. Derolez, ed., *Anglo-Saxon Glossography: Papers Read at the International Conference held in the Koninklijke Academie voor Wetenschappen Letteren en Schone Kunsten van België. Brussels, 8 and 9 September, 1986* (Brussels, 1992), 77–95.

61. Page, "On the Feasibility of a Corpus of Anglo-Saxon Glosses," 83.

62. See note 57. There appears to be some link between the Corpus 23 glosses and the commentary on Prudentius (perhaps by Remigius of Auxerre) preserved in MS Valenciennes 413, as Page has noted: "On the Feasibility of a Corpus of Anglo-Saxon Glosses," 84. In particular the second of the scholia quoted is found verbatim in that text, which also offers much other allegorical commentary on Abraham's activities, the significance of Melchisedech, and the mystical meaning of the 318 warriors. See John M. Burnam, ed., *Commentaire anonyme sur Prudence d'après le manuscrit 413 de Valenciennes* (Paris, 1910), 85–88.

63. Page, "On the Feasibility of a Corpus of Anglo-Saxon Glosses," 87–88. As Page indicates, two further Anglo-Saxon manuscripts of the *Psy-chomachia* (London, BL Cotton Cleopatra C. viii and Cambridge,

University Library Gg.5.35) also demonstrate the same variant "uinctum."

64. Cf. Orchard, *The Poetic Art of Aldhelm*, 47–54 and 119–25

65. P. Verbraken, ed., *Sancti Gregorii Magni Expositio in Librum Primum Regum*, *CCSL* 144 (Turnhout, 1963), 47–614, 471; cf. Peter Hunter Blair, *The World of Bede* (Cambridge, 1970), 286.

Christian Tradition in
the Old English *Exodus*

JAMES W. EARL

This essay first appeared in NM *71 (1970), 541–70. Notes have been renumbered consecutively, and translations in square brackets have been supplied by the editor.*

The only critical judgment concerning the Old English *Exodus*[1] which has not been debated is that it is an extraordinarily difficult poem. Besides the usual textual problems which plague all OE poetry, the poem's structure is highly problematic as well. There seem to be numerous lacunae; questions of interpolation are frequent; the narrative is often jumbled; and the Biblical parallel which supposedly underlies the whole conception of the poem is often tenuous and at times willfully distorted. The problems of dealing with the poem are illustrated dramatically in its latest edition, that of Irving.[2] The liberties which this editor has felt compelled to take with the MS text are perhaps unique in modern OE scholarship. His frequent (and sometimes arbitrary) emendations, and the gross rearrangement of the poem's lines stand as a monument of resistance to the recent trend toward the defense of MS readings whenever possible. But the edition certainly does attest to the difficulties involved in trying to deal with the poem as a whole.

The history of the criticism of *Exodus* is short and unhappy. The only extended pieces of literary criticism dealing with the poem before 1950, which remain significant contributions today (outside the editions of Blackburn[3] and Krapp), are Moore's "The Sources of the Old English *Exodus*"[4] and Bright's "Relationship of the Cædmonian *Exodus* to the Liturgy."[5] And whether even these two pieces can survive our close scrutiny today is certainly debatable. The rest of the early *Exodus* scholarship belongs to that genre most accurately described by the title of one of Ernst Kock's innumerable contributions to the field: "Jubilee Jaunts and Jottings: 250 Contributions to the Interpretation," etc.[6] The age of such scholarship, valuable as it may be, is hopefully over; that freedom with which scholars might indulge themselves by dog-trotting through the whole corpus of Germanic literature, and making notes and emendations in phonological flights of fancy, seems to be now out of style.

The results of such "jaunts and jottings" in *Exodus* can be seen in Krapp's edition of the poem. The format of the *ASPR* series does not include much in the way of a literary study of the poem, and the task of establishing the poem's text proceeds without the advantage of a critical understanding of the poem as a whole. Individual lines and words have their own personal histories, and emendations which do not depend on any general interpretation of the poem have been proposed and accepted. Emendations thus may conflict with their own implications regarding their larger context. For example, Krapp and Irving both follow Gollancz's emendation *dægweorc > dægword* in line 519. This change is supposedly justified by the "ingenious surmise" that the poet was trying to refer to Deuteronomy, but mistakenly used the equivalent of the title "Chronicles," a common confusion due to the similarity of the two words in their translation from the Hebrew.[7] Both editions, however, are quick to point out that the reference to Deuteronomy must be "momentary" and "very brief," since the events being described certainly do not occur in the Biblical narrative. Thus they have gratuitously added a Biblical reference which would seem to have no structural relevance to the imaginative framework of the poem as they understand it. And indeed, when Moses finally does speak, in lines 554–64, they insist that this speech is not the Deuteronomic *dægword* earlier referred to—even though it can be seen as a pretty fair summary of the themes of Deuteronomy. This particular problem will be raised again later; suffice it to say that the old tradition of making such notes can actually impede our understanding of a poem, unless a coherent critical attitude toward the poem can be presupposed. The task of the present paper is not to "solve" *Exodus*, but only to provide such a critical attitude, which may serve as a prolegomenon to a more exhaustive treatment of the poem.

Such a coherent approach toward *Exodus* has only begun to emerge in the last few years. Two attempts have been made to explain the difficulties of the poem without falling back upon what has always been considered the ineptitude of the poet. Bernard Huppé's treatment of the poem in his book *Doctrine and Poetry: Augustine's Influence on OE Poetry*[8] and Cross and Tucker's "Allegorical Traditions and the OE *Exodus*"[9] have begun the task of understanding *Exodus* in the context of Medieval Christian tradition. Although this approach has not been carried far, it holds the most promise for producing a unified interpretation, which could clarify the poem's perennial cruces as well.[10] The essential correctness of this approach seems clear for this particular poem: the puzzling details which have defied understanding on the literal level beg for an allegorical (or at least some form of spiritual) interpretation; and the common Medieval Christian traditions, as embodied especially in Scriptural exegesis, answer this need very satisfactorily.

The necessity for an exegetical approach is illustrated at the very opening of the poem.

> Hwæt! We feor and neah   gefrigen habað
> ofer middangeard   Moyses domas,
> wræclico wordriht   wera cneorissum
> (in uprodor   eadigra gehwam
> æfter bealusiðe   bote lifes,
> lifigendra gehwam   langsumne ræd)
> hæleðum secgan.   Gehyre seðe wille!   (1–7)
> [Lo! far and wide throughout the world we have heard men tell of the laws of Moses, a wondrous code for the race of men—reward of life for all the blessed after the fateful journey, and lasting instruction for every living soul. Let him hear it who will!]

This passage raises several important questions. First, how is the reference to "Moyses domas" related to a poem which seems to concern the passage of the Red Sea? If the poem concerns the Law at all, it is either in one of the lacunae, or on a level other than the narrative itself. After all, the Red Sea episode unambiguously precedes the giving of the Law at Sinai in the Biblical narrative. Yet the poet apparently introduces his poem as being about "Moyses domas," rather than the Red Sea. Second, and more to the point, the subject of the parenthesis seems even more irrelevant to the poem's literal meaning, and indeed it does not even seem very clearly related to the sentence which it interrupts. The relationship between Mosaic Law and heavenly salvation here seems to depend solely on the double meaning of the word "ræd," which may either refer back to the "counsel" of Moses or to the "benefit" of "bote lifes." But no matter how the line is read, the idea of "in uprodor . . . bote lifes" clearly stands outside the poem's literal narrative.

Within the context of Christian exegetical tradition, however, this passage is not especially problematical, and is indeed very relevant. Even the most general symbolic interpretation of the exodus story involves the idea of salvation which is referred to here. From earliest times, the exodus story has been interpreted as an allegory of man's journey from this world to the next, from the earthly "land of bondage" to the Promised Land, from a state of sin to the salvation of heaven, with the Red Sea marking the beginning of the spiritual journey at baptism. We will examine this tradition in some detail further on.

Our poem, however, seems to concern only the beginning of the exodus, up to the Red Sea. Cross and Tucker, who outline the traditions of the whole exodus, do not see in the traditions concerning the Red Sea any justification for the poem's emphasis on salvation: "Naturally enough an exposition of these biblical events in the commentaries on 'Exodus' never places such emphasis on the crossing of the Red Sea as does the poem— baptism is only a beginning after all."[11] But there is a tradition in Medieval exegesis, which interprets the passage of the Red Sea as a "type" or allegory very similar to the one outlined above, involving the entire exodus: The single episode in itself represents the journey of the Christian soul as it moves toward salvation by means of Christ and the Church.

Denique illi post mare ad eremum pervenerunt: nos post baptismum ad paradisum pervenimus . . . Illis in deserto suavitas lactis et mellis exhibita est: nobis vero, quod plus est melle dulcior ac lacte candidior, aeternae vitae beatitudo Dei tribuetur in regno.[12]

[Then after the sea they came to the desert: we after baptism come to paradise . . . to them in the desert was shown the sweetness of milk and honey: but to us is granted, sweeter than honey and whiter than milk, a life of eternal blessedness in the kingdom of God.]

Ille populus per mare Rubrum salvatus est, Pharaone demerso, ita Ecclesia gentium per baptismum de diaboli servitio liberata, et ad veram repromissionis terram et evangelicam libertatem introducta est.[13]

[That people was saved and Pharaoh drowned in the Red Sea; likewise the Church has saved the nations by baptism from servitude to the devil, and led them into the true land of promise and the freedom of the Gospel.]

We hardly need turn to the Fathers for the association of the desert with earthly and heavenly Paradise—it is a very common idea in the Bible itself. The prophets looked back on the years in the desert as that time when Israel enjoyed her most intimate and desirable relationship with God.[14] Augustine himself makes it clear that at the Red Sea the Kingdom of God is attained in a spiritual sense, even though the Jordan is still far away:

> *Et abstulit sicut oves populum suum, et perduxit eos tanquam gregem in deserto. Et deduxit eos in spe, et non timuerunt, et inimicos eorum operuit mare.* Tanto fit hoc melius, quanto interius, ubi eruti de potestate tenebrarum in regnum Dei mente transferimur, et secundum pascua spiritualia efficimur oves Dei, ambulantes in hoc saeculo velut in deserto, quoniam nemini est fides nostra conspicua.[15]
> ["And He took away His people like sheep, and led them like a flock in the desert; and He led them down in hope, and they did not fear, and the sea covered their enemies." This comes about to so much the greater good, the more it is an inward thing, wherein being delivered from the power of darkness we are mentally carried into the Kingdom of God, and in spiritual pastures we are made to become sheep of God, walking in this world as if in a desert, for our faith is visible to no one.]

One has only to remember that baptism, in the early church, was intimately associated with Easter, to understand the profoundly anagogical nature of the sacrament. Jean Daniélou, in his book *From Shadows to Reality*, summarizes the "primitive approach to Baptism and the Redemption" by stressing this aspect of baptism which has been practically lost in the modern Church: "The Exodus gives us the type for this theology: what God did once by the mystery of water to free an earthly people from an earthly tyrant and so pass from Egypt into the desert, he still does by the mystery of water when he frees a spiritual people from a spiritual tyrant and leads them from the World into the Kingdom of God."[16] Ambrose brings this concept out clearly by means of contrast, in a different use of the traditional typology:

> Quid praecipuum quam quod per mare transiit Judaeorum populus? ut de baptismo interim loquamur. Attamen qui transierunt Judaei, mortui sunt omnes in deserto. Caeterum qui per hunc fontem transit, hoc est, a terrenis ad coelestis; hic est enim transitus, ideo pascha, hoc est transitus ejus,

transitus a peccato ad vitam, a culpa ad gratiam, ab inquinamento ad san-
tificationem qui per hunc fontem transit, non moritur, sed resurgit.[17]
[In what are we superior to the people of the Jews who passed through the
sea, that we may speak meanwhile of baptism? Yet the Jews who passed
through all died in the desert. But he who passes through this font, that is
from the earthly to the heavenly; for this is a passage, thus "Easter," that is
"his passage," the passage from sin into life, from guilt into grace, from
defilement to sanctification—he who passes through this font does not die
but rises again.]

The parenthesis of lines 4–6, then, is directly relevant to our poem of the
Red Sea crossing, and the whole poem's emphasis on the theme of sal-
vation (which we will examine below) is quite central to our understand-
ing of the narrative. The introduction of this theme so early in the poem
should indicate to us the necessity for reading the whole poem with an
eye to the traditional Christian symbolism of the exodus. Huppé is cor-
rect in pointing out that in this context the word "bealusið" (5) means
more than simply "death," but refers to the "baleful journey" of earthly
life as well, that journey of life and death which precedes our entrance
into heaven, and which is most conventionally symbolized by the exodus
story, and most concisely in the story of the Red Sea crossing. The word
"bealusið" summarizes a long exegetical tradition that interprets the
wanderings in the wilderness which precede the entrance into the
Promised Land (or the life of bondage in Egypt which precedes the sal-
vation of the Red Sea) as the period of temptation and sin in this life.
This tradition is of course closely tied to the theme of "in
uprodor . . . bote lifes" by the shape of the exodus narrative itself. It
should be pointed out, however, that Huppé's analysis of these opening
lines is marred by both an extravagance of interpretation and a dubious
translation.[18] It is enough to say that the real significance of these lines is
that they introduce the subject of the poem, but do so by summarizing
that subject allegorically.

The traditions referred to in this opening passage are only a small
part of the complex symbolism of the exodus in Patristic exegesis which
informs the entire poem. Such difficulties as the continual depiction of
the Israelite army in nautical terms, the seemingly incongruous use of
battle imagery to describe the "retreat" into the Red Sea, the Noah and
Abraham digression, the many complexities of the poem's last eighty
lines, and many individual problematical lines and images can be fitted

with some success into the traditional understanding of the exodus story and its allegorical meanings. Irving's attitude toward this approach to the poem clearly indicates the necessity for a detailed argument. He says:

> In this poet we find a radical departure from such a tradition. He is interested primarily in facts, in recreating historical events as accurately as possible. It is necessary to emphasize this point because of the impression created by Moore to some extent and Gollancz to a much greater extent that the poet of *Exodus* is following rather ignorantly the allegorical tradition. A few phrases in the poem suggest that he was aware of it . . . but the whole poem shows decisively that he was not interested in it.[19]

In many ways, the most difficult of the passages I want to examine is the poem's conclusion, lines 519–590. A detailed commentary on these lines might best indicate just what it is that the poet was interested in, and best illustrate the intellectual framework in which the poet was working. It is for the sake of clarity, and not out of perversity, that I begin my argument at the end of the poem. These lines contain ambiguities of language and reference which have prevented critics, commentators, editors, and translators from finding any satisfactory explanation of the structure, meaning, or relevance of the passage to the rest of the poem. Irving's treatment of this passage illustrates perfectly the state of confusion which even recent scholarship represents. He emends frequently (thirteen times in these seventy-four lines, four times changing the meanings of words) in order to eliminate apparent incongruities, and then restructures the passage by dividing it into segments which he feels must be rearranged. Although he is actually modifying Gollancz's even more elaborate treatment, this part of his edition has not met with much sympathy (see C. L. Wrenn's review[20]). But no one has felt up to the task of arguing the case for the passage's integrity. The commentary which follows should demonstrate that within the context of the traditions of Medieval Scriptural exegesis, the original structure of the passage is perfectly comprehensible and meaningful.

> þanon Israhelum   ece rædas
> on merehwearfe   Moyse sægde,
> heahþungen wer   halige spræce,
> deop ærende.   Dægweorc nemnað,
> swa gyt werðeode   on gewritum findað:

doma gehwilcne   þara þe him drihten bebead
on þam siðfate   soðum wordum.   (516–522)
[Then on the shore of the sea Moses, that man of high virtue, spoke to the
Israelites in holy words, eternal wisdom, a profound message. They call it
the day's work, as still men find it in Scripture: every law which God gave
him on that journey with words of truth.]

The only way we can begin to understand the poet's approach to his sub-
ject is to examine the narrative parts of not only Exodus 13 and 14, as is
the usual method,[21] but also the rest of the exodus story, contained
mostly in Exodus, Numbers, and Deuteronomy. What this approach
amounts to is an amplification of the suggestion first made by Cosijn[22]
(and discussed briefly by Blackburn, Gollancz, Irving, and Krapp[23])
concerning the role of Deuteronomy in the poem. Although the "dæg-
word" emendation which has inspired most of this discussion seems to
me unacceptable, the commentary on that crux has been useful. Irving's
theory is that the lines quoted above constitute a "momentary glance for-
ward" to Deuteronomy. But it might be more fruitful and accurate to say
that throughout the ending of the poem, the poet has systematically dis-
torted the chronology of his Scriptural source, in accordance with cer-
tain exegetical traditions, and has incorporated great amounts of material
from other books of the Bible, in a more meaningful (though for the
modern reader a somewhat uneasy) rendering of the scene at the shore of
the Red Sea. This interpretation will become more clear as we proceed.

   This general approach to the poem's conclusion is made necessary
by such lines as those quoted above, for it is painfully obvious that the
Law (if we can thus interpret "ece rædas" and "doma gehwilcne") was
not spoken by Moses "on merehwearfe," as the Israelites emerged from
the Red Sea. There have been two lines of criticism which try to explain
this problem. The one reads "ece rædas," "deop ærende," and "doma
gehwilcne" as references to the speech of Moses in lines 554–64, and
debate has raged as to whether these references are to the Decalogue or
to the *Canticum Moysis* of Exodus 15. Moore summarizes the arguments
for both interpretations and opts for the *Canticum*, arguing convincingly
that the speech in no way resembles the Decalogue.[24] (He fails to note,
however, that it also bears little resemblance to the *Canticum*.) The other
explanation is that referred to above, which reads the above lines as a
reference to Deuteronomy. By understanding "þanon" as "at a later

time," it would be possible to eliminate the confusion of thinking that the deuteronomic speech was made on the shore of the Red Sea. But such a sudden and brief shift in the poem's time sequence is certainly awkward. It has been pointed out before that this misconception which introduces the deuteronomic speech at the Red Sea may have been inspired by the wording of the Vulgate itself: "Haec sunt verba, quae locutus est Moyses ad omnem Israel, trans Jordanum, in solitudine campestri, contra mare Rubrum" (Deut. 1:1). [These are the words which Moses spoke to all Israel, across the Jordan, in the plain of the wilderness, over against the Red Sea.] The peculiar phrase "contra mare Rubrum" receives much exegesis in the Middle Ages, and it might even be said that the Church Fathers give some support to the idea that "haec verba" were spoken by the Red Sea. St. Jerome interprets this particular passage in a short piece called *Decem tentationes populi in deserto*:

> Haec sunt verba, quibus corripuit Moyses filios pro decem tentationibus, quibus Domini tentaverunt. Unde Dominus in libro Numerorum dicit: At omnes homines qui viderunt majestatem meam, et signa quae feci in Aegypto et in solitudine, et tentaverunt me jam per decem vices, nec obedierunt voci meae, non videbunt terram pro qua juravi patribus eorum (Num. 14:22).[25]
>
> [These are the words by which Moses reproached his children for ten temptations, by which they tempted the Lord. From whence the Lord says in the book of Numbers: but all the men who have seen my majesty, and the signs which I worked in Egypt and in the desert, and have tempted me now ten times, and have not heard my voice, shall not see the land for which I swore an oath to their fathers.]

Among these *tentationibus* is the event which accounts for the reference to the Red Sea:

> Tertia tentatio continetur in eo quod ait: "In campestri contra mare rubrum." In quo loco murmurasse dicuntur contra Dominum, quia peremptos Aegyptios fuisse, Moysi non crediderunt sibi de verbo Domini dicenti, sed potius eos se subsequi timuerunt.[26]
>
> [The third temptation is contained the passage in which it is said: "In the plain over against the Red Sea." In which place they are said to have grumbled against the Lord, asking why they had not been slain in Egypt, they would not believe that Moses himself was speaking the word of the Lord, but rather feared to follow him.]

That is, "haec verba" (Deuteronomy) were understood in part as a response to the behavior of the Israelites at the Red Sea crossing. Not only is Deuteronomy related to the Red Sea episode in this way, but "contra mare Rubrum" is also understood spiritually, and the chronology of the whole exodus narrative is collapsed in the allegory which results.

> Solitudo vero Ecelesiam significat, spiritualiterque ab omnibus intus soli-
> tudo est contra Rubrum mare. In hoc significatur, quod hi quibus haec
> verba historialiter dicuntur, fuissent contrarii baptismo, sive veritatis
> legis, quae illis data est.[27]
> [The desert signifies the Church, and spiritually the desert interior to all is
> across the Red Sea. In this is signified that those to whom these words
> were said historically were opposed to baptism, or the truth of the law
> which was given to them.]
> Contra videlicet mare Rubrum, quia dura mens reproborum ablutionem
> peccatorum in sanguine Christe fieri nullo modo credidit.[28]
> [Against the Red Sea, because the hard mind by no means believed in the
> cleansing of false sinners in the blood of Christ.]

Whether or not the poet was aware of the traditions which associate Deuteronomy with the Red Sea, the appropriateness of Deuteronomy to the lines in question is clear. That book consists of the farewell speeches of Moses to Israel before the entrance into the Promised Land. The situation of the speeches, which summarize the exodus from beginning to end and the laws which God gave to Moses ("doma gehwilcne þara þe him drihten bebead"), parallels the situation of our poem, especially in the context of that tradition which understood the crossing of the Red Sea as a crossing into the Promised Land Itself.

The mysterious "dægweorc" of line 519 would seem to refer to the actual "day's work," the march through the sea (the word is used this way elsewhere in the poem, ll. 151, 315, 507). But, as has been noted before, there is a possible source for this word in the opening of Deuteronomy. The speeches of Moses might themselves be considered the "day's work," as the Vulgate perhaps suggests: "Quadragesimo anno, undecimo mense, prima die mensis, locutus est Moyses ad filios Israel omnia, quae praeceperat illi Dominus" (Deut. 1:3). [In the fortieth year, the eleventh month, the first day of the month, Moses spoke to the children of Israel all that the Lord had commanded him.] So the deutero-nomic speeches are a "day's work" in a sense. And the possible relationship of the "prima die mensis" and the "dægweorc" is strengthened by the fact that line 521b is a perfectly natural translation of the last phrase of the Vulgate verse. In fact, Ælfric translates "quae praeceperat illi Dominus" as "þe drihten him bebead."[29]

If we have only been tempted to read lines 1–7 and 516–522 in the light of such exegetical traditions as I have suggested, then the lines which follow practically instruct us to do so.

> Gif onlucan wile   lifes wealhstod
> (beorht in breostum   banhuses weard)
> ginfæsten god   gastas cægon,
> run bið gerecenod,   ræd forð gæð.   (523–526)
> [If life's interpreter, the body's guardian radiant within the breast, will
> unlock with the keys of the spirit this lasting good, then the mystery will
> be explained and counsel shall go forth.]

Even Irving concedes, with Moore, that this is "clearly a reference to the universal medieval distinction between the letter and the spirit. The learned Christian is able to interpret any part of scripture in order to bring to light the spirit, the allegorical or symbolical meaning."[30] But Irving does not attempt to explain why the poet would have included this passage in a poem which is supposedly a "radical departure" from the allegorical tradition.

The internal logic of the poem suggests that the "scripture" which the poet had in mind (and its interpretation) is that which is paraphrased for us in the lines which follow immediately:

> Hafað wislicu   word on fæðme,
> wile meagollice   modum tæcan
> þæt we gesne ne syn   godes þeodscipes,
> metodes miltsa.   He us ma onlyhð,
> nu us boceras   beteran secgað
> lengran lyftwynna.   þis is læne dream . . .   (527–532)
> [It has words of wisdom in its keeping; it earnestly desires to teach the
> heart, that we may not lack the law of God or the mercy of the Maker. He
> enlightens us further, now that writers tell us of a better place, the more
> lasting joys of heaven. This is a fleeting joy . . .]

Now if the possible references of this passage are (1) the *Canticum Moysis* of Exodus 15, (2) the Decalogue, or (3) Moses's deuteronomic speech, we have reached an impasse, for none of these possibilities is very clearly related to the theme stated here. Many critics have found these lines, and the "sermon" which follows, inappropriate to the poem's narrative. Craigie says of the whole passage, lines 523–548, "We have here a concluding portion of a moralizing poem which has no connection with the theme of *Exodus*."[31] Irving is not so violent, but concludes that the passage "seems to have no direct connection with Exodus . . . it is the kind of general statement which could be attached to almost any Christian poem."[32]

But we must turn once more to the exegesis upon the exodus story as a whole as it is developed in commentary and sermon. The most commonplace interpretation of the story constitutes a great popular tradition and a natural source for the theme expressed here. The interpretation of the exodus as a type for the Christian life stresses heavily the "læne dream" theme. Between the baptism of the Red Sea and the crossing of the Jordan into the Promised Land, the wanderings of the Israelites in the wilderness, their sins, and the *tentationes* referred to earlier constitute a type for the transitory life which must be led in the meantime. Augustine summarizes this allegory in his *Enarrationes in Psalmos*:

Et attendite jam breviter ipsam figuram nostram. Populus Israel sub Pharaonis et Aegyptiorum dominatione (Ex. 1:10); populus Christianus ante fidem praedestinatus jam Deo, et adhuc serviens daemonibus et diabolo principi eorum: ecce populus subjugatus Aegyptiis, serviens peccatis suis; non enim nisi per peccata nostra potest diabolus dominari. Liberatur populus ab Aegyptiis per Moysen; liberatur populus a praeterita vita peccatorum per Dominum nostrum Jesum Christum. Transit populus ille per mare Rubrum; iste per Baptismum. Moriuntur in mari Rubro omnes inimici populi illius (Ex. 14:22, 23); moriuntur in Baptismo omnia peccata nostra. Intendite, fratres. Post mare illud Rubrum non continuo patria datur, nec tanquam jam hostes desint, secure triumphatur; sed restat eremi solitudo, restant hostes insidiantes in via: sic et post Baptismum restat vita Christiana in tentationibus. In illa eremo suspirabatur patriae promissae; quid aliud Christiani suspirant abluti Baptismo? Num quid jam regnant cum Christo? Nondum ventum est ad terram promissionis nostram . . . Omnes fideles sciant ubi sint: in eremo sunt; patria suspirant.[33]

[Now listen briefly to this figure of ours. The people of Israel under the domination of Pharaoh and the Egyptians; the Christian people before faith soon predestined for God, and until now serving demons and the Devil their prince: behold this people subjugated to the Egyptians, serving their sins; for only through our sins is the Devil able to dominate. The people were freed from Egypt by Moses; people are freed from their former life of sin through our Lord Jesus Christ. That people crossed through the Red Sea; this one through baptism. All the enemies of that people were slain in the Red Sea; all our sins are slain in baptism. Listen, brothers. After the Red Sea a homeland was not given to that people immediately, nor did enemies cease, safely triumphant; but the desert wasteland remains, and enemies still lie in wait for them along the way: likewise after baptism the Christian life remains among temptations. In that desert they longed for the promised land; what else do Christians washed in baptism long for? Do they now reign with Christ? We have not yet come to our promised land . . . Let all faithful know where they are—they are in the desert; they long for their homeland.]

The theme of the transitory nature of life which is superseded by the eternal bliss of heaven is hardly an inappropriate reflection at that point in the poem when the Israelites have just crossed through the sea. And the traditional diction of OE moralizing upon this popular theme is in beautiful harmony with the exegetical tradition being expressed.

> þis is læne dream,
> wommum awyrged, wreccum alyfed,
> earmra anbid. Eðellease
> þysne gystsele gihðum healdað,
> murnað on mode, manhus witon
> fæst under foldan, þær bið fyr and wyrm,
> open ece scræf yfela gehwycles.
> Swa nu regnþeofas rice dælað,
> yldo oððe aerdeað. (532–554)

[This joy is fleeting, cursed with sin, granted to exiles, a time of waiting for wretched ones. Homeless we hold this guest-hall with sorrow, mourning in spirit, mindful of the dungeon fast under the earth wherein are fire and the worm, the open eternal pit of every evil. So now those archthieves, old age and early death, divide up their dominion.]

Almost invariably, the commentaries on Exodus express a similar idea after the Red Sea episode; Isidore, Bede, and lesser figures all follow Augustine in interpreting the events identically.

Jam dehinc ducitur post maris transitum populus per desertum. Baptizati scilicet omnes per mundum, non perfruentes promissa patria; sed quod

non vident, sperando, et per patientem expectando, tanquam in deserto
sunt, et illi laboriosae et periculosae tentationes . . . [34]
[Soon after the crossing of the sea that people is led into the desert, that is
to say all baptized into the world, not fully enjoying their promised home-
land; but hoping for what they do not see, and awaiting in patience, while
they are in the desert, and with great labors and dangers of temptation . . .]

Life is for the Israelites "wommun awyrged" (cursed with sins), because
it was for their sins that they were required to wander in the wilderness
forty years, until the generation perished. In the case of Israel, life is
"wreccum alyfed" (granted to exiles) in a very real sense, as well as in
the metaphorical sense so common to OE poetry. Life is "earmra anbid"
(a wretched waiting alone) before being allowed to enter into the Land
of Promise. In line 534, man (allegorically Israel) is called "eðellease,"
an extraordinarily fresh use of a common OE poetic theme, used in both
its literal and allegorical senses.

Of course, in our analysis we have already made use of two distinct,
and to some degree contradictory, exegetical traditions concerning the
Red Sea. I have argued that the poem's emphasis on heavenly salvation
is appropriate to its subject, because the crossing of the sea is itself often
interpreted anagogically (p. 169, n. 12–14). Yet the "læne dream" pas-
sage is appropriate, I have said, in the context of the interpretation which
sees the Red Sea as only the beginning of that journey toward salvation.
It is the confusion of these two traditions which accounts for the appar-
ent confusion in the poem's narrative. Both traditions involve the same
themes and the same general meaning, but in the one case they are
applied to the whole exodus story, and in the other to the story of the Red
Sea alone. We must simply keep in mind when reading the poem that the
crossing of the sea is a miniature version of the whole exodus. Thus the
appearance of Deuteronomy at the Red Sea is understandable and the
many details of the poem which seem to refer far beyond the Red Sea
crossing can be explained.

As for the "læne dream" theme, it fits comfortably into its place in
the poem, whether we understand it as relating to the wanderings which
end at the Jordan or the Egyptian exile which ends at the Red Sea, or
both. But the homiletic passage does not end at line 540, of course. The
allegory (or more correctly, the typology) of the poem would be incom-
plete if it ended on such a negative note. Any exegetical treatment of the

exodus, especially as it was introduced in lines 1–7, must finally dwell upon the theme of salvation, the entrance into the Promised Land. Lines 540–548 accomplish this necessary conclusion to the "moralizing" passage. Maintaining the allegorical viewpoint, and making no explicit reference to the exodus itself, the poet describes the Day of Judgment, and pictures God himself leading the souls of the blessed into Heaven. Certainly the image of God leading a journey to the other world is a carefully drawn parallel to the exodus.

> Eftwyrd cymð,
> mægenþrymma mæst   ofer middangeard,
> dæg dædum fah.   Drihten sylfa
> on þam meðelstede   manegum demeð,
> þonne he soðfæstra   sawla lædeð,
> eadige gastas,   on uprodor,
> þær [is] leoht and lif,   eac þon lissa blæd;
> duguð on dream   drihten herigað,
> weroda wuldorcyning   to widan feore.   (540–548)
> [The requital is coming, the greatest of all glories in the world, a day marked by deeds. The Lord Himself will judge the multitude in the assembly, when He will lead the souls of the righteous, blessed spirits, to heaven above, where there is light and life and joy of bliss; in joy that host shall praise the Lord, Glory-king of hosts, for ever and ever.]

It should be pointed out that the *Canticum* of Exodus 15 does contain lines which might justify such an anagogical idea. Moses looks forward to the completion of the exodus in words which Medieval commentators expectably interpret as a reference to the soul's salvation.

> Introduces eos, et plantabis in monte hereditatis tuae, firmissimo habitaculo tuo quod operatus es, Domine, sanctuarium tuum, Domine, quod firmaverunt manus tuae. Dominus regnabit in aeternum et ultra. (Exodus 15:17–18)[35]
> [You will bring them in, and plant them on the mountain of your inheritance, in the most firm habitation which you have made, o Lord, your sanctuary, Lord, which your hands have established. The Lord shall reign forever and ever.]

The basic structure of this section of the poem should now be clear. A speech by Moses has been introduced, which would seem to refer to the

Deuteronomic speech, i.e., a speech of summary and conclusion rather than the more topical *Canticum Domino* or the Decalogue. Then a short passage follows, concerning the importance of Scriptural interpretation; then we are given an interpretation of the whole exodus narrative according to its most common exegetical traditions. There has been, in this part of the poem, a sudden tendency toward generalization, accompanied by a collapse, or telescoping, of the Biblical chronology. We are being presented an overview of the significance of the whole exodus, in the dual themes of judgment and salvation. The scene of the poem remains fixed at the shore of the Red Sea, but the poet feels free to expand his scope to include developments and significances still far removed from that scene.

This ambiguity, which in effect conflates the remainder of the exodus story into the episode described in the poem, is systematically developed in the lines which follow. Lines 549–553 reintroduce Moses' speech—a speech of eleven lines in which the poet's method, as we are beginning to understand it, is made most clear and meaningful.

> Swa reorode,   ræda gemyndig,
> manna mildost,   mihtum swiðed,
> hludan stefne;   here stille bad
> witodes willan;   wundor ongeton,
> modiges muðhæl;   he to mænegum spræc:
> "Micel is þeos menigeo   mægenwisa trum,
> fullesta mæst,   se ðas fare lædeð;
> hafað ufon Cananea   cyn gelyfed,
> burh and beagas,   brade rice.
> Wile nu gelæstan   þæt he lange gehet
> mid aðsware,   engla drihten,
> in fyrndagum   fæderyncynne,
> gif ge gehealdað   halige lare,
> þæt ge feonda gehwone   forð ofergangað.
> Gesittað sigerice   be sæm tweonum,
> beorselas beorna.   Bið eower blæd micel!"   (549–564)

[Thus he spoke, mindful of counsel, the mildest of men, made mighty in power, in a loud voice; the army awaited silently the leader's will; they perceived the wonder, the brave one's words of salvation; he spoke to the multitude: "Mighty is this multitude and great our Leader, strongest support, who leads our journey; He hath given to us the tribes of Canaan, their cities and treasure, their broad kingdom. He will now fulfill what He long ago promised with oaths, Lord of angels, in ancient days to our ancestors, if you will hold His holy teaching, so that we can overcome all of our enemies, occupy in triumph the beer-halls of men between the two seas. Great shall be your glory!"]

The debate over whether this passage resembles more the Decalogue or the *Canticum* is misguided: There is not a distant echo of either. But to even the casual reader of Deuteronomy, the speech must bring to mind numerous passages from that book which closely parallel these lines. For example, in Deut. 1:8 the Lord speaks to Moses concerning the land of Canaan: "En, inquit, tradidi vobis; ingredimini et possidete eam, super qua juravit Dominus patribus vestris, Abraham et Isaac et Jacob, ut daret illam eis, et semini eorum post eos" [Behold, he said, I have given it to you; enter and possess it, about which the Lord swore to your fathers, Abraham and Isaac and Jacob, that He would give it to them and to their seed after them]. Note also Deut. 6:17-19:

Custodi praecepta Domini Dei tui ac Testamonia et ceremonias, quas praecipit tibi, et fac quot placitum est et bonum in conspectu Domini, ut bene sit tibi et ingressus possideas terram optimam, de qua juravit Dominus patribus tuis, ut deleret omnes inimicos coram te, sicut locutus est.
[Keep the precepts of the Lord your God and the testimonies and ceremonies which He has commanded you, and do what is pleasing and good in the sight of the Lord, that it may be well with you, and going in you may possess the best land, about which the Lord swore to your fathers, that He would destroy all your enemies before you, as he has spoken.]

Many passages in Deuteronomy which repeat this "aðswaru fæderyn-cyn" theme have an even more direct bearing upon our poem. For the mention of the covenant made to Abraham (which was introduced into *Exodus* in ll. 432–446) is very often made in connection with the wonder worked by God at the Red Sea ("wundor ongeton"); and often these passages also stress the day of the crossing of the sea or the day of Moses's speech—an emphasis which might help explain the use of "dægweorc" earlier. For example:

Cognoscite hodie . . . signa et opera, quae fecit in medio Aegypti, Pharaonis regi et universae terrae eius; omnique exercitui Aegyptiorum, et equis ac curribus; quomodo operuerint eos aquae maris rubri, cum vos persequerentur, et deleverit eos Dominus usque in praesentem diem . . . Oculi

vestri viderunt omnia opera Domini magna, quac fecit, ut custodiatis uni-
versa mandata illius, quae ego hodie praecipio vobis, et possitis introire et
possidere terram, ad quam ingredimini, multoque in ea vivatis tempore,
quam sub juramento pollicitus est Dominus patribus vestris. (Deut.
11:2–4, 7–9)[36]
[Know today . . . the signs and works which He did in the midst of Egypt
to Pharaoh the king and all his land, and all the host of the Egyptians, and
their horses and chariots; how the waters of the Red Sea covered them
when they pursued you, and the Lord destroyed them unto the present
day . . . Your eyes have seen all the great works which the Lord has done,
that you may keep all the commandments which I command you today,
and you may go in and possess this land you are entering, and may live in
it a long time, which the Lord promised your fathers under oath.]

The diction and tone of Moses' speech in lines 554–564 support the
impression that it is deuteronomic. The implication of accomplishment
in lines 556–557 would lead us to think that the covenant has been ful-
filled. But of course the conquest of the "burh and beagas, brade rice" is
very distantly removed from the action of the poem. In the Biblical nar-
rative, it is not until Numbers 12 that the Israelites get their first glimpse
of the Promised Land, and it is not until forty years later (on the day of
Deuteronomy) that a reference to such a conquest is plausible. Also, the
use of the perfect form of the verb in line 556, "hafað gelyfed," adds to
the feeling that the speech is not the *Canticum*, but is made much later
than the Red Sea setting would imply. Another detail which would seem
to support this view is a possible Biblical source for line 563. Although
the phrase "be sæm tweonum" occurs elsewhere (four times in *Beowulf*,
for example), its use here gains meaning from a parallel idea in Exodus
23:31:

Ponam autem terminos tuos a mari Rubro usque ad mari Palestineorum, et
a deserto usque ad fluvium; tradam in manibus vestris habitatores terrae,
et ejiciam eos de conspecto vestro.
[I will set your bounds from the Red Sea to the sea of the Palestinians, and
from the desert to the river; I will deliver the inhabitants of the land into
your hands, and drive them out before you.]

I am not suggesting that what we have here is a momentary, or even
extended, "glance forward." Rather, the poet has simply compressed the
events of the entire exodus into the episode of the crossing of the sea. In

a sense, the covenant has been fulfilled. When the poet says in line 567 that "folc wæs on lande," the implication is not just that the Israelites have finally reached dry ground, but that they have reached the Promised Land at the same time.

> Æfter þam wordum   werod wæs on salum,
> sungon sigebyman,   segnas stodon
> on fægerne sweg;   folc was on lande:
> hæfde wuldres beam   werod gelæded,
> halige heapas,   on hild godes.   (565–569)
> [After these words the host was glad; the trumpets sang a song of triumph, and banners rose to strains of joyful music; the folk was in the land. The beam of glory had led the host, the holy troop, in God's battle.]

That the "beam of glory" had led the "holy troop in God's battle" is more reminiscent of the series of holy wars conducted later in the exodus than the crossing of the sea. The same is true of the martial imagery throughout the poem, including the division of spoils in the concluding lines. It should be remembered that the Israelites were not formed into an army until the book of Numbers. While it has been noticed that the details of the size and structure of the army as it is described in the poem are taken from Numbers,[37] it should be further noted that the concept of God's army at the Red Sea is itself anachronistic.

Earlier, the poet manipulated the themes of judgment and salvation, in lines 540–548, to refer triply to the entrance of the Christian soul into Heaven, to the crossing into the land of Canaan, and also to the salvation of the Israelites from the Egyptians as expressed in the song of Exodus 15. Here, by placing the deuteronomic speech at the scene of the Red Sea, the poet has composed the speech in such a way that the crossing of the Red Sea is identified with the eventual crossing of the Jordan. This identification is hardly surprising since both events are important types for baptism.

The baptismal traditions which interpret the Red Sea and the Jordan help clarify the fact that the *Exodus* poet, in conflating the exodus as he does, is working within a well-developed tradition. (An examination of these traditions will, incidentally, also help to clarify further the "dæg-weorc" crux.) I have already noted passages from Zeno, Cassiodorus, and Augustine, as well as the Bible itself, which point to the close relationship between baptism and salvation, the entrance into the desert and the entrance into the Promised Land and Paradise. These typological traditions are associated, as Bright first pointed out, with Holy Saturday and the Easter vigil, when new members were grafted onto the body of Christ by baptism. St. Augustine, in his homily *De exodo, in vigilia Paschae*, stresses the historical–typological significance of the day on which the homily was to be delivered. He opens:

> Hodie populus Israel et vere homo videns Deum (hoc quippe interpretatur Israel) egredi iubetur ex Aegypto. Hodie agnus Dei, qui tollit peccata mundi, pro omnium salute iugulatur. Hodie sanguine illius postes domorum, id est, frons nostra depingitur. Hodie occiduntur Aegyptii, et de servitute Pharaonis Dei populus liberatur. Hodie percutimur primitiva Aegyptiorum, et Israelitarum non solum liberi sed etiam inrationabilia iumenta servantur.[38]
>
> [Today the people of Israel and the true man seeing God (for this is what Israel means) are called out of Egypt. Today the Lamb of God, who takes away the sins of the world, is slaughtered for the health of all. Today the blood of that Lamb is painted on the house posts, that is, on our foreheads. Today the Egyptians are slain, and the people of God freed from slavery to Pharaoh. Today the firstborn of the Egyptians are struck down, and not only the Israelites but even their dumb beasts are delivered to freedom.]

Here the Paschal lamb is identified with Christ the sacrificed *Agnus Dei*—and thus the emphasis on liberation and salvation long before the Red Sea, not to mention the conquest. Typology knows no chronology outside that of the liturgy. And the liturgy draws together all of the themes and events we have been examining, and makes them into one "day's work." This way of organizing events and their significances within the structure of the liturgical calendar provides us with a new understanding of the exodus, as it is explained, for example, in Ælfric's famous sermon *In die sancto Paschae*:

> On þissum dæge ferde Godes folc fram Egipta lande ofer þa rædan sæ, fram þeowte to þam behatenan earde.
>
> Ure Drihten ferde eac on þisne timan, swa swa se Godspellere Iohanes cwæþ, fram þissum middanearde to his heofonlican fæder. We sceolon fylian urum hæfde, and faran fram deofle to Criste, fram þissere unstaþþigan worulde, to his staþelfæstan rice . . . fram unþeawum to godum þeowum, gif wc willað, after ðisum lænan life, faran to þam ecan.[39]
>
> [On this day the people of God traveled from the land of Egypt over the

Red Sea, from slavery to the promised land. Our Lord traveled also at this
time, as the evangelist John says, from this world to his heavenly Father.
We should follow our leader, and journey from the devil to Christ, from
this unstable world to his stable realm . . . from misdeeds to good deeds, if
we are willing, after this fleeting life, to travel to the eternal one.]

The whole complex of ideas in this passage is clearly related to our
poem. Israel is seen to cross through the Red Sea directly into the "beha-
tenan earde" in one day; this exodus is seen as a type for Christ's victo-
rious resurrection, and for the promise held out to each Christian that
after this "lænan life" there is an eternal heavenly kingdom which
awaits. Here, the homiletic themes of line 527–548—the transitory
nature of this life, the eternal joy of heaven, and the journey from one to
the other—are linked to the poem's narrative by the exegetical signifi-
cance of the Red Sea crossing. Ælfric even uses the image of God lead-
ing the spiritual exodus to Heaven. Ælfric and the *Exodus* poet have
tapped the same exegetical and liturgical traditions in their respective
sermonizings.

The last twenty lines of the poem do not present so many problems,
because they refer less to events which occur later in the exodus. The
scene is consistent, and the action consists of the singing (at last) of the
Canticum Domino, and the spoiling of the dead Egyptians. The identifi-
cation of the "hildespelle" of line 574 and the "fyrdleoð" of line 578
with the *Canticum* has been made convincingly by Robinson in his note
on the "Afrisc meowle" crux of line 580.[40] The parallel between lines
574–579 and the song of Moses is reinforced by the detail that the men
and women sing separately: "weras wuldres sang, wif on oðrum" (l.
577). This peculiar addition to the Biblical narrative is nearly universal
in the exegesis upon Exodus 15. For example, Isidore says:

Choros idem Moyses post transita Rubri maris primus instituit, et
utrumque sexum, distinctis classibus, se ac sorore praesente, canere
Domino in choris carmen triumphale perdocuit.[41]
[After the Red Sea was crossed Moses first instituted that same chorus,
and with each sex in a separate group before him or his sister, taught them
how to sing a song of triumph to the Lord in chorus]

Irving cites Philo Judaeus for the same detail.[42] That this tradition
appears as a line in *Exodus* is strong evidence that the *Exodus* poet was

well aware of the details of the exegesis upon his subject. Robinson's article amply demonstrates the poet's debt to exegetical traditions in these last lines of the poem. I would add another detail in this same vein. I would suggest that line 581 could be read "on geofones staðe golde geweorðod," with the second half of the line modifying the first. This reading is based upon the possibility that this line could represent another use of Deut. 1:3, quoted earlier: "in solitudine campestri contra mare rubrum . . . ubi auri est plurimum."

It would certainly be foolish to suggest that the *Exodus* poet has used as sources the many passages I have cited. Nor would it be correct to suggest that he has intended to echo consciously this passage, or refer to that one, or cleverly reconstruct meanings by tampering with or com-bining ideas from patristic exegesis. But the Scripture which I have cited here, from Exodus, Numbers, and Deuteronomy, is either central to the exodus story, or consists of often-repeated motifs which could not fail to impress themselves upon the memory of a careful reader of the Bible. And those exegetical ideas which influence the poem are large and wide-spread enough to be considered commonplace to a learned Medieval writer.

This examination of the concluding passage of the poem is only a beginning in understanding the difficulties which *Exodus* presents. But the ideas which inform the structure and imagery of these lines are the controlling ideas of the poem—the concepts of judgment and salvation as they are expressed in the traditions surrounding the Old Testament types for baptism. Irving's classic statement that "no sane reader would be likely to call *Exodus* a poem about baptism"[43] is certainly undebat-able on a certain literal level, but it should be pointed out that no less sane a person than Augustine (among innumerable others) thought that the story of the Red Sea is about baptism. Any Medieval treatment of the story is then in a sense about baptism, because baptism was recognized as the historical–typological significance of the event, and the traditions concerning this interpretation provide structural and thematic unity to our poem. I will examine three of the perennial cruces of the poem from this point of view—the strange image of the Israelites as sailors and their journey as a sea voyage, which is used many times in the poem; the depiction of the entrance into the sea as a battle, though none takes place; and the Noah and Abraham digression.

The nautical imagery which is used so frequently and casually throughout the poem to describe the Israelites and the exodus (viz. ll. 80–85, 105–106, 133, 179, 223, 331–333, 479) can be understood easily in relation to the themes of the poem as we have found them expressed in the lines we have examined. The wilderness, which has been interpreted thus far as both Paradise (on the anagogical level) and the transitory life (on the tropological level), is commonly allegorized by the Fathers as a type of the Church.[44] This interpretation is in perfect accord with the others for obvious reasons, and its fits neatly into the baptismal traditions we have seen, since baptism marks the entrance into Christian life, and into the Church, and has its own anagogical aspect as well. All of these meanings and levels of interpretation overlap and flow together in exegesis, of course. For example, the passage quoted from Zeno, above, included the statement "nos post baptismum ad paradisum pervenimus" (p. 169, n. 12). A later writer attempted to clarify this typology by providing a lengthy etymology of the word "paradisum" and explaining its ambiguity. He concluded: "Paradisum hoc loco non coelum, sed Ecclesiam auctor vocat, quam quidam per baptisma ingredimur"[45] [the author calls this place Paradise, not in heaven but in the Church, into which we enter through baptism]. Cassiodorus makes the same identification (p. 169, n. 13). Daniélou makes it clear that this interpretation can be said to be a commonplace.[46] The people of Israel, then, as the people of God wandering in the wilderness before entering the Promised Land, are a type for the Church in this world.

Now one of the most common symbols for the Church in Medieval exegesis is the ship. That this image is also a commonplace has been pointed out thoroughly enough by R. E. Kaske.[47] The tradition he has examined is that of the Church as a ship, with the cross as its stabilizing mast. But there is another tradition of the ship image which is also pertinent to our poem, and that concerns the other great type for baptism which is included in *Exodus*, the story of Noah. For Noah's ark is universally interpreted as a type for the Church, by means of which the faithful are saved, while those outside perish. The relationship between this idea and the typology of the exodus is obvious. Daniélou has thoroughly examined and documented this tradition in early Christian exegesis, citing Tertullian, Cyprian, Jerome, and many others, as well as liturgical and iconographical evidence.[48] It might incidentally be noted that the Junius MS illustrations include three drawings of the Ark, which is represented as a stone building in the Romanesque style, complete with towers, columns, and portals, supported on a Viking-type wooden ship, with Christ opening and closing the doors.

In the light of these common traditions, the sailing imagery in our poem makes clear sense. The Israelites are sailors on the "mystical ship, the Church,"[49] guided by the "halige seglas, lyftwundor leoht" (ll. 89–90) which is identified in line 96 as "heahþegnunga haliges gastes." Their "sea journey" is all the more mysterious to them, because

> Hæfde witig god
> sunnan siðfæt   segle ofertolden,
> swa þa mæstrapas   men ne cuðon,
> ne ða seglrode   geseon meahton,
> eorðbuende   ealle crafte,
> hu afæstnod wæs   feldhusa mast.   (80–85)
> [Wise God had tented over the course of the sun with a sail, so that men did not know those mast ropes, nor could they, earth dwellers, see by any cunning that sail-yard, how the greatest of tents was fastened.]

This image suggests that the Israelites do not seem to fully understand the nature of their "voyage." Perhaps Israel does not know the rigging or the mast because this journey is, after all, only a type for the journey of the Church in the world; unlike the anti-type, she cannot actually know Christ and the cross. There are many Medieval traditions which describe rather literally the role of the cross in the exodus,[50] but our poem participates in such a tradition only symbolically. The cross is an operative image in the poem, as it is brought to mind in the term "beam," used four times in the poem to describe the pillar of fire and cloud. And certainly the cross is evoked in the phrase "wuldres beam" in line 568—a phrase used unambiguously to describe the cross elsewhere (*Dream of the Rood*, 97; *Elene*, 217).

> Folc was on lande
> hæfde wuldres beam   werud gelæded,
> halige heapas,   on hild godes.   (567–569)

The Israelites as sailors on the ship of the Church led by Christ and the Cross would indeed be a wild interpretation, if it did not fit perfectly into the larger context of the poem's exegetical meanings. The image is perfectly appropriate to the theme of baptism and its Old Testament typology and its liturgical use in the Easter season. Needless to say, the plausibility of this reading is increased by the fact that the story of Noah, from which the ship–Church typology is principally drawn, is conspicuously included in the poem. This interpretation complements Cross and Tucker's examination of the sea voyage as a common image of "man's life as a journey."[51]

There is no doubt that the Noah and Abraham digression is related to the Red Sea narrative by the typology of baptism and the liturgy of Easter and the themes of covenant and salvation, all of which are inextricably interrelated in patristic exegesis. One would wish, of course, that there were a single coherent tradition which would explain clearly the relationship between the Red Sea and the episodes of the digression—a tradition linking Noah, Abraham and Isaac, Moses at the Red Sea, Solomon ("Dauides sunu") and the Temple; but we look in vain for such a tradition that would bear upon our poem and aid our understanding of it. Rather, the traditions involved are many, large, and amorphous.

Many traditions can be isolated which relate the various figures in the poem and the digression, and which thus provide us with simple grounds for associating them with each other. The most obvious of these is the theme of the covenant, for the history of the covenant in the Bible consists of the covenants made with Noah, Abraham, Moses, David, and of course the New Covenant in Christ. This idea is so basic that we must at least agree that the grouping together of these figures is not unexpected or unintelligible at the simplest structural level of understanding. And the fact that the poem deals with the fulfillment of the covenant makes the appearance of these figures at least partially relevant to the narrative, but it hardly justifies the digression satisfactorily.

The covenant tradition inspired another set of traditions, which at first would seem to be a neat source for the digression's structure: that is, the concept of the "world ages."[52] One common way of outlining the six ages which have preceded the one to come is in accordance with the covenant history: The six ages are begun by Adam, Noah, Abraham, Moses, David or the building of the Temple, and Jesus.[53] But this common theory provides us with little more than a proof that the association of these figures it perfectly natural; unfortunately, the idea of the world ages itself does not really clarify the poem's significance.

It is the typology of the digression and its relation to the liturgy which finally justifies the passage. The relation of the exodus to the

Easter celebration has been noted, as has the baptismal significance of the Flood, and the interpretation of the ark as a type for salvation through the Church and the cross. And the relation of the sacrifice of Isaac to the Passion of Christ is so well known that it does not need documentation. It is this concentration on the typology of the Easter celebration and the baptism ceremony which lies behind Bright's argument concerning the Holy Week liturgy and *Exodus*. The story of Abraham and Isaac is not included in the baptismal rite just as an example of the strong faith necessary to Christian life, as Kennedy suggests[54]; the story is there because it prefigures the Easter celebration, which is tied to baptism by the twin doctrines of rebirth and resurrection. Even the brief reference forward to the building of the Temple (lines 389–396), which has no specific baptismal or Paschal meaning, relates to the poem typologically, for in the earliest writers the Temple signifies (on various "levels") the life of the good man, the Church, and the *patria coelestis*.[55] Rupert of Deutz, writing about four centuries later than our poet, makes explicit what is perfectly implicit in these early interpretations of the Temple, when he says: "Baptismus est ostium per quod intratur in templum Dei"[56] [baptism is the gate through which the temple of God is entered]. Here the *templum Dei* signifies both the Ecclesia and the *patria coelestis*, which are inaccessible except through baptism.

It might also be pointed out that Noah, Isaac, Moses, and Solomon are among the most prominent types for Christ in the Old Testament, and the stories included in *Exodus* all speak directly of redemption and salvation. The reference to Solomon may seem far removed from these themes, but Augustine's interpretation of the building of the Temple along these lines became commonplace in later writers:

> Salomon Christi praenuntiat figuram, qui aedificavit domum Domino in coelesti Hierusalem, non de lignis et lapidis, sed de sanctis hominibus.[57]
> [Solomon prefigures Christ, who built the house of the Lord in the heavenly Jerusalem, not of wood and stone but of holy men.]

No matter how elaborate the texture of meanings which relates the digression to the poem's narrative, it must finally be admitted that the digression does seem unprepared for and abrupt. No amount of interpretation will ever explain the suddenness and awkwardness of the transition in lines 361–362, and the unusual placement of the passage within the action of the poem. But our criticism should be qualified by the evidence of a considerable lacuna after line 446, which may have included some clarification of the digression's intent and a transition back to the main narrative.

The third crux I want to examine, the description of a battle at the Red Sea, also involves the traditions of baptism in the early Church. But this problem can be approached from many directions, as was the structure of the poem's conclusion. The description of the Israelites as an army is begun at the very opening of the poem:

> And him hold frea
> gesealde wæpna geweald   wið wraðra gryre,
> ofercom mid þy campe   cneomaga fela,
> feonda folcriht.   (19–22)
> [And the loyal Lord gave them control over their weapons against the terror of hostile ones; they overcame in battle many tribes, the sovereignty of their enemies.]

These lines certainly cannot refer directly to the action of the poem, and all the similar diction and imagery throughout the poem must be understood in some other than a literal fashion. For the Israelites never go into battle, and indeed are described as fearful and woeful as they are pursued:

> Forþon wæs in wicum   wop up ahafen,
> atol æfenleod . . .   (200–201)[58]
> [Therefore in the camps wailing arose, a terrible evening-song . . .]

The seeming inconsistency between the action of the poem and its descriptive imagery comes to a climax as the Israelites march into the divided sea. The long passage (lines 310–346) in which this march is described possesses an extraordinarily incongruous tone for a description of what must be admitted to be a retreat from battle. For example:

> Be þam herewisan   hynðo ne woldon
> be him lifigendrum   lange þolian,
> þonne he to guðe   garwudu rærdon
> ðeode ænigre.   Þracu wæs on ore,
> heard handplega,   hægsteald modige

    wapna wælslihtes,   wigend unforhte,
    bilswaðu blodige,   beadumægnes ræs,
    grimhelma gegrind,   þær Iudas for.   (323–330)

[On account of that leader they would not long endure oppression from any people while he lived, while they raised a spear in battle. The charge was in the front, hard hand-play, young warriors brave in the slaughter of weapons, undaunted fighters, bloody wounds, the rush of battle and the crash of helmets, when Judah advanced.]

It was noted earlier that the image of the Israelites as an army at the Red Sea is itself anachronistic, since such organization does not take place in the Bible until the book of Numbers. The scriptural exodus story does abound in battle scenes, often preceded by descriptions of the formation and movements of the tribes, as in the poem; and the Israelites as a fighting army is certainly an inescapable impression upon reading Numbers and Deuteronomy.[59] These battles, however, occur long after the Red Sea crossing. This whole line of imagery may be seen as another aspect of the conflation of the exodus story into the one episode, according to the exegetical traditions which were examined in our analysis of lines 516–590.

    Cross and Tucker advance a simpler but more esoteric theory regarding this problem, developed out of the same exegetical traditions we have examined. They point to the baptismal traditions associated with the Red Sea, which speak of both the enemies behind (the Egyptians), and those *ante faciem*, the sins and temptations in the wilderness which still face the catechumen after baptism. They conclude, "It is a short step from enemies *a tergo* and *ante faciem* in the allegorical expositions to the unrealistic situation in the Old English *Exodus*."[60] We might recall Augustine's warning in a passage quoted earlier: "Sed restat eremi solitudo, restant hostes insidiantes in via: sic et post baptismum restat vita Christiana in tentationibus."[61] Judah's "heard handplega" may be in reference to these insidious enemies *in via*, although in the Bible and in the allegory they are quite removed from the Red Sea. Their appearance here might also be explained by the typology which makes the compression of Biblical events the basis for the poem's narrative.

    A third approach to this problem is sketched out in Cross and Tucker's article. It concerns the theology of the baptismal rite itself, which is often explained by the Fathers in a more violent imagery than we are likely to associate with the ceremony today. "In the Christian

view the catechumen comes to his baptism as a soldier to the colours—
sacrament has not lost all its military meaning."[62] This idea comple-
ments the exodus tradition outlined above, in which baptism, like the
Red Sea, is the initiation into the struggle of this transitory life. But there
is perhaps a more directly relevant tradition, not mentioned by Cross and
Tucker, which speaks of the struggle at the baptismal font itself.
Daniélou discusses this idea fully and documents it well enough.[63] Bap-
tism is here seen as the struggle between Christ and Satan (or the
Dragon) beneath the waters; predictably, sin and the devil are always
defeated (as God, through Moses's rod, slays the Pharaoh). The central
typological fact here is the prefiguration of the Easter story in the exo-
dus; and Christ's death, the descent into Hell, and the resurrection all
play a necessary part in this theology of baptism. This idea originates in
the Syriac Fathers (Daniélou points out that "for Oriental theology
Christ's descent into Hell is the central fact of redemption"), but passes
into the West very early. For Origen, the "mystery of baptism" is con-
tained in the "three days' journey into the wilderness and the Paschal
triduum of the Lord." The first day is for the Lord's Passion; the second
that of the descent into Hell; the third that of the Resurrection.[64] Thus the
baptismal rite is joined to the traditions of the battle of cosmic forces at
the Harrowing of Hell.

Gregory, in his *Moralia in Job*, goes so far as to associate the cross-
ing through the sea with the descent to the underworld, because Satan
lives in the "depths":

> Quod profundum maris Dominus petiit, cum inferni novissima, electorum
> suorum animas erepturus, intravit. Unde et per prophetam dicitur: *Posuisti
> profundum maris viam, ut transierent liberati* (Is. 51:10) . . . Quod tamen
> profundum viam Dominus posuit, quia illuc veniens, electos suos a claus-
> tris inferni ad coelestia transire concessit.[65]
>
> [Because the Lord sought to rescue the souls of his chosen ones he
> entered into the depth of the sea, being the lowest region of Hell. Whence
> is said by the prophet: You have made the depth of the sea a way for the
> ransomed to pass over . . . But yet the Lord has made a way in the depth,
> by coming thither he allowed his chosen ones to pass from the bonds of
> hell to the heavens.]

The parallel between the crossing of the Red Sea and the Harrowing of
Hell is perfectly clear: Moses leads the Hebrew captives through the sea

to the Promised Land, just as Jesus leads the captives of Hell through "a claustris inferni ad coelestia." And Origen's explication of the *Canticum Domino* makes the descent into Hell the central significance of the deliverance from Egypt. In commenting on Exodus 15:14–15, he says:

> Sed, spiritualiter, invenies quia Philisthiim, id est cadentes populo; et Edom, scilicet terrenus, trepidant: et eorum princeps cursitant et pavent constricti doloribus, cum vident regna sua, quae in inferno sunt, penetrata ab eo qui descendit in inferiora terrae, ut eripuit eos qui possidebantur a morte . . . Veniat ergo super eos timor, et tremor: tremunt et timent daemones crucem Christi, in qua triumphati sunt, et exuti principatus eorum et potestate.[66]
>
> [But spiritually you will find that "the Philistines," that is people who fall; and "Edom," which means earthly, are anxious: and their princes run about and are terrified, gripped by distress, when they see their kingdoms, which are in a lower realm, penetrated by him who descended into the lower parts of the earth, that he might snatch away those who were possessed by death . . . Therefore fear and trembling will fall upon them: the demons tremble at and fear the cross of Christ, in which they have been conquered, and in which their principalities and powers have been stripped.]

This passage was familiar enough to have found its way into the *Glossa Ordinaria* later.

The typology of the Red Sea and the Harrowing of Hell is the most dramatic example of the martial aspect of the baptismal rite. But the relationship of this tradition to the "battle" scene in *Exodus* is perhaps not as direct as the other two suggestions I have outlined: Judah's role in the battle, for example, cannot be clearly defined by this tradition. But this complex of typological relations may incidentally clarify another perennial crux in the poem. The Harrowing of Hell may be the concept underlying these puzzling lines[67]:

> Wæron hleahtorsmiðum   handa belocene,
> alyfed laðsið   leode gretan;
> folc ferende,   feond wæs bereafod,
> hergas on helle;   heofon hider becom,
> druron deofolgyld.   Dæg waes mære
> ofer middangeard   þa se mengeo for.   (43–48)
> [The hands of the laughter-smiths were shackled, a hateful journey

allowed to strike the people; the folk traveled, the enemy was despoiled, their hellish shrines; Heaven came thither, devil-idols toppled. The day when that multitude went forth was famous throughout the world.]

"Heofon þider becom" points directly to our interpretation, and all other details support it. The laughter-smiths are bound and sent packing on some sorrowful journey. This image is generally interpreted as the death (*laðsið*) of the Egyptian firstborn, but that reading is certainly awkward. We have only to compare the description of the Harrowing in the OE *Christ and Satan* to see more clearly the symbolic meaning of the image:

Let þa up faran   ece drihten;
wuldre hæfde   wites clomma
feondum oðfæsted,   and heo furðor sceaf
in þæt neowle genip,   nearwe gebeged.   (441–444)
[Then the eternal lord let them ascend; in glory he had fastened the bonds of punishment on the enemies, and thrust them deeper into that awful darkness, tightly crushed.]

Both the "laðsið" and "belocene" motifs are also in the description of the Harrowing in *Christ II*:

þa he hellwarena   heap forbygde
in cwicsusle,   cyning inne gebond.   (731–732)[68]
[then he humiliated the inhabitants of hell in perpetual torment, bound their king within.]

These details traditionally associated with the *descensus* are derived from the account in the apocryphal *Gospel of Nicodemus* (22:2), in which Christ binds Satan's hands and sends him off to Hades for safe-keeping until the second coming.[69]

The diction throughout the lines from *Exodus* is evocative of the Harrowing, and perhaps even somewhat conventional. Likewise, the hyperbole "ofer middangeard" emphasizes the cosmic aspect of the event. Just as the Cross is to be discovered in our poet's description of the pillar, the Harrowing is subtly evoked in the poem as one of the underlying significances of the flight from Egypt.[70]

The use of Christian traditions such as the ones we have examined here provides us with a necessary key to understand the OE *Exodus*. The strange historiography of the early Church, and its fantastic body of Biblical study, most of which is now long forgotten, are an elaborate frame of reference which must be reckoned with whenever we approach Medieval Christian literature. It is possible to reconstruct the basic historical and religious concepts which must be taken into account before we can confront the details of the text. Once we can define the themes of the poem in terms of covenant and fulfillment, judgment and salvation, baptism and Easter, we can fit the awkward-looking pieces of this ancient puzzle together. But of course, our final judgments should not be counted very final; our conclusions are always qualified by the fact that the poem is incomplete—and may indeed be very incomplete. We have no way of knowing what has been lost after the central digression; and the final line of the poem raises some suspicion. Although p. 171 of the MS (the last page of *Exodus*) contains only thirteen and a half lines of verse, leaving the bottom two-thirds of the page blank, and though the last word in the poem appears itself to be incomplete, and though p. 172 is the only blank page in the MS between poems, and though the poem must be admitted to end abruptly by any standard, it has never been seriously argued that the poem has been left unfinished to an extent which might significantly affect its structure and meaning. Irving's method for handling this problem—by restructuring the poem's conclusion—cannot be defended. We must just live with the fact that any critical comment on the poem's larger structure or intention can only be inconclusive.[71]

NOTES

1. Unless noted otherwise, all references to the poem are to the edition by G. P. Krapp, *The Junius Manuscript*, ASPR 1 (New York, 1931). I have altered punctuation and restored MS readings without note. Line references to other OE poems are to the ASPR texts.
2. E. B. Irving, Jr., *The Old English Exodus*, Yale Studies in English 122 (New Haven, 1953).
3. Francis A. Blackburn, *Exodus and Daniel* (Boston and London, 1907).
4. *MP* 9 (1911), 83–108.
5. *MLN* 27 (1912), 97–103.
6. *Lunds Universitets Årsskrift*, N. F., Avd. I, Bd. 14, Nr. 26 (1918). Cf. also his "Plain Points and Puzzles: 60 Notes on OE Poetry," ibid., Bd. 17, Nr. 7 (1922).
7. Krapp, xxix, 216.

8. Bernard Huppé, *Doctrine and Poetry: Augustine's Influence on OE Poetry* (New York, 1959), 217–223.

9. J. E. Cross and S. I. Tucker, "Allegorical Tradition and the OE *Exodus*," *Neophil.* 44 (1960), 122–127.

10. Within this interpretation Fred Robinson has convincingly defended some MS readings in his discussion of many cruces of the poem, "Notes on the OE *Exodus*," *Anglia* 80 (1962), 363–378. See also his "Significance of Names in OE Literature," *Anglia* 86 (1968), 14–58; his discussion of *Exodus* on pp. 25–29 clarifies a number of cruces with particular reference to patristic onomastics.

11. Cross/Tucker, 123.

12. Zeno, *PL* 11, 519.

13. Cassiodorus, *PL* 70, 1059. Cf. Ambrose, *PL* 16, 421.

14. E.g. Isaiah 51:3:

> Consolabitur ergo Dominus Sion,
> et consolabitur omnes ruinas ejus,
> et ponit desertum ejus quasi delicias,
> et solitudinem ejus quasi hortum Domini.
> Gaudium et laetitia invenietur in ea,
> gratiarum actio et vox laudis.
> [For the Lord will comfort Zion, and comfort all her ruins; and make her deserts like a place of delight, and her wasteland like the garden of the Lord. Joy and gladness shall be found in her, and thanksgiving and the voice of praise.]

Cf. also Is. 43:16–21, 63:11–14, Hos. 2:14ff, Amos 5:25, *et passim*.

15. *Enarratio in Psalmum LXXVII*, *CCSL* 39, 1091.

16. Jean Daniélou, *From Shadows to Reality* (London, 1960), 177–178.

17. *PL* 16, 439.

18. Huppé, 220–222.

19. Irving, 20.

20. C. L. Wrenn, *RES* n.s. 6 (1955), 184–189.

21. E.g. Krapp, xxvii: "The main source of *Exodus* is the second book of the O. T., but of the O. T. narrative, the poem uses only chapters xii and xiv, with some brief allusions to earlier and later events in the life of Moses." Also Charles W. Kennedy, *Early English Christian Poetry* (New York, 1952), 15: "Only a portion of the Biblical Exodus serves as material for the narrative, namely Exodus xii 17–xiv 31 and Exodus xv 1–21."

22. Peter J. Cosijn, "Anglosaxonica II," *Beiträge* 20 (1895), 105.

23. The fullest expression of this line of thought to date is in Irving, 97.

24. Moore, *op. cit.*

25. *PL* 23, 1319.

26. Ibid. Cf. col. 1321: "Prima tentatio in mare Rubro: unde Scriptum est in Psalmo, 'Et irritaverunt ascendentes in mari, mari Rubro.' "

27. Variously ascribed to Bede or Pseudo-Bede, probably the latter. Thus this quote may be later than our poem. *PL* 90, 380.

28. Rhabanus Maurus, *PL* 108, 841.

29. S. J. Crawford, ed., *The OE Version of the Heptateuch*, EETS 160 (London, 1922).

30. Irving, 98.

31. "Interpolations and Omissions in A-S Poetic Texts," *Philologica* 11 (1925), 9.

32. Irving, 12.

33. *Enarratio in Psalmum LXXII*, *CCSL* 39, 989–990.

34. Isidore, *PL* 83, 296. Cf. Bede *PL* 91, 312; 95, 571.

35. Cf. the *Vetus Latina* variant, which seems to have been more familiar in Anglo-Saxon England: "Inducens plantas eos in montem hereditatis tue in preparato habitaculo tuo quod preparasti domine; Sanctimonium tuum domine quod preperaverunt manus tuæ . . ." See *Der Altenglische Regius-Psalter*, ed. Roeder (Halle, 1904), 282; *Eadwine's Canterbury Psalter*, ed. Harsley, EETS 92 (1889), 250; and the same text is found in the Vespasian, Cambridge, and Bosworth Psalters.

36. Cf. Deut. 6:23–24, 8:12, *et passim*.

37. Irving, 17.

38. *PL* 40, 1201.

39. *Anglo-Saxon Homily and Prayers*, ed. E. Thomson, (London, 1875), 53–54.

40. Robinson, "Notes," 373–378.

41. *PL* 83, 741.

42. Irving 96.

43. Ibid., p. 15.

44. Daniélou, 90ff.

45. *PL* 11, 519. Who is responsible for the "annotationibus perpetuis" in this edition is a bit of a mystery. Indeed, who the editor of the *Tractates* is, is unclear from Migne's description. But this footnote is certainly still instructive.

46. Daniélou, 175–201.

47. R. E. Kaske, "A Poem of the Cross in the Exeter Book," *Traditio* 23 (1969), 41–71. The discussion of this image is on pp. 54–55.

48. Daniélou, 20–29, 90–91, 97–102.

49. Ibid., p. 102.
50. The most extraordinary example of the Cross legend is the *History of the Holy Rood-Tree*, ed. A. S. Napier, EETS 103 (London, 1894). Napier's introduction discusses many other versions of the legend, most of which are admittedly later than our poem.
51. Cross/Tucker, no. 12.
52. For a complete discussion of this concept see Roderich Schmidt, "*Aetates Mundi*: die Weltalter als Gliederungsprinzip der Geschichte," *Zeitschrift für Kirchengeschichte* 67 (1955–56), 288–317. See also Morton L. Bloomfield, *Piers Plowman as a Fourteenth-Century Apocalypse* (New Brunswick, 1962), 207 n. 7.
53. Origen, Jerome, and Gregory, among others, share this interpretation. See Schmidt.
54. Kennedy, 15. See also Stanley Greenfield, *A Critical History of OE Literature* (New York, 1965), 157.
55. For the Temple as the *patria coelestis* see Augustine, *PL* 37, 1668; Isidore, *PL* 83, 113; as the Church see Ambrose, *PL* 15, 1585; as the *viri sancti* see Rhabanus Maurus, *PL* 112, 1064.
56. *PL* 167, 1151.
57. *PL* 37, 1668.
58. Cf. Numbers 14:1, "igitur vociferans omnis turba flevit nocte illa . . ."
59. Numbers 21:1–3, 21–25, 31–35; 31; Deut. 2, 3, *et passim*.
60. Cross/Tucker 125.
61. See p. 148-a.
62. Cross/Tucker, 125.
63. Daniélou, 184ff.
64. *Homilies on Exodus* (V, 2), quoted by Daniélou, 186.
65. *Moralia in Job*, *PL* 76, 489.
66. Quoted in *Glossa Ordinaria*, *PL* 113, 230.
67. Cf. Huppé, 222, on these lines. Robinson, "Notes," 361–365, offers another (though less satisfying) exegetical explanation of line 46b.
68. Cf. also *Christ and Satan*, ll. 460–461, and also the description in *Christ II*, ll. 558–570, which has some similarities of diction with *Exodus*, ll. 43–50.
69. W. Schneemelcher ed., *New Testament Apocrypha*, trans. J. B. Higgens *et al.* (Philadelphia, 1963), 474.
70. Another detail of our poem which brings to mind the Harrowing of Hell (though it is apparently not derived from a patristic tradition) is the poet's description of the journey through the Red Sea with the phrase "ofer grenne grund" (l. 312a). Krapp remarks that *grene* is "not an appropriate adjective

here" (after all, in line 284 the *herestræta* is described as *haswe*—gray). But perhaps the phrase should remind us of a similarly curious use of the color in the Harrowing scene in *Christ and Satan*:

> Gemunan symle on mode   meotodes strengðo;
> gearwian us togenes   grene stræte
> up to englum,   þær is almihtiga god.   (285–287)
> [Let us always keep in mind the Creator's strength; let us prepare ourselves for the green street upwards to the angels, where Almighty God is.]

See the note on this line by Merrel Clubb, *Christ and Satan, an OE Poem* (New Haven, 1925), for other similar references. It is possible that this use of the color green gives support to Holthausen's reading of the crux in *Genesis*,

> siððan Adam stop
> on grene græs   gaste geweorðad   (1136–37)
> [after Adam trod the green grass, honored in spirit]

which he interprets "since Adam died" (*Die ältere Genesis*, Heidelberg, 1914, 94). More likely, perhaps, the reference here is to the path of green grass which traditionally leads to and from Paradise, and which, in later Cross legends, Seth is instructed to follow to Eden before Adam's death. See references in Robinson's "The OE Genesis, ll. 1136–1137," *Archiv* 204 (1967), 267–268. In any case, if the road to Heaven/Paradise is a green road, then the *grenne grund* across the Red Sea is perfectly appropriate in the context of the poem's typology as I have outlined it.

71. I am indebted to professors R. E. Kaske and T. D. Hill of Cornell University for their many helpful suggestions and criticism.

The Patriarchal Digression in the Old English *Exodus*, Lines 362–446

STANLEY R. HAUER

This essay first appeared in Studies in Philology 78 (1981), 77–90.

The Old English *Exodus* relates the well-known story of the Israelites' delivery from bondage, their miraculous dry-land crossing of the Red Sea, and the destruction by water of their Egyptian pursuers.[1] The poem is laden with difficulties, syntactic, lexical, and interpretive, but perhaps no problem in reading the poem is more acute than that shrouding the interpretation of the eighty-five-line passage called here the patriarchal digression. At line 361, as the Israelites are crossing the dry bed of the Red Sea, the narrative breaks off rather suddenly into a digressive section relating the stories of Noah and the Flood[2] and of Abraham and Isaac;[3] interpolated within the latter story is yet a third episode on the building of the temple of Solomon in Jerusalem.[4] The conclusion to the digression is missing because of a lacuna in the manuscript,[5] and the text resumes abruptly with the attempted flight and slaughter of the Egyptians (based on Exodus 14:25), already well in progress. This patriarchal digression has long been the object of critical controversy.

Earlier scholars almost unanimously rejected the passage as incongruous and unrelated to the main body of *Exodus*. Terming the lines a "störende Interpolation," Balg suggested retitling the digression separately as *Exodus B*, recalling the analogous bifurcation of *Genesis A* and *B*.[6] Similarly, Alois Brandl proposed the independent title "Noah und andere Patriarchen."[7] Sedgefield omitted the passage entirely from his edition[8] and in a review criticized Krapp sharply for including it in the

ASPR text of *Exodus*.[9] W. P. Ker called the digression "intolerable," stating that "no reader will hesitate to cut this out as an interpolated passage."[10] And Charles Kennedy has written, "It can hardly be denied that these lines constitute a definite interruption of sequence and deal with material whose relation to the narrative seems extremely remote."[11] Mürkens, who found the digression "durchaus störig und fremdartig," so that it "kann unmoglich zum Exoduslied gehort haben," believed that the lines are a self-contained independent poem interpolated either by mistake or through a gross lapse in taste by a later compiler.[12] Craigie, however, suggested the more elaborate theory that the lines (originally part of another, longer poem—perhaps indeed a part of *Genesis* itself) were inserted by a befuddled scribe who had confused the pages of his exemplar and copied the passage "without noticing its irrelevance." When he did observe his mistake, he simply stopped at the bottom of the manuscript page and continued afresh with the true *Exodus* material; thus, reasons Craigie, the abrupt halt to the passage in line 446 does not at all indicate the presence of a lacuna, but merely the scribe's realization of his error and his return to the major work at hand.[13]

Certainly there are marked differences between the patriarchal digression and the main section of the poem which make its rejection by these early scholars comprehensible. Perhaps the most immediately noticeable are the lexical and stylistic differences. Balg, for example, has observed that of the nine terms in the digression for the name of God only two (*wereda god* and *metod*) occur elsewhere in *Exodus*.[14] Likewise Groth has compared the use of substantive compounds in the different parts of *Exodus*: In the main body of the poem there is a compound every two or three lines; in the digression, however, there are only sixteen compounds in eighty-five lines, or only one to every five lines—a marked stylistic change, says Groth.[15] On the whole, the style of the patriarchal digression often resembles the straightforward chronicle style of *Genesis A* more than it does the rest of *Exodus*. Critics also point to metrical differences between *Exodus A* and *B*. Groth found that the digression contains more two-stave (instead of three-stave) alliteration than the rest of the poem; subsequently Graz[16] and Mürkens[17] used this and other metrical evidence to prove that *Exodus B* is younger than *Exodus A*. Furthermore, the passage has a number of admitted poetic weaknesses. Speaking of the Abraham and Isaac story, Creed has objected especially to three aspects: (1) the abrupt (Creed calls it "vitiating") interruption of the reference to the temple of Solomon, (2) an overabundance of "puzzling or even embarrassing parentheses" (e.g., 399, 408b), and (3) the seeming inability of the poet "to resist reminding us that God will intervene in time," thus spoiling the dramatic effect of the denouement of the sacrifice. Creed compares the *Exodus* version of the story to that in *Genesis* 2846–936 and finds the former much inferior to the emotionally charged impact of the latter.[18] Even James W. Earl, otherwise a great admirer of *Exodus*, concludes that the digression is only barely justified thematically and is awkwardly introduced into the narrative: "No amount of interpretation will ever explain the suddenness and awkwardness of the transition in lines 361–2, and the usual placement of the passage within the action of the poem."[19]

Nevertheless, as the two most recent editors of the poem suggest,[20] the integrity and relevance of the patriarchal digression can indeed be defended on a number of grounds, and it is surprising that the topic has yet to be thoroughly explored in a comprehensive study. This article, therefore, will attempt to lay the groundwork for future investigations, showing how the digression is related to the main text in the following four ways: (1) through a common interest in genealogy, (2) by certain major thematic parallels, (3) with several consistent strains of imagery, and (4) by means of a similar focus on Christological typology.

I

As early as 1860 Götzinger countered the rejection of the passage by viewing it as an extended genealogical reference,[21] like the *Þulur* in *Widsith*[22] or the meticulously detailed ancestries preserved in the sagas;[23] the poet is presenting the pedigree, as it were, of Israel as an insight to its national character. In 1882 Adolf Ebert was the first to recognize in the Abraham and Isaac incident the broader thematic import of the original bestowal of the covenant of Canaan, which is mentioned elsewhere in the poem; the Noah story serves as a preface to this but, says Ebert, "hat weiter keinen zweck."[24] Since that time, however, readers have learned more about the salient thematic function of both stories and their calculated location in the plan of the poem. The patriarchal digression is a subplot enriching the narrative complexity of the work and adding needed thematic weight to reinforce the broader implications of the main narrative. The abrupt shift at this point to a simpler style may be explained as a deliberate device whereby the poet echoes in his syntax the reversion to earlier narrative material. Says Krapp, "The poet of *Exodus*, with his sensitiveness to style, consciously reverted in this passage of falling action in his poem to that older manner of Cædmonian poetry as appropriate to an episode properly belonging to the story of *Genesis*."[25] Or perhaps this material was actually borrowed from earlier lays on the previous history of Israel and the poet only adapted it for his purposes in this digression. But the fact remains that, contrary to the views of many earlier critics, the passage is skillfully and neatly woven into the main fabric of the poem through the use of the genealogical motif. Early in *Exodus* the Hebrew tribes are termed *Abrahames sunum* (18b), and when telling of the crossing of the Red Sea, the poet explains that all of the tribes were related through a common ancestry *(Him wæs an fæder* [353b]) and that each knew his lineage therefrom, just as Moses had taught them (356–61). At this point the narrative glides smoothly into the story of Noah (362–76), which in turn is linked to the lines on the life of Abraham, the father of the Israelite nation (380–83), through a further genealogy tracing briefly the ten successive generations between the two patriarchs (377–79); then the poet commences the tale of the sacrifice of Isaac (384–446). Due to the present fragmentary state of the manuscript, unfortunately one can no longer discern how the original text of *Exodus* would have emerged from the end of the digression to rejoin the principal narrative of the crossing, and how these or further genealogical relationships would have been emphasized.[26]

II

A careful reading of *Exodus* could demonstrate also how the patriarchal digression is related integrally to several other major themes of the poem, three of which could be cited as of special interest. First, both the stories of Noah and Abraham are clear instances of the help of God sent to those in time of need.[27] *Exodus* makes full use of the Old Testament concept of Yahweh as a God of great physical power, both over human affairs and over the forces of nature. With his own hand he protects Israel. *Þis is se ecea Abrahames god . . .* , proclaims Moses, *se ðas fyrd wereð, / modig and mægenrof, mid þære miclan hand* ([273–75] "This is the eternal god of Abraham, mighty and renowned in strength, who protects the army with a great hand"). And at the height of their distress, with his right hand he opens the sea for his chosen people, and with the return blow destroys their enemies. God's interest in the Israelites is personal and immediate; at the theophany on Horeb (Ex. 3:1–4:17) he even discloses *his sylfes naman, / ðone yldo bearn ær ne cuðon* ([27b–28] "his own name, which the children of men had not known earlier"). The digression, however, presents us with a precedent to these events; for just as he was to do later with the Hebrews at the time of the exodus, so God had earlier revealed himself directly to Noah before the Flood and to Abraham at the climax of the sacrifice, intruding at the last moment to prevent what otherwise seemed fated death. All of these episodes are clear manifestations of the omnipotence of God and his divine intervention into mortal affairs.

Second, Noah and Abraham are analogous examples of the virtue of abiding faith and its reward.[28] Throughout most of the poem the Israelites are praised for their steadfastness in abiding by their oaths (*fæstum fleðmum freoðowære heold* [306]) and contrasted with the Egyptians who violate theirs (*Wære ne gymdon* [140b]; *wære fræton* [147b]). The Hebrews learn to be humble and obedient to God, but the Egyptians are proud and boastful. *Hie wið god wunnon!* (515b) exclaims the poet, for inevitably annihilation can be the only result of such vanity. Pharaoh learns only too late the mortal limits of his royal power:

> He onfond hraðe,
> siððan grund gestah   godes ansaca,
> þæt wæs mihtigra   mereflodes weard;
> wolde heorufæðmum   hilde gesceadan,
> yrre and egesfull.   (502b–506a)
> [After God's adversary reached the bottom, he soon found out that the guardian of the sea was greater; he wanted to deal out battle in deadly embraces, angry and fearsome.]

The patriarchal digression pinpoints Noah and Abraham as forerunners of the faithful among the Jews. In the apocryphal Book of Ecclesiasticus 44:17–21 Abraham is immediately preceded by Noah in a catalogue of the righteous, and in Hebrews 11 both of the patriarchs, as well as Moses, are cited as proof of the thesis *Sine Fide autem impossibile est placere Deo* ([11:6a] "Without faith it is impossible to please God"). Noah is said to bear in his breast *halige treowa*, "holy Faiths" (366b), and Abraham is praised for his *fæste treowa* (423a). The two patriarchs are, in short, paragons of faith to whom both the Hebrews of the exodus and the Christian auditors of the poem can turn as models of the upright life.

Third, both stories are in different ways precursors of the covenant of Moses, which was comprised of both the law and the promise of Canaan. A covenant is a new beginning, a fresh start in man's relationship with God; the law of Moses, with its obvious Christian typology,[29] represents just such an enterprise:

> in uprodor   eadigra gehwam
> æfter bealusiðe   bote lifes,
> lifigendra gehwam   langsumne ræd.   (4–6)
> [a remedy of life after the terrible journey (death?) for each of the blessed
> in heaven, a lasting counsel for each of the living.]

Similarly, the flood of the Noah story was associated with a new creation and a renewal of life and hope on earth.[30] And though the incident is not specifically related in *Exodus*, Noah was shown the covenant of the rainbow (Gen. 9:8–17), an important forerunner of the promise of Canaan and a typological prophecy of the coming of Christ.[31] More overtly, and directly concerned with the larger narrative of *Exodus*, Abraham received the important covenant of the nationhood of Israel and of the hope for a promised land in Canaan (432–46), all of which Moses would later see fulfilled. Abraham is even given a new name (*niwan naman asceop* [381a]) to symbolize his exalted state.[32] This theme is directly tied to the exodus story most strongly through Moses's words after the crossing:[33]

> hafað us on Cananea   cyn gelyfed
> burh and beagas,   brade rice;
> wile nu gelæstan   þæt he lange gehet
> mid aðsware,   engla drihten,
> in fyrndagum   fæderyncynne,
> gif ge gehealdað   halige lare.   (556–61)
> [he has granted to us the cities and rings of the tribe of the Canaanites, a
> wide kingdom; if you hold to the holy teachings, the lord of angels will
> carry out what he promised in oaths long ago to our ancestors in days
> past.]

The promise made to Abraham in the digression represents something like the title deed to Canaan, the *onwist eðles*, "habitation of a native land" (18a), which the Israelites begin to take possession of at the end of the poem.

III

In addition, each of the digressive stories is related to the main narrative through a number of incidental details and recurrent images. The Noah story, like the *transitus*, is a miracle of salvation by water. The Israelites, as "sailors" (*sæmen* [105b], *flotan* [133a, 223a, 331b]), pass unharmed over the flood of the Red Sea; Noah floats over a "different" flood (*Niwe flodas* [362a]), and appropriately his story recalls the seafaring imagery so important in *Exodus* when the poet refers to him as *snottor sæleoðu*, "wise seaman" (374a).[34] On the other hand, Abraham is said to have lived *on wræce* (383b), a prominent reference recalling the complementary images of exile and spiritual pilgrimage in the poem. Like Abraham wandering from the city of Ur, Moses and the Israelites are *eðelleas* (139a) and *wræcmen* (137b); their journeys resemble the allegorical *peregrinatio ad Deum* of *The Wanderer* and *The Seafarer*; and their quest is the Old Testament type of the Christian life.[35]

Another significant detail in the digression is the eight-line insert on the building of the temple (389–96). Far from being merely intrusive or vitiating, as Creed thought it, this passage represents an important though subtle thematic statement, both for the Abraham and Isaac story separately and for the poem as a whole. The building of the temple suggests the erection of the tabernacle, of which the temple is but a more permanent manifestation; the elaborate instructions for creating the tabernacle occupy the latter half of the Book of Exodus, and hence the poet was able to suggest in these lines much of the material in the book that takes place chronologically after the crossing.[36] Through these associations the temple becomes a type of the Christian church, a thesis well borne out by Bede's exhaustive allegorical expositions *De Tabernaculo et Vasis Eius* (*PL* 91, 393–498) and *De Templo Salomonis Liber* (*PL* 91, 755–808). But the poet modifies scriptural tradition (where the sacrifice takes place on Mt. Moriah[37]) to follow a Hebrew legend in locating the offering of Isaac on Mt. Zion (*on Seone beorh* [386b]), well known as the site of Jerusalem and the later-day temple of Solomon. In context then the temple represents a monument to Abraham's faith, following the dictum of 1 Corinthians that the true temple of God abides in the heart of the upright believer: *Templum enim Dei sanctum est, quod estis vos.*[38] The temple is also a physical embodiment of the Hebraic covenant, a sign of God's presence among his people.[39] Further, these lines on the temple (like those on the treasure of Joseph [580–90]) may look forward to the next poem in the manuscript, *Daniel*, where, as a result of Israel's unfaithfulness to the Lord, the temple of Jerusalem is ravaged by Babylonian invaders and its treasures plundered. Like the whole of the patriarchal digression, these lines on the temple are well integrated through significant thematic and imagistic echoes into the main body of the *Exodus* narrative.

IV

The patriarchal digression is also related to *Exodus* through a consistent Christological typology, for like Moses (see Heb. 3:5–6) both Noah and Isaac are important Old Testament figures of Christ.[40] Noah's preservation of life on earth from destruction is analogous to the Savior's crucifixion; the flood suggests Christian baptism, and the ark is the church.

> Noe autem per omnia significat Christum . . . Noe solus justus, Christus solus sine peccato est . . . Noe per aquam et lignum liberat suos, Christus per crucem et baptismum liberat Christianos. Arca construitur de lignis non putrescentibus, Ecclesia instruitur hominibus in sempiternum victuris. Arca enim ista Ecclesiam significat, quæ natat in fluctibus mundi huius. (Bede, *PL* 91, 222)
>
> Moreover in all things Noah signifies Christ . . . Noah alone is just, but Christ alone is without sin . . . Noah delivers his people by means of water and wood; Christ delivers Christians through the cross and baptism. The ark is constructed of wood which does not rot; the Church is built for men about to live in eternity. For this ark signifies the church, which sails on the waters of this world.

Furthermore Noah, whose name was thought to mean *requies*, "repose," in Hebrew, resembles Christ in giving the world peace from God's curse on its wickedness and in his taking upon himself the sins of mankind.[41] Obviously then the Noah story is linked with the baptismal overtones of the exodus legend, just as 1 Peter 3:18–21 indicates,[42] and the poet's juxtaposition of the story in the midst of narrating the Red Sea crossing is intended to make such an association abundantly clear in *Exodus*.

The Abraham and Isaac story is rather more complex in its typology. The sacrifice by Abraham of Isaac, his only legitimate son and heir, represents God's similar offering of his firstborn as the Christ to be crucified. Isidore explains, *Nam sicut Abraham filium et dilectum Deo victimam obtulit, ita Deus Pater unicum filium suum pro nobis omnibus tradidit*.[43] Here too there is a subtle relationship to the undercurrent of baptismal typology running through *Exodus*, for (as J. H. Wilson has noted[44]) the story of Isaac emphasizes the concept of sacrifice that in the early church was central to the sacrament of baptism, whereby the catechumen renounced his old life, acknowledged his role in the death of the Savior for the sins of mankind, and accepted the promise of a greater life in heaven after his earthly exile was completed. The story of Isaac brings to the typology of this poem an essential connection between baptism and the passion. But perhaps of even greater importance to the structure and meaning of *Exodus* is the poet's use of the tale of Abraham and Isaac to suggest the otherwise unnoticed ritual of the Hebrew passover.

The *Exodus* poet's thorough reworking and adaptation of his primary biblical source, Ex. 13–15, has often been noted, especially his additions to this source. But the poem also features a striking omission: in the account of the passover (30–53) there is no mention at all of the passover feast so prominent in the biblical chapters 12–13. This is especially noteworthy since the paschal lamb is so rich in typological associations and was much emphasized in the exegeses of the fathers. Furthermore, other vernacular treatments of the exodus story, such as those found in Middle English and Middle High German, contain a full exposition of the subject.[45] But the Old English poet confines his focus to the events of the death of the firstborn and the rejoicing on the morning of the exodus. Nevertheless, a strong argument might be made that the Christological, thematic function of the passover has been assumed in *Exodus* by this digressive story of the sacrifice of Isaac. Since it is lost in the lacuna, readers can only surmise the ending of the tale, but probably it concluded, like the source in Genesis, with some brief reference to Isaac's being replaced on the altar with the ram found trapped in the thicket. In Hebrew theology, this ram is analogous to the lamb offered on the evening of the passover, and both are prominent types of Christ and the crucifixion.[46] Typologically then the two incidents, the passover and the sacrifice of Isaac, carry basically the same significance, and the poet may very well have used the one to suggest the other. Perhaps he deliberately omitted the passover ritual, knowing full well that its thematic, Christological, and sacramental functions would be taken over by the later digression. In this view a separate reference to both would be merely redundant, and as the narrative moves very swiftly in the passage on the passover and the exodus from Egypt (30–53), any detailed reference at that point to the ritual meal might seem only to obstruct the rapid, excited progress of the lines. Furthermore, the sacrifice story contained additional thematic elements, such as the covenant and the help of God, which could not be represented in the passover supper alone. The poet's choice to compact or "telescope" both events into a single story is a boldly ingenious device whereby he was able to eliminate any overt reference to the passover ritual at its chronologically appropriate point early in the poem but still imply the essential thematic significance of the event by means of its common typological associations with the material on Abraham and Isaac related in the digression more than 300 lines later.[47]

In short, the patriarchal digression embedded in the center of *Exodus* is not the poetic excrescence or scribal intrusion that scholars once thought. Rather, it is a skillfully introduced and poetically effective subplot reinforcing through its parallels much of the significance of the material in the main story. Both the tales of Noah and of Abraham and Isaac are analogous instances of the help of God, the virtue of faith, and the precursors of both the Old and New Covenants. There are also consistent strains of imagery throughout all the stories, and they share with the main body of *Exodus* important typological similarities, most notably a common Christological and sacramental emphasis. *Exodus* and *Beowulf* alone in Old English employ the epic convention of the structural use of digression, and the stories of Noah and Abraham here are as germane thematically as the Finn digression is to understanding the deep-lying fermentation in the court of Heorot.[48] Thus thematically, typologically, and structurally the patriarchal digression is at the heart of *Exodus*.

NOTES

1. Citations from *Exodus* are to the text edited by George Philip Krapp, *The Junius Manuscript*, *ASPR* 1 (New York, 1931), 91–107.

2. *Exodus* 362–76; see Gen. 6:5–8:22. Actually the Noah story in Exodus is not so much told as merely alluded to. The technique recalls that of the Sigemund digression in *Beowulf*.

3. *Exodus* 377–446; see Gen. 22.

4. *Exodus* 389–96; see 1 Kings 6, 2 Chron. 3–4.

5. After line 446 of the poem, two and a quarter pages of the manuscript have been left blank and a folio has been cut out. Line 446 ends about three-quarters of the way down p. 163, and its last words, *folca selost*, are followed by the usual pointed positura (;) indicating the end of a fitt or section (number XLVII). Page 164 (the verso) is completely blank except for the random jotting in a later hand *tribus annis transactis*, clearly irrelevant to *Exodus*. The facing page, 165, is also blank, and 166 begins a new fitt, with the number XLVIII centered at the top and a capital F(*olc*). There is evidence that a leaf has been cut out between the present pages 164 and 65, and the knife marks are still visible. See Sir Israel Gollancz, *The Cædmon Manuscript of Anglo-Saxon Biblical Poetry, Junius XI in the Bodleian Library*, facsimile edition (London, 1927). Despite the blanks and the missing folio, it is impossible to calculate exactly how much text has been lost, since the manuscript frequently leaves blank spaces for illustrations, many of which were never completed.

6. Hugo Balg, *Der Dichter Cædmon und seine Werke* (Bonn, 1882), 24–27.

7. Alois Brandl, *Geschichte der altenglischen Literatur* (Strassburg, 1908), I, 1029.

8. W. J. Sedgefield, *Specimens of Anglo-Saxon Poetry* (Edinburgh, 1923).

9. W. J. Sedgefield, *MLR* 26 (1931), 352–55.

10. W. P. Ker, *The Dark Ages* (New York, 1904), 260–61.

11. Charles Kennedy, *The Earliest English Poetry* (Oxford, 1943), 176.

12. Gerhard Mürkens, "Untersuchungen über das altenglische Exoduslied," *Bonner Beiträge* 2 (1899), 65.

13. W. A. Craigie, "Interpretations and Omissions in Anglo-Saxon Poetic Texts," *Philologica* 2 (1925), 5–19.

14. Balg, 24–37.

15. Ernst J. Groth, *Composition und Alter der altenglischen (angelsächsischen) Exodus* (Göttingen, 1883), 21–22.

16. Friedrich Graz, *Die Metrik des sog. Cædmonischen Dichtungen mit Berücksichtigung der Verfasserfrage* (Weimar, 1894), 37–40.

17. Mürkens, 67.

18. Robert P. Creed, "The Art of the Singer," *Old English Poetry: Fifteen Essays* (Providence, RI, 1967), 72–73.

19. James W. Earl, "Christian Traditions in the Old English *Exodus*," *NM* 71 (1970), 563–65 [reprinted in the present volume—*ed.*]; the quotation is from p. 565.

20. Edward B. Irving, Jr., "Exodus Retraced," in *Old English Studies in Honor of John C. Pope*, ed. Robert B. Burlin and Edward B. Irving, Jr. (Toronto, 1974), 204. This is one of two articles in which Irving updated his edition of 1953 (see note 26); the other, "New Notes on the Old English *Exodus*," appeared in *Anglia* 90 (1972), 289–324. Peter J. Lucas, *Exodus* (London, 1977), 31.

21. Ernst Götzinger, *Über die Dichtungen des Angelsachsen Cædmon und deren Verfasser* (Göttingen, 1860), 25–26.

22. Kemp Malone, *Widsith* (1936; rpt. Copenhagen, 1962), 27.

23. See Theodore M. Andersson, *The Icelandic Family Saga: An Analytic Reading* (Cambridge, MA, 1967).

24. Adolf Ebert, "Zum Exodus," *Anglia* 5 (1882), 409–10.

25. Krapp, xxviii.

26. See note above. Irving (*The Old English Exodus*, Yale Stds. in English, 122 [New Haven, 1953], 10) estimated that about sixty lines of text have been lost at this point, encompassing all of fitt XLVIII.

27. On this theme see Charles W. Kennedy, *The Cædmon Poems. Translated into English Prose* (London, 1912), 182–83; Robert T. Farrell, "A Reading of OE *Exodus*," *RES* 20 (1969), 401–17.

28. In his edition, Peter J. Lucas raises a similar point, though with an altogether different focus; "the most powerful unifying factor in the poem," writes Lucas, is "the central theme of salvation by Faith and Obedience" (61). The same thesis had earlier been argued for the entire Junius manuscript by J. R. Hall in his dissertation "The Old English Book of Salvation History" (Diss., Notre Dame, 1974) and in a recension of it, "The Old English Epic of Redemption: The Theological Unity of MS Junius 11," *Traditio* 32 (1976), 185–208 [reprinted in the present volume—*ed.*].

29. On the typology of the law, see for example Gal. 3:23–26, 29; (Pseudo-) Bede, *In Pentateuchum Commentarii, PL* 91, 295; and Ælfric's homily for Midlent Sunday, in *The Homilies of the Anglo-Saxon Church*, ed. Benjamin Thorpe (London, 1844–46, 1:186–88. Father Zacharias P. Thundy's monograph *Covenant in Anglo-Saxon Thought . . .* (Madras, 1972) offers a full exposition of this matter, though unfortunately without reference to *Exodus*.

30. J. R. Hall, "'Niwe Flodas': Old English 'Exodus' 362," *N&Q* 22 (1975), 243–44.

31. On the Hebrew interpretations and legends of Noah as a precursor of Abraham in his role of covenant-bearer with Yahweh, see Leo Lieberman, "Old English *Exodus* and *Sefer Shemoth*: A Comparative Study" (Diss., Fordham, 1969), 95–96.

32. Gen. 17:5. The patriarch's original name *Abram* (of which *Abraham* is actually but a dialectical variant) is never used in Old English; even in *Genesis*, before the speech of God's promise to him (2306–37), the character is consistently termed *Abraham*.

33. The association between Abraham, the covenant, and the exodus is made explicit in an important scriptural precedent in Neh. 9:7–12.

34. This nautical metaphor is pervasive in *Exodus*. Unlike the Israelite *sæmen* who cross the sea, the Egyptians are *landmen* (179b) who drown in it. The famous kaleidoscopic imagery of the pillar of cloud as a ship (71b–92) is also related to this cluster. The typology of the metaphor has been much discussed; see for example Peter J. Lucas, "Old English Christian Poetry: The Cross in *Exodus*," *Famulus Christi: Essays in Commemoration of the Thirteenth Centenary of the Venerable Bede*, ed. Gerald Bonner (London, 1976), 193–209.

35. James H. Wilson, *Christian Theology and Old English Poetry* (The Hague, 1974), 110–40.

36. Indeed, the poem suggests and alludes to many incidents in the Book of Exodus that occur after the *transitus*. For this reason the present title (first given the poem by Grein in 1857) is not as inappropriate as some critics would lead us to believe (e.g., Krapp, xxvii).

37. See Irving's note on this passage in his edition, p. 90.

38. "For God's temple is holy, and that temple you are" (1 Cor. 3:17b; tr. RSV); see also 6:19: "An nescitis quoniam membra vestra, templum sunt Spiritus sancti, qui in vobis est, quem habetis a Deo, et non estis vestri?" ("Do you not know that your body is a temple of the Holy Spirit within you, which you have from God? You are not your own."—RSV)

39. See 1 Kings 8:16–21, 2 Chron. 5:10.

40. The typological analysis of *Exodus*, and especially its relationship to the symbology of baptism, seem well established in current criticism. See, for instance, the seminal article by James W. Bright, "The Relationship of the Cædmonian *Exodus* to the Liturgy," *MLN* 27 (1912), 97–103; and J. E. Cross and Susie I. Tucker, "Allegorical Tradition in the Old English *Exodus*," *Neophilologus* 44 (1960), 122–27; also Bernard F. Huppé, *Doctrine and Poetry* (Albany, 1959), 217–23. The spiritual and allegorical signifi-

cance of the rite of baptism is exhaustively documented by the late Cardinal Jean Daniélou, *The Bible and the Liturgy* (Notre Dame, 1956), 19–113. The traditional allegorical interpretation of *Exodus* has been questioned by Ruth M. Ames ("The Old Testament Christ and the Old English *Exodus*," *Studies in Medieval Culture* 10 [1977], 33–50), but see Hall's remarks in *Old English Newsletter* 12 (Fall, 1978), 48–49. Paul F. Ferguson's "The Old English *Exodus* and the Patristic Tradition" (Diss., SUNY at Binghamton, 1978) provides a brief but interesting discussion of the problem and its literary ramifications.

41. On the patristic typology of Noah see especially Origen, *in Genesim Homilia*, II: "De Fabrica Arcæ," *PG* 12, Cols. 161–75; Isidore, *Quæstiones in Vetus Testamentum*, *PL* 83, 229.

42. "Quia et Christus semel pro peccatis nostris mortuus est, justus pro injustis: ut nos offerret Deo, mortificatus quidem carne, vivificatus autem spiritu. In quo et his, qui in carcere erant, spiritibus veniens prædicavit: Qui increduli tuerant aliquando, quando expectabant Dei patientiam in diebus Noe, cum fabricaretur arca: in qua pauci, id est octo animæ salvæ factæ sunt per aquam. Quod et vos nunc similis formæ salvos facit baptisma: non carnis depositio sordium, sed conscientiæ bonæ interrogatio in Deum per resurrectionem Jesu Christi." ("For Christ also died for sins once and for all, the righteous for the unrighteous, that he might bring us to God, being put to death in the flesh but made alive in the spirit; in which he went and preached to the spirits in prison, who formerly did not obey, when God's patience waited in the days of Noah, during the building of the ark, in which a few, that is, eight persons, were saved through the water. Baptism, which corresponds to this, now saves you, not as a removal of dirt from the body but as an appeal to God for a clear conscience, through the resurrection of Jesus Christ."—RSV.)

43. "For just as Abraham offered up to God his son and most beloved as a sacrifice, so God the Father delivered his only son for us all." Isidore, *PL* 83, 250; see also Bede, *PL* 91, cols. 245–46. A very full allegorical exposition of the story appears in Origen's *In Genesim Homilia*, VIII, "De Eo Quod Obtulit Abraham Filium Suum Isaac" (*PG* 12, 203–10), and IX; "De Repromissionibus Secundis ad Abraham Factis" (*PG* 12, 210–15).

44. Wilson, p. 139.

45. Edgar Papp, ed., *Die altdeutsche Exodus* (München, 1969), ll. 2443–626; Richard Morris, ed., *The Story of Genesis and Exodus: An Early English Song*, EETS 7 (London, 1865), ll. 3133–58.

46. Isidore's commentaries on the Pentateuch clarify this point very well. He says of the ram: "Deinde Isaac, ligatis pedibus, altari superponitur, et Dominus in ligno suspensus cruci affligitur. Sed illud, quod figuratum est

in Isaac, translatum est ad arietem. Cur hoc, nisi quia Christus ovis? ipse enim filius, ipse agnus. Filius, quia natus; aries, quia immolatus" (*PL* 83, 251: "Thereupon, Isaac, with feet bound, is placed upon the altar, even as the Lord is afflicted while suspended on the wood of the cross. But that which has been figured in Isaac has been transferred to the ram. But why so, if not because Christ is the sheep? For that very son is himself the lamb. The son, because he was born; the ram, because he was sacrificed."). The identification of the paschal lamb is equally specific: "In occisione agni occiditur Christus, de quo Evangelia dicitur: *Ecce Agnus Dei, ecce qui tollit peccata mundi (Joan.* i)" (*PL* 83, 294: "in the slaying of the lamb, Christ is slain, about whom it is said in the gospels, 'Behold the lamb of God, behold him who takes away the sins of the world' [John 1:29]").

47. This "telescoping" of disparate events and their significance is not at all uncommon in *Exodus*. For example, Moses's homily on the law (516–48), though ostensibly representing the giving of the decalogue and the Hebrew covenant, is actually a typological exposition of the New (Christian) Covenant, with its implications of Christ's saving grace for man at doomsday. And the final scene of the poem on the opposite shore of the Red Sea seems fused with a similar scene of rejoicing later in the Pentateuch where the Israelites have crossed the Jordan and celebrate at long last having attained the Promised Land (Josh. 3:14–17).

48. See, for example, the classic study by Adrien Bonjour, *The Digressions in Beowulf* (Oxford, 1950).

The Lion Standard in *Exodus*: Jewish Legend, Germanic Tradition, and Christian Typology

CHARLES D. WRIGHT

This essay first appeared in Archiv für das Studium der neueren Sprachen und Literaturen *227 (1994), 138–45. It has been revised by the author.*

In the Old English *Exodus*, as the Israelites prepare to cross the Red Sea, the poet describes the battle standard carried by the tribe of Judah, which leads the host:

> Hæfdon him to segne,   þa hie on sund stigon,
> ofer bordhreoðan   beacen aræred
> in þam garheape   gyldenne leon,
> drihtfolca mæst,   deora cenost.   (319–22)[1]
> [When they descended upon the sea that greatest of tribes had a beacon raised up for a banner above the shield-wall, a golden lion, bravest of beasts, amid that spear-host.]

The essential elements of the poet's description have biblical precedent. Judah, *þæt feorðe cyn* (line 310; cf. Gen. 29:35), is first in the order of battle, Reuben having by sin forfeited the primacy to his younger brother, as the poet relates in lines 335b–339 (cf. Gen. 49:3–4).[2] That the Israelites carried standards (*vexilla*) is attested by Num. 2:2,[3] although, as James W. Earl reminds us, the military organization of the tribes was not instituted until after the crossing of the Red Sea, making the poet's use of such details apparently anachronistic.[4] As for the emblem of the lion, Groth recognized an allusion to Gen. 49:9 ("catulus leonis Iuda ad

superbos mole praedarum graves, 1. 27). Equally "heroic" is the focus of interest on the booty, which is lavishly detailed (ll. 30–31) and, as in *Genesis*, consists largely of specifically female items: *aurum puellas paruulos monilia / greges equarum uasa uestem buculas* [gold, maidens, small boys, necklaces, herds of mares, vessels, clothing, cows]. A third feature of this passage is the way in which verbal and structural parallels are employed. So the description of Christ, the true priest (*sacerdos verus*, 1. 59), born of a single unutterable source (*parente natus alto et ineffabili*, 1. 60), offering food to the blessed victors in the struggle of life (*cibum beatis offerens uictoribus*, 1. 61), deliberately recalls the earlier picture of Melchisedech, the priest of God (*sacerdos . . . dei sacerdos*, ll. 39–40), whose own origins are obscure (*origo cuius fonte inenarrabili*, 1. 41), bestowing heavenly sustenance on the warrior (Abraham) fresh from the field of battle (*adhuc recentem caede de tanta uirum / donat sacerdos ferculis caelestibus*, ll. 38–39). In drawing out these parallels Prudentius is simply aligning himself with a common patristic and exegetical tradition which saw in Melchisedech a prefiguration of Christ, an identification founded ultimately on Hebrews 7:1–3.[54] Prudentius also employs a number of rhetorical techniques, including paronomasia and alliteration, underlining the artfulness of his recasting of the biblical narrative.[55] Finally, one might point to the way in which Prudentius implicitly moves beyond the plain story and hints at the exegetical penumbra of tradition. The identification of Christ and Melchisedech through repeated diction already noted provides one example, and a similar dependence on exegetical tradition surely explains Prudentius's otherwise puzzling (and quite unbiblical) insistence that the defeated Lot is chained and bound, a notion repeated throughout the passage.[56] It seems likely here that Prudentius is alluding to the sacred etymology of Lot's name, which Jerome identified as *uinctus* ("bound").[57] For Prudentius, as for Jerome, Lot is not simply conquered (*uictus*, as in 1. 15), but constrained (*uinctus*). The allegorical possibilities presented seem powerful, and in the course of a sensitive and detailed study Macklin Smith has demonstrated the subtlety with which Prudentius has depicted "the first *psychomachia* of sacred history."[58]

That the allegorical significance of this episode from Prudentius was well recognized in Anglo-Saxon England is also clear. It is intrigu-

praeda fili mi, ascendisti / requiescens accubuisti ut leo et quasi leaena quis suscitabit eum"),[5] and Blackburn added Rev. 5:5 ("ecce vicit leo de tribu Iuda radix David . . .").[6] These verses, of course, do not specifically account for the detail that the standard of the tribe bore a lion device. Stanley Hauer, following Groth, has argued that the poet's description reflects a native tradition of adorning standards with images of animals.[7] Hauer points out that a banner with a raven device is mentioned in the Anglo-Saxon *Chronicle*, and that Constantine in the Old English *Elene* is said to have an *eofurcumbol* (l. 76), the boar emblem being particularly significant in Germanic tradition. Hauer concludes that "The lion standard in *Exodus* then appears to be an adaptation of the old tribal emblem of the boar into the Biblical image of a lion."[8]

Hauer's suggestion is plausible and attractive, and the Germanic background of the poet's description of the lion standard is clearly relevant. The advance to battle under a lion standard is strikingly paralleled in a passage from Widukind of Corvey's *Rerum Gestarum Saxonicarum Libri Tres*, in which an old warrior named Hathagat, exhorting his companions to battle, seizes a sacred standard surmounted by lion, dragon, and eagle devices: "Hic arripiens signum, quod apud eos habebatur sacrum, leonis atque draconis et desuper aquilae volantis insignitum effigie."[9] But the poet probably did have a more immediate source, since the idea that the Israelite tribes' standards each had its proper emblem, including the lion of Judah, is attested in Jewish tradition and can be paralleled in a Latin biblical gloss as well as in Irish vernacular sources. Louis Ginzberg has documented the Jewish lore concerning the standards of the four tribes Reuben, Judah, Dan, and Ephraim, corresponding to the four angels surrounding the throne of God.[10] As Ginzberg explains, "The four standards were distinguished from one another by their different colors, and by the inscriptions and figures worked upon each."[11] Of the details cited by Ginzberg, only the emblem is relevant to the Old English poem: "Judah's standard bore in its upper part the figure of a lion, for its forefather had been characterized by Jacob as 'a lion's whelp,' and also sword-like hooks of gold."[12] A Midrash on Numbers also assigned a distinctive flag to each of the twelve tribes, including Judah's upon which was embroidered the lion.[13]

When a Midrashic tradition provides an analogue for a motif in an Anglo-Saxon poem, it is best to assume transmission through a Christian intermediary, even when none can be identified.[14] The precedence of Judah was applied to the procession through the Red Sea in Jewish tradition, for example, but Irving has pointed out that this tradition is transmitted in a

Latin commentary on Hebrews.[15] The poet's statement in lines 314ff. that
God rewarded Judah with the primacy for his courage in entering the sea
first is also paralleled in a Hiberno-Latin commentary on Matthew:

> Cur per Iudam portatur genealogia (ms. gelogia) Christi specialiter?
> Hier[onymus]: Tradunt Hebraei huiuscemodi fabulam: In exitu Israel de
> Aegypto, quando ex alia parte mons, ex alia parte rubrum mare, ex alia
> Pharaonis cingebatur exercitus et inclusus populus tenebatur, ceteris (ms.
> ceterae) tribubus desperantibus salutem et aut reverti in Aegyptum aut bel-
> lare cupientibus, solus Iuda fideliter ingressus est in mare, unde et regnum
> meruit accipere et Christum nascentem a se.[16]
> [Why is the genealogy of Christ borne by Judah in particular? Jerome:
> The Jews have a legend of this sort: during the exodus from Egypt, when
> the Israelites were surrounded on one side by a mountain, on another by
> the Red Sea, and on another by the army of the Pharoah, the other tribes
> gave up hope of rescue, wishing either to return to Egypt or to fight; Judah
> alone entered faithfully into the sea, for which reason he merited to
> receive both the kingship and the birth of Christ from his line.]

The tradition is also found in later Christian sources, including Peter
Comestor's *Historia Scholastica* and an eleventh- or twelfth-century
Irish poem.[17] As for the motif of the standards of the Israelites and their
emblems, analogues exist in both Latin and Irish. The Latin parallel
occurs in a *Glossarium* on the Bible preserved in a thirteenth-century
manuscript in Erlangen. A list of the tribal standards and emblems from
this commentary has been printed by Elias Steinmeyer:

> Tradunt hebrei hec fuisse in uexillis tribuum israhel singularum.
> in Ruben mandragoram. in symeone hastam. in leui archam testamenti. *in*
> *iuda leonem.* in ysachar asinum. in zabulo nauim. in neptalim ceruum. in
> gad leenam. in ioseph taurum. In beniamin lupum. in dan serpentem.[18]
> [According to the Jews, these were the standards of each of the tribes of
> Israel: for Ruben, a mandrake; for Simeon, a lance; for Levi, the ark of the
> testament; *for Judah, a lion*; for Isacar, an ass; for Zabulon, a ship; for
> Nephtalem, a stag; for Gad, a lioness; for Joseph, a bull; for Benjamin, a
> wolf; for Dan, a serpent.]

Though considerably later than the Old English poem, this Latin gloss
does suffice to show that the tradition—specifically acknowledged as a
Jewish one—circulated in Christian exegesis in the Middle Ages. That

the same tradition was known in Ireland is attested by a prose biblical history preserved in the fourteenth-century Irish manuscript known as the *Leabhar Breac*, which gives a closely similar list of the banners of the Israelite tribes, together with a fourteen-stanza poem on the same subject.[19] Keating included the poem and a version of the list in his *History of Ireland*[20]:

> Now there were twelve tribes of them, and each tribe had a separate division of an army and a separate emblem.
> The tribe of Ruben, a mandrake on its standard as an emblem;
> The tribe of Simeon, a javelin on its standard as an emblem;
> The tribe of Levi, the ark on its standard as an emblem;
> *The tribe of Juda, a lion on its standard as an emblem;*
> The tribe of Isacar, an ass on its standard as an emblem;
> The tribe of Zabulon, a ship on its standard as an emblem;
> The tribe of Nephtalem, the figure of a [stag] on its standard as an emblem;
> The tribe of Gad, the figure of a lioness on its standard an an emblem;
> The tribe of Joseph, a bull on its standard as an emblem;
> The tribe of Benjamin, a wolf on its standard as an emblem;
> The tribe of Dan, a serpent on its standard as an emblem;
> The tribe of Aser, an olive branch on its standard as an emblem.

From the poem, which Keating claims to have read "in the old Book of Leacaoin, in Urmhumha, and in many other old books," I quote only the stanza on Judah[21]:

> The ensign of the noble tribe of Juda,
> The figure of a powerful lion;
> The tribe of Juda, in the hour of wrath
> Proud hosts following a good ensign.

The association of the tribes with their respective emblems, though not specifically in the military context of emblazoned standards, even appears in Anglo-Saxon iconography. Thomas Ohlgren's *Anglo-Saxon Textual Illustration*[22] has made available a previously unpublished representation of the twelve tribes and their emblems. The Bury Psalter (Vatican City, Biblioteca Apostolica, MS Reg. lat. 12), produced at Canterbury for Bury St. Edmunds in the first half of the eleventh century,[23] contains on fol. 109rv depictions of twelve bearded figures repre-

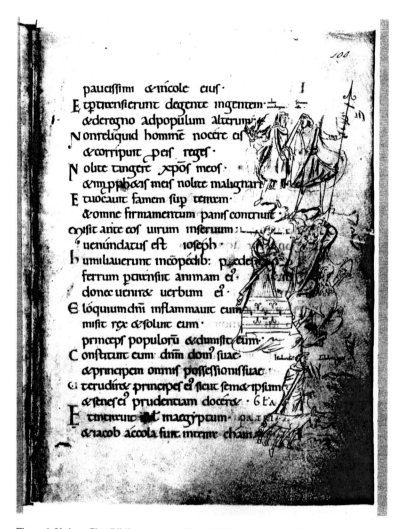

pauaffimi & incole eiuf ·
Et transierunt degente ingentem
& de regno ad populum alterum
Non reliquid homine nocere ei
& corripuit per reges ·
Nolite tangere xpos meos ·
& in pphetis meis nolite malignari
Et uiocauit famem fup terram ·
& omne firmamentum panif contriuit
Misit ante eof uirum in seruum
uenundatuf est ioseph ·
humiliauerunt in compedib: pedes
ferrum pertransit animam ei.
donec ueniret uerbum ei ·
Eloquium dni inflammauit eum
misit rex & soluit eum ·
princeps populorum & dimisit eum·
Constituit eum dnm domi suae
& principem omnis possessionis suae ·
Ut erudiret principes ei sicut semet ipsum
& senes ei prudentiam docere · 6 Et
Et intrauit isrt in aegyptum · & ia
& iacob accola fuit in terra cham

Figure 1. Vatican City, Biblioteca Apostolica, MS Reg. lat. 12, fol. 109r. Reproduced by permission of the Vatican Library. © Biblioteca Apostolica Vaticana.

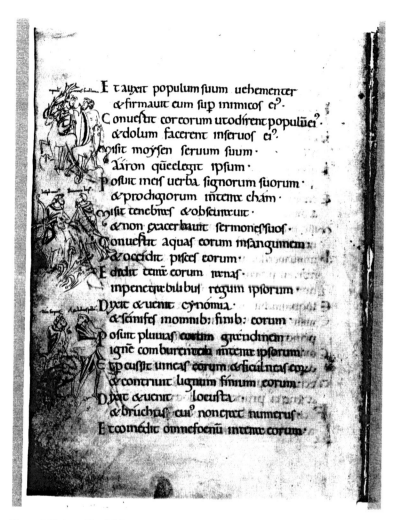

E tauxir populum fuum uehementer
&firmauit cum fup inimicos ei?.
Conueſtit corcorum utodirent populũei?.
&dolum facerent inſeruos ei?.
miſit moÿſen ſeruum ſuum ·
Aaron quĕeelegit ipſum ·
poſuit meiſ uerba ſignorum ſuorum ·
&prochigiorum inteinx chám ·
miſit tenebriuſ &obſcuruit ·
& non exacerbauit ſermoneſſuoſ ·
Conueſtit aquaſ eorum inſanguinem ·
&occidit piſceſ eorum ·
Edidit teinx corum ranaſ ·
inpenetrebulibuſ regum ipſorum ·
Dixit &uenit cÿnómia ·
&ſcinifeſ momnibuſ finibuſ eorum ·
poſuit pluuiaſ eartin grandinem ·
igñ comburentem inteinx ipſorum ·
& percuſſit uineaſ eorum &ſiculneaſ eoụ ·
&contriuit lignum finium eorum ·
Dixit &uenit loeuſta ·
&bruchuſ cui? non erat numeruſ ·
& comedit omnefoenũ inteinx eorum ·

Figure 2. Vatican City, Biblioteca Apostolica, MS Reg. lat. 12, fol. 109v. Reproduced by permission of the Vatican Library. © Biblioteca Apostolica Vaticana.

senting each of the *filii Iacobi* of Ps. 104:6, accompanied by literal
images of their respective emblems and identified by inscriptions giving
their names and attributes (figs. 1 and 2). The inscriptions read as follows:

ruben mandragora
Symeon asta
Leui arca testamenti
Iudas leo
Isachar asinus
Zabulon nauis
neptali ceruus
Gad leena
Ioseph taurus
Beniamin lupus
Dan serpens
Aser habens pellum

In the illustration, Judah (fig. 1: fol. 109r, second row) stands frontally
behind his lion and carries in his right hand a foliate scepter while point-
ing with his left to a crown on his head, denoting his rulership over the
twelve tribes. Although the Bury Psalter illustration postdates the Old
English poem and does not portray the sons of Jacob with emblazoned
battle standards, it does provide striking documentary and iconographic
confirmation that the tradition of the tribal emblems, including the lion
of Judah, was known in late Anglo-Saxon England.

It seems likely, then, that the *Exodus* poet drew upon a biblical
gloss or commentary for his description of the lion standard of Judah,
and believed that the Israelite tribes did actually carry such emblazoned
banners during the Exodus.[24] His use of the image, therefore, is not sim-
ply a case of "Germanicizing" the biblical text but is also a piece of "his-
torical" exegesis. No doubt the similarity of Hebrew and Germanic
military customs appealed to the poet, who so vigorously adapted the
martial imagery of Germanic poetry to the expression of spiritual war-
fare,[25] and who elsewhere in the poem was alert to coincidences of Ger-
manic and biblical traditions.[26]

There is more to the poet's use of the image, however, than mere
syncretism of Jewish legend and Germanic tradition, for the lion of
Judah, with its well-established Christological interpretation,[27] makes
for a pointed contrast with the totemic animals of Germanic tradition
and their inevitably pagan associations. The boar in particular seems to

have been recognized as a specifically heathen symbol by other Anglo-Saxon poets. Fred C. Robinson has argued that the *Beowulf* poet takes pains to remind his audience "of the protective power which pagan Germanic people attributed to the boar images," only to expose the image as "an epitome of the tragic delusions of the heroic society."[28] In Cynewulf's *Elene*, the boar banner (*eofurcumbol*) of Constantine, to which Hauer drew attention, gives way to the sign of the Cross as a consequence of the Roman general's divinely inspired dream.[29]

As Widukind of Corvey's description of the standard as "holy" (*sacrum*) suggests, in Germanic tradition the battle standard itself, whatever its insignia, seems to have had cultic significance,[30] and William A. Chaney has suggested that "It may well have been this heathenism-associated antiquity of the royal standard that barred its acceptance by the Church when it substituted an ecclesiastically blessed Christian kingship for the sacral king-cult of paganism of which the banner was an emblem."[31] In Christian tradition, moreover, the image of the royal standard, taken as a symbol of the Cross, is often contrasted with the military standards of paganism, especially by early Christian authors such as Tertullian, for whom military service by Christians in the pagan Roman army was still a serious issue to be resolved. In the words of Adolf Harnack, "the military standards appeared to be heathen *sacra*; to reverence them was hence idolatry."[32] Tertullian was uncompromising: "There is no agreement between the divine and the human sacrament, the standard of Christ and the standard of the devil, the camp of light and the camp of darkness."[33] Yet as Tertullian's remark shows, the Church Militant pressed into its own service the technical terms of the Roman legions, including *vexillum* and *signum*.[34] Against the flag of the devil the Christian soldier advanced into spiritual combat under the banner of Christ. The most famous example of the Christian appropriation of the image of military standards is of course Venantius Fortunatus's hymn "Vexilla regis prodeunt."[35] Other Christian authors explicitly opposed the *vexillum* or *signum crucis* to the military standards of the legions with their animal emblems.[36] Thus Ambrose, recalling the vision of Constantine, contrasts the images of eagles and dragons displayed by the banners of the legions with the sign of the Cross carried into battle by the Christian soldier: "scit exercitata mens quos ad proelium consummandum adhibeat sibi, quibus armis instruat, quibus ducat vexillis. non aquilarum praefert imagines nec dracones, sed in cruce Christi et Iesu nomine progreditur ad proelium, hoc signo fortis, hoc vexillo fidelis" ("the disciplined mind knows whom to call upon to accomplish the battle, with which arms to array them and under which standards to lead them. He does not display images of eagles, or dragons, but advances to battle with the cross of Christ and in the name of Jesus, strong under this ensign, faithful under this banner").[37]

Prudentius, who in one poem praises two legionaries who abandoned their dragon standards for the sign of the Cross,[38] elsewhere ascribes the same emblems to the armies of Pharaoh in pursuit of the Israelites:

> densetur cuneis turba pedestribus,
> currus pars et equos et volucres rotas
> conscendunt celeres, signaque bellica
> praetendunt tumidis clara draconibus.[39]
> [The multitude forms up in serried ranks of foot; others swiftly mount
> their horses and flying wheels, and display their banners of war with their
> famous dragons.]

The *Exodus* poet has contrived a similar opposition between pagan and Christian standards. The Israelites are at first cast into terror and despair by the sight of the Egyptian host, led by the Pharaoh, who is significantly termed their *segncyning*, riding *wið þone segn foran* (l. 172). But arrayed against the standard of Pharaoh is the *segn* of Judah, which the poet has previously mentioned in lines 126–29:

> Gesawon randwigan   rihte stræte,
> segn ofer sweoton,   oðþæt sæfæsten
> landes æt ende   leomægne forstod,
> fus on forðweg.
> [The shield-bearers followed the straight path, a banner above the troop,
> until that lion-host stood against the stronghold of the sea at the land's
> end, eager on their way forth.]

According to Fred C. Robinson, "The *segn ofer sweoton* is the lion banner of the host of Juda, which is leading the way for the tribes following," the tribe itself here designated as the "lion host" (*leomægne*, line 128b, emended by Lucas and Irving to *leodmægne*).[40] Lucas, however, interprets the *segn* in line 127 as the pillar of cloud, elsewhere termed a *fana* (l. 248b), "seen as a *labarum*, a battle standard incorporating the Cross."[41] The two apparently conflicting readings may be reconciled at the level of typology. As Lucas suggests, "by employing the same words for different concepts (pillar, Cross, standard) the poem compels its audience to consider how these concepts are linked, and indeed to realize that the links are to be found through symbolism and allegory."[42] Hauer likewise interprets the lion standard in lines 319-22 (also a *segn*) typologically, representing Christ crucified and echoing the earlier symbolism of the pillar as a *segn* signifying the Cross.[43] The *segn* of line 127 may thus refer at once to both "standards," with the Cross as the unifying referent. In the typological structure of the poem the *signum crucis*, the standard of Christ, is raised against the standard of the devil, the *segn* of the Egyptian host and their *segncyning* Pharaoh, as the Israelites, with renewed courage, advance into the Red Sea behind the standard of Judah and its emblem, the golden lion, *deora cenost*.[44]

NOTES

1. All quotations from *Exodus* are from the edition by Peter J. Lucas, *Exodus*, rev. ed. (London, 1994), by line numbers, although I do not accept Lucas's emendation of l. 128b, as discussed later.
2. For the relevant scriptural passages see Lucas's note to these lines.
3. For the poet's use of details from Num. 2 see Irving's edition, *The Old English Exodus* (1953; rpt. New York, 1970), 17.
4. "Christian Tradition in the Old English *Exodus*," *NM* 71 (1970), 541–70, at 557–58 and 566 [reprinted in the present volume—*ed.*]. Earl explains the anachronism in terms of the poem's patristic typology. The tradition I outline below suggests that the poet was convinced of the historicity of the Israelite's use of banners at the crossing; cf. Keating's remark cited in note 26.
5. [Judah is a lion's whelp: to the prey, my son, thou art gone up: resting thou hast couched as a lion, and as a lioness, who shall rouse him?] Ernst J. Groth, *Composition und Alter des altenglischen (angelsächsischen) Exodus* (Göttingen, 1883), 20, cited by Hauer (see note 7), 307. Biblical quotations are from *Biblia Sacra iuxta Vulgatam versionem*, 2 vols., ed. R. Weber, 3rd ed. (Stuttgart, 1983).
6. [Behold, the lion of the tribe of Judah, the root of David, has overcome . . .] Francis A. Blackburn, *Exodus and Daniel* (Boston, 1907), note to line 361.
7. "The Lion Standard in *Exodus*," *Archiv* 221 (1984), 306–11.
8. Hauer, p. 308. Irving, in "*Exodus* Retraced," in *Old English Studies in Honour of John C. Pope*, ed. Robert B. Burlin and Edward B. Irving

(Toronto, 1974), 203–23, at 215, suggests similarly that the lion is "the epitome of animal courage like the boars on a Germanic warrior's helmet."

9. This passage has been cited in a different connection by Fred C. Robinson, "Some Aspects of the *Maldon* Poet's Artistry," *JEGP* 75 (1976), 25–40, at 39. As Robinson remarks, Widukind's late-tenth-century narrative "draws heavily on Germanic songs and heroic legends for its matter."

10. Ginzberg, *The Legends of the Jews*, 6 vols. (Philadelphia, 1909-38) III, 230–36.

11. Ginzberg, 233.

12. Ginzberg, 234.

13. Ginzberg, 237–38. See further the *Encyclopaedia Judaica*, 16 vols. (Jerusalem, 1971–72) VI, 1334–35 (art. "Flag") and IV, 181–82 (art. "Banner"). The latter article reproduces an illumination from a Hebrew manuscript of *ca.* 1300 showing the banners of the four tribes, including the lion standard of Judah. Here Reuben's standard bears an eagle rather than the mandrake.

14. Despite the optimistic assessment of A. S. Cook, "Old English Literature and Jewish Learning," *MLN* 6 (1891), 71–77, I am aware of no convincing demonstration of direct influence of Jewish sources on Old English literature. See now also Frederick M. Biggs and Thomas N. Hall, "Traditions concerning Jamnes and Mambres in Anglo-Saxon England," *ASE* 25 (1996), 69–89, at 85–87. For a thorough survey of the knowledge of Hebrew in the early Middle Ages, see Matthias Thiel, "Grundlagen und Gestalten der Hebräischkenntnisse des frühen Mittelalters," *Studi Medievali* 3rd ser. 10 (1969), 3–212.

15. Aaron Mirsky, "On the Sources of the Anglo-Saxon *Genesis* and *Exodus*," *ES* 48 (1967), 385–97, had cited parallels from Hebrew sources. For the Latin parallel, see Irving, "New Notes on the Old English *Exodus*," *Anglia* 90 (1972), 289–324, at 311, and "*Exodus* Retraced," 208. Irving's statement in the latter article that this commentary was "probably composed in Ireland between 650 and 800" is mistaken. Although he cites F. Stegmüller, *Repertorium Biblicum Medii Aevi*, 11 vols. (Madrid, 1940-80) III, 8, Stegmüller in fact attributes it to Haymo of Auxerre. Irving has confused this commentary (Stegmüller III, no. 3114) with another Hebrews commentary (Stegmüller IV, no. 6368, and IX, no. 11028,1); cf. Michael Lapidge and Richard Sharpe, *A Bibliography of Celtic-Latin Literature 400–1200* [Dublin, 1985], nos. 760–61). See further Alexander Souter, *The Earliest Latin Commentaries on the Epistles of St. Paul* (Oxford, 1927), 209–10.

16. *Eine Würzburger Evangelienhandschrift*, ed. (partial) Karl Köberlin (Augsburg, 1891), 33. The manuscript attribution of this comment to

Jerome is incorrect. On this commentary, see Dáibhí Ó Cróinín, "Würzburg, Universitätsbibliothek, M.p.th.f. 61 and Hiberno-Latin Exegesis in the VIIIth Century," in *Lateinische Kultur im VIII. Jahrhundert. Traube-Gedenkschrift*, ed. Albert Lehner and Walter Berschin (St. Ottilien, 1989), 209–16.

17. Holthausen drew attention to the parallel from Comestor (see Irving's edition, note to lines 310ff.). The Irish poem, by Echtgus Úa Cúanáin, reads: "The tribe of Juda preceded all upon the wonderful unusual path. By reason of that sudden guidance they won kingship in their home in the north." I cite from the translation by Gerard Murphy, "Eleventh or Twelfth Century Irish Doctrine concerning the Real Presence," in *Medieval Studies Presented to Aubrey Gwynn, S.J.*, ed. J. A. Watt et al. (Dublin, 1961), 19–28, at 25. For the Irish text see A. G. van Hamel, "Poems from the Brussels MS. 5100-4," *Revue Celtique* 37 (1919), 345–52, at 345–49.

18. *Die Althochdeutschen Glossen*, ed. Elias Steinmeyer and Eduard Sievers, vol. 5 (Berlin, 1922), 234 (emphasis mine). The manuscript is Erlangen, Universitätsbibliothek 83 (Irm. 242), fol. 30b. See H. Fischer, *Katalog der Handschriften der Universitätsbibliothek Erlangen*, I: *Die lateinischen Pergamenthandschriften* (Erlangen, 1928), 90–91.

19. The *Leabhar Breac* biblical history has never been published in full, but can be consulted in the lithograph facsimile published by the Royal Irish Academy, *Leabhar Breac, The Speckled Book* (Dublin, 1876). According to Robin Flower, *Catalogue of Irish Manuscripts in the British Museum*, vol. 2 (London, 1926), 534, the Old Testament section of the *Leabhar Breac* biblical history "is a free, amplified prose rendering of the Saltair na Rann," but the information on the banners does not appear in that poem. See also James F. Kenney, *The Sources for the Early History of Ireland: Ecclesiastical* (1929; rpt. New York, 1966), 739 (no. 616). Kenney states that much of the biblical material in the *Leabhar Breac* dates back to the twelfth century.

20. *The History of Ireland by Geoffrey Keating*, ed. and trans. Patrick S. Dinneen, Irish Texts Society, vol. 9, pt. 3 (London, 1908), 125 and 127 (emphasis mine; for the Irish text, see pp. 124 and 126).

21. Keating, 127 (Irish text, p. 126; for Nephtalem's emblem Keating's Irish text reads *dam allaid*, which means "stag" rather than "wild ox," as Keating's translator has it. See the *Dictionary of the Irish Language: Compact Edition*, ed. E. G. Quin (Dublin, 1983), s.v. "dam" II. The editor prints the *Leabhar Breac* text of the poem in the textual notes, pp. 375–77. A seventeenth-century translation of the poem from Keating was printed by John O'Daly in the *Transactions of the Kilkenny Archaeological Society* 2 (1853), 379–80. Its flavor may be conveyed by quoting the stanza on Judah: "The Rampant Lyon did Juda Tribe, / With honour in the field

maintain; / Which free from feare and vndaunted mynes, / Their Banners
still kept from staine." John O'Donovan, *The Banquet of Dun na n-Gedh
and the Battle of Magh Rath* (Dublin, 1842), 343ff., printed Keating's
remarks on the standards along with a Latin rendering by John Lynch.
The stanza on Judah here reads, "Vexillis sobolis Judæ procera ferocis /
Forma leonis erat, stirpem hanc impunè lacessat / Nemo, lacertorum
magno, nam robore præstat."

22. Ohlgren, *Anglo-Saxon Textual Illustration: Photographs of Sixteen Manu-
scripts with Descriptions and Index* (Kalamazoo, MI, 1992), 291–92
(plates 3.43 and 3.44), with descriptions at p. 49. Robert Mark Harris, in an
unpublished dissertation on the marginal drawings of the Bury Psalter,
referred to Ginzberg for the tradition of the tribal emblems and standards,
and cited the OE *Exodus* for the lion standard of Judah: "The Marginal
Drawings of the Bury St. Edmunds Psalter (Rome, Vatican Library MS
Reg. lat. 12)," (diss., Princeton University, 1960), 467–69 and 538–39, n.
213. I was unaware of the Bury Psalter illustration and Harris's dissertation
when the original version of this essay was published in 1990. Harris does
not refer to the Latin and Irish parallels I have noted here, or discuss the
significance of the motif in *Exodus*.

23. Date from Helmut Gneuss, "A Preliminary List of Mansucripts Written or
Owned in England up to 1100," *ASE* 9 (1981), 1–60, at 58 (no. 912); Elz-
bieta Temple, *Anglo-Saxon Manuscripts 900–1066*, A Survey of Manu-
scripts Illuminated in the British Isles, 2 (London, 1976), 100, dates the
manuscript to the second quarter of the eleventh century.

24. Keating thought that the Irish "began the practice of having emblems, in
imitation of the children of Israel, who employed them in Egypt . . . when
thc children of Israel passed through the Red Sea, with Moses as their
chief leader" (*The History of Ireland*, 125). On the use of banners in Irish
tradition prior to the Norman invasion see G. A. Hayes-McCoy, *A History
of Irish Flags from Earliest Times* (Dublin, 1979), 15–18. Donald E.
Meek, "The Banners of the Fian in Gaelic Ballad Tradition," *Cambridge
Medieval Celtic Studies* 11 (Summer 1986), 29–69, at 33–36, surveys the
use of banners in Germanic and other cultures as well as Irish. Neither
Meek nor Hayes-McCoy refers to the tradition discussed here.

25. See J. E. Cross and S. I. Tucker, "Allegorical Tradition and the Old En-
glish *Exodus*," *Neophilologus* 44 (1960), 122–27, at 125–26.

26. See my note, "Moses, *manna mildost (Exodus*, 550a)," *NQ* 224 (1984),
440–43.

27. If the poet knew a list such as quoted above giving the emblems of each of
the tribes, he may have omitted reference to the standards of Reuben and
Simeon in order to stress the Christological significance of the Lion of
Judah, although Irving ("*Exodus* Retraced," 215) downplays the possible

spiritual interpretations of Judah's lion: "That it materializes here to stand for his tribe's newly found bravery and selfhood seems more important dramatically than any of the myriad meanings the exegetes assigned to this famous symbol."

28. *Beowulf and the Appositive Style* (Knoxville, 1985), 70. For a thorough study of the boar image in Germanic culture see Heinrich Beck, *Das Ebersignum im Germanischen*, Quellen und Forschungen zur Sprach- und Kulturgeschichte der Germanischen Völker, N.F. 16 (140) (Berlin, 1965), esp. 37–41 and 113 on banners with emblems of boars and other animals. In a paper entitled "The Boar on the Helmet" read at the 35th International Congress on Medieval Studies, Kalamazoo, MI, May 2000, Roberta Frank discussed the use of boar images as military insignia in Old English and Old Norse poetry, pointing to classical and early Germanic analogues. For the use of battle standards and animal emblems in Germanic tradition see further O. Schräder, "Fahne," in *Reallexikon der indogermanischen Altertumskunde*, 2 vols. (Berlin, 1917–29) I, 207–9; H. Reichert and K H Krüger, "Feldzeichen," in *Reallexikon der Germanischen Altertumskunde*, 2nd ed. (Berlin, 1973–) VIII, 307–26; and N. Lukman, "The Raven Banner and the Changing Ravens," *Classica et Medievalia* 19 (1958), 133–51.

29. Cf. Rosemary Cramp, "*Beowulf* and Archaeology," in *The Beowulf Poet: A Collection of Critical Essays*, ed. Donald K. Fry (Englewood Cliffs, NJ, 1968), 114–40, at 118 n. 13. Constantine does not abandon the boar image, for his troops still carry it when they approach the Holy Land (ll. 258–59). But the *eoforcumbol* is clearly subordinated to the Cross in the crucial opening scene. A similar contrast between the lion and boar emblems appears in *Exodus* if we accept Lucas's (and Blackburn's) emendation of MS *ofer holt* in line 157a to *eoferholt*, for by this reading the Israelites see behind them the pursuing force of the Pharaoh equipped with "boar-spears." Fred Robinson, however, has defended the manuscript reading *oferholt* as meaning "an overwhelming forest" of spears. See his "Two Aspects of Variation in Old English Poetry," in *Old English Poetry: Essays on Style*, ed. Daniel G. Calder (Berkeley, 1979), at 136–37. If *eoforholt* is correct, "boar-spear" would probably designate the *signum* type of standard, an inverted lance to which the emblem was affixed. The Egyptian banner is a *segn* (l. 172).

30. See William A. Chaney, *The Cult of Kingship in Anglo-Saxon England* (Manchester, 1970), pp. 121-47.

31. Chaney, pp. 144-45.

32. Adolf Harnack, *Militia Christi: The Christian Religion and the Military in the First Three Centuries*, trans. David McInnes Gracie (Philadelphia, 1981), p. 65.

33. *De Idolatria* 19, cited by Harnack, p. 76. (As the translator notes, Harnack renders the technical term *sacramentum* as "military oath"). Harnack (p. 56, n. 46) refers to two further passages from Tertullian in which "the military flags are expressly the rivals of the flag of Christ."

34. The Cross is frequently termed a *vexillum* or *signum*, specifically the military standard; see, in addition to Harnack, W. Seston, "Feldzeichen," in *Reallexikon für Antike und Christentum* (Stuttgart, 1950-) VII, 706-8; G. Q. Reijners, *The Terminology of the Holy Cross in Early Christian Literature* (Nijmegen, 1965), pp. 146, 157, and 192-93.

35. Ed. F. Leo, *Monumenta Germaniae Historica*, Auctores antiquissimi 4.1 (Berlin, 1881), p. 34.

36. The animal emblems which decorated the standards of the legions, the eagle and the dragon, were well-known to the Middle Ages through Isidore's *Etymologies* XVIII.iii, *De Signis*. This passage is cited by F. P. Pickering, *Literature and Art in the Middle Ages* (Coral Gable, Fl., 1970), pp. 260-61, part of an excellent discussion of the Christian use of the terms *signum* and *vexillum*. I owe the reference to Lucas, "The Cross in *Exodus*," p. 208, n. 32.

37. *De Abraham* 2.7.42, CSEL 32.1 (Vienna, 1897), 597; cited by Seston, "Feldzeichen," col. 706.

38. *Peristephanon*, ll. 134ff., cited by Pickering, 262. On the other hand, since Moses raised the brazen serpent in the wilderness *pro signo* (Num. 21:8), he is represented on the Meuse Valley Cross with a *draco* standard; here the serpent-dragon prefigures Christ (cf. John 3:14). See Pickering, 260–61.

39. *Liber Cathemerinon* V, ll. 53–56, ed. and trans. H. J. Thomson, *Prudentius*, 2 vols. (Cambridge, MA, 1949), I, 40–41.

40. Robinson, "Notes and Emendations to Old English Poetic Texts," *NM* 67 (1966), 356–64, at 358; rpt. in Robinson, *The Editing of Old English* (Oxford, 1994), 116–21, at 116–17.

41. Lucas, *Exodus*, note to line 127.

42. "Old English Christian Poetry: The Cross in *Exodus*," in *Famulus Christi: Essays in Commemoration of the Thirteenth Centenary of the Birth of the Venerable Bede*, ed. Gerald Bonner (London, 1976), 193–209, at 200.

43. Hauer, 308.

44. I would like to thank J. P. Hermann of the University of Alabama and J. R. Hall of the University of Mississippi for their comments on this paper.

The Structure
of the Old English *Daniel*

ROBERT T. FARRELL

This essay first appeared in NM *69 (1968), 533–59. Translations have been supplied by the editor in square brackets; notes have been renumbered consecutively.*

I

My purpose in this paper is to examine the internal structure of Old English *Daniel*. All of the poems in the Junius Manuscript were once associated with the name of Cædmon,[1] but differences in style indicate to most scholars that the attribution of *Genesis*, *Exodus*, *Daniel* and *Christ and Satan*[2] to a single author is incorrect. While each of the three companion pieces to the *Daniel* found in the manuscript has been edited separately or commented upon in some detail over the course of the past forty years,[3] little attention has been given to *Daniel*, other than two brief discussions in the course of larger works.

Gollancz gave some attention to the poem and the problems involved in the criticism of it in his facsimile edition of the Junius Manuscript (1927),[4] and Krapp presented his briefly stated views in the introduction to his edition of the text, which appeared in 1931.[5] Neither Krapp nor Gollancz had a high opinion of *Daniel*, especially in comparison with *Exodus*, which immediately precedes *Daniel* in the manuscript. Sir Israel Gollancz's opinion is as follows:

> The former [the author of the *Exodus*] stands alone by reason of his strongly marked characteristics of personality and style; for the latter [the author of *Daniel*] no great claim can be made for a high place among the

Biblical poets of Old England. His paraphrase and exposition are merito-
rious, but his poetical talent is slight.[6]

Krapp is much of the same mind, although his remarks are more of an
account of the contents of the poem than a criticism:

> It opens with a conventional epic formula, followed by a short account of
> the Jews in Jerusalem (1–45) as introductory to the main narrative . . . .
> The story moves along in regular order, except that ll. 279–439 have the
> appearance of being an interruption.[7]

Theodore Blackburn had something to say on the structure of *Daniel* in
1907, when he edited *Exodus and Daniel*:

> The *Daniel*, on the other hand, [as contrasted with the *Exodus*] lacks these
> elements of strength and originality, and cannot he ranked high in poetic
> quality. It is a collection of stories, well told, to be sure, but in a rather
> prosaic way, and owing their merit as stories, when all is said, chiefly to
> the original. The author makes use, as a matter of course, of the amplifi-
> cations that are the stock in trade of all the Old English versifiers of Latin
> stories. But his additions are chiefly repetitious. Even a situation so dra-
> matic as that of the Hebrew youths in the furnace does not seem to rouse
> his imagination.[8]

The general impression gained from a reading of these criticisms is that
the *Daniel* poet follows his source closely, and in an uninspired way. The
art of the poem, such as it is, is due to the source, not the poet. This view
is not solidly based. As study of the relations of the poem with the Old
Testament Book of Daniel reveals, the poet follows the general order of
events as they take place in the course of the first chapters of the book,
but he has made important changes in stress. The poem has a sharply
defined structure of its own which is at best only implicit in the Bible
account. The poet probably did not use the Vulgate, but rather some Old
Latin text.[9] However, since a comparison of the extant fragments of the
Old Latin with the Vulgate reveals no difference in the order of events or
in other essentials, the Vulgate will be used throughout for purposes of
comparison.

   Opinions have differed as to the importance of the Book of Daniel
for Christians. Jerome felt that the book was most important for the
prophecies it contained, most especially those about the Messiah.[10]

Jerome seems to have considered the narrative portions of the text (chapters 1–6) as less important. The major prophecies are found in chapters seven to twelve.[11] The difference between the earlier and later chapters of *Daniel* has led modern scholars to divide the book into two parts. Father Cuthbert Lattey, S.J., describes the structure of *Daniel* as follows:

> The main division of the book is into narratives (cc. i–vi) and visions (cc. vii–xii). There are six main narratives, corresponding to the first six chapters, and four visions, of which the last occupies three chapters.[12]

The Old English poet clearly saw this division, and based the construction of his poem on the narrative rather than on the prophetic chapters. If it is true, as Father Robert McNally, S.J., holds, that Jerome's *Commentary on the Book of Daniel* was "the traditional interpretation of Daniel in the early Middle Ages,"[13] then the poet is displaying considerable freedom of mind in his interpretation.[14] The poet's cursory treatment of the only major prophetic passage to appear in the course of the first six chapters, Nabuchodonosor's dream of the statue and Daniel's subsequent interpretation of it, further indicates his lack of interest in the prophetic matter in the book.[15] It is quite possible that the poet intended to limit his material still further, to the first five, rather than the first six, chapters of the Book of Daniel. If this is so, then the poem is complete, or nearly complete, as we have it. There is a balanced narrative in the first five chapters. The first four deal with the struggle of forces of good and evil, with Daniel and the three children as protagonists, and Nabuchodonosor as antagonist. Chapter five gives an account of the end of Baltassar, Nabuchodonosor's descendant, after the prophecy of his fall given by Daniel. The sixth chapter, while it undoubtedly must be counted as a part of the narrative portion, has quite a different topic, the trials of Daniel under Darius the Mede. The first five chapters, then, have a unity of their own, since they have as their subject the struggle of Daniel and the three children, as they oppose the wickedness of the last two Chaldean kings of Babylon. The poem, as it stands, has a balance of beginning and end, since it opens with the fall of the Jews and ends with the fall of Baltassar.[16]

The manuscript offers no definite indication that the poem is ended at leaf 212 of the book, the last page on which the text of *Daniel* appears. There is no reason to expect any such indication, since neither *Genesis* nor *Exodus* (the two poems which precede *Daniel*) has any clear indication of ending. It is only after the last poem in the manuscript, which is

called (not with great accuracy) *Christ and Satan*, that the notation
"Finit Liber II. Amen" appears. Since this poem was probably added at a
later time, and since it was copied by other scribes than the person who
copied *Genesis, Exodus,* and *Daniel*,[17] such a notation has little meaning
for the student of *Daniel.* Gollancz suspected that there is a leaf missing
between what are now numbered leaves 212 and 213 of the manuscript.
He felt that "the conclusion of Liber I should have been indicated, even
if merely by a scribal addition of the word 'finit.' "[18] Two considerations
cast doubt on this contention. First of all, there are many indications that
the Junius XI manuscript was never finished. The earlier poems in the
manuscript, particularly *Genesis,* have many illustrations, and occa-
sional illuminated initial letters appear. The leaves on which *Daniel* was
written often have vacant spaces, undoubtedly left for similar illustra-
tions which were never completed. If neglect for such larger considera-
tions is evident, little can be made of so small a point as the inclusion or
omission of a scribal *finit.* Secondly, it is also quite possible that the
scribe of *Genesis, Exodus,* and *Daniel* never considered his work as a
"first book." The "Finit Liber II. Amen." at the end of *Christ and Satan*
may represent *only* the viewpoint of one of the scribes of the later poem,
as he completed the task of adding this last work to the already copied
poems.

Krapp offered other suggestions as to the contents of the "missing
leaf." He felt that the poem "is incomplete at the end, probably through
loss in the manuscript. The subject matter of the missing part was pre-
sumably Daniel's interpretation of the writing on the wall and the slay-
ing of Belshazzar. This would have made a fitting climax for the
poem"[19] Krapp obviously proposed, then, that the poet meant to present
only the first five chapters of the Old Testament book as his subject mat-
ter. Both Krapp and Gollancz do not seem to think that more than a sin-
gle page at most is missing from the poem as we have it.[20] There is some
reason to suppose that no part of the poem has been lost. No immedi-
ately evident indication of incompleteness can be seen, such as a break
in the middle of a word or phrase. The last lines are the completion of a
sentence spoken by Daniel, as he castigates Baltassar for his sins:

and þu lignest nu   þæt sie lifgende,
se ofer deoflum   dugeþum wealdeð.   (763–64)[21]
[And you deny now that He exists, who rules in majesty over the devils.]

A comparison of the Vulgate with the Old English text shows that lines 675–764 are derived from the fifth chapter of the Bible account. In the Vulgate version the progression of events is chronological. In the poem there is an anticipation of the destruction of Babylon, as a punishment for the sins of its ruler. An outline of events as they take place in the fifth chapter of the Vulgate and in the last eighty-nine lines of the poem makes this clear:

The Poem	**Vulgate, Daniel, Chapter 5**
1. The first mention of Baltassar is combined with a forecast of his destruction (675–679)	1. Baltassar has a feast, using the sacred vessels of the Jews (1–4).
2. The Medes and Persians are to destroy Babylon, and the plots of the king of the Medes (presumably Darius) are discussed in some detail (680–694).	2. The writing appears, which none can interpret until Daniel comes to the council (5–16)
3. Baltassar commits his acts of impiety (695–716).	3. Daniel explains the power God and the nature of Baltassar's offense (17–24) and interprets the writing on the wall (25–28).
4. The handwriting appears and Daniel is summoned (717–740)	4. Daniel is rewarded, and Baltassar killed; Darius the Mede succeeds him (29–31).
5. Daniel explains why Baltassar and his people will be destroyed (740–764).	

What the poet has done is to change the order of events so that the destruction of Babylon is forecast in some detail, although the actual event is not reported in its proper chronological order, as the story goes in the Bible. The only detail left out is the text of the writing on the wall, and Daniel's interpretation of it. The writing is described as *worda gerynu, baswe bocstafas* (722b–723a), that is, riddles in words, bright red letters. Perhaps this description indicates that the poet is more inter-

ested in the symbolic content of the writing than in the literal interpreta-
tion.[22] The conclusions that can be drawn from the above discussion are
as follows: (1) The poem may be complete as it has come down to us.
(2) The missing portion, if indeed the work is incomplete, is very proba-
bly of no great length. (3) It would seem possible that the poet did intend
to limit the subject matter of his poem to the first five chapters of the Old
Testament book, those narratives which deal with the struggle of Daniel
and the three children as protagonists, with Nabuchodonosor and Baltas-
sar as antagonists. A close study of the text reveals that it is the conflict
between these principals which is the real source of the structure of Old
English *Daniel*.

II

The first thirty-two lines of the poem have no source in the Bible.[23]
These lines are particularly important, because they introduce central
themes about which the action of the poem devolves. What is more, the
words used to describe the actions of the Jews in the opening portion of
the poem are to appear time and again in the text. As the passage is
developed, an opposition is set up between the deceits of the Devil and a
knowledge of God's law. The Jews have lived happily, as long as they
kept the covenant (*hyra fæder wære*, 10b–11a), but they swiftly fell from
grace when they turned from their skills in the law (*æcræftas*, 19a) and
chose to follow the deceits of the Devil (*curon deofles cræft*, 32b). They
did so while they were drunk at a banquet[24] and pride took control of
their minds:

> . . . hie wlenco onwod   æt winþege
> deofoldædum,   druncne geðohtas. (17–18)
> [Pride and drunken thoughts took control of them at their feasting with
> devilish deeds]

Though God offered them His wisdom through angels,[25] they main-
tained their faith only until a desire for earthly bliss overcame eternal
counsel:

> Hie þære snytro   soð gelyfdon
> lytle hwile,   oðþæt hie langung beswac
> eorðan dreamas   eces rædes.   (28–30)

[They believed in the truth of that wisdom for a little while, until longing
for earthly pleasure defrauded them of eternal wisdom.]

The progression of the Jews towards evil, then, might be outlined as
follows:

1. Happiness and final salvation are the result of the faithful
   observance of *æ* (Divine law) and the maintenance of the
   covenant, *wær*.
2. Divine counsel and knowledge are required for the continu-
   ance of such a state of happiness, and for the attainment of
   final salvation.
3. The Jews fell from grace when they took up dissolute habits of
   drunken feasting.
4. Their fall is described as a turning from their practice of God's
   law, *æcræft*, to the deceits of the Devil, *deofles cræft*.

As the action progresses, it becomes clear that some such pattern as
this is the basis of the poet's moral theme. Daniel and the three children
represent a positive morality; Nabuchodonosor, Baltassar, and the Jews
(as they are presented being led into the captivity) are depicted as evil-
doers. The conflict is made more explicit by the use of a series of
weighted words which appear throughout the poem, always in similar
contexts. Through the frequent use of these terms, the poet gives them a
specific semantic importance, a limited and particular meaning. This
device is a major unifying element in his work.

The main words which are used in this way are those which deal
with wisdom and divinely inspired knowledge. The principal terms are
gleaw (adj.), *ræd* (noun), *soð* (noun/adj.), *snotor* (adj.), *wis* (adj.), *wis-
dom* (noun), and *lar* (noun). Another pair of words deals with the law, *æ*,
and the covenant, *wær*. One word, *cræft*, is interesting since it is devel-
oped in two directions during the course of the poem, by a distinction
between *godes cræft* and *deofles cræft*. Each of these words will be
taken up in turn. In each case the passage from the first thirty-two lines
which employs the key word will be quoted at the head. Throughout, the
words to be discussed will be italicized, for emphasis.

Words for Divine Counsel and Wisdom (*gleaw, ræd, soð, snotor,
wis, wisdom, lar*)

Oft he þam leodum   to *lare* sende,
heofonrices weard,   halige gastas,
þa þam werude   *wisdom* budon.
Hie þære *snytro   soð* gelyfdon
lytle hwile,   oðþæt hie langung beswac
eorðan dreamas   eces *rædes*.   (25–30)
[Often he, Guardian of the heavenly kingdom, sent that people holy spir-
its for instruction, who offered wisdom to the host. They believed in the
truth of that wisdom for a little while, until longing for earthly pleasure
defrauded them of eternal wisdom.]

As we scan the poem, many references are made to such divinely
inspired knowledge as the Jews refused. Nabuchodonosor orders that the
youths who were most learned in the books of the commandments be
brought to him:

Het ða secan   sine gerefan
geond Israela   earme lafe,
hwilc þære geogoðe   *gleawost wære*
boca bebodes,[26]   þe þær brungen wæs.   (79–82)
[Then he ordered his officials to seek out among the wretched remnant of
the Israelites which of the youths that had been brought there were wisest
in the books of the law.]

The king's retainers find three young men[27] who are wise in godly
knowledge (*freagleawe*, 88). Their duty will be to reveal wisdom to the
king:

þa hie þam wlancan   wisdom sceoldon,
weras Ebrea,   wordum cyðan,
higecræft heane   þurh halig mod.   (96–98)
[Then the men of the Hebrews were required to reveal to the proud king in
words their wisdom and their profound thoughts, through a holy mind.]

When Nabuchodonosor seeks an interpretation of his first dream of the
statue, his retainers are unable to help him. Their learning has a specific
quality. They are the devil's sorcerers, who are outstanding for their
practice of witchcraft (*þa wiccungdom widost bæron*, 121), and their
knowledge is useless,[28] until Daniel arrives, the Lord's chosen one, wise
and steadfast in truth (*se wæs drihtne gecoren, / snotor and soðfæst*,

150b–151a). He has been inspired through the prophecy of a holy spirit, who had been sent by God:

> him God sealde   gife of heofnum
> þurh hleoðorcwyde   haliges gastes.   (154–155)
> [God gave him grace from heaven, through the prophecy of the Holy Spirit.]

Despite Daniel's best efforts, Nabuchodonosor will not believe in the Lord's might (168–70). The king sets up an idol, because he is not wise, but fierce and without counsel:

> *for þam þe gleaw ne wæs,*   gumrices weard,
> reðe and rædleas,   riht . . . [29]   (176–177)

The same sort of ignorance is the lot of Nabuchodonosor's people. The poet displays what appears to be sympathy toward them, which calls to mind the *Beowulf* poet's description of the Danes in their return to heathen worship under the stress of Grendel's attacks;[30] the Babylonian people followed their lord and knew no better counsel:

> Onhnigon to þam herige   hæðne þeode,
> wurðedon wihgyld,   *ne wiston wræstran ræd*
> *efndon unrihtdom,*   swa hyra aldor dyde,
> *mane gemenged,   mode gefrecnod.*
> Fremde folcmægen,   swa hyra frea ærest,
> *unræd efnde,*   (him þæs æfter becwom
> yfel endelean),   *unriht dyde.*   (181–187)
> [The heathen people bowed down before the image, honored an idol— knowing no better wisdom they wrought wickedness, as their lord did, entangled in sin, emboldened in mind. The tribes of people did as their lord before them, carried out their folly (later an evil reckoning befell them for that) and did wrong.]

The young bearers of God's word (*godes spelbodan*, 229), Annanias, Azarias, and Misael, refuse to worship the idol because they know the eternal Lord Almighty on high (*wiston drihten / ecne uppe, ælmihtigne*, 194b–195). After Nabuchodonosor's speech expressing astonishment at seeing four men walking about in the fire, that is, the three and the angel who protected them, the poet adds a speech by a character who does not even exist in the Bible account. He is a high official at the court, and his particular abilities are indicated by his title, *cyninges ræswa.*[31] The speech is sufficiently important to quote in full:

Ða cwæð se ðe wæs   cyninges ræswa,
wis and wordgleaw: "þæt is wundra sum
þæt we ðær eagum   on lociað.
Geðenc, ðeoden min,   þine gerysna!
ongyt georne   hwa þa gife sealde
gingum gædelingum!   Hie god herigað,
anne ecne,   and ealles him
be naman gehwam   on neod sprecað,
ðanciað þrymmes   þristum wordum,
cweðað he sie ana   ælmihtig god,
witig wuldorcyning,   worlde and heofona.
Aban þu beornas,   brego Caldea,
ut of ofne.   Nis hit owihtes god
þæt hie sien on þam laðe   leng þonne þu þurfe."   (416–429)
[Then counselor of the king spoke, wise and prudent of speech: "This is a great marvel which we behold with our own eyes. Consider, my lord, your proper duty! Understand who it is that has given this grace to the youths! They worship God, One and Eternal, and call on Him earnestly with every name, praise His majesty with eager words, say that He alone is Almighty God, Wise King of glory, of earth and heaven. Summon these men forth from the furnace, prince of the Chaldeans! It is not at all good that they should linger in that torture longer than you have need."]

It must be noted that this is the only time in the poem that a character other than Daniel and the three children is spoken of as *wis and word-gleaw,* wise and inspired in word. This invention of a character is perhaps necessary because the king and all of his people have been pictured as deeply involved in evil deeds. At any rate, the point of the advice is significant in the structure of the poem: The king is urged to recognize the power of the Lord God, to follow the example of the three youths, who call upon him by every name, and are thus protected. When the wise young men (*gleawmode guman,* 439) came forth from the furnace, they instructed the heathens in true speech, and by many miracles and signs.[32] Only then did Nabuchodonosor accept the true God. This is a considerable change from the Bible version, where the king is presented as being converted just by seeing the miracle of the preservation of the youths. In the poem, Nabuchodonosor then goes on to seek a true account of how God's messengers (*godes spelbodan,* 464) escaped from the fire. The king closes his exhortation with a reference to Daniel, having commanded his people to believe in the might and miracles of God.[33] He praises the prophet's true interpretations, and explains how the inspiration for them had come to him:

> forþam ælmihtig   eacenne gast
> in sefan sende,   *snyttro cræftas.*   (484–485)
> [because the Almighty send a more ample spirit and the skill of wisdom into his breast.]

When Nabuchodonosor has another dream, he calls upon Daniel once more, because his skill in wisdom and the great extent of his knowledge are known to the prince:

> Þa wæs to ðam dome   Daniel haten,
> *godes spelboda.*   Him wæs gæst geseald,
> hulig of heofonum,   oo hio hyge trymede
> *On þam drihtenweard   deopne wisse*
> *sefan sidne geþanc   and snytro cræft,*
> *wisne wordcwyde.*   (531–536a)
> [Then Daniel, God's messenger, was summoned to judgment. A holy spirit was given to him from heaven, which strengthened his mind. The lord knew that in him was a deep spirit, broad thought and the skill of wisdom, wise speeches.]

After Daniel has finished the account of the king's dream of the Tree[34] he advises the king to call to mind firmly establish counsel (*Gehyge þu, frea min, fæstlicne ræd,* 585). When the Babylonians had followed their lord in the worship of a golden statue, they too were unaware of a better counsel: *ne wiston wræstran ræd* (182b). When we turn back to the beginning of the poem, we find that the Jews did have *ræd,* but that they lost it when they deliberately chose other values:

> Hie þære snytro   soð gelyfdon
> lytle hwile,   *oðþæt hie langung beswac*
> *eorðan dreamas   eces rædes* . . .   (28–30)

There is still another important later appearance of the term *ræd.* After the king had undergone his punishment, he accepted the true God. It is only after his conversion, the end result of a long and hard process of education, that the poet tells us:

> him frean godes,   in gast becwom
> *rædfæst sefa*,   ða he to roderum beseah.   (650–651)
> [in his spirit came, from the Lord God, a spirit fast in counsel, when he
> looked up to the heavens.]

The selective application of these terms for wisdom is maintained with
absolute consistency. Daniel and the three are always *snotor, soðfæst,
wis, wordgleaw*: They alone have divinely inspired knowledge. The
description of the invented *ræswa* as *wis and wordgleaw*, coupled with
the tone and import of his speech, show the importance of this series of
interrelated weighted words, since the division between the two oppos-
ing forces is made even more evident by this newly inserted character.
When Nabuchodonosor is described as having a *rædfæst sefa*, only after
his extended punishment, the evidence in favor of the semantic impor-
tance given to these words by the poet becomes extremely striking.[35]

III

Words for the Law and the Covenant (*æ* and *wær*)

> þa hie [*the Jewish people*] æcræftas   ane forleton,
> metodes mægenscipe,   swa no man scyle
> his gastes lufan   wið gode dælan.   (19–21)
> [Then they abandoned at once the teachings of the law, the authority of
> the Lord, as a man should never separate his spirit's love from God.]

The interrelated set of words denoting divinely inspired wisdom is the
most important in the poem; but, in addition, the poet's careful use of
words for the law, *æ*, the covenant, *wær*, and skill, *cræft* (both godly
and infernal), can also be observed. In the case of his use of *æ*, the Old
English author makes it clear that he has a particular meaning in mind.
Æ is a general law of good conduct, the observance of divine com-
mandments. It is a rule for all men to follow, not just a particular sect.
For the Jews, *æ* is related to the particular agreement (*wær*) made
between them and God. As long as they maintained their pledges, they
were favored:

> þenden þæt folc mid him   hiera fæder wære
> healdan woldon,   wæs him hyrde god   (10–11)

The three youths are keepers of the covenant:

> Wæron wærfæste;   wiston drihten
> ecne uppe,   ælmihtigne   (194–195)

Neither of these details can be paralleled in the corresponding por-
tions of the Vulgate account. But although the law (*æ*) is related with
the covenant when the Jews are dealt with, the Old English poet shows
that the divinely established law, though not the covenant, was the rule
for all men. The Jews fell when they left off *æcræftas*, skills in the
law:

> þa hie æcræftas   ane forleton,
> metodes mægenscipe;   swa no man scyle
> his gastes lufan   wið god dælan!   (19–21)

Annanias, Azarias, and Misael are often described as attentive to the
rules of conduct proper under *æ*. When the three children first appear in
the poem, they are characterized as noble lads, steadfast in the law,
young and good:

> þa hie þær fundon   þry freagleawe
> æðele cnihtas   and æfæste,
> ginge and gode   in godsæde.   (88–90)
> [Then they found there three wise, noble, and pious youths, young and
> good in their divine lineage.]

When they refuse to worship the idol which the pagan king has just set
up, the poet makes their motivation clear in two passages. They are the
children of Abraham, keepers of the covenant, who recognize the true
God; they wish to remain in God's favor,[36] and do not fail to persevere in
their belief, even in the face of the most dire persecution:

> Hogedon georne
> þæt æ godes   ealle gelæste,
> and ne awacedon   wereda drihtne,
> ne þan mæ gehwurfe   in hæðendom,
> ne hie to facne   freoðo wilnedan,
> þeah þe him se bitera deað   geboden wære.   (218b–223)
> [They eagerly sought to keep entirely the law of God, and not forsake the

Lord of hosts; no more would they convert to paganism, nor ask for truce
with that evil thing, though a bitter death were proclaimed for them.]

These lines have no explicit parallel in the Vulgate.

Daniel is conscious of the law, just as his countrymen are. He is
described as *æcræftig* in line 741, and, if Krapp's emendation of
arcræftig ar in line 550 to *æcræftig* be accepted, as seems plausible from
the other appearances of this phrase in the text, this epithet is applied
twice to the prophet. By his excision of Vulgate material, the poet gives
some indications that the *æ* followed by Daniel and the three is not to be
particularized as the Old, or Mosaic, Law. The first chapter of the Vul-
gate has an account of the dietary problems of Daniel and his brethren
which is some nine verses in length (1:8–16). This is left out entirely in
the poem. There is positive evidence for the extension of *æ* as a rule for
non-Jews as well. In a passage which has no source in the Vulgate,
Nabuchodonosor is accused of not following the law:

> þa wæs breme   Babilone weard,
> mære and modig   ofer middangeard,
> egesful ylda bearnum.   *No he æ fremede,*
> *ac in oferhygde   æghwæs lifde.*   (104–107)
> [then the ruler of Babylon was infamous, notorious and proud over the
> earth, terrifying to the sons of men. He kept no law, but lived in arrogance
> in every way.]

There are other indications that the author intended a relationship in kind
between the offenses of the Jews and those of the two rulers of Babylon.
In his greatly compressed version of the canticle of the three children,
the particular nature of the offence of the Jewish nation is made clear,
though this specific charge is not made in the Vulgate:

> We þæs lifgende
> worhton on worulde,   eac þon wom dyde
> user yldran;   for oferhygdum
> bræcon bebodo   *burhsittendum**
> had oferhogedon   halgan lifes.   (295b–299)
> [We the living wrought this in the world, and likewise our ancestors com-
> mited sin; in their arrogance they broke the covenant for city-dwellers and
> scorned the calling of a holy life.]

*MS form; Krapp emends to *burhsittende.*

The same sort of crime was performed by the rulers of Babylon who fell from their high states because of pride; they, too, broke the commands for dwellers in cities and were driven from their walled fortresses for their respective boasts. The poet of *Daniel* sees *æ* as a universal set of precepts; he is interested in the continuity of the moral implications of the law, rather than in Judaic ritual observance, and he feels that this law is a rule of conduct for all men.

IV

Skill (*cræft*)

> sylfe forleton
> drihtnes domas, curon deofles cræft. (31b–32)
> [they themselves abandoned the Lord's judgments, and chose the devil's craft.]

The first appearance of this term, and the essential opposition set up in the very first lines of the poem, are discussed above. The next appearance of *cræft*, in line 83, is ambiguous. Nabuchodonosor wanted the young men to learn skills: *wolde þæt þa cnihtas cræft leornedon*. This seems natural enough. The corresponding passage in the Vulgate helps to make the situation even clearer. The pagan king sent his retainer, Asphenez, to bring in the most noble and learned of the young Hebrews, that they might serve as his retainers:

> Et ait rex Asphenez praepositio eunuchorum ut introduceret de filiis Israel et de semine regio et tyrannorum pueros in quibus nulla esset macula, decoros forma et eruditos omni sapientia, cautos scientia et doctos disciplina, et qui possent stare in palatio regis, ut doceret eos litteras et linguam Chaldaeorum. (1:3–4)
> [And the king spoke to Ashpenaz the master of the eunuchs, that he should bring some of the children of Israel, and of the king's seed and of the princes, children in whom there was no blemish, well favored, and skillful in all wisdom, acute in knowledge, and instructed in science, and such as might stand in the king's palace, that he might teach them the learning and the tongue of the Chaldeans.]

The boys are to learn the secular skills of the Chaldeans who are described as the devil's sorcerers (*deofolwitgan*, 128).[37] The youths are to reveal their skill of mind to the prince (*hygecræft*, 98). The next

use of *cræft*, in line 225, is sufficiently clear. The youths are con-
demned to the furnace because they defied the cræftas of Nabu-
chodonosor. In line 327, God is called upon to display his *cræft* and
miht.[38] In line 393, the poet gives a curious modification of his source
in the use of *cræft*:

> And þec haligra   heortan cræftas,
> soðfæstra gehwæs   sawle and gastas,
> lofiað liffrean.[39]   (393–395a)
> [And let the hearts' virtues of holy men, souls and spirits of every righ-
> teous man praise you, Lord of life.]

Save for the use of *runcræftig* (skilled in mysteries, or magic, 733) as a
description of Baltassar's counselors, all other instances of *cræft* are
applied to Daniel. He has *snytro cræft* (skill in wisdom),[40] God's *cræft*
(737), and is skilled in the law (*æcræftig*, 550[41] and 741). Though some
of the contexts and uses of *cræft* are ambiguous, there is sufficient evi-
dence that an opposition is carried out, and that there are two forms of
cræft that are in conflict, God's and the devil's.

V

The author's use of certain terms as constants is not his only modi-
fication of the Bible story. There are important themes which are devel-
oped in detail and which add much to the structural unity of the work. A
point-for-point similarity can be seen in the author's sketching of the
causes leading up to the fall of the Jews, and the falls of the two leaders
of Babylon. The major fault of Nabuchodonosor is sufficiently clear, as
the trials he has experienced are recounted in the fourth chapter of the
Vulgate Daniel. The prophet had interpreted the king's dream of the tree
stripped of its branches and cut back to the roots as a prediction of the
punishments Nabuchodonosor would have to endure. One year later, the
ruler of Babylon, walking about in his garden, asserted his pride of pos-
session. It was then that his punishment was meted out:

> Omnia haec venerunt super Nabuchodonosor regem. Post finem mensium
> duodecem, in aula Babilonis deambulabat. Responditque rex, et ait:
> "Nonne haec est Babylon magna, quam ego aedificavi in domum regni, in
> robore fortitudinis meae, et in gloria decoris mei?" Cumque sermo adhuc

esset in ore regis, vox de caelo ruit: "Tibi dicitur, Nabuchodonosor rex:
regnum tuum transibit a te." (4:25–28)
[All these things came upon king Nabuchodonosor. At the end of twelve
months he was walking in the palace of Babylon. And the king answered,
and said: "Is this not the great Babylon, which I have built to be the seat of
the kingdom, by the strength of my power, and in the glory of my excel-
lence?" And while the word was yet in the king's mouth, a voice came
down from heaven: "To thee, O king Nabuchodonsor, it is said: Thy king-
dom shall pass from thee."]

The modification which the poet has made of these lines indicates very
well the degree of freedom with which he reworked his materials:

No þæs fela Daniel   to his drihtne gespræc
soðra worda   þurh snytro cræft,
þæt þæt a oo rion   reccan wolde,
middangeardes weard,   ac his mod astah,
heah fram heortan;   he þæs hearde ongeald!
Ongan ða gyddigan   þurh gylp micel
Caldea cyning   þa he ceastergeweorc,
Babilone burh   on his blæde geseah,
Sennera feld   sidne bewindan,
heah hlifigan;   þæt se heretyma
werede geworhte   þurh wundor micel,
weard ða anhydig   ofer ealle men,
swiðmod in sefan,   for ðære sundorgife
þe him god sealde,   gumena rice,
world to gewealde   in wera life:
"Ðu eart seo micle   and min seo mære burh
þe ic geworhte   to wurðmyndum,
rume rice.   Ic reste on þe,
eard and eðel,   agan wille."
Ða for ðam gylpe   gumena drihten
forfangen wearð   and on fleam gewat
ana on oferhyd   ofer ealle men.   (593–614)

[Daniel did not speak to his lord so many true words through his power of
wisdom that this powerful lord, lord of the earth, would ever pay him
heed; instead his pride grew, lofty in his heart; he paid cruelly for that!
Then the king of the Chaldeans began to brag with great boast when he
saw the great city walls, the fortress of Babylon in its prosperity, stretched
out broadly across the plain of Shinar, towering aloft, that he, warrior

king, had built for that host as a great marvel, he became arrogant above
all men, headstrong in his heart on account on the special gift that God
had given him, the power over men and a world to wield in this human
life: "You are the mighty and famous city of mine, which I have built to
my own honor, a spacious kingdom. I will have rest in you, a dwelling and
a home." Then for his boasting the lord of men was stricken and went off
in flight, alone in his pride above all men.]

What was in the Vulgate account a simple narration of events becomes a
highly dramatic passage. Before the utterance of the king's prideful
boast, the poet adds a passage which intensifies the impression of Nabu-
chodonosor's hardness of heart. Despite Daniel's divinely wise words of
advice (*snytro cræft*) the king's pride mounts up, and he begins to make
boasts about his kingdom. The important note that this high-towering
citadel is held only as a gift from God is added at this point by the poet,
after he had again stressed the king's pride by the use of the intensifying
adjectives *anhydig* and *swið mod*. Another new note is added in Nabu-
chodonosor's speech (which was in the form of a simple question in the
Vulgate) when the poet has the king state: "Ic reste on þe, / eard and eðel
agan wile" (610b–611). These words are to become profoundly ironic in
the course of the events which follow. As a final point, the Old English
poet again stresses the reason for the king's plight, and the wretchedness
of his solitary state:

> þa for ðam gylpe   gumena dryhten
> forfangen wearð   and on fleam gewat,
> ana on oferhyd   ofer ealle men.   (612–614)

In the course of this passage, the king of Babylon had lost that which
was most precious to him, his homeland and ancestral kingdom, the
eðel.

When Nabuchodonosor comes to see the true position of the Lord
God, he is restored to his throne and established in a state which would
suit the tastes of a Germanic *dryhten* very well indeed:

> Siððan weardode   wide rice,
> heold hæleða gestreon   and þa hean burh,
> frod, foremihtig   folca ræswa,
> Caldea cyning,   oðþæt him cwelm gesceod.   (664–667)

[He afterwards guarded his broad kingdom, held the treasures of men and the lofty city, old, very mighty ruler of his people, king of the Chaldeans, until death destroyed him.]

Old and wise (*frod*), the advisor of the people (*folces ræswa*), he comes back to his citadel and has control over the treasures of men. The pride which plays so important a role in this description of the fall of Nabuchodonosor is stressed elsewhere in the poem, both through the characterizing adjectives which are applied to the ruler and in more extended passages of description. The connective passage which the poet has supplied to join the materials drawn from the first and second, then the third and fourth chapters of the Vulgate are examples of this sort of amplification.[42] The development of the parallel themes of the king's absolutely solitary wanderings and his later conversion to truth is considerably more explicit in the poem than in the Bible[43] and the Old English author enlarges upon the other unpleasant character traits of the king, such as his fierceness. In both the Bible account and the poem, Nabuchodonosor and Baltassar are punished because of their offenses against God and his people. They commit acts of impiety because of their great pride. As I have indicated in the course of the above discussion, the *Daniel* poet sets out several major themes in the course of the first thirty-two lines of the poem. These give an account of the fall of the Jews, couched in language which is of particular significance and weight. The Jews fell because they turned to evil deeds, under the influence of drink, in a state of pride. These three notes are also found in the description of the falls of Nabuchodonosor and Baltassar. Though no charge of drunkenness is made against Nabuchodonosor in the Bible, the poet describes him in a besotted state (*þa onwoc wulfheart, se æt wingal swæf*, 116). Baltassar's offense is made more striking than it is in the Vulgate as well. The king's pride is indicated when he is first mentioned. Baltassar's particular offense is dual in the poem: He profanes the sacred vessels of the Jews (as he does in the Vulgate version), but he also maintains that his gods are more powerful than the Lord God of the Israelites:

Ða wearð bliðemod   burga aldor,
gealp gramlice   gode on andan,
cwæð þæt his hergas   hyrran wæron
and mihtigran   mannum to friðe
þonne Israela   ece drihten.   (712–716)
[So the lord of cities grew happy, boasted greatly to the anger of God, said

that his idols were higher and more mighty in protecting the people than
the eternal Lord of the Israelites.]

This further darkening of Baltassar's character seems to accomplish two
ends. First, it makes him more evil than his predecessor, which helps to
explain his destruction, while Nabuchodonosor escaped with a lighter
punishment. Secondly, it adds a climatic quality to the major events in
the poem: The Jews were saved after their long suffering, Nabu-
chodonosor was granted divine knowledge (*ræd*) after he recognized the
true God, but Baltassar fell, for he blasphemed without repenting.

There is a balance of beginning and end in the Old English poem,
as a number of similarities can be noted when the fall of the Jews and the
end of Chaldean Babylon are compared. Daniel lists the offenses of the
pagan king, in a passage which comes very close to the end of the poem
as we now have it:

> "þu for anmedlan   in æht bere
> huslfatu halegu,   on hand werum.
> On þam ge deoflu   drincan ongunnon,
> ða ær Israela   in æ hæfdon
> æt godes earce,   oðþæt hie gylp beswac,
> windruncen gewit,   swa þe wurðan sceal."   (747–752)
>
> ["In your arrogance you put the holy sacrificial vessels into the hands of
> men. You devils began to drink from those vessels which the Israelites
> kept according to the law by the ark of God, until boasting betrayed them,
> a wit drunk with wine, as shall happen to you."]

The Jews were accused of turning to devilish acts (*deofoldædum*, 18)
and choosing the *cræft* of the devil (32). The Babylonians under Baltas-
sar, in their drunkenness, *are* devils, *ge deoflu*. Both the Jews and Bal-
tassar's people fell because of this drunken boasting. In addition to the
triple conditions of drunkenness, pride, and impious acts, close similar-
ities in external situation can be seen when the falls of the three peoples
are compared. The precise locale of Baltassar's final banquet is devel-
oped in the poem, while it remains no more than an unspecified splen-
did palace in the Bible. Once more, the walled city is the place of
protection for Baltassar, as it had been for Nabuchodonosor, and for the
Jews:

> . . . alhstede eorla,   þær æþelingas
> under wealla hleo   welan brytnedon.
> þæt wæs þam fæstna   folcum cuðost,

mæst and mærost,   þara þe men bun,
Babilon burga,   oðþæt Baldazar
þurh gylp grome   godes frasade.
Sæton him æt wine   wealle belocene,
ne onegdon na   orlegra nið,
þeah ðe feonda folc   feran cwome
herega gerædum   to þære heahbyrig
þæt hie Babilone   abrecan mihton.   (689–699)

[. . . the city of warriors, where the princes enjoyed their wealth in the shelter of the walls. Of all the fortresses known to men that was the mightiest and most widely known of all that men inhabit, the city of Babylon, until Baltassar in his furious boasting provoked God. They sat at wine within their walls, never fearing the hate of any foe, though a nation of enemies should come advancing in an army's trappings to that lofty city of Babylon to destroy it.]

As was to happen with Baltassar, both the Jews and Nabuchodonosor had been deprived of the protection of a walled city (*burh*) when they were punished by the Lord God.

VI

The conclusion that can be arrived at on the basis of this investigation is clear. The *Daniel* poet is an original craftsman, who may well deserve the name of artist. He has composed a moral poem with clearly evident lessons, a climatic order of events, and a skilful development of themes in his reworking of the first five chapters of the narrative portion of the Book of Daniel. He displayed considerable freedom from accepted tradition in this reworking, since his interpretation of the Book of Daniel differs radically from that of St. Jerome. The Old English poet's introduction sets out the themes he is to develop, and his conclusion carefully balances the opening of the poem. Through the use of a series of interrelated terms for wisdom, for the law, for godly or infernal skills and knowledge, the poet indicates oppositions between two major forces which clarify the moral lesson of the Bible text. An investigation of his work as compared with the Bible reveals that the *Daniel* poet was in no sense a mere translator and that even the title of "paraphrase" is not correct when applied to his work. The *Daniel* poem is a careful, conscious reworking of the first part of the Old Testament Book of Daniel, and its author was endowed with considerable originality and poetic skill.[44]

NOTES

1. Francis Junius clearly showed his views on this point when he prepared the first printed edition of the work in 1655, describing the manuscript as *Caedmonis Monachii Paraphrasis Poetica Genesios ac praecepuarum Sacrae paginae Historiarum* . . . . The source for the attribution of the poems to Cædmon was the account of the poet's works given in Bede's *Ecclesiastical History of the English People* 4:24–25.

2. For brief discussion of Cædmon and the Cædmonian poems, see C. L. Wrenn, "The Poetry of Cædmon," *Proceedings of the British Academy* 32 (1946), 247–95, and Kemp Malone, "The Old English Period," in *A Literary History of England* (New York, 1948), 64–68. In a recent history of Old English literature, Stanley B. Greenfield states the currently accepted view that Cædmon's *Hymn*, a nine-line poem found in a great number of manuscripts dating from the early eighth to the late fifteenth century, is the "only authentic work of the first English Christian poet." See his *A Critical History of Old English Literature* (New York, 1965), 168.

3. See *Christ and Satan*, ed. Merrel D. Clubb (New Haven, 1925); *The Old English Exodus*, ed. Edward B. Irving (New Haven, 1953). Though no recent edition has appeared there is an extended discussion of *Genesis* in Bernard F. Huppé's *Doctrine and Poetry* (New York, 1959), 131–216.

4. *The Cædmon Manuscript of Anglo-Saxon Biblical Poetry, Junius XI in the Bodleian Library*, ed. Sir Israel Gollancz (Oxford, 1927).

5. *The Junius Manuscript, ASPR* 1.

6. Gollancz, *Junius Manuscript*, xxxi.

7. Krapp, *Junius Manuscript*, xxxi.

8. Theodore Blackburn, ed., *Exodus and Daniel* (Boston, 1907), xxxliii.

9. The evidence for this conclusion is based on a study of such materials as are extant from the older version. See Samuel Berger, *Histoire de la Vulgate pendant les premières siècles du moyen-age* (Paris, 1893). Chapter 3 of this work is a study of the texts of the Bible in use in the Celtic and English churches. Berger's conclusion is that the Old Latin versions of the Old Testament would have been most common in English and Irish churches up to the ninth century, though readings from the Vulgate would have influenced these texts more and more as time went on. There are fragments of the Old Latin Book of Daniel extant, collected by Alban Dold in his *Konstanzer altlateinische Bruhstücke*, Texte und Arbeiten herausgegeben durch die Erzabtei Beuron, I Abt. Heft 19 (Leipzig, 1923). The Vulgate edition used in citation is *Biblia Sacra Vulgate Editionis*, Sixti V Pont. Max. Iussu recognita et Clementias VIII auctoritate edita (Rome, 1965).

10. Jerome, *Commentarius in Daniel*, PL 25, 491: "Verum quia nobis propositum est, non adversarii calumniis respondere . . . sed ea quae a propheta dicta sunt nostris disserere, id est, christianis, illus in praefatione commoneo, nullum prophetarum tam aperte dixisse de Christo. Non enim solum scribit cum esse venturum, quod est commune cum caeteris, sed etiam quo tempore venturus sit docet; et reges per ordinem digerit, et annos enumerat, ac manifestissima signa praenuntiat."

11. The only major exception is that of Nabuchodonosor's dream of the statue in the second chapter, which is, except for incidental mention, omitted from the poem. See note 15.

12. *The Book of Daniel* (Dublin, 1948), xv.

13. Rev. Robert McNally, S.J., *The Bible in the Early Middle* Ages (Westminster, MD, 1959), 45.

14. It may well be that the poet depended on other commentaries than Jerome's; a number of interesting similarities seem to link the poem with the commentary on the book of Daniel written by Hippolytus of Rome. I have developed the similarities between the two in an article which will be published in this journal. ["A Possible Source for Old English *Daniel*," *NM* 70 (1969), 84–90—*ed.*]

15. The dream is merely summarized in an epitome which does not lay a great deal of stress on the statue symbolic of the descent of the power of tile kings of Babylon; cf. Dan. 2:31–45. The poet is not interested, either, in the detailed description which the Vulgate provides of the great statue, "caput ex auro optimo . . . pectus autem et brachia argento, porro venter et femora ex aere, tibia autem ferreae, pedum quaedam pars erat ferra, quaedam erat fictilis" (2:32–33). The poet merely summarizes the import of the dream (108–115). He takes no more than five lines to tell us that Daniel interpreted the dream; no indication is given of Daniel's interpretation and prophecy, both of which Jerome found so important.

16. The precise nature of this interrelationship between Jewish heroes and Chaldean villains will he treated in greater depth in a later section of this paper.

17. See the introduction to Krapp's edition for a discussion of the reasons for the contention that the *Christ and Satan* was added later, and the evidence for the supposition that different scribes copied this later poem.

18. Gollancz, *Cædmon Manuscript*, lxxxix.

19. Krapp, *Junius Manuscript*, xxxi.

20. Even the term "a single page" is somewhat misleading, since the natural inference would be that a full page (i.e., some twenty-six full lines of text) has been lost. Though there are pages in the manuscript with this amount of material on them, the average number of lines per page would be much smaller, since so much space had been left for illustrations.

21. All quotations are from Krapp, *Junius Manuscript*, unless specific note is made to the contrary.

22. Or perhaps the poet foresaw difficulties in trying to fit the Aramaic words (if Aramaic was indeed the language of the inscription; cf. Lattey, *The Book of Daniel*, xvii–xxii, for a discussion of this language problem) into his text.

23. The next section, lines 33–78, corresponds to verses 1 and 2 of the first chapter of the Old Testament Daniel. The destruction of Jerusalem is described, but only *after* an account of Nabuchodonosor's plottings to destroy his enemies and the gathering of his forces is described in some detail. While the Bible verses merely recount the fact of the capture of the city, the poet gives a dramatic importance to the event, both by the greater breadth of his description, and by his characterization of Nabuchodonosor as arrogant and fierce. The rhetorical skill of the poet is also displayed in his choice of words, for example, the triple use of intensified verbs: "Gesamnode þa . . ." (52a); "gestrudan gestreona under stanhliðum" (61); "gehlodon him to huðe hordwearda gestreon" (65).

24. The verb in line 17 might well be interpreted as an instance of the continued preterite. If it is interpreted as such, then a series of drunken banquets, a gradual decline from a state of grace can be postulated for the Jews.

25. *Halige gastas* (line 26): the phrase might well mean holy visitants, or prophets, though the appearance of angels at so many other points in the text where none appear in the Bible lends support to the first translation.

26. This specification of the sort of learning the three possess is not made in the Bible. In Daniel 1:3–4, Nabuchodonosor orders his retainers to search out "de filiis Israel, et de semine regio et tyrannorum, pueros in quibus nulla esset macula, decoros forma, et *eruditos omni sapientia, cautos scientia, et doctos disciplina*" (emphasis added).

27. Daniel is not included. Evidently, the poet wishes to treat Daniel and the three as distinct from one another. Daniel does not even appear in the poem until line 150, which corresponds to the later part of chapter 2 of the Vulgate, when he is to interpret the king's dream of the statue. By treating Daniel and the three separately, the poet avoids the perplexing question which has troubled some of the commentators on the Book of Daniel: Where was Daniel when the three children were being persecuted for their beliefs? See, for example, the commentary of Hippolytus: "Mais on dira: 'Daniel, en qualité d'ami du roi, ne pouvait-il rien dire en leur faveur et obtenir leur grace?'—Il le pouvait. Mais pour que soient mises en lumière les grandes œuvres de Dieu, et que les Babyloniens apprennent à craindre de Dieu, il se tut. De cette manière, éclatait leur foi, et Dieu était glorifié en eux. Si en effet il avait parlé, les Babyloniens seraient alles dire: 'Daniel n'aurait pas parlé en leur faveur au roi, qu'aujourd'hui même ils

seraient morts dans les flammes!' Et l'on aurait attribué leur salut à la faveur humaine et non à la puissance de Dieu." I cite Hippolytus from the edition and translation of M. Maurice Le Fèvre (Paris, 1947), II, XXV, 115. The French translation is cited because it is the most readily available version.

28. Jerome and Hippolytus have similar commentaries on the Bible verses which underlie these lines, Dan. 2:9–10. Jerome states: "Confitentur magi, confitentur harioli, et omnis scientia saecularis litteraturæ, praescientiam futurorum non esse hominum, sed Dei. Ex quo probatur prophetas Dei spiritu locutos, qui futura cecinerunt" (*Comm. in Danielem*, 499). Hippolytus states: "Le songe vu par le roi n'était donc pas un songe de la terre que les sages du monde eussent pu interprêter; mais c'était un songe du ciel qui devait se réaliser en son temps selon la volonté et la prévoyance de Dieu. C'est pourquoi il resta caché aux hommes qui n'ont que des pensées terrestres afin que seuls les chercheurs des choses célestes aient la révélation des mystères célestes." (II, II, Le Fèvre, 98.)

29. There is a break in the MS at this point; apparently, a single page has been cut out between those now numbered 180 and 181. The missing lines apparently correspond to Dan. 3:2–6.

30. See *Beowulf*, lines 171b–183a.

31. The word also implies high advisory ability, related as it is with *ræd* and *ræswan*. It is also interesting to note that Nabuchodonosor is described as *werodes ræswa* (486), *se ræswa* (639), and *frod, foremihtig folces ræswa* (666). In all three instances, the king recognizes the true God, if only for a short time. The first instance is just after he had praised the Lord for His power in saving the three children (cf. 486–488a). The other two instances in which he is described as *ræswa* are *after* his conversion, and his final complete acceptance of the eternal Lord God of the Israelites.

32. See lines 445–447:
   septon hie soðcwidum   and him sædon fela
   soða tacna,   oðþæt he sylfa gelyfde
   þæt se wære mihta waldend   se þe hie of ðam mirce generede.
   [they enlightened him with true statements, and told him many true signs, until he himself believed that he who saved them from the darkness was a ruler of powers.]

33. See lines 472–485.

34. Corresponding to Dan. 4:15–24.

35. It may be remarked in passing that the poem which precedes *Daniel* in the Cædmon MS, *Exodus*, shows a similar use of *ræd*, and also develops other terms in the series found in *Daniel*. I have dealt with the *Exodus* structure in another paper, which will appear elsewhere. ["A Reading of OE *Exodus*," *RES* n.s. 20 (1969), 401–17—*ed.*]

36. Ða wæron æðelum god   Abrahames bearn,
    wæron wærfæste;   wiston drihten,
    ecne uppe,   ælmihtigne.
    Cnihtas cynegode   cuð gedydon,
    þæt hie him þæt gold   to gode noldon
    habban ne healdan,   ac þone hean cyning,
    gasta hyrde,   ðe him gife sealde.   (193–199)
    [These were by good lineage sons of Abraham, they were true to the
    covenant; they knew the Lord, eternal on high, the Almighty. These noble
    youths made it known that they would not take or hold that gold as a god,
    but rather the high King, shepherd of souls, who gave them grace.]

37. But the problem is not completely solved. The youths are described as
    "eruditos omni sapientia, cautos scientia, et doctos disciplina" in the Vul-
    gate, immediately before this point in the action. In the poem this exten-
    sive knowledge becomes highly particularized. Nabuchodonosor is
    spoken of as seeking out whoever among the youths was most wise in the
    books of the Law: *hwylc þære geogoþe gleawost wære boca bebodes*
    (81–82a). Further on they are described as noble, steadfast in the law and
    endowed with godly wisdom (88–90). They are to reveal skill of mind to
    the king. Apparently their role is seen in the following way by the poet:
    They are to learn as much secular knowledge as is necessary to reveal
    wisdom to their lord.

38. See Dan. 3:44.

39. See Dan. 3:86.

40. Lines 485, 535, 595.

41. The manuscript reads *arcræftig ar*. I accept Krapp's emendation to
    æcræftig ar.

42. See lines 104–107, and 486–494.

43. This difference can be seen by a comparison of lines 612–656 of the poem
    with the corresponding passage in the Vulgate, 4:30–34.

44. I wish to thank Professor A. Campbell, Rawlinson and Bosworth Profes-
    sor of Anglo-Saxon at Oxford, Professor Charles Donahue of Fordham
    University, Dr. R. Bruce Mitchell, university Lecturer in English Lan-
    guage and Fellow of St. Edmund Hall, Oxford, and Christopher Ball, Fel-
    low of Lincoln College, Oxford, all of whom read and commented on this
    paper in the course of its preparation.

Style and Theme in the Old English *Daniel*

EARL R. ANDERSON

This essay first appeared in *English Studies* 68 (1987), 1–23.

Critical discussion of the Junius MS *Daniel* has centered primarily on problems of structure. Is the poem complete, or nearly complete, in its present form on pages 173–212 of the manuscript? Are lines 279–361, that is, the Song of Azarias in the fiery furnace, and the narrative material just preceding the Song of the Three Children (lines 362–408) originally part of the poem, or are they an interpolation adapted from some other poem the remains of which appear as *Azarias* in the Exeter Book? Discussions about theme in *Daniel* have sometimes been undertaken in relation to these questions about structure (or at least in relation to the second question), but at other times, scholars have adduced "themes" from the prologue (lines 1–78) or from the poet's habit of repeating words that have key thematic importance, without regard to structure. At the most general level, the theme of *Daniel* has been thought of in terms of oppositions between the "way of righteousness," which is rewarded, and the "way of the world," which is punished, but most critics have viewed this opposition in the more precise moral terms of humble obedience, exemplified by Daniel and the Three Children, and arrogant pride, exemplified by Nabochodonossor and Baldazar. This approach to theme assumes that Nabochodonossor and Baldazar are tropological examples of "Everyman" who must be warned against pride and admonished to practice Christian humility. But Nabochodonossor and Baldazar were not examples of "Everyman"—not in history, not in biblical exegesis, and not in *Daniel*. They were the world's most powerful magnates, and their activities had implications for the fortunes of nations. It is true, of course, that pride versus humility, along with good counsel versus foolishness and observance of law versus idolatry, are moral issues in *Daniel*, but in my view the organizing theme of the poem, which encompasses these moral issues, has to do with the medieval historiographical and political concept of *translatio imperii*, and with the closely related tradition about the Hebrews as the *populus Dei* who through sin lost their favored position and eventually were superseded by the *populus christianus*. In this paper I propose to deal briefly with the poem's structural problems and then discuss the development of style and theme in *Daniel*.

As to the question about the poem's ending, the most recent editor, R. T. Farrell, suggests on the basis of manuscript evidence, and to some extent on the basis of narrative structure, that the Junius MS presents the complete poem, or nearly all of it,[1] but P. J. Lucas has convincingly reasserted the traditional view that we are missing an account of Daniel's interpretation of the angelic writing on the wall at Baldazar's feast (Dan. 5:17–19), and also of the slaying of Baldazar and the conquest of Babylon by Darius the Mede (Dan. 5:30–1).[2] If this is so, the *Daniel* poet would have had to improvise his own details for the conquest of Babylon, since the biblical account provides none; but since the poet had improvised details in the prologue (lines 1–78), perhaps borrowing details from II Kings 25:11, Chron. 36, and Jer. 52,[3] it may be that the poem once possessed an equally improvised epilogue about the downfall of Babylon.

Because of the similarity between lines 279–370 of *Daniel* and the first 79 lines of the Exeter Book *Azarias*, it probably was inevitable that from a time early in its critical history (as early, indeed, as Ernst Götzinger's 1860 dissertation[4]) *Daniel* should be thought of in terms of composite authorship; according to this view, an earlier, mainly narrative poem, called *Daniel A*, was combined with the "lyrical" Song of Azarias, called *Daniel B*, in order to form the poem as we have it in the Junius MS.[5] The interpolation theory has been argued mainly on grounds of narrative logic: *Daniel B* is said to be a lyrical interruption of an otherwise economical narrative, and, moreover, as Gollancz states the matter, "the interpolation of the prayer [of Azarias], which asks for deliverance, is made after the deliverance"[6] since an angel already had appeared to protect the Three Children from flames at line 237; but Farrell has made the point that the poet was only following his biblical source, which similarly duplicates details relating to the deliverance of the Three Children.[7] Moreover, in the poem the Three Children are not actually released from the furnace until lines 416–29; hence the prayer of Azarias does not disrupt narrative logic—at least not badly enough to justify the interpolation theory. As for the supposed "double appearance" of the angel in the furnace, at lines 271–73a and 335b–39a, together with the two similes comparing the environment within the furnace to a pleasant summer breeze or a warm summer shower (lines 273a–78; 345–51a), these should be regarded as a frame or "envelope pattern"[8] encircling the prayer of Azarias and marking it off as a set piece, and not as the inelegant seams of interpolative stitching. There are other such "set pieces" in the poem, as N. Isaacs has noted: the Song of the Three Children (lines 362–408); Daniel's interpretation of Nabochodonossor's dream (lines 551–92); Daniel's interpretation of the writing on the wall at Baldazar's feast (lines 743–64, incomplete).[9] G. Krapp felt that the interpolated part of the poem included the Song of the Three Children as well as Azarias's prayer,[10] but this Song, which is based not on the "cantus trium puerorum" in Dan. 3:52–90 but rather on a "Hymnum trium puerorum" the text of which appears in the Vespasian Psalter,[11] seems consistent with the relative freedom that the *Daniel A* poet takes with his biblical source elsewhere—in the prologue, for example. The beginning of the Song (lines 362–70), it is true, has a direct connection with *Azarias* lines 73–79; Krapp's view is certainly simpler than Kemp Malone's proposal that whereas *Daniel B* was influenced by both the Vulgate and *Azarias*, *Azarias* in turn had been influenced by *Daniel A*.[12] This hypothetical coincidence is too complicated to bear the weight of literary history. Much unnecessary complexity could be avoided, it seems to me, by abandoning the interpolation theory and regarding *Azarias* as a poem based (in its first 79 lines) on *Daniel*.[13]

Malone, to be sure, had taken into account not only the problem of *Azarias*, but also a stylistic difference between *Daniel A*, which exemplifies "the early stages of the run-on style,"[14] in contrast to *Daniel B* where end-stopped lines are more frequent; but, as Farrell notes, this stylistic difference may be due to the psalm-like character of the biblical source for Azarias's prayer (Dan. 3:26–45), in contrast to the prose used for the narrative portions of the Vulgate Daniel.[15] In other respects, moreover, *Daniel B* may have stylistic affinities with *Daniel A* as against *Azarias* even in passages where the contents of *Daniel B* and *Azarias* are nearly identical. *Daniel* as a whole is characterized by what might be called a "ragged style" that often deviates from the "norms" of alliterative poetry.

Features of this style include not only the sporadic use of hypermetric lines (admittedly only in *Daniel A*), but also "mixed lines" in which one verse is normal and one hypermetric (eighteen examples in *Daniel A*; one in *Daniel B*, line 283), and also seven single half lines (variously normal or hypermetric), five in *Daniel A* (lines 38, 207, 238, 240, 459) and two in *Daniel B* (lines 288, 369). In *Azarias* there are no single half lines, and only one hypermetric verse (77a).[16] Single half lines have been shown to be rhetorically appropriate in the Exeter and Cotton *Maxims* since half lines also are used in the *ljóðaháttr* meter of Old Norse gnomic poetry,[17] but no particular rhetorical function has been suggested for the half lines in *Daniel* or other Old English poems. Hypermetric lines function variously to mark the beginnings or endings of sections, to slow the pace, or to express emphasis or solemnity, though it should be cautioned that in the Old Saxon *Heliand* the main function of hypermetric lines was merely to bear the weight of function words that in earlier alliterative poetry had been avoided.[18] Most of the hypermetric lines in *Daniel* appear, as Farrell points out, in the account of "the angel's descent into the furnace and the salvation of the three youths" (lines 207–73) and in the account of Nabochodonossor's conversion "because of this manifestation of God's power" (lines 432–57).[19] In these passages the hypermetric lines have a specific rhetorical purpose, but hypermetric and "mixed" lines appear sporadically and with no particular purpose elsewhere in *Daniel*, as do, also, the single half lines, perhaps for no more reason than because the poet likes metrical variety. *Azarias*, in contrast, is consistently "normal" in metrical appearance, except in line 77 as noted above.

The first 79 lines of *Azarias* duplicate more or less the contents of *Daniel* 279–370, although with discrepancies in detail that might often be referred to the imperfection of memory or to the instability inherent in the oral transmission of poetry.[20] Thereafter the *Azarias* poet alternates between improvisation relatively independent of *Daniel* (especially lines 81–138 and 176–91), and passages that duplicate parts of *Daniel*: *Azarias* 140–57 and 170–75 are based on *Daniel* 386–401 and 411–15. The improvised passages result from artistic independence at least to some extent: They enlarge the Song of the Three Children and provide *Azarias* with a suitable narrative ending. But most of *Azarias* may properly be described as the result of a faulty recollection of *Daniel*.

However this may be, some of the most significant discrepancies between *Daniel* and *Azarias* reflect differing stylistic preferences rather than faulty memory. In general the *Azarias* poet seems bent on "normalizing" some of the stylistic quirks that comprise the "ragged" style of *Daniel*. Thus where *Daniel* reads (lines 287–89)

soðe and geswiðde   and gesigefæste,
swa þu eac sylfa eart.
Syndon þine willan   on woruldspedum

the *Azarias* poet omits the single half line (*Az.* 9–10):

soðe geswiðde   and gesigefæste
eac þinne willan   in woruldspedum.

For the single half line "eallum, ece drihten" (*Dan.* 396), *Azarias* substitutes a full line, "and, ece god, eaðmodheorte" (line 152). The hypermetric verse "hwæt, þu eart mihtum swið" (*Dan.* 283b) in *Azarias* is normalized by omitting "hwæt": "þu eart meahtum swið" (*Az.* 5b). At line 281 *Daniel* reads "dæda georn drihten herede." Here the *a* verse is metrically defective, possibly by scribal error, and editors have emended it to "dæda geornful." The *Azarias* poet must have seen "dæda georn," since he attempts his own correction: "dreag dædum georn, dryhten herede" (*Az.* 3). Later on the excessively "light" verse "and Misael" (*Dan.* 398a) is corrected to "and Misahel, meotud" (*Az.* 154a). For the "light" verse "ut of ofne" (*Dan.* 428a), *Azarias* substitutes "Het þa of þam lige" (182a). At least one minor change in diction may be a "correction." Twice the *Daniel* poet repeats a substantive word in two consecutive verses in a "variation" series: "metode dyrust, / dugoða dyrust" (*Dan.* 36b–7a), and "oðþe brimfæroþes, / sæfaroða sand" (*Dan.* 321b–22a). This sort of repetition usually is avoided in Old English poetry, and in the second instance *Azarias* substitutes "oð brimflodas, / swa waroþa sond" (lines 38b–39a). There is evidence of some confusion in the sentence where this appears (*Az.* 32–41), most notably the repetition of the verse "þæt swa unrime" (*Az.* 34b and 40b), but "brimflodas" for "brimfæroþes" may reflect an attempt to avoid repetition.

Not all differences are related to stylistic preference. In seventeen verses the difference between *Daniel* and *Azarias* consists mainly in the addition or omission of function words. In seven verses, *Azarias* adds function words that were not present in *Daniel*: *Dan.* 298a, 317b, 325a, 328a, 331b, 350b, 397a = *Az.* 19a, 34b, 42a, 45a, 48b, 65b, 153a. In ten verses *Azarias* omits function words: *Dan.* 291a, 314a, 315a, 326b, 330a, 341a, 341b, 390a, 391a, 393a = *Az.* 12a, 31a, 32a, 43b, 45a, 59a, 59b, 146a, 147b, 151a. A strong tendency to add function words, or conversely to avoid them, would have implications for style, but that is not the situation here.

The same must be said about the "formulaic" character of verses in *Daniel* and *Azarias* in places where there are differences in diction. Thus "wer womma leas" (*Dan.* 282a) is a common formula (cf. "wer womma leas," *Menologium* 209a; "þa ic womma leas," *Christ III*, 1451a; "wlitig womma leas," *Christ III*, 1464a; "womma lease," *Christ I*, 188a, etc.) substituted in *Azarias* by "wis in weorcum" (cf. "weorces wisan," *Genesis* 1689a), and this substitution, in the context of the full line in *Azarias*, "wis in weorcum and þas word acwæð" (*Az.* 4), reflects the frequent Old English collocation of *weorc*, *word*, and *wis*. The formulaic verse "rihte and gerume" (*Dan.* 290a; cf. "rihte and rume," *Lord's Prayer II*, 15a) is replaced by equally formulaic "ryhte mid ræde" (*Az.* 11a; cf. "ryht mid wisum" *Maxims I*, 22b). "Folca manegum" (*Dan.* 303b; cf. "folca mæste," *Gen.* 747b; "folca maenegum," *Psalm* 143, 18.2) is replaced by "foldbuendum" (*Az.* 24b; cf. *Beowulf* 309b, 1355a, 2274b, and at least fourteen verses in other poems). "On cneorissum" (*Dan.* 318b; cf. "on þas cneorisse," *Andreas* 207b; "þurh cneorisse," *Fates of the Apostles* 26a, etc.) is replaced by "on cynerice" (*Az.* 35a; cf. "ofer cynericu," *Exodus* 318a).[21] This list could easily be expanded, but additional examples would only illustrate a point that is already clear: Differences in diction between *Daniel* and *Azarias* do not represent a drift toward or away from "formulaic" quality, but instead tend merely to substitute one formula for another.

This is not to say, of course, that systematic study of the changes in diction might not be useful for other reasons. The verse "herran þinne" (*Dan.* 392b), as an example, defies translation in its manuscript form and is plausibly emended by editors to "heran þine," "your servants," on the basis of Vulgate Daniel 3:85, "servi Domini"[22]; it is helpful to compare this with the corresponding verse in *Azarias* 150a "and þine þas," probably a scribal error for "and þine þeowas." The *Azarias* poet may have intended to replace an obscure word, *hera*, with the much more familiar *þeow*. Again, the verses "and for ðeonydum" and "þeowned þoliað" in

Daniel (lines 293b and 307a) are replaced by "and for þreanydum" and "þreanyd" [followed by a hiatus in the Exeter Book] (*Az.* 14b and 28a), seemingly an innocuous substitution. But *þeownyd*, "enforced servitude," applied to the adversities of the Hebrews in Babylon is far more precise than the general term *þreanyd*, "unavoidable suffering." The idea that the Hebrews' adversities took the form of slavery does not appear in *Azarias* but it is well established in *Daniel*: the Babylonian captivity was the Hebrews' second period as slaves ("to weorcþeowum," *Dan.* 74b), a return to the condition that they had known in Egypt (cf. *Dan.* 7a). Thus the choice of words in *Daniel* 293b and 307a should be preferred to *Azarias* 14b and 28a on grounds of thematic development.[23]

The earliest scholarship on *Daniel* did not include any serious discussion of theme. F. A. Blackburn's view on this matter was representative: "*Daniel*," he wrote, "contains several stories . . . united by general identity of characters and place as well as source . . . the subject being the history of the captive Hebrews in Babylon," but since in the poem "the source is followed rather closely and to the exclusion of all outside matter," the historical material was not thought of as having been shaped to emphasize a theme.[24] Modern critics of *Daniel* believe, in contrast, that the poem does depart from its biblical source in many details, and that the poet thus goes beyond biblical paraphrase to develop a theme at least partly independent of his Latin source. This view of the poem, however, did not appear in the criticism until B. F. Huppé's *Doctrine and Poetry* (1959). Huppé sought the theme of *Daniel* through analysis of its prologue (especially lines 1–24), and emphasized the poet's "Augustinian playing with words" like *modig*, which can mean both "magnanimous" (as in line 7, describing the faithful Hebrews) and "arrogant" (as in line 105, describing Nabochodonossor). In Huppé's view the *Daniel* poet uses wordplay to "develop the theme of obedience" to God's way and to contrast this with arrogant disobedience and self-love.[25] Farrell, however, pointed us in the right direction when he argued that theme in *Daniel* is developed not through wordplay but through the poet's frequent repetition of "a series of weighted words which appear throughout the poem, always in similar contexts"; through "thematic word-use" the poet develops contrasts between the wisdom and good counsel (*wisdom, lar, ræd*, adjectives *gleaw, snotor, wis*) of those who keep God's law and the covenant (*æ, æcræft, wær*), and the foolish counsel of those who instead follow the deceits of the devil, "deofles cræft."[26] In a different context, I have referred to this pattern in diction as "thematic repetition" and related it to the "reflective" style in which the poet "holds a mirror," as it were, "to the events and images [of his story], allowing a sharp clarity in the development of ideas through chronological and logical sequence," as Cynewulf does in his poems, whereas frequent use of wordplay is more often a feature of the "illuminative" style exemplified in the Advent Lyrics, where the poet "holds a lamp," as it were, "to the events and images associated with Christ's nativity, allowing varying degrees of light and shadow through the suggestiveness of diction."[27] The "reflective" style is best suited to poets like Cynewulf whose aim is mainly didactic, whereas the "illuminative" style of poems like the Advent Lyrics or *The Dream of the Rood* best suits poems that embody a mystical experience. *Daniel* readily exemplifies the "reflective" style and is very similar to Cynewulf's poetry in its patterns of diction, although, of course, Cynewulf does not share the *Daniel* poet's liking for the "raggedness" of metrical irregularity discussed above.

Notwithstanding the comprehensive range of moral issues that Farrell saw interrelated through "thematic repetition" in *Daniel*, several critics have wanted to define the theme of the poem more narrowly (or perhaps more sharply) in terms of the humble obedience of the Three Children and of Daniel, in contrast with the foolish pride of their antagonists, Nabochodonossor and Baldazar. G. D. Caie believes that *Daniel* links three *exempla*—the stories about the captive Hebrews, Nabochodonossor, and Baldazar—to warn against the dangers of pride, and to support this view he calls attention to thematic repetition (Nabochodonossor is described as "proud" fifteen times in the poem and only twice in the Vulgate Daniel) and to symbolism (he associates the drunkenness of the Hebrews, lines 17–18, and of the Chaldeans, lines 695–702, with pride).[28] Isaacs believes that "*Daniel* is an *episodic-narrative exemplum* on the *sin of pride* and the *virtue of humble obedience*," and he argues this view on the basis of details found in the poem's four "set-pieces" that retard the otherwise quickly-paced narrative: the songs of Azarias and of the Three Children, which are "*exempla* of humble obedience," and Daniel's interpretations of Nabochodonossor's dream (lines 551–92) and of the writing on the wall at Baldazar's feast (lines 743–64), which are "preachments against pride."[29] J. W. Kirkland and C. E. Modlin agree that the Exeter Book *Azarias*, like the corresponding songs in *Daniel*, exemplifies the virtues of humble obedience,[30] and J. Gardner[31] and A. Lee[32] have argued that narrative details, some of them nonbiblical, point to a contrast between humble obedience and foolish pride. There has been some unrest in the ranks, to be sure: H. J. Solo has wanted to see the poem in the light of the familiar exegetical association of Babylon with "confusio" (which usually means "the confusion of sin") and of Jerusalem with "visio pacis,"[33] and R. E. Bjork, through analysis of thematic repetition and symbolism, has redirected our attention to the themes originally proposed by Farrell: "good counsel" and "keeping the covenant."[34] But in the main the emphasis in criticism has been on pride and humble obedience.

Although *Daniel* is first and foremost a paraphrase of the first five chapters of the Vulgate Daniel, it is true that the poet omits some biblical details and adds some nonbiblical ones. Major omissions include the role of Malassar and the prince of the eunuchs ("praepositus" or "princeps eunuchorum" Dan. 1:7 and 11; the "gerefa" of *Dan*. 79b) in changing the names of Daniel, Ananias, Misael, and Azarias to Baltaooar, Sidrach, Misach, and Abdenago (Dan. 1:6–7); the episode about the Hebrews' dietary restrictions, which also involves Malasar (Dan. 1:8–17); the symbolic details of Nabochodonossor's first dream (Dan. 2:31–45); and Nabochodonossor's idolatrous worship of Daniel (Dan. 2:46-7). Alterations or additions of detail could have their sources variously in biblical exegesis, in Old English poetic tradition, or in the poet's own imagination, and although nonbiblical details at times might point to a particular theme, at other times they might simply reflect the poet's understanding of the biblical story. The drunken feast of the Hebrews just prior to the Babylonian captivity (*Dan.* 17–18), comparable to Holofernes's drunken feast in *Judith* 15–34a, probably reflects an Old English poetic tradition; attempts to relate this detail to Jerome's commentary on Daniel 1:8 and 9:14 have not been successful.[35] Since later on the poet describes Baldazar as "medugal" at his feast (*Dan.* 702a, based on Daniel 5:1–2), it seems reasonable to claim both thematic and structural functions for "drunkenness," which is associated symbolically with pride and foolishness, and which appears at the beginning and again at the end of the poem.

The addition of a speech by the unnamed "cyninges ræswa" (*Dan.* 416b), who counsels Nabochodonossor to release the Three Children from the fiery furnace (lines 417b–29), seems to be the poet's own invention, in part at least, and perhaps calls attention to the theme of

"good counsel" in the poem, but critics have exaggerated both the sub-
stance and the significance of the poet's originality here. According to
Farrell, "This *ræswa* and his speech have no source in the Vulgate,"
and he speculates that the poet had in mind some artistic principle
regarding characterization: "Such a character [sc. the *ræswa*] was per-
haps necessary because the king had been pictured as deeply involved
in evil."[36] Bjork takes this line of reasoning further by relating it to
theme:

> The appearance of the *wis and wordgleaw* . . . counselor (lines 416–39)
> further underscores the importance of the *gast* [referring to the angel that
> appeared in the furnace, line 155] and its relationship to those who keep
> the covenant. Because Nabuchodonosor has broken God's law and repre-
> sents the confused philosophy embodied in Babylon, he does not have the
> spiritual insight brought by an attendant *gast* and necessary for under-
> standing the miracle of the Three Children. Consequently he must be
> instructed, and a human *ræswa* fulfills that function.[37]

If this is so, the thematic point seems to depend on too complicated a
calculation, and on too fragile a balance of narrative details. But we need
not concern ourselves with the intricacies of detail here, since arguments
about the "thematic" function of the *ræswa* fail at a much more funda-
mental level. These arguments assume that (1) nonbiblical "additions"
are sensational and require extraordinary explanations in terms of aes-
thetics or theme, and that (2) the *ræswa* is one such "addition." But the
speech by the *ræswa* is anything but sensational: He merely counsels
Nabochodonossor to release the Three Children, nothing more. He does
not even suggest that Nabochodonossor should worship the true God. I
doubt that the Anglo-Saxons would have thought of this passage as a
thematically significant deviation from the Vulgate Daniel—nor should
they have done so, since on the authority of Daniel 3:91–92 the poet
could have supplied the poem with any number of counselors had he
wanted to:

> Tunc Nabuchodonosor rex obstupuit: et surrexit propere, et ait optimati-
> bus suis: Nonne tres viros misimus in medium ignis compeditos? Qui
> respondentes regi, dixerunt: Vere, rex. Respondit, et ait: Ecce ego video
> quatuor viros solutos, et ambulantes in medio ignis, et nihil corruptionis
> in eis est, et species quarti similis filio Dei.[38]

The poet's phrase, "cyninges ræswa, wis and wordgleaw" (*Dan.* 416b–17a), represents an attempt—and a successful one I think—to render fully the implications of the Latin "optimatibus suis." The speech of the *ræswa* has its counterpart in the conversation between Nabochodonossor and his counselors, reported in part in the Vulgate verses. It seems unreasonable to me to characterize the *ræswa* episode in *Daniel* as anything other than an attempt to represent faithfully the poet's understanding of his biblical source.

This issue requires emphasis because the *ræswa* episode is not the only allegedly "nonbiblical" detail that turns out to have a basis in the Vulgate after all. In his account of Nabochodonossor's furnace, for example, the poet twice remarks that the fire was immoderately large: "Æled wæs ungescead micel . . . micle mare þonne gemet wære" (lines 243a, 250). Farrell claims that "Neither passage has a source in the Vulgate" and finds it thus "significant that the fire kindled by those who do not possess *ræd* is unreasonably, or immoderately, large."[39] But at Daniel 3:19 we are told that Nabuchodonosor, "repletus furore" ("hreohmod," *Dan.* 242a), ordered the furnace heated up seven times more than was necessary: "et praecepit ut succenderetur fornax septuplum quam succendi consueverat." Our poet has merely chosen to express this idea less vividly. True, the immoderate fire points to the theme of "good counsel" (which Nabochodonossor lacked at this time), and perhaps also to wrath,[40] but this came about because the poet thought that he found these themes in the Vulgate Daniel—not because the poet had introduced extraneous material to support a nonbiblical theme.

Some nonbiblical details in *Daniel* may have had their origin in biblical exegesis, and thus may reflect the poet's effort to represent the meaning, if not the literal detail, of the Vulgate Daniel. In his speech at Baldazar's feast, for example, Daniel refers to the Chaldeans as "devils" because they had dishonored the sacred vessels taken from Solomon's temple: "On þam ge deoflu drincan ongunnon" (line 749). No such detail appears in the Vulgate (Dan. 5:17–28), but the Chaldeans are sometimes called devils in theological and tropological analyses of the Babylonian captivity. Bede, for example, in the first book of his commentary *In Ezram et Neemiam*, develops an interpretation according to which Judaea is symbolic of "confession," Babylon of the "confusion of sin" which detracts from the spiritual state proper to confession, and the Chaldeans as devils who lead men astray into the captivity of sin: "Hierusalem quoque esse in Iudaea, hoc est in confessione, memoratur ut qui obliuionem Dei captiuari a Chaldeis qui interpretantur quasi daemonia."[41]

An early third-century commentary on Daniel by the Greek exegete Hippolytus of Rome has been proposed as the source for some of the nonbiblical details in *Daniel*,[42] and if this is so the poem provides unique evidence for Anglo-Saxon knowledge of Hippolytus, whose work survives only in fragments. In my view the evidence does not point to Hippolytus, although the influence of Bede and Jerome might be contemplated. Thus according to Daniel 1:2 the Chaldeans carried off only part of the vessels from Solomon's temple, "et partem vasorum domus Dei," while according to the poet all the treasures were taken (*Dan.* 61–2 and 706b, "clæne genamon"). Jerome quotes Daniel 1:2, "partem uasorum," and regards the vessels as symbols of true doctrines, "dogmata ueritatis," never wholly accessible to pagan philosophers.[43] Hippolytus quotes Daniel 1:2 early in his commentary (I, 6; ed. Le Fèvre, 73), but later relates the passage to Isaias 39:3–8 where Isaias tells Ezechias that all the treasures of his ancestors, "tous les trésors," will be carried off to Babylon (I, 10: ed. Le Fèvre, 77). However this may be, Bede, at the conclusion of a lengthy discussion about the meaning of the captured treasures (*In Ezram et Neemiam* I, 108–78) relates them to Colossians 2:3 where Christ is spoken of as one "in quo sunt omnes thesauri sapientiae et scientiae absconditi" (*In Ezr.* I, 174–75); thus the idea that all the treasures were taken could have come from Bede rather than Hippolytus.

Again, in *Daniel* 675–76 Baldazar is said to belong to the third generation of Nabochodonossor's descendants ("his þæt þridde cneow," 675b) whereas in Daniel 5:2, 11, and 22, Nabuchodonosor is referred to as Baltassar's father ("Nabuchodonosor, pater eius," v. 2; "pater tuus," v. 11; "filius eius, Baltassar," v. 22). G. Steiner once suggested that *Daniel* may have been influenced by Eusebius, who, on the basis of IV Kings 25:27 and Jeremias 52:31, mentions Evil-Marodach as a king who ruled between the times of Nabuchodonosor and Baltassar.[44] Farrell notes that Hippolytus also mentions Evil-Marodach as a single intervening ruler.[45] Jerome, with greater historical accuracy, mentions several intervening rulers (*In Danielem* II, 1–15, p. 820), and interprets the biblical references to Nabuchodonosor as Baltassar's "pater" as the appropriate honorific for a royal predecessor (*In Dan.* II, 26–42, p. 821). The *Daniel* poet seems closer to Jerome than to Eusebius and Hippolytus on this point, since he refers vaguely to an intervening generation, rather than specifically to a single intervening ruler.

A third argument for the influence of Hippolytus remains to be considered: that while Daniel and the Three Children were chosen to serve in Nabuchodonosor's court because of their learning "in omni libro et sapientia" (Daniel 1:17), the poet specifies that they were learned in books of the law, "gleawost wære / boca bebodes" (*Dan.* 81b–82a), a detail seen also in Hippolytus, who describes them as learned in "science de l'Ecriture."[46] Jerome, in contrast, describes their learning as "artem grammaticam" (*In Dan.* I, 113, p. 781). This detail in *Daniel*, notwithstanding the similarity to Hippolytus, may well be related to the poet's thematic purpose rather than to an exegetical influence. Knowledge of law, *æ*, and loyalty to covenant, *wær*, are important values in the poem. These themes also appear in Cynewulf's *Elene*, where the Jews summoned by Elene in Jerusalem are noted for their knowledge of "rihte æ" (281a), "Moyses æ" (283b), but Cynewulf found this in his Latin source, the *Vita Cyriaci*, which refers to the Jews' knowledge of "legis scientiam" and "de sanctis libris propheticis."[47] *Daniel* and *Elene*, however, share a wider thematic interest in the concept of the Hebrews as the *populus Dei*, and the emphasis on "æ" thus appears in both poems as an integral part of this theme.[48]

Some nonbiblical details appear in the poem not as the result of exegetical or thematic influences, but merely as compositional accidents. One example would be the poet's description of the writing on the wall at Baldazar's feast as scarlet letters, "baswe bocstafas," 723a. Farrell compares this with the *Grettis Saga* (ch. 79) where "the witch Þurðr carves runes into the roots of a tree, reddening them with her own blood and reciting spells over them to bring disaster to Grettir," and on the basis of this analogue and other evidence for Germanic associations of the color red with magic, he suggests that the *Daniel* poet uses color symbolism, describing the letters as "mysterious and magical writing, inscribed in bright red to show their importance and to demonstrate their mystic and sacred nature."[49] A reading of the Vulgate Daniel, however, reveals how "baswe" got into the poem. Although the biblical text does not attribute color to the inscription on the wall (Dan. 5:5), two verses later Baltassar is represented as promising to clothe in purple ("purpura vestietur'), that is, to invest with regal authority, anyone who can read and interpret the letters. Latin "purpura" often is glossed in Old English as "read" or even "felleread" which is close to "basu,"[50] and in at least one Old English poem, *The Phoenix*, the word "basu" has its basis in Latin "purpura": Where the *Carmen de ave phoenice* says of the phoenix that "in cuius maculis purpura mixta rubit" (line 132),[51] the Anglo-Saxon poet renders "sum brun sum basu sum blacum splottum / searo-lice beseted."[52] In *Daniel* the color "baswe" was transferred from Baltassar's promised raiment to the angelic inscription, not because of some obscure Germanic color symbolism, but by a compositional acci-dent—either by a loose association of ideas, or by a sort of *trompe l'oeil* as the poet's eye glanced over the Latin text.

Thus it appears that analysis even of the nonbiblical details in *Daniel* supports the thesis that the poet endeavored to create a faithful representation of his biblical source. If any pattern dominates the poet's deviations from the Vulgate, it can be found not in sensational interpola-tions, but, on the contrary, in the poet's tendency to tone down some of the vivid details that he found in his biblical story. We have already noted one clear example of this: Where the Vulgate describes the fiery furnace as seven times hotter than usual (Dan. 3:19), the poet describes it in more general terms as "ungescead micel" (*Dan.* 243a). Other exam-ples can be found throughout the poem. Whereas in IV Kings 25:8 Nabuzardan "princeps exercitus," captain of the guard, was the officer in charge of organizing the sack of Jerusalem and the Hebrews' subsequent march into captivity, *Daniel* mentions only Chaldean counselors, "wit-gan" (41b), and their army, "werod" (44b), who attack the city.[53] The officer in charge of the learned Hebrew captives was Malasar, whose superior was the prince of the eunuchs, "princeps eunuchorum" (Dan. 1:3–4 and 9–11), but *Daniel* 79b mentions only an unnamed *gerefa*. The poet omits the symbolic details of Nabuchodonosor's first dream about the destruction of a bright image with a head of gold, breast and arms of silver, belly and thighs of brass, legs of iron, and feet of iron and clay (Dan. 2:31–5), and gives only the meaning of the dream: that every king-dom must come to an end (*Dan.* 114–15). He represents the king as threatening his counselors because of their inability to expound the dream (*Dan.* 134–44), but omits the role of Arioch captain of the praeto-rian guard in this episode (*Dan.* 2:14–18 and 24–25). The counselors are described in general terms as the "witigdom" (*Dan.* 146a), "witgum sinum" (136a), as in Dan. 2:14, "sapientes Babylonis," but the poet avoids the Vulgate's more specific representation of them as astrologers, magicians, and sorcerers, "arioli, et magi, et malefici" (Dan. 2:2). The vivid punishments that Nabuchodonosor proposes for his "sapientes," that they should be cut in pieces and their houses made into a dunghill ("peribitis vos, et domus vestrae publicabuntur" Dan. 2:5), are generalized to an unspecified threat of death ("Ge sweltað deaðe," *Dan.* 142a). In place of the several musical instruments used to summon the people to worship of Nabuchodonosor's brazen image—the cornet, flute, harp, sackbut, psaltery, dulcimer, and others, "sonitum tubae, et fistulae, et citharae, sambucae, et psalterii, et symphoniae, et universi generis musicorum" (Dan. 3:5, 10)—the poet mentions only the first item in the series, "byman stefne" (*Dan.* 179a). Here and at line 192b, "byman sungon," the poet uses synecdoche, in contrast to Bede, who simplifies the catalogue of musical instruments by generalizing to "voce symphoniarum et musicorum" (*In Ezram et Neemiam* II, 1028–9, p. 313). In general *Daniel* avoids catalogues of details although these appear often in its biblical source. Thus, for example, Nabuchodonosor's animal-like appearance and behavior during his period of madness are described vividly in the Vulgate, "et foenum, ut bos, comedit, et rore caeli corpus eius infectum est, donec capilli eius in simulitudinem aquilarum crescerent, et ungues eius quasi avium,"[54] but in the poem, these lurid details are replaced by the more conventionalized sufferings of a traditional exile: The king endured hardship in the wilderness of beasts ("susl þrowode, / wildeora westen" *Dan.* 620b-la)[55] and was a companion of wild beasts ("wilddeora gewita," *Dan.* 622a).

We may wonder why the poet passed by these opportunities to liven up his poem with exotic or even lurid details. The *Pearl* poet encountered the same material in the Vulgate while working on *Cleanness*, and not only included it, but added to it, for example, in his description of Nabugo-de-nozar in bestial state:

He fares forth on alle faure, fogge watȝ his mete,
& ete ay as a horce when erbes were fallen,
þus he countes hym a kow, þat watȝ a kyug ryche,
Quyle seuen syþeȝ were ouer-seyed someres I trawe.
By þat, mony þik thyȝe þryȝt vmbe his lyre,
þat alle watȝ dubbed & dyȝt in þe dew of heuen:
Faxe fyltered, & felt flosed hym vmbe,
þat schad fro his schulderes to his schyre wykes,

& twenty-folde twyna*n*de hit to his tos raȝt
þer mony clyuy as clyde hit clyȝt to-geder.
His berde I-brad alle his brest to þe bare vrþe,
His browes bresed as breres about his brode chekes;
Holȝe were his yȝen & vnder campe hores,
& al watz gray as þe glede, *with* ful gry*m*me clawres
þat were croked & kene as þe kyte paune.[56]

Elsewhere, as here, *Cleanness* presents catalogues of details, often on the authority of no more than a hint in the biblical source, but the *Daniel* poet's interests, in contrast with those of the *Pearl* poet, are predominantly conceptual rather than visual. It may be, too, that in this regard *Daniel* was influenced by Jerome's *In Danielem* or at least by exegetical ideas that are traceable to Jerome. The poet's idea that Nabochodonossor was in the wilderness for seven years ("seofon winter samod," *Dan.* 620a) reflects Jerome's understanding that "septem tempora" in the Vulgate (Dan. 4:20 and 29) means "septem annos" (*In Danielem* I, 782 and 782, p. 810)—evident also in "seuen . . . som*er*es" in *Cleanness* (line 1686). This detail by itself proves nothing, since the interpretation "septem annos" was widely accepted and did not come to be challenged until the twelfth century,[57] but *Daniel* agrees with Jerome on other points also: that the king suffered from madness, not bestial transformation (hence *In Dan.* I, 782–803, offers no tantalizing details of animalism, but instead notes that many madmen live in the wilderness like beasts); that his dementia was inflicted as a punishment for pride, "superbiam" (I. 802); that during his madness God preserved the kingdom for him intact ("imperium reseruatum sit regnumque potentissimum absque rege tanto tampore fuerit" etc., I, 785 sqq., probably the source for *Dan.* 636–39); and that he was fated to dwell among beasts, "inter bruta animalia uixerit" (I, 771–72), "inter bestias uixerat" (I, 784), as a "wilddeora gewita" (*Dan.* 622a). This, perhaps, reflects a medieval tradition according to which wild beasts leave madmen unharmed because madmen are lacking in reason, like themselves.[58] Throughout all of this it is the understanding of concepts associated with Nabuchodonosor's madness, and not his physical appearance, that comes to the fore.

If *Daniel* was influenced by biblical exegesis in its representation of particular episodes, very likely this influence extended to the general conception of theme in the poem. The exegetical tradition, however, does not impose a single view of the "meaning" of Daniel, but rather it allows for approaches variously theological, moral, or political in emphasis, and this complexity is evident within particular commentaries as well as in the exegetical tradition taken as a whole. Thus while Jerome interprets the stories of Nabuchodonosor and Baldasar in a moral sense as warnings against pride, he also develops a theological interpretation according to which the vessels taken from Solomon's Temple are symbolic of religious doctrines; thus, the misuse of these vessels at Baldasar's feast is sacrilege on the literal or historical level, and heresy on the allegorical level (*In Dan.* I, 30–41, and II, 43–71). Bede accepts Jerome's interpretation of the vessels as doctrines (*In Ezr.* I, 164–78), but develops his own moral interpretation of the Babylonian captivity as an allegory of the "confusion" of sin that diverts the Christian from that proper "confession" that leads to the liberating vision of peace and light ("ad uisionem liberae pacis et lucis" *In Ezr.* I, 245–6). This, of course, is based upon the traditional etymologizing of Babylon as "confusio peccatorum" and of Jerusalem as "visio pacis" (*In Ezr.* I, 233 sqq ; Ierome, *In Dan.* I, 28–30).[59] On the historical level, the Persians brought about the destruction of the "Chaldeorum imperium" in order to liberate the "populum Dei," so that under Cyrus they could return to Jerusalem to rebuild the temple (*In Ezr.* I, 178-82), and on the mystical level, Cyrus is symbolic of Jesus Christ who frees the *populus Dei* from the tyranny of the devil (*In Ezr.* I, 148–95). Bede's emphasis is on the role of Cyrus as a prefiguration of Christ, but this typology is based upon the linkage of two political concepts: the *populus Dei*, and *translatio imperii*. By divine plan the *imperium* of the Chaldeans is transferred to Persia, so that the *populus Dei* might be liberated.

The *populus Dei* as a political concept has its roots in the Old Testament representation of the Hebrews as God's chosen people, but the Hebrews, deceived by the devil, brought about Christ's crucifixion and thereby lost their special status as the *populus Dei*; in this role they were superseded by the *populus christianus*. For Augustine, Jerome, and Isidore of Seville, as well as in Anglo-Saxon and Frankish political thinking, the idea of a *populus christianus* was the basis for the authority of Christian governments, and also for the medieval ideal of kingship.[60] Cicero had declared that there is a *res publica*, a *populus*, only where there is justice; without justice there is no community of interest, but only a multitude lacking any common sense of right.[61] This argument is recapitulated by Augustine in *De civitate Dei* 2.21, and the definition of *populus* is repeated by Isidore. But for Augustine, Rome was never a *res publica*, because true justice never had a place in it. The only true republic is the one founded by Christ, the *populus christianus*. True kingship, according to this view, is a *ministerium*; the ideal king is a *minister Dei* who governs and corrects the *populus christianus* or *populus Dei*.[62] The king, as *minister Dei*, must be enlightened by Christian teaching, for as it is the duty of the Church to teach Christian principles, it is the duty of the ruler to learn them.[63]

In the alternative, when a ruler or a peoples adopt evil practices, God intervenes in history by transferring military and political power—the *imperium*—from one nation to another. The *translatio imperii* thus was seen as God's instrument to provide for the "correction" of a people, and this concept, like those of the *populus Dei* and of kingship as a *ministerium Dei*, was thought to have biblical authority. Passages cited in medieval accounts of *translatio imperii* included (among others) Proverbs 14:34, Amos 1–2, Jonah 3:5–10, Habakkuk 1:5–11, and Ecclesiasticus (Jesus Sirach) 10:10,[64] but the true foundation of the concept was the story of Nabuchodonosor and Baltassar in the first five chapters of Daniel.[65] Particularly useful was Nabuchodonosor's first dream, which, on the basis of Daniel's observation that God "mutat tempora et aetates; transfert regna atque constituit"[66] (Dan. 2:21), could be interpreted symbolically as a prophecy of the "course of empire" from Babylon (the golden head of Nabuchodonosor's image) to Media-Persia (the silver breast and arms) to Greece (the brass belly and thighs) to Rome (the iron legs). This, indeed, though with various elaborations of detail, was the interpretation not only of Hippolytus (*In Dan.* II. 11, 1-13), but also of Jacobus Nisebenus (*serm.* V) and of his disciple Ephraem of Syria as well as of other early Christian writers,[67] and the theme had its counterpart in the pro-Roman historiographical theme of the succession of four kingdoms, for example in a second-century B.C. fragment of Aemilius Sura preserved by Velleius Paterculus, and in the fourth Sibylline Oracle.[68] Jerome follows a tradition already well established when he quotes Dan. 2:31–5 and interprets the details symbolically as referring to the succession of Babylonians, Medes and Persians, Macedonians under Alexander, and Romans (*In Dan.* I, 370–414). The biblical account of Baltassar's feast and the conquest of Babylon by Darius the Mede, of course, was understood literally as an example of *translatio imperii* (*In Dan.* II, 159–74 and 187–216). Bede, as we have seen, links this example of *translatio imperii* (*In Ezr.* I, 95–98, alluding to Dan. 5:30–31) with the idea of divine intervention in history to preserve the *populus Dei*.

Elsewhere I have argued that Cynewulf's *Elene* was influenced by the political and historiographical ideas summarized here. The historical basis for that view had to do with the expanded role that Cynewulf gives Constantine, compared with the minimal role that Constantine plays in his Latin source, the *Vita Cyriaci*. Constantine, as the earliest Christian ruler, in early medieval political thought embodied the ideal of the king as a *minister Dei* who must govern and correct the *populus Dei* or *populus christianus*. In his representation of the establishment of a Christian *ordo* under Constantine, Cynewulf also makes use of the idea of a *translatio legis* or *translatio religionis* or *translatio studii*, according to which, through the conversion of Judas and through the miraculous recovery of the true Cross, the Hebrews relinquished to the Christians their ancient control of the traditions of learning and law. These concepts of *translatio legis, religionis, studii* or *artium* have complex histories in and of themselves,[69] but are modeled on the *translatio imperii* idea and often are implicated in the development of the *translatio imperii* as a theme.

As with *Elene*, so with *Daniel*, there is a historical basis for the view that the poem develops the themes of the *populus Dei* and *translatio imperii* in relation to each other—for the first five chapters of *Daniel*, on which the Old English poem is based, functioned in medieval historiography as the *locus classicus* for the idea of *translatio imperii*. These themes are developed more or less systematically throughout *Daniel*.

In the prologue, the Hebrews' special status as the *populus Dei* is mentioned in connection with the idea of *wær*, "covenant":

þenden þæt folc mid him   hiera fæder wære
healdan woldon,   wæs him hyrde god,
heofonrices weard,   halig drihten,
wuldres waldend.[70]   (10–13a)

"Wær" here calls to mind God's promise to Abraham that "benedicam tibi, et multiplicabo semen tuum sicut stellas caeli, et velut arenam quae est in littore maris"[71] (Gen. 22:17), which provided the basis for Dan. 3:35–36 in Azarias's prayer:

Neque auferas misericordiam tuam a nobis,
Propter Abraham, dilectum tuum,
Et Isaac, servum tuum,
Et Israel, sanctum tuum,
Quibus locutus es pollicens quod multiplicares semen eorum
Sicut stellas caeli,
Et sicut arenam quae est in littore maris.[72]

The poet incorporates this material into his version of Azarias's prayer for deliverance, changing "Israel" to "Iacobe" (line 314a) to reflect the three-name formula that appears often in Genesis in connection with the "covenant" theme:

Ne forlet þu usic ana,   ece drihten,
for þam miltsum   ðe ðec men hligað,
and for ðam treowum   þe þu, tirum fæst,
niða nergend,   genumen hæfdest
to Abrahame   and to Isaace
and to Iacobe,   gasta scyppend.
Þu him þæt gehete   þurh hleoðorcwyde,
þæt þu hyra frumcyn   in fyrndagum
ican wolde,   þætte æfter him
on cneorissum   cenned wurde,
and seo mænigeo   mære wære,
hat to hebbanne   swa heofonsteorran
bebugað bradne hwyrft,   *oð*þe brimfaroþes,
sæfaroða sand,   geond sealtne wæg
in eare gryndeð,   þæt his unrima
in wintra worn   wurðan sceolde.
Fyl nu frumspræce,   ðeah heora fea lifigen![73]   (309–25)

The verse "ðeah heora fea lifigen" contrasts with the remark in the prologue that the "Israela cyn" carried off to Babylon were a countless number of men, "beorna unrim" (lines 69a and 70b).

Azarias's prayer is for deliverance not of himself and his companions from the furnace, but for the Hebrews, the *populus Dei*, from their captivity in Babylon, and he acknowledges that this captivity came about because the Hebrews had broken the covenant upon which their special status was based:

> We þæs lifgende
> worhton on worulde,   eac ðon wom dyde
> user yldran.   For oferhygdum
> bræcon bebodo   burhsittendum,
> had oferhogedon   halgan lifes.[74]   (295b–9)

It is clear from the text, however, that Azarias and his companians had
not sinned, but

> Ða wæron æðelum   Abrahames bearn,
> wæron wærfæste[75]   (193–4a)

and Azarias is said to be "wer womma leas"[76] (282a). This accords with
Jerome's interpretation of Dan. 3:29 "Peccavimus enim, et inique
egimus recedentes a te"[77]—for Jerome writes:

> Et certe tres pueri non peccauerunt, nec eius aetatis erant quando ducti
> sunt in Babylonem ut propter sua uitia punirentur. Ergo quomodo hi ex
> persona populi loquuntur . . . [78]

Azarias's prayer, indeed, recalls the poet's observation in the prologue
that the Hebrews, although they

> wæron mancynnes   metode dyrust,
> dugoða dyrust,   drihtne leofost[79]   (36-7)

nevertheless they "in gedwolan hweorfan" (lines 22b) and "curon
deofles cræft"[80] (line 32b), and for this reason God allowed the Baby-
lonian *imperium* to prevail against them. So long as the Hebrews kept
the covenant, they possessed an *imperium*, "þæt hie oft fela folca feore
gesceodon"[81] (*Dan.* 15), but when they broke the covenant, Nabo-
chodonossor, God's instrument of punishment, carried them off as
slaves, "to weorcþeowum" (line 74b).

But Babylon, like Jerusalem before her, will lose her power through
the process of *translatio imperii*, as is foretold in the first of Nabo-
chodonossor's dreams, about

> hu woruld wære   wundrum geteod,
> ungelic yldum   oð edsceafte.

> Wearð him on slæpe   soð gecyðed,
> þætte rices gehwæs   reðe sceolde gelimpan,
> eorðan dreamas,   ende wurðan.[82]   (111–15)

The poet omits the details of the broken image that the king saw, with
its symbolic metals, wood, and clay, and also omits the usual interpre-
tation of these in terms of the "course of empire" from Babylon to Per-
sia to Greece to Rome, and his summary of Nabochodonossor's first
dream could, indeed, be said to reflect the generalized theme of
"mutability," rather than the more specific one of *translatio imperii*,
were it not for details elsewhere in the poem that point to the latter
theme. Nabochodonossor's second dream, about the fallen tree, fore-
shadows his period of madness, and Daniel in his interpretation of it
warns that the king's position is insecure even though he has no
earthly enemies:

> Nis þe wiðerbreca,
> man on moldan,   nymðe metod ana.
> Se ðec aceorfeð   of cyningdome . . . [83]   (565b–67)

Again, the poet reminds us of God's power to make and unmake kings
even when he reports Nabochodonossor's death after a long reign: The
king had ruled peacefully "oðþæt him god wolde / þurh hryre hreddan
hea rice"[84] (lines 669b–70). Then when he begins his account of Bal-
dazar's feast, the poet announces the theme of *translatio imperii* in the
most explicit terms possible:

> Ða wæs endedæg
> ðæs ðe Caldeas   cyningdom ahton.
> Ða metod onlah   Medum and Persum
> aldordomes   ym lytel fæc,
> let Babilone   blæd swiðrian,
> þone þa hæleð   healdan sceoldon.
> Wiste he ealdormen   in unrihtum,
> ða ðe ðy rice   rædan sceoldon.[85]   (678b–85)

There follows a description of the "Meda aldor" sitting at home—"ham-
sittende" (line 686b), designing the ruin of Babylon, just as Nabo-
chodonossor, earlier, had taken counsel in Babylon, "on his burhstede"
(line 47b), designing the ruin of Jerusalem. Repetition of detail in these

two places, both on the eve of military conquest, calls attention to the idea of the *translatio imperii* as a continuing process of divine intervention in history.

A final comment must be made about the vessels from Solomon's temple, and the Babylonians' use of them at Baldazar's feast, which brings down God's wrath. Notwithstanding the influence of Jerome and the near-contemporaneity of Bede, the poem provides no support for the idea that the vessels represent "doctrines" or that the abuse of them symbolizes heresy, although, of course, abuse of the vessels is a literal example of sacrilege. The poet, it may be, thinks of Baldazar's "Last Supper" as a sort of parody of Communion:

> Gesæt þa to symble   siðestan dæge
> Caldea cyning   mid cneowmagum;
> þær medugal wearð   mægenes wisa.[86]   (700–2)

However this may be, in *Daniel* the role of the temple treasures calls to mind a "forbidden treasure" motif inspired partly by Daniel 5 and partly by the spoliation of the temple by the Romans under Titus, according to which ownership of Solomon's treasures brings ruin upon a people. This theme is developed in a dramatic way by Procopius in his account of the old-style Roman triumph that Justinian observed in the streets and hippodrome of Byzantium in A.D. 534, to celebrate his victory over the Vandal kingdom. Among the booty brought from Carthage and exhibited in the hippodrome were "the treasures of the Jews, which Titus, the son of Vespasian, together with certain others, had brought to Rome after the capture of Jerusalem." These, in turn, had been seized by the Vandals under Gizeric when they despoiled the Palatium in Rome, in A.D. 455. Seeing the treasures on display, one of the Jews in the hippodrome gave warning to Justinians officers:

> "These treasures I think it inexpedient to carry into the palace in Byzantium. Indeed, it is not possible for them to be elsewhere than in the place where Solomon, the king of the Jews, formerly placed them. For it is because of these that Gizeric captured the palace of the Romans, and that now the Roman army has captured that of the Vandals."[87]

Upon hearing this, Justinian became fearful and had the treasures conveyed to Christian sanctuaries in Jerusalem. The story from Procopius, of course, is but a distant analogue; the poet's source is the Vulgate *Daniel*. But in the matter of the symbolic associations of the treasure, the distant analogue may give us better guidance than Jerome's commentary on Daniel or Bede's on the Babylonian captivity. Both the *Daniel* poet and Procopius link ownership of the temple treasures with national ruin and thus with the concept of *translatio imperii*.

In my analysis of theme in *Daniel*, I have not reviewed in detail the moral concepts of pride versus humble obedience, idolatry versus loyalty to the covenant, and drunkenness versus good counsel, because these have been discussed adequately in the published criticism of the poem, and I do not wish to repeat material that is readily available elsewhere. Critics have disagreed about which of these themes should be thought of as central or most important in the poem, but it seems to me that they are equally important as secondary concepts that complement the companion themes of *populus Dei* and *translatio imperii*. God's care for His *populus* enhances the moral life of man; and the *translatio imperii* is an instrument through which He provides for the correction and salvation of His *populus*, while also bringing nations to ruin as a punishment for wickedness. Thus, the moral concepts are necessary and inevitable adjuncts to the historiographical themes of the poem.

In my analysis of style and theme generally, I have tried to identify the most distinctive qualities of *Daniel*. Two features of style require special attention. In terms of versification, the *Daniel* poet develops a "ragged style" that deviates from the "norms" of alliterative poetry through the use of hypermetric lines and verses, "light" verses, and single half lines. Some features of this "ragged style" have at times been thought of as aesthetic lapses, but I am inclined to a sympathetic alternative: The apparent lapses result not from incompetence, but from a studied indifference to the "norms" of versification. In terms of content development, the *Daniel* poet, like Cynewulf, exemplifies the "reflective" style in that his aim is mainly didactic: He wants to tell a story clearly, and through "thematic repetition" he points to the thematic issues that arise from the story.

Above all else, the poet aims for a faithful representation of the first five chapters of the Vulgate Daniel, according to his understanding of the significance of this material. "Faithful representation" is not the same thing as "biblical paraphrase." The poet does more than repeat the contents of his biblical source. From a background of learning, influenced by Jerome and perhaps also by Bede, he creates a poetic narrative that represents the medieval significance of Daniel.[88]

NOTES

1. *Daniel and Azarias*, ed. Farrell (London, 1974), 3–6 and 32–33; earlier, "The Structure of Old English *Daniel*," *NM* 69 (1968), 533–59, especially pp. 536–41 [reprinted in the present volume—*ed*]. Farrell's edition is used for all quotations.

2. P. J. Lucas, "On the Incomplete Ending of *Daniel* and the Addition of *Christ and Satan* to MS Junius 11," *Anglia* 97 (1979), 46–59. This would be similar to the ending of ME *Cleanness*, lines 1755–1812; in *Early English Alliterative Poems in the West-Midland Dialect of the Fourteenth Century*, ed. R. Morris, EETS OS 1, 2nd ed. (Oxford, 1869), 35–88.

3. D. A. Jost, "Biblical Sources in the Old English *Daniel* 1–78," *ELN* 15 (1978), 257–63.

4. *Über die Dichtungen des angelsächsen Cædmon und deren Verfasser* (Göttingen, 1860); so noted by Farrell, ed., 23, n. 60. So also H. Balg, *Der Dichter Cædmon und seine Werke* (Bonn, 1882).

5. The most important discussions have been G. Steiner, *Über die Interpolation im angelsachsichen Gedichte "Daniel"* (Leipzig, 1889); W. J. Craigie, "Interpolations and Omissions in Anglo-Saxon Poetical Texts," *Philologia* 2 (1923), 5–19 (for an argument based on section divisions in the manuscript); Sir Israel Gollancz, ed., *The Caedmon Manuscript of Old English Poetry* (Oxford, 1927), lxxv–xcvii.

6. Gollancz, ed., *Caedmon Manuscript*, lxxxvi.

7. Farrell, "The Unity of Old English *Daniel*," *RES* 18 (1967), 117–35; again in his edition, 23–26.

8. For "envelope patterns" in general see A. C. Bartlett, *The Larger Rhetorical Patterns in Anglo-Saxon Poetry* (New York, 1935), 9–29; C. B. Hieatt, "Envelope Patterns and the Structure of *Beowulf*," *English Studies in Canada* 1 (1975), 249–65; H. W. Tonsfeldt, "Ring Structure in *Beowulf*," *Neophilologus* 61 (1977), 443–52; Walter H. Beale, "Rhetoric in the Old English Verse-Paragraph," *NM* 80 (1979), 133–42.

9. N. D. Isaacs, *Structural Principles in Old English Poetry* (Knoxville, TN, 1968), 149–50.

10. G. P. Krapp, ed., *The Junius Manuscript*, ASPR 1 (New York, 1931), xxxii; so also E. E. Wardale, *Chapters on Old English Literature* (London, 1935), 135.

11. *The Oldest English Texts*, ed. Henry Sweet, EETS OS 83 (London, 1885), 414–15.

12. Albert Baugh and Kemp Malone, *A Literary History of England, vol. 1: The Middle Ages*, 2nd ed. (New York, 1948), 66–67.

13. Alternatively, it is possible that both *Daniel* and *Azarias* were influenced by a lost poetic "Proto-Daniel," but it seems pointless to clutter the scene with an imagined "Proto-Daniel" if this in the main is to be regarded as the equivalent of the Junius MS *Daniel*.

14. Baugh and Malone, *Literary History*, 66.

15. Farrell, "Unity of Old English *Daniel*," 122. The Song of the Three Children (Dan. 3:52–90) also has this psalm-like character, but, as noted above, the Daniel poet did not use this section of the Vulgate.

16. See Farrell, ed., 18–22, and the index of hypermetric lines prepared by A. J. Bliss in *The Metre of Beowulf* (Oxford, 1958), 167–68. Farrell states that there are no hypermetric "lines" in *Azarias*, which is true, but line 77 must be regarded as a "mixed" line according to his terminology.

17. A. J. Bliss, "Single Half-lines in Old English Poetry," *N&Q* 216 (1971), 442–49.

18. B. J. Timmer, "Expanded Lines in Old English Poetry," *Neophilologus* 35 (1951), 226–30; and further, Bliss, "The Origin and Structure of the Old English Hypermetric Line," *N&Q* 217 (1972), 242–48. For *Heliand*: W. P. Lehmann, *The Development of Germanic Verse Form* (Austin, Texas, 1956), 111–12.

19. Farrell, ed., 19.

20. A. Jones, "*Daniel* and *Azarias* as Evidence for the Oral Formulaic Character of Anglo-Saxon Poetry," *MÆ* 35 (1966), 95–102.

21. Poems are quoted from *The Anglo-Saxon Poetic Records*, ed. G. P. Krapp and E. V. K. Dobbie, 6 vols. (New York, 1931–53).

22. O. Hofer, "Über die Entstehung des angelsächsischen Gedichtes *Daniel*," *Anglia* 12 (1889), 199–204; Farrell, ed., 136.

23. Farrell, "Some Remarks on the Exeter Book *Azarias*," *MÆ* 41 (1972), 1–8, develops a similar argument for the priority of *Daniel* using other details.

24. F. A. Blackburn, ed., *Exodus and Daniel* (Boston, 1907), xix–xx.

25. *Doctrine and Poetry* (New York, 1959), 224–27. In *The Web of Words* (Albany, 1970), 137, Huppé notes that *Daniel*, like the OE *Judith*, is "selectively thematic." Wordplay in *Daniel* is discussed further by Roberta Frank in her Harvard University dissertation, "Wordplay in Old English Poetry" (1968), 80–100. Stanley B. Greenfield, in *A Critical History of Old English Literature* (New York, 1965), 160, cites Huppé's interpretation with approval, while cautioning that Huppé's comments are based "really on only the beginning of the poem."

26. Farrell, "The Structure of Old English *Daniel*," 541–49; ed., 34–35.

27. *Cynewulf: Structure, Style, and Theme in His Poetry* (Madison, NJ, 1983), 46.

28. "The Old English *Daniel*: A Warning Against Pride," *English Studies* 59 (1978), 1–9. Caie argues further that the Junius Manuscript is unified by this theme, since pride provides motivation for human evil in *Genesis* and *Exodus*, and the pattern of pride and sin is "not resolved until the final poem in the manuscript, *Christ and Satan*, in which Christ sets the example of how the cycle can be broken" (9). This approach to the Junius Manuscript is not possible, however, because of the nature of the manuscript's composition; scholars generally agree that *Genesis*, *Exodus* and *Daniel* originally were gathered in one manuscript, to which *Christ and Satan* was added later to form the enlarged Junius MS.

29. Isaacs, *Structural Principles*, 145 and 150.

30. J. W. Kirkland and C. F. Modlin, "The Art of *Azarias*," *MÆ* 41 (1972), 9–15.

31. J. Gardner, *The Construction of Christian Poetry in Old English* (Carbondale, IL, 1974), 34–37.

32. A. Lee, *The Guest-hall of Eden* (New Haven, 1972), 52–53.

33. H. J. Solo, "The Twice-Told Tale: A Reconsideration of the Syntax and Style of the Old English *Daniel*, 245–429," *Papers on Language and Literature* 9 (1973), 347–64, especially pp. 358 sqq., but Solo does not succeed in relating details from *Daniel* to his exegetical materials.

34. R. E. Bjork, "Oppressed Hebrews and the Song of Azarias in the Old English *Daniel*," *SP* 77 (1980), 213–26.

35. Caie, "A Warning Against Pride," 4, and Bjork, "Oppressed Hebrews," 216–17, discuss the associations of drunkenness and sin in *Judith* and in *Juliana* 483b–90a. Bjork, 217–19, argues tentatively for the possible influence of Jerome's *In Danielem* (of which more below), but the connection is remote.

36. Farrell, edition, 35 and 73n.; earlier. "The Structure of Old English *Daniel*," 546–49.

37. Bjork, "Oppressed Hebrews," 219.

38. Then Nabuchodonosor the king was astonished: and he rose up in haste, and said to his best [counselors]: Did we not cast three men bound into the midst of the fire? They answered the king and said. True, King. He answered and said: Indeed. I see four men loose, and walking in the midst of the fire, and they have no injury, and the form of the fourth is like the son of God.

39. Farrell, edition, 61n.

40. Jerome makes this symbolic connection in his commentary on Dan. 3:19: Nabuchodonosor's *furor*, which approximates madness ("sed furor et ira, quae insaniae proxima est"), has a concrete parallel in the immoderate fire

of the furnace: *In Danielem* I, iii, 19a–c: in *S. Hieronymi presbyteri opera pars 1. 5*: *Commentariorum in Danielem Libri III (IV)*, CCSL 75A (Turnhout, 1964), 802, lines 576–91. Jerome's view, that Nabuchodonosor's wrath was something like madness, was developed in later biblical exegesis (beyond the reach of our poet) by distinguishing between *ira* (reasonable wrath) and *furor* (insane wrath); this, at any rate, is the analysis of Richard of St. Victor, in *De eruditione hominis interioris*, *PL* 196, 1241

41. *Bedae Venerabilis opera, pars. 2, opera exegetica, 2A,* ed. D. Hurst, CCSL 119A (Turnhout, 1969), 247, lines 241–44.

42. Farrell, "A Possible Source for Old English *Daniel*," *NM* 70 (1969), 84–90; for translations: Hippolyte, *Commentaire sur Daniel,* ed. and trans. M. Le Fèvre (Paris, 1947); and *Fathers of the Third Century: Hippolytus, Cyprian, Caius, Novatian,* ed. A. Roberts and J. Donaldson, in *The Ante-Nicene Fathers,* vol. 5 (Grand Rapids, MI, 1965), 177–91.

43. *In Danielem* I, 23–41, on Dan. 1:2b, pp. 777–78. Later on, in his commentary on the use of the vessels at Baltassar's feast (*In Dan.* II, 43–71, on Dan. 5:4; pp. 821–82). Jerome refers to "uasa templi Dei" rather than to "partem uasorum," although he continues to regard the vessels as symbols of doctrines, and the misuse of them as symbolic of heresy.

44. G. Steiner, *Über die Interpolation im angelsächsischen Gedichte "Daniel"* (Leipzig, 1889), 31–32.

45. Farrell, "A Possible Source for Old English *Daniel*," 88–9; Hippolytus, ed. Le Fèvre, 227.

46. Farrell, "Possible Source," 87; Hippolytus, ed. Le Fèvre, 91.

47. *Cynewulf's Elene,* ed. P. O. F. Gradon (London, 1958); for the *Vita Cyriaci*: *Cynewulf's Elene,* ed. C. W. Kent (Boston, 1891), 31 and 29.

48. For the *populus Dei* concept in *Elene* see Anderson, *Cynewulf,* 125–33.

49. Farrell, ed., 135.

50. For "purpurescit" glossed as "readode" see Thomas Wright, *Anglo-Saxon and Old English Vocabularies,* 2nd ed., ed. R. P. Wülcker [1884] (Darmstadt, 1968), 466, line 37, and 507, line 23. For "purpura" (noun) and "purpureus" (adj.), glossed as "felleread" (n. and adj.), see A. S. Cook, *A Glossary of the Old Northumbrian Gospels* (Halle, 1894), 56. For the place of *basu* in the OE color vocabulary, see N. F. Barley, "Old English colour classification: Where do matters stand?," *ASE* 3 (1974), 18–19 and 25.

51. Text in *The Phoenix,* ed. N. F. Blake (Manchester, 1964), 91; of the tail of the phoenix, "in her spots the blended purple reddens."

52. The beautifully variegated tail of the phoenix thus is described as "partly brown, partly crimson, and partly covered artistically with bright spots."

53. Hippolytus understood Nabuzardan's office to be that of chief of the

slaughterers, or chief cook (I, 10: ed. Le Fèvre, 77). Farrell, ed., 49n., regards the "witgan" as "magicians." Since it is "somewhat unusual for a group of magicians to attack a city," Farrell regards the detail as symbolic of the "arcane learning" of the Chaldeans in contrast with "effectual knowledge (*ræd*)." *Witga*, however, is a general term and not usually a pejorative one. C. W. Kennedy, in *The Cædmon Poems Translated Into English Prose* (London, 1916), 122, translates as "wise men." The epithet "witga" is applied to Daniel at line 149b.

54. "He ate grass like an ox, and his body was wet with the dew of heaven, until his hairs grew like eagles' [feathers], and his nails like birds' [claws]."

55. S. B. Greenfield, "The Formulaic Expression of the Theme of Exile in Anglo-Saxon Poetry," *Speculum* 30 (1955), 200–6, discusses this tradition. For Nabuchodonosor's beastly appearance see Émile Mâle, *L'art réligieux du VIIe siècle en France* (Paris, 1928), 4–17.

56. *Cleanness*, lines 1683–97. In *Cleanness* the poet modifies the structure by allowing Daniel to recall Nabugo-de-nozar's madness in his long address to Baltazar. Thus through a sort of "flashback" the contents of Daniel 4 are enclosed within a story based mainly on Daniel 5.

57. Peter Comestor, *Hist. scholastica, PL* 198, 1452, argues that the seven-year punishment intended for Nabuchodonosor was reduced to seven months through Daniel's intercession. This, of course, lacks biblical authority and is disputed by Nicholas de Lyra, *Biblia sacra cum glossa ordinaria*, 7 vols. (Paris, 1590), IV, 304. The point is discussed briefly by P. B. R. Doob, *Nebuchadnezzar's Children: Conventions of Madness in Middle English Literature* (New Haven, 1974), 71n.

58. Nicholas de Lyra, *Glossa ordinaria*, IV, 304: noted by Doob, *Nebuchadnezzar's Children* 70–71, although Doob does not deal with the OE *Daniel* in her analysis.

59. For Jerusalem as "visio pacis" see further J. E. Cross, "*Halga Hyht* and Poetic Stimulus in *The Advent Poem (Christ 1)*, 50–70," *Neophilologus* 53 (1969), 194–99.

60. See Jeremy Adams, *The Populus of Augustine and Jerome* (New Haven, 1971), and Adams, "The Political Grammar of Isidore of Seville," *Actes du quartrième Congrès Internationale de la Philosophie Médièvale*, Montreal, August–September 1967: *Arts liberaux et philosophie au moyen âge* (Montreal, 1969), 763–75. The concept of a *populus* in Anglo-Saxon political thought is brought out by E. E. Stengel, "Imperator und Imperium bei den Angelsachsen," *Deutsches Archiv für Erforschung des Mittelalters* 16 (1960), 15–72. For Carolingian France, see J. M. Wallace-Hadrill, "The *Via Regia* of the Carolingian Age," in *Trends in Medieval Political Thought*, ed. Beryl Smalley (Oxford, 1965), 22–41, especially pp. 37 sqq.

61. M. Tullius Cicero, *De re publica* I, 25, and II, 42.

62. The idea of the king as *minister* over a *populus Dei* was first expressed by Gregory the Great; see Wallace-Hadrill, *Early Germanic Kingship in England and on the Continent* (Oxford, 1971), 31. The concept is prominent in Bede's *Hist. ecclesiastica* 1.32 and in Wulfstan's *Institutes of Polity*; see my *Cynewulf*, 126–31.

63. See W. Ullmann, *The Growth of Papal Government in the Middle Ages* (London, 1955), 19, for this "*discere–docere* antithesis," which goes back to Gelasius.

64. The influence of Ecelesiasticus was emphasized by E. R. Curtius, *Europäische Literatur und lateinisches Mittelalter* (Bern, 1954), 38–39.

65. The best discussion of this is Werner Goez, *Translatio Imperii: Ein Beitrag zur Geschichte des Geschichtsdenkens und der politischen Theorien im Mittelalter und in der frühen Neuzeit* (Tübingen, 1958), 4–17.

66. "[God] changes times and ages: He removes and sets up kings."

67. The tradition is discussed by H. H. Rowley, *Darius the Mede and the Four World Empires in the Book of Daniel* (Cardiff, 1959); see especially pp. 184–85.

68. See J. W. Swain, "The Theory of the Four Monarchies: Opposition History under the Roman Empire," *Classical Philology* 35 (1940), 1–21, and D. Flusser, "The Four Empires in the Fourth Sibyl and in the Book of Daniel," *Israel Oriental Studies* 2 (1972), 148–75.

69. *Cynewulf*, 121–33; for extensions of the *translatio imperii* idea, see F. J. Worstbrock, "Translatio Artium: Über die Herkunft und Entwicklung einer kulturhistorischen Theorie," *Archiv für Kulturgeschichte* 47 (1965), 1–22, and D. L. Gassman, "*Translatio Studii*. A Study of Intellectual History in the Thirteenth Century" (diss., Cornell University, 1973).

70. "As long as the people kept their fathers' covenant with Him, God was their guardian, the Lord of the heavenly kingdom, the holy Lord, the Ruler of glory."

71. "I will bless you, and multiply your seed as the stars of heaven, and as the sand on the seashore." Cf. Gen. 13:16, 15:5, and 26:4.

72. "Do not withdraw your mercy from us, for the sake of Abraham, your beloved, and Isaac, your servant, and Israel, your holy one, to whom you promised to make their seed multiply as the stars of heaven, and as the sand on the seashore."

73. "Forsake us not, eternal Lord, for the sake of the mercy that men attribute to You, and for the sake of the covenant which You, fast in glory, Savior of men, had compacted with Abraham and with Isaac and with Jacob, Creator of souls. You promised them through prophecy in days of old that You would increase their lineage, so that after them in (their) descendants

would be begotten, and the multitude become illustrious, a nation ("hat" = *had*) to be raised up like the stars of heaven (that) turn in a wide arc, (or) like the sand of the seashore, of sea coasts, that throughout the salt sea serves as a foundation for the ocean, so that an uncountable number (of the race) should come into being in the course of years. Fulfill now the ancient prophecy, though few of them are living!"

For discussion of this difficult passage see E. Fulton, "The Anglo-Saxon *Daniel* 320–5," *MLN* 16 (1901), 122–23. From the point of view of pragmatics, the complex syntax signifies the deferential attitude of the petitioner.

74. "We the living wrought this (adversity) in the world: our fathers, also, did evil. Because of pride they broke the covenant for city-dwellers: the nation arrogantly scorned a holy life."

75. "These were noble descendants of Abraham, (who) were faithful to the covenant."

76. "A man innocent of sin."

77. "We have sinned . . ."

78. *In Dan.* I, 634–7 (p. 804): "And certainly the three youths did not sin, nor were they old enough when they were led into Babylon that they were being punished because of their own sins. Thus, they were speaking as representatives of the people." See Bjork, "Oppressed Hebrews," 224–25, for further discussion of this passage and its possible influence on *Daniel*.

79. "Were the dearest of mankind to the Lord, dearest of hosts most beloved to the Lord."

80. "Turned to error . . . chose the devil's craft."

81. "So that they often 'harmed the life' of many peoples."

82. "How the world would be wondrously shaped (sc. "transformed"), a new creation unlike to (previous) ages. The truth was made known to him in sleep, that an end must cruelly befall every kingdom (and all) earthly joys."

83. "No man on earth is an adversary to you, but only God. He will cut you off from the kingship." The poet is influenced by the contents of Daniel's interpretation of the dream, in Dan. 4:22, where Nabuchodonosor is warned that he will be punished with exile "donec scias quod dominetur Excelsus super regnum hominum, et cuicumque voluerit det illud" ("until you know that the Most High rules in the kingdom of men, and gives it to whomsoever He will").

84. "Until God desired to take the high kingship from him through death."

85. "Then the Creator granted the *imperium* to the Medes and Persians for a little time, caused the prosperity in Babylon to vanish, (the prosperity)

which the heroes 'should have held' (= had been caused [by God] to hold). He knew that the princes were unrighteous, those who should [otherwise] have ruled the kingdom." This material has no immediate source in Dan. 5 but the concept was expressed in earlier chapters in the Vulgate Daniel, as we have noted above.

86. "On the last day, the king of the Chaldeans sat at the feast with his kinsmen: there, the leader of the host became drunk with mead."

87. Procopius, *History of the Wars*, V. ix, 4–10, trans. H. B. Dewing, 7 vols. (Cambridge, MA, 1913–35), II, 281.

88. I should like to dedicate this study to my son, Daniel.

Nebuchadnezzar's Dreams in the Old English *Daniel*

ANTONINA HARBUS

This essay first appeared in English Studies *75 (1994), 489–508.*

The Old English poem *Daniel*, which paraphrases the first part of
the Old Testament Book of Daniel, has an emphasis so divergent from its
source that its modern title is hardly appropriate.[1] *Nebuchadnezzar*
would have been a more suitable title, because the focus of the poet's
attention is the king and his moody spiritual fluctuations, not the
prophetic abilities of Daniel on which the biblical writer concentrates.
Daniel deals specifically with the pride and humbling of Nebuchadnez-
zar,[2] and when the narrative does not concern him, his failings—pride
and drunkenness—are reflected in other characters, such as the Israelites
in the opening scene, and Belthazzar at the end of the poem. The poet
actively diminishes the role of Daniel in the story in order to concentrate
on the king. This new agenda is nowhere more evident, or more effec-
tively pursued, than in the treatment of Nebuchadnezzar's dreams and
their interpretation.

The modern title *Daniel* may have been suggested to early editors
by analogy with the source text in which the Daniel's prophetic abilities
are foremost. Medieval commentaries on the Book of Daniel concentrate
on its prophetic material, influenced by Jerome's early commentary[3] in
which this Church Father defends the book's revelatory purpose.[4] As a
result of this treatment of a text in which dreams are so prominent, the
prophet Daniel traditionally has been the scriptural figure most associ-
ated with dreams and their interpretation. Medieval dream interpretation
handbooks, especially those listed alphabetically, were often attributed

to him. The *Somniale Danielis* is the generic title for these alphabetic works, which were known to the English, for three vernacular versions are extant.[5] Daniel was firmly associated with dream interpretation thanks to the widespread distribution of this work, "one of the most popular books in the Middle Ages."[6]

There is other evidence which suggests that Nebuchadnezzar's dreams and Daniel's prophetic abilities held a fascination for medieval people. Extant illuminated manuscripts of Jerome's commentary include illustrations to Nebuchadnezzar's dreams,[7] and there are many references to Daniel's interpretive powers in a wide range of literature. Middle English accounts of Daniel and Nebuchadnezzar are numerous: Chaucer's *Monk's Tale*,[8] *Parson's Tale*,[9] and *House of Fame*[10]; Gower's *Confessio Amantis*[11]; *Piers Plowman*[12]; and *Cleanness*[13] reflect the traditional approach, focusing on Daniel's prophetic skill rather than Nebuchadnezzar's penitence and humility.[14]

Old English texts have a different emphasis. Homiletic accounts concentrate on Nebuchadnezzar, not Daniel, usually in order to stress the king's power and cruelty or his salvation through grace and penitence. In some instances, Nebuchadnezzar is a negative exemplum and his evil nature is emphasized: "[He] getacnode þone deofol"[15] (He signified the devil). Another example of this role is in an account of the burning of the three youths.[16] In most references, however, his positive characteristics are foremost; he is either the mighty conqueror of the Jews or the king humbled by God,[17] and Daniel is often not mentioned even in the context of Nebuchadnezzar's dreams.

In view of this homiletic material, it is not surprising that the poet of the Old English poem *Daniel* has changed the emphasis of the biblical story to concentrate on the character of Nebuchadnezzar rather than Daniel the prophet. A major element in this new focus is the poet's alteration of the accounts of Nebuchadnezzar's dreams. He changes both the elements and proportions of the biblical narrative in order to provide a commentary on the Vulgate version rather than a mere translation of it. In a story famous for its lengthy and thematically important dream sequences, the version wrought by the *Daniel* poet strikingly reduces the significance of dreams in the conversion of Nebuchadnezzar and diminishes Daniel's participation in the narrative. The result is more a psychological portrait of redemption than a tale of prophecy. The poet retains the narrative structure of his original, but changes the details, foreshadowing events and allusively referring to elements of the biblical story.

He presupposes the reader's intimate knowledge of the source text. This approach allows the poet to tell the story of Nebuchadnezzar and Daniel from a new perspective, while taking full advantage of his aptitude for the verbal echoes and etymological puns which many critics have noticed.

The *Daniel* poet's intentions and methods are most evident in the account of Nebuchadnezzar's first dream. He has radically changed the Vulgate account, greatly expanding the context of the dream without reporting its images, but his method is not based solely on expansion. He omits the divine dream sent to Daniel which enables the prophet to interpret Nebuchadnezzar's unremembered dream (Dan 2:19). Many details of the king's dream, including the famous image of the statue with legs of iron and feet of clay, are also omitted (Dan 2:31–5). Instead, the poet focuses on aspects of the scene which are absent from the biblical account, the arrival of the dream itself and Nebuchadnezzar's reaction to it. The Vulgate merely says that Nebuchadnezzar had a dream which terrified his spirit, and which he promptly forgot:

> In anno secundo regni Nabuchodonosor, vidit Nabuchodonosor somnium et conterritus est spiritus eius et somnium eius fugit ab eo. (Dan 2:1)
> [In the second year of the reign of Nebuchadnezzar, Nebuchadnezzar saw a dream and his spirit was quite terrified and his dream escaped him.]

The *Daniel* poet, however, commences the scene with Nebuchadnezzar's retirement to bed, and introduces the dream as a moving, noisy entity:

> þa þam folctogan   on frumslæpe,
> siððan to reste gehwearf   rice þeoden,
> com on sefan hwurfan   swefnes woma.   (108–10)
> [Then the disturbance of a dream came turning into the mind of that chieftain in his first sleep after the powerful prince had turned to his rest.]

The entrance of the dream, expressed by *hweorfan* (to turn), reiterates the movement of turning to rest, "to reste gehwearf" (109), and introduces a term which will become significant later in the poem with the theme of turning one's mind to God. The use of *hweorfan* here communicates the infiltration of the dream entity, twisting its noisy way into the dreamer's consciousness. The verb is particularly evocative in this context, as it has connotations of roaming and is used elsewhere in the OE corpus to refer to the activity of the mind and thought, the venue and faculty respectively of the dream.[18] It is clear that the repetitive phrasing of these lines is intended to emphasize the movement of the dream.

The dream is introduced here as a *woma*, a tumult or disturbance, as it is described later at lines 118 and 538, and is in opposition to *rest*. The collocation "swefnes woma" occurs only once outside *Daniel*, in *Elene* (71), and specifically refers to an aural disturbance.[19] It is not clear, however, how dreams were considered to be noisy, except in their properties as a waking stimulus to the sleeping consciousness. The use of this phrase in collocation with *hweorfan* stresses the arrival of the dream as an external entity with a prophetic potential which interrupts the king's moral apathy.

But the actualization of that potential is undermined in the poem. The *Daniel* poet again departs from his source text in summarizing the general import of the dream rather than reporting its images. He says it signifies

> hu woruld wære   wundrum geteod
> ungelic yldum   oð edsceafte.   (111–12)
> [how the world would be made wondrously to a new creation unlike in previous ages.]

The poet immediately reiterates and clarifies the general eschatological threat of the dream:

> Wearð him on slæpe   soð gecyðed,
> þætte rices gehwæs   reðe sceolde gelimpan,
> eorðan dreamas   ende wurðan.   (113–15)
> [In sleep the truth was made known to him, that the end of each kingdom would happen harshly, the end of earthly joy would come about.]

By providing an emphatic interpretation of the dream at this early point, the poet anticipates Daniel's prophetic role in the narrative and draws attention to the dream itself. This summary also gives the impression that the reader is experiencing the dream simultaneously with Nebuchadnezzar and thereby undermines Daniel's explanation by allowing the reader to understand the dream before the prophet himself does.

While the poet gives the dream only brief attention, he gives Nebuchadnezzar a good deal more. Unlike the Old Testament writer, the poet emphasizes throughout this scene that Nebuchadnezzar has been asleep, giving the circumstances of the dreamer more consideration than the dream's message. In order to give further stress to the occurrence of the dream, he adds a comment on the king's waking which is not in the Vulgate: "þa onwoc wulfheort, se ær wingal swæf" (116) (Then the wolf-hearted one awoke, he who had previously slept flushed with wine). This remark is included to relate the king's newfound sobriety and to focus the reader's interest on him rather than on Daniel. It is also one of the many occasions when the *Daniel* poet emphatically qualifies the character of the king. He is called *wulfheort* (116), a term which occurs only in *Daniel*, here and at lines 135 and 246. It is a critical appellation, used when Nebuchadnezzar is either frightened by his dream or bullying his understandably perplexed prophets:

þa him unbliðe andswarode
wulfheort cyning, witgum sinum.   (134–35)
[Then ungraciously the wolf-hearted king answered them, his prophets.]

The adjective is also used when he is making arrangements to burn the three children: "Wolde wulfheort cyning wall onsteallan" (246) (The wolf-hearted king intended to create a wall). Since classical and medieval bestiaries characterize the wolf as rapacious and bloodthirsty, and in Christian typology he represents the devil prowling around the flock of the faithful, here the poet is probably using the rare word *wulfheort* to suggest the greed and ferocity of the pagan king. In view of the fact that in OE poetry the wolf is one of the beasts of battle,[20] and *wulf* is a Germanic name element with positive connotations of strength, the poet here also communicates Nebuchadnezzar's power and belligerence, his arrogant nature engaged in reprehensible behavior. This is precisely the picture which the *Daniel* poet paints throughout the story.

As a further departure from the biblical text, the poet adds that the king has slept *wingal* (116) (flushed with wine). *Wingal* is a poetic word, occurring elsewhere only in the collocation *wlonc and wingal* (proud and drunk) in two poems, *The Seafarer* (29) and *The Ruin* (34).[21] *Wlonc* is not used in *Daniel* in conjunction with *wingal* (although it does describe the king at 96), but the connection between pride and drunkenness is made nevertheless in the many references to the king's arrogance. These are far more numerous in the poem than in the biblical account in a ratio of fifteen to two, and demonstrate the poet's preoccupation with the king's pride.[22] Just prior to the dream, for example, we are told that

Nebuchadnezzar "in oferhygde æghwæs lifde" (107) (lived wholly in a state of pride). In this context, it is clear that *wingal* carries negative connotations, specifically of moral weakness and spiritual unreceptiveness, as well as wolf-like physical greed. Its full significance, however, can be understood only with reference to the use of *frumslæp* (108) (first sleep).

The poet uses *frumslæp* in the introduction to the dream (108) discussed above. This word occurs only twice elsewhere in Old English, both times in prose works, where it is employed to establish the time of night.[23] In *Daniel*, *frumslæp* replaces the remark in the Vulgate that the dream occurred in the second year of the king's reign, "In anno secundo" (2:1). The poet has subtly changed the time reference from the regnal year to the part of the night in which the dream occurs. This alteration highlights the dream's prophetic significance to the drunken Nebuchadnezzar. Traditionally, true dreams occur after the first sleep, that is, after midnight.[24] According to Macrobius's influential catalogue of dream types, only fleeting nightmares occur in the first period of sleep:

> Fantasma vera, hoc est visum, cum inter vigiliam et adultam quietem in quadam, ut aiunt, prima somni nebula adhuc se vigilare aestimans qui dormire vix coepit . . . ad nullam noscendi futuri opem.[25]
> [But a *fantasma*, that is an apparition, occurs between wakefulness and advanced sleep in, as they say, that certain first mist of sleep, when he who has barely begun to sleep imagines himself to be still awake . . . to no avail in knowing the future.]

The consumption of food or strong drink just prior to sleeping can also affect the dream's prophetic qualities: "[Somnia] a vino et a cibis proxima . . . vana esse visa prope convenit."[26] (It is almost certain that [dreams] occurring just after food or drink . . . are useless.) Artemidorus, a second-century cataloguer of dreams, claims that prophetic dreams can occur before midnight provided that the dreamer has not indulged in excessive eating:

> There is no difference with regard to prediction between night and day, or between late evening and early evening, if a man falls asleep after consuming a moderate amount of food. For immoderate eating prevents one from seeing the truth even at dawn.[27]

The proviso about excessive food (and by implication drink) accounts for the presence of prophetic dreams occurring in the "first sleep" in classical literature.[28] The *Daniel* poet would have been familiar with this common classical distinction.[29] Merely by the inclusion of the appellations *wingal* and *frumslæp*, he suggests that Nebuchadnezzar was in a drunken first sleep, with drunkenness's attendant pride, unable to derive any prophetic significance from the dream by which the truth should have been made known to him ("soð gecyðed"). The introduction of this reason for Nebuchadnezzar's neglect of the dream is a major innovation by the OE poet. It demonstrates a desire to account for the king's behavior through the exposition of psychological and physical factors.

In the context of this new portrait of a drunken and decidedly proud king in *Daniel*, Nebuchadnezzar's dream has an impact on him which is different from that portrayed in the biblical story. The OE poet has replaced the Vulgate comment on the fear of the dream instilled into the king's spirit (*conterritus est spiritus eius*) with a threefold reference to the disturbing influence of the dream: "Næs him bliðe hige, / ac him sorh astah swefnes woma" (117–18) (He was not happy in his mind, but sorrow assailed him, the disturbance of the dream). The two aspects of *sorh*, grief and anxiety, are reinforced by the other two referents *næs . . . bliðe and woma*. The combination of the three terms expresses the state of complete and saddening turmoil produced by the experience of the dream, which is dramatically different from the Old Testament's "terror."[30] It suggests that Nebuchadnezzar has been shaken out of his proud drunkenness by the dream, particularly because the verb *astigan* (to mount up), often used with reference to pride (in e.g., *Dan* 494 and 596), is used here with *sorh*. The king is vulnerable to the unsettling influence of the dream even after his waking, not fearful of the dream's message as he is in the biblical story.

The poet has moved quickly over the dream to concentrate on the king's reaction to it. Claire Fanger has accounted for the reduction of the account of Nebuchadnezzar's first dream in *Daniel* with the explanation that, in his preference for personal over historical material, the poet has dealt with it briefly "because its content was not as personal or immediate as the content of later miracles" and concerns the king only "indirectly."[31] But the poet does more than this implies: to make the historical aspect of his source personal, he has introduced Nebuchadnezzar's emotional reaction to the dream itself, in the context of his salient characteristics at the time of the dream (drunkenness and pride), as well as introducing a commentary on the spiritual ramifications of the king's behavior.

The cause of the king's susceptibility to sorrow is made clear in the following line where we are told that he is unmindful of God: "No he gemunde þæt him metod wæs" (119) (He did not remember at all that he had a lord). This makes perfectly good sense in the new context created by the *Daniel* poet of sorrow visited upon the proud king. Despite this logical development, most editors of the poem emend the MS reading *metod* (lord) to *meted* (dreamed), so the sentence reads: "He did not remember what he had dreamed."[32] Blackburn believes that the greater frequency of *metod* in the poem has caused a mistranscription of *meted*.[33] But this does not adequately account for the presence of *meted* at this point, The emendation has also been justified on the basis that it reflects the meaning of the Latin at this point: "Et somnium eius fugit ab eo" (2:1) (And his dream escaped him). Yet, in a poem which exhibits so many conscious deviations from the Latin, this is not a sound argument, especially when the MS reading reflects a significant theme of the poem, the relationship between grace and memory.

Forgetfulness of divine omnipotence is an issue on which the *Daniel* poet concentrates in his rendition of the biblical story of Nebuchadnezzar's journey towards grace. The Augustinian expression of the acknowledgement of God in terms of memory at line 119 is repeated at line 624, in almost the same terms: "Gemunde þa on mode þæt metod wære" (He remembered then in his mind that there was a Lord) and again at line 629 when "his gast ahwearf in godes gemynd" (his mind came around to the memory of God). The poet consistently describes Nebuchadnezzar's arrogance in terms of mnemonic failure. Prior to the dream, he remarks that Nebuchadnezzar did not remember to thank God for his gifts:

> Nales ðy þe he þæt moste   oððe gemunan wolde
> þæt he þara gifena   gode þancode.   (85–86)
> [Not at all that he could or would remember that he should have thanked God for those gifts.]

The theme of forgetfulness as a theme of Nebuchadnezzar's distance from God provides thematic support for the reading *metod*, the Lord the king has forgotten. Lexical arguments also oppose the popular emendation of *metod* to *meted* at line 119. *Meted* is a reconstructed past participle from *mætan* (to dream), not attested elsewhere without the *ge*-prefix. While the past participle spelling *gemæted* at line 157 is also unique, it both represents the manuscript reading and retains the *æ* spelling of the infinitive (*ge*)*mætan*, as does the preterite form *gemætte* at line 122.[34]

Syntactic patterns also support this MS reading. The accusative referent is used at line 122, "Hwæt hine gemætte" (What he dreamed), and at line 157, "Swa his mandrihten gemæted wearð" (That his lord had dreamed). This suggests that at line 119 the poet would have used the accusative *hine* and not the dative *him* if *meted* (dreamed) were intended. (*Ge*)*mætan* can take the accusative or dative of the person dreaming, but the *Microfiche Concordance* records that the accusative was used more frequently.[35] There is no basis, then, for altering the MS reading *metod*. The reader expects a comment on Nebuchadnezzar's unremembered dream; with considerable rhetorical effect, the poet substitutes a remark on Nebuchadnezzar's pride,[36] of which the neglect of God is the most serious manifestation.

The poet has diminished the role of Daniel in the story in order to concentrate upon Nebuchadnezzar. This change of focus is achieved by several alterations to the Vulgate account. Daniel's first appearance is delayed in the poem until line 150, when he arrives to interpret the first dream, whereas in the biblical account he is mentioned many times prior to this episode, as one of the four children of Judah brought to Nebuchadnezzar and as the spokesman in the food episode, which is not recounted in *Daniel* (Dan 1:8–16). The reduction of the prophet's status is most evident, however, when his interpretive powers are introduced, in the first dream scene in *Daniel*. In the biblical account, Daniel prays for the ability to interpret the dream, in response to which he receives a dream himself. But the *Daniel* poet omits these elements of the story and substitutes a means of enlightenment both less indicative of Daniel's prophetic prowess and less flatteringly recounted. An angel, invented by the poet, tells the eponymous hero the matter and interpretation of the dream:

> Him god sealde   gife of heofnum
> þurh hleoðorcwyde   halige gastes,
> him engel godes   eall asægde
> swa his mandrihten   gemæted wearð.   (154–57)
> [God gave him a gift from heaven through the prophecy of the holy spirit,
> an angel of God told him all just as his lord had dreamed it.]

Daniel's subservience to the king, "his mandrihten," is striking here, as is his reliance on the holy spirit for the prophetic material. There is no mention of any dream context for this transfer of information. The allusive reference to the dawning of day, "Þa dæg lyhte" (158) (When day dawned), as Daniel goes to recount the dream to Nebuchadnezzar, is the only reminder of the dream that is missing from the OE account. The poet's omission of this dream signals his conscious reduction of both Daniel's role in the story and the stature of the dream as a device of revelation.

The poet further truncates Daniel's involvement in the episode by paraphrasing his recital of Nebuchadnezzar's dream and its interpretation in three lines:

> [Daniel] sægde him wislice   wereda gesceafte,
> þætte sona ongeat   swiðmod cyning
> ord and ende   þæs þe him ywed wæs.   (160–62)
> [(Daniel) wisely told him the destiny of hosts so that soon the proud king perceived the beginning and the end of all that was shown to him.]

This incident is related from Nebuchadnezzar's point of view rather than from Daniel's. In the Vulgate the content of the dream and its interpretation are recounted separately and at considerable length by Daniel.[37] In the poem, the omniscient narrator, not Daniel, pronounces the prophecy at this point; moreover, the poet had anticipated this information and further undermined Daniel's prophetic role by paraphrasing the significance of the dream while Nebuchadnezzar was asleep (111–15). In this emphatic reiteration of the moral of the first dream, the poet stresses Nebuchadnezzar's intellectual involvement rather than Daniel's prophetic role.

In this scene, the poet reaffirms the king's persistent arrogance in order to account for the nonassimilation of the dream's message. He adds a comment here that Nebuchadnezzar is *swiðmod* (161) (proud) when he hears Daniel's interpretation of the dream, and therefore is unaffected by its meaning. The poet consolidates his portrayal of the king's obliviousness to grace when he says that Nebuchadnezzar could not apprehend the meaning of the dream "for fyrenum" (166) (on account of [his] sins).[38] Nebuchadnezzar may have understood the message of the dream, but, firm in his pride, will not necessarily assimilate it and alter his behavior. By adding this comment, the poet suggests that the ability to interpret the dream depends less on any positive possession of grace in the character of the interpreter than on the absence of sin in the recipient. The explanation also provides an element of psychological validity to the king's imminent backsliding.

The Old Testament Nebuchadnezzar is humbled, if only temporarily, by his first dream, but in the OE *Daniel* the king's pride is undiminished. In the Book of Daniel, Nebuchadnezzar falls down and worships Daniel, admitting that the latter's God is supreme:

> Tunc rex Nabuchodonosor cecidit in faciem suam et Daniehelem adoravit et hostias et incensum praecepit ut sacrificarent ei, loquens ergo rex ait Danieli: vere Deus vester Deus deorum est et Dominus regum et revelans mysteria quoniam potuisti aperire sacramentum hoc. (2:46–7)
> [Then king Nebuchadnezzar fell on his face and worshipped Daniel and commanded that captives and incense should be sacrificed to him. Therefore, speaking, the king said to Daniel: "Truly your God is the God of gods and the lord of kings and the revealer of mysteries, since you were able to recount this secret."]

Daniel is made governor of Babylon and otherwise richly rewarded for his services. The OE poet omits all these details, merely stating that Daniel had much glory among scholars:

> þa hæfde Daniel   dom micelne,
> blæd in Babilonia   mid bocerum.   (163–64)
> [Then Daniel had great glory, renown in Babylon amidst the scholars.]

By summarizing the outcome of events in this way, the poet alters the roles of both Nebuchadnezzar and Daniel, Nebuchadnezzar's pride continues, unaffected by the first dream, and Daniel's prophetic prowess is seen by the king as the intelligent insight of a merely clever man who is rewarded with temporal glory. Responsibility for change cannot be assumed by the prophet: Daniel's attempts to convince Nebuchadnezzar of the import of the dream are ineffectual in the face of Nebuchadnezzar's own failings:

> No hwæðere þæt Daniel   gedon mihte
> þæt he wolde metodes   mihte gelyfan.   (168–69)

[Daniel, however, could not bring it about that he (Nebuchadnezzar) would believe in the might of the Lord.][39]

This remark, which is not in the Book of Daniel, summarizes the poet's view of the story which he is telling and characteristically concentrates on the results rather than the details of actions. The comment denies the external imposition of moral responsibility and anticipates Nebuchadnezzar's persistence in error, which is directly caused by his undaunted pride.

These major alterations to the Vulgate story of the repercussions of the king's first dream rely on the reduction of Daniel's glory and the accentuation of Nebuchadnezzar's pride. This change in focus from the Old Testament story is the primary means by which the poet creates a study of the workings of the king's mind throughout his experiences. A secondary means is wordplay. Critics have remarked upon the *Daniel* poet's use of similar-sounding words in close proximity to forge associations of ideas across the syntax of his poetry.[40] A good example of this device occurs in this first dream account in the use of the stressed alliterating terms *swefn* (or *swefnian*) (dream) with *sefa* (mind):

Cam on sefan hwurfan   swefnes woma (110);
On sefan þinne,   hu ðe swefnede (131);

and

Soðan swefnes,   þæs min sefa myndgað   (144).[41]

This collocation is unique to *Daniel*. It reminds the reader of the strong association between dream and mind without any change in the narrative pace. *Sefa* is mainly a poetic word.[42] It is conceivable that in poetry the mind as individual volition is distinguished from the conscious self by the use of such terms.[43] In addition to his use of the collocation, the poet reiterates his themes of consciousness and will by repetition of the individual terms of the collocation throughout the poem. *Swefn* and the verb *swefnian* are found sixteen times,[44] and *sefa* occurs twelve times,[45] while the compound *modsefa* appears eleven times.[46]

Like the first dream in *Daniel*, the second one (lines 495–592) is much altered, and is introduced in association with Nebuchadnezzar's pride. Again, *oferhygd* is mentioned in the line prior to the account of the dream (494), just after a lengthy description of the king's hubris in which the mind once again figures prominently:

Ac þam æðelinge   oferhygd gesceod
wearð him hyrra hyge   and on heortan geðanc
<mara on> modsefan   þonne gemet wære.   (489–491)[47]
[But pride injured that prince, his mind was loftier and the thought in his
heart, in his understanding, was greater than was fitting.]

In the Vulgate, Nebuchadnezzar is undoubtedly proud, but this charac-
teristic is not expressed so emphatically. It appears that the *Daniel* poet
is not only stressing the stubborn arrogance of the king, but is also
attempting to provide psychological validity for Nebuchadnezzar's
behavior and some depth to his own new perspective in the poem.

The account of the second dream does more than make "a few
changes of emphasis" which "emphasize Daniel's role."[48] It is most
strikingly different from the biblical version in the change from first- to
third-person narration. In the Bible, Nebuchadnezzar recounts his dream
experience himself and admits immediately, "Somnium vidi quod pert-
erruit me" (4:2) (I saw a dream that terrified me greatly). In *Daniel*, how-
ever, the dream is told by the omniscient narrator, who also interprets its
prophetic significance at the outset:

þa him wearð on slæpe   swefen ætywed,
Nabuchodonossor;   him þæt neh gewearð.   (495–96)
[Then a dream was revealed in sleep to him, to Nebuchadnezzar; it
concerned him closely.]

Again, the context of sleep is stated to emphasize the occurrence of a
dream, but this time, the dream does not roam or turn; it merely appears.
But it does retain the status of a discrete entity which it had in the
account of the first dream. We are told less of its nature and effect at this
point, although later it is called a terrifying spirit from God: Nebuchad-
nezzar is said to experience "gryre fram ðam gaste ðe þyder god sende"
(525) (terror from that spirit which God sent thither). This diminution in
detail concerning the entrance of the dream is accompanied by a corre-
sponding increase in the quantity of its images reported by the narrator.

Consequent upon the change of voice in *Daniel* is a change in nar-
rative sequence. In the biblical account, Nebuchadnezzar acknowledges
his terror and relates his dream, and Daniel's interpretation follows. In
Daniel, the occurrence and images of the dream are reported first so that
the reader is exposed to this dream, as if he was the first, together with
Nebuchadnezzar. But the poet reproduces some degree of the Vulgate's

first person account by relating the images of the dream from the king's viewpoint. To do this, he uses an impersonal construction, *þuhte him* (it seemed to him), which is frequently employed in OE accounts of dreams. This method of narration is employed for the pleasant part of the dream during which Nebuchadnezzar sees the glorious and firmly secured tree which signifies his reign:

> þuhte him þæt on foldan   fægre stode
> wudubeam wlitig,   se wæs wyrtum fast.   (497–98)[49]
> [It seemed to him that a beautiful forest-tree, one which was firm in its roots, stood beautifully in the earth.]

The construction is used again for the description of the tree as the provider for wild beasts and for the arrival of the angel (503–10). Yet the poet simulates an abrupt change in the tone of the dream by changing to an indicative, personal construction to report the angel's commands. The use and reiteration of *hatan* (510, 513, and 518) (to command) present the images of the felling and shackling of the tree dramatically. The removal of the intermediary, the king's thought, brings the terror of the scene a step closer to the reader, intensified by the lexical repetition. Nebuchadnezzar's inability to control his own destiny is suggested vividly by the poet through this change from *þuhte him* to *hatan*, a change from his own perception to the direct commands of God's angel. It highlights the king's empty pride, for now he is subject to the will of God, and is presented as the recipient of ordered blows, not the commander of his temporal empire.

In the Vulgate version, the king recounts his dream and asks for an interpretation (4:1–15), but in *Daniel* the prophetic significance of the images of the second dream is summarized by the narrator within the dream. The poet demystifies the dream's revelatory power and spiritual potential by explaining that the king is shackled

> þæt his mod wite   þæt mihtigra
> wite wealdað   þonne he him wið mæge.   (521–22)
> [so that his mind may know that one, mightier than he may avail against, wields punishment.]

The images of the dream demonstrate the outcome of denying the incontrovertible nature of God's omnipotence, but the poet's presentation of the scene communicates something quite different. By presenting an already interpreted dream, the poet ensures that the reader understands it before the king, or even Daniel, does, and thereby removes the need for prophetic explanation. He makes the message appear obvious in order to stress the willfulness of Nebuchadnezzar's imminent negligence of the dream.

The end of the second dream, unrecorded in the Vulgate, is mentioned unambiguously in *Daniel*: "þa of slæpe onwoc—swefn wæs æt ende" (523) (Then he awoke from sleep—the dream was over). Like the first dream, the abrupt announcement of the cessation of this dream is matched by its inability to hold the king's attention or warrant his earnest consideration. It does not exert a spiritual influence over Nebuchadnezzar after he wakes and therefore the poet stresses its conclusion. The only reaction the dream produces is emotional: It provokes terror in its recipient: "Him þæs egesa stod" (524) (The terror of that remained for him). The poet emphasizes this reaction, repeating the terrifying aspect of the dream when Nebuchadnezzar recounts it to Daniel:

> þa he secgan ongan   swefnes woman,
> heorhheort and hæðen   heriges wisa,
> ealne þone egesan   þe him eowed was.   (538–40)
> [Then the proud and heathen leader of the troop began to recount the tumult of the dream, all the terror that had been shown to him.]

The poet calls this dream, like the first, a *woma* (disturbance), its aspect from the king's perspective of fear. Again, he qualifies the king's character and anticipates his backsliding through unambiguously negative appellations, *heorhheort* and *hæðen*. The combination of these terms produces a picture of sinful unenlightenment. The warning dream has been unhelpful because Nebuchadnezzar may be terrified but is spiritually unprepared to undertake any necessary reform.

Daniel's interpretation of the dream is as spiritually ineffective as the dream itself and Nebuchadnezzar remains as weak and sinful as beforehand. Immediately after Daniel recounts and interprets the dream, Nebuchadnezzar's pride reasserts itself: "His mod astah / heah fram heortan" (596–97) (His mind grew proud, lofty from the heart). The poet takes further steps to clarify the reasons for the king's downfall. Nebuchadnezzar's final act of pride, his boast of Babylon, "min seo mære burh" (608) (my glorious city), occurs immediately after he dismisses the warning of the second dream, whereas in the Vulgate, it occurs twelve months later: "Post finem mensuum duodecim" (4:26) (After a space of twelve months). In contracting the time between dream and fall, the *Daniel* poet has kept Nebuchadnezzar's overweening pride at the forefront of his story and has increased the narrative pace. He has also created a sounder logical progression from sin to fall, providing psychological causes for Nebuchadnezzar's change of behavior. By altering the emphasis of the biblical story, the *Daniel* poet has stressed the immediate resurgence of sin rather than the temporarily salvific effect of the dream and its interpretation, and made Nebuchadnezzar immediately responsible for his pride.

The poet's lexical skill is as prominent here as in the first dream account, where it is employed to assist in the creation of a new focus. The poet is apparently aware of the fact that the name Daniel means "the judgment of God."[50] He uses it and *dom* (judgment) in close proximity as an etymological pun throughout the poem, including the second dream scene: "Þa wæs to ðam dome Daniel haten" (531) (Then Daniel was called for the interpretation) and "Daniel at þam dome" (546) (Daniel at the interpretation). This collocation occurs elsewhere in Old English[51] and in Middle English to affirm the prophet's ordained role.[52] In the last and most conspicuous use of the collocation in the text, the poet changes it to undermine the supremacy of Daniel's judgment. Judgment itself is absolute and Daniel is merely its emissary:

> Wyrd was geworden,   wundor gecyðed,
> swefn geseðed,   susl awunnen,
> dom gedemed,   swa ær Daniel cwæð,
> þæt se folctoga   findan sceolde
> earfoðsiþas   for his ofermedlan.   (652–56)
> [Fate was brought about, a wonder made known, the dream fulfilled, torment endured, judgment appointed, just as Daniel had said, that the leader should encounter troubles for his pride.]

Here, *dom* is emphatically linked with the terms *wyrd*, *wundor*, *swefn*, and *susl*, and only parenthetically with *Daniel*. The role of *Daniel* in the euphonic collocation with *dom* is shared with the etymologically related *gedemed*. Judgment, like the other manifestations of God's interaction with Nebuchadnezzar, is still within the sphere of Daniel's influence, but his prophetic voice has been subordinated thematically to the divine manifestations of judgment. The poet places the entire responsibility for Nebuchadnezzar's troubles on the king's sin of pride; Daniel is removed from the moral equation. His unheeded warnings are as peripheral to

Nebuchadnezzar's experience as is his own name to this comment from the author.

The poet has made it quite clear that Nebuchadnezzar's change of heart is the result more of his own tribulations than of the prophetic significance of his dreams or the warnings administered by Daniel. He contrasts the two modes of enlightenment through lexical reiteration. It is not until "gemunde þa on mode þæt metod wære" (624) (he remembered then in his mind that there was a lord), and that God is "ana ece gast" (627) (the single eternal spirit) that his reason is restored: "His gast ahwearf in godes gemynd" (629) (His spirit reverted to the memory of God). He who "gleaw ne wæs" (176) (was not wise) is restored to sanity and power when "in gast becwom / ræd-fæst sefa" (650–61) (wise thought came into his spirit), The poet uses the term *gast* for both God and the spirit of one who turns to Him to suggest the divine potential of the soul. He also suggests, in the repetition of *gast*, one of the terms for "dream," that Nebuchadnezzar now has means of enlightenment more effectual than his potentially prophetic experiences.

The poet's careful use of significant words in transferred contexts is evident elsewhere. To complete his picture of cerebral activity and to stress the engagement of the will necessary for atonement, he has employed "turning" words, characteristic of the first dream experience, to express change inspired by the will: "[Nebuchadnezzar] onhwearf / wodan gewittes" (626–67) (Nebuchadnezzar recovered from his insane reason), and "þa his gast ahwearf in godes gemynd" (629) (then his spirit came around to the memory of God). Here it is Nebuchadnezzar's spirit, not the spirit of a dream, which turns, and here it is active, personal, and more effective. In the latter example, which occurs at the high point in the narrative, the moment of revelation and salvation, three terms are used with meanings transferred from the dream to the conscious act of acknowledging God: *gast*, *-hwearf*, and *-mynd*. The very repetition of terms previously associated with the king's dreams highlights the active nature of this revelation.

Thematic repetition and contrast are also employed on a larger scale throughout the poem. The poet continues to emphasize Nebuchadnezzar's great failing and sustains his theme of drunken oblivion and pride in the final scene dealing with Belthazzar's defilement of the sacred vessels. He compares Belthazzar with Nebuchadnezzar by the reiteration of prominent motifs and expressions. Belthazzar is ruling when "him wlenco gesceod / oferhyd egle" (677–78) (arrogance, hateful pride injured him).[53] He is also a drunkard: *medugal* (702) (which recalls *wingal*), and *windruncen* (752). The poet balances his work by recalling in this conclusion the vices initially introduced into the story in the condemnation of the proud and drunken Israelites:

> . . . hie wlenco anwod   æt winþege
> deofoldædum,   druncne geþohtas.   (17–18)
> [. . . pride, drunken thoughts, seized them with evil deeds at the wine banquet.]

The scenario acted out by Nebuchadnezzar in the poem is repeated in miniature when Daniel confronts the similarly proud and drunk Belthazzar. Yet, while an initial comparison is drawn between the two in the final scene, it is only to introduce Nebuchadnezzar as a positive exemplum of a man who overcame the failings which Belthazzar is exhibiting. Daniel says that Nebuchadnezzar finally revered God's omnipotence:

> Siððan him wuldres weard   wundor gecyðde,
> þæt he wære ana   ealra gesceafta
> drihten and waldend,   se him dom forgeaf.   [759–62]
> [After the guardian of glory made known a wonder to him, that he alone was lord and ruler of all creation, he who gave him power.]

These lines have changed the emphasis of the Vulgate verse in which Daniel berates Belthazzar for neglecting to glorify God: "Porro Deum qui habet flatum tuum in manu sua et omnes vias tuas non glorificasti" (5:23) (Moreover, God, who has your breath in his hand and all your ways, you have not glorified). At the conclusion of his text, the OE poet has couched Belthazzar's need to acknowledge God's power in terms of a wondrous revelation, reminiscent of the change experienced by Nebuchadnezzar. The *wundor* referred to at line 759, the enlightenment of the king, contrasts with the earlier miracles of vision, prophecy, and salvation of the youths in the oven, as well as the matter at hand, the writing on the wall. It is the revelation of God's supremacy which Nebuchadnezzar experiences in the wilderness. This active acquisition of knowledge is described as the outcome of fate, the enactment of the meaning of the dream, when "swefn [wæs] geseðed" (653) (the dream was fulfilled). The dream could only foreshadow, not effect, the necessary change in Nebuchadnezzar's outlook, because his punishment and rehabilitation were the working out of the plan of providence. That the king chose to ignore this plan was prophesied by the dream itself and was likewise necessary for its fulfillment. The poet takes advantage of the incompatibility of the prophetic accuracy of the dream and its inevitable inefficacy by reducing its revelatory role and highlighting Nebuchadnezzar's negligence of it, for he is more concerned with Nebuchadnezzar's human motivations than with his participation in revelatory activities.

The final lines of the poem, Daniel's words of reproach to the arrogant Belthazzar, are a fitting conclusion to a work centering on the sin of pride and its manifestation in the refusal to acknowledge the absolute supremacy of God:

And þu lignest nu   þæt sie lifgende,
se ofer deoflum   dugeþum wealdeð.   (763–64)
[And now you deny that he is the living one, who rules powerfully over devils.][54]

We are not shown Belthazzar's change of heart, for this scene is included only to draw a moral from Nebuchadnezzar's experiences. While focusing on Nebuchadnezzar's pride, the poet has shown that the responsibility for turning to God comes from the individual, not from prophetic admonition, a theme not derived from the Vulgate account. The wakeful demonstration of his sin is more efficacious to the erring Nebuchadnezzar than somniatic warning. In *Daniel*, it is clear that enlightenment is not gained passively, but requires the suppression of pride and the conscious resolution of the will.

The *Daniel* poet has brought his own meaning to the biblical story of the prophet's encounter with the proud king by means of dramatic editing of the Vulgate and ingenious word choice in his "translation" into the vernacular. He has changed the emphasis from the miracle of Daniel's God-given prophecy to the need for the conscious reception of revelation. The changes demonstrate that Nebuchadnezzar's human failings, his typical reaction of fear to his dreams, and his backsliding are more interesting to the Anglo-Saxon poet than the orthodox concentration on the prophet Daniel. This preference accounts for the diminution of Daniel's role in the poem and the absence of those elements which are considered to be the hallmarks of the story, the statue and Daniel's own dream. The change in

narrative focus is also achieved by the poet's careful selection of vocabu-
lary and lexical patterns, which allows him to fashion a commentary on
pride from a biblical story without altering the narrative too radically.

By his reduction of the famous dream sequences in this story noted
for its prophetic visions, the poet manages to suggest that dreams render
ineffective warnings, that the positive effects of dreams as signs of
divine providence evidenced throughout history are useless if unheeded.
He stresses Nebuchadnezzar's emotional reactions to what are poten-
tially prophetic experiences as well as his obliviousness to God's warn-
ings, rather than the inherent value of those dreams and Daniel's
miraculous understanding of them. In his examination of psychological
processes, the poet changes the biblical narrative in order to discuss how
consciousness and memory are related to volition and atonement. He
achieves this by locating the focus of the narrative in the mental sphere
through his reiteration of terms for "mind" and "dream," and by trans-
ferring the sense of terms for "turning," "spirit," and "memory" from
sleeping to conscious behavior. His didactic agenda is also served
semantically by his use of rhetorically effective references to the cir-
cumstances of the dream and its recipient, such as *frumslæp* and *wingal*,
whereby he communicates additional information on the king's unrecep-
tivity to his dreams.

The *Daniel* poet has altered the Vulgate account of the proud king
and his prophet quite consciously and consistently in terms of his own
design for a commentary on the biblical narrative. He has changed the
exemplary force of the original story about the Jewish prophet's God-
given superiority into an exposition of the psychological motivations
behind Nebuchadnezzar's actions and an account of the reform of his
pride. The result is a didactically effective behavioral model for the con-
temporary Anglo-Saxon audience, for whom pride and active atonement
were more pertinent than Old Testament prophecy.

NOTES

1. The poem is untitled in the manuscript. It is difficult to ascertain precisely
    when the title was given to the poem. The text is always called *Daniel*
    when named in printed editions, including: Theodore W. Hunt, ed., *Cæd-
    mon's Exodus and Daniel Edited from Grein* (Boston, 1888); Francis A.
    Blackburn, ed, *Exodus and Daniel* (Boston and London, 1907); G. P.
    Krapp in *The Junius Manuscript*, ASPR 1 (New York, 1931), 111–32;

and, more recently, Robert T. Farrell, ed., *Daniel and Azarias* (London, 1974). Benjamin Thorpe, *Cædmon's Metrical Paraphrase of Parts of the Holy Scriptures in Anglo-Saxon* (London, 1832), however, considers the *Junius Manuscript* to contain a single work and consequently does not assign separate names to the individual poems. According to Farrell, 23, the division into separate poems, and into the "original" and "interpolated" sections of *Daniel*, was first made by Ernst Götzinger, "Über die Dichtungen des angelsächsen Cædmon und deren Verfasser," Ph.D. Thesis (Göttingen, 1860).

2. See also Graham Caie, "The Old English *Daniel*: A Warning Against Pride," *English Studies* 59 (1979) 1–9, 2, where it is argued that "[Nebuchadnezzar], the personification of *wlenco* and *oferhygd*, is undoubtedly the central figure of the poem," and his name alone is capitalized in the manuscript (at line 618, just underneath a space for a picture).

3. *Commentarii in Danielem*, CCSL 75A (Turnhout, 1964).

4. Jerome's commentary is designed to condemn the claim of the third century Neo-Platonist Porphyry that the Book of Daniel was in fact written much later than its purported date of composition in the sixth century B.C. Porphyry's argument, that the text was composed around 165 B.C. in order to encourage the Jews being persecuted by Antiochus Epiphanes, and that, therefore, it describes events of the past rather than future prophecies, has been accepted by later biblical scholars on the basis of historical and linguistic evidence within the text (J. N. D. Kelly, *Jerome: His Life, Writings, and Commentaries* [London, 1975], 300).

5. Edited by Max Förster, "Beiträge zur mittelalterlichen Volkskunde II," *Archiv* 120 (1908), 302–5; "IV," *Archiv* 125 (1910), 47–70; and "IX," *Archiv* 134 (1916), 270–93.

6. Gabriel Turville-Petre, "Dream Symbols in Old Icelandic Literature," *Festschrift Walter Baetke* (Weimar, 1966), 349.

7. Penelope B. R. Doob, *Nebuchadnezzar's Children: Conventions of Madness in Middle English Literature* (New Haven and London, 1974), 75.

8. The monk refers to Nebuchadnezzar as one of the men who have fallen from high degree, and it is Daniel's wisdom and interpretation of the dream which dominate the dream episode:

> Amonges othere Daniel was oon
> that was the wiseste child of everychon
> for he the dremes of the kyng expowned,
> wereas in Chaldeye clerk ne was ther noon
> that wiste to what fyn his dremes sowned. (2154–58)

(All Chaucerian quotes are from Larry D. Benson, ed., *The Riverside Chaucer*, 3rd ed. [Boston, 1987]).

9. The Parson refers to Nebuchadnezzar's second dream when he compares penitence to a tree: "This tree saugh the prophete Daniel in spirit, upon the avysioun of the kyng Nabugodonosor, whan he conseiled hym to do penitence" (125).

10. Here, the exceptionally blessed nature of Nebuchadnezzar's vision entitles it to be mentioned along with other famous dreams:

> . . . so sely an avisyon,
> that Isaye, ne Scipion,
> ne kyng Nabugodonosor,
> Pharoo, Turnus, ne Eleanor,
> ne mette such a drem as this. (513–17)

11. Gower recounts Nebuchadnezzar's first dream in his prologue (585–669), emphasizing Daniel's interpretation, "that swevene hath Daniel unloke" (654) (G. C. Macaulay, *The Complete Works of John Gower*, 4 vols [Oxford, 1901], vol. 2).

12. In Passus VII, Langland relates:

> how Daniel diuined þe dremes of a kyng
> that Nabugodonosor nemneþ þise clerkes.   (158–59)
> (George Kane and E. Talbot Donaldson, eds., *Piers Plowman: The B-Version* [London, 1975]).

13. The *Cleanness* poet does mention Nebuchadnezzar's humility, yet he attributes the change of heart to Daniel's prophetic prowess:

> and al þurg dome of Daniel, fro he devised hade
> þat all goudes com of God, and gef hit hym bi samples,
> þat he ful clanly bicnu his carp hi þe laste,
> And ofte hit mekned his mynde, his masterful werkkes. (1325–28)
> (*Purity*, ed. Robert J. Menner [New Haven, 1920]).

14. This is contrary to Doob's opinion that "although Nebuchadnezzar occasionally appears as a just conqueror or prophet, most frequently he is a proud king who falls into bestiality to be saved eventually by penance and grace" (*Nebuchadnezzar's Children*, p. 74). This could refer to *Cleanness*, but not the other Middle English accounts given above, where Nebuchadnezzar's dreams rather than his reactions to them are of prime importance, along with Daniel's interpretation of them.

15. All OE citations are drawn from the editions used, and cited according to the conventions and short titles listed, in A. diP. Healey and R. L. Venezky, eds., *A Microfiche Concordance to Old English: The List of Texts and Index of Editions*, Publications of the Dictionary of Old English 1 (Toronto, 1980). This citation: ÆCHomII, 4 37.230.

16. ÆHom4 127.

17. For example, ÆCHomII, 33 252.95.

18. *Hweorfan* is used specifically of the movement of the mind and thought in *The Seafarer*: "Min hyge hweorfeð . . . min modsefa . . . hweorfeð" (58–60) (My thought turns . . . my mind turns); and *Beowulf* "[God] læteð hworfan monnes modgeþonc" (1728–29) (God allows a person's thought to wander).

19. Cf. "wiges woma" (*Elene* [18], *Andreas* [1355]) (clash of battle), "wuldres woma" (*Exodus* [100]) (sound of glory), and "wintres woma" (*The Wanderer* [103]) (tumult of winter), which attest the "noise, disturbance" connotations of *woma*. The idea of dreams making a noise may have extended into the Middle English period. In Chaucer's *Monk's Tale* in the section concerning Nebuchadnezzar, it is said that the prophets could not understand "to what fyn his dremes *sowned*" (2158) (to what end his dream signified). Although *MED* lists "to express, indicate" as one of the definitions of this word, it is the same verb as that used to express the creation of noise, either musical, vocal, or other. *MED* lists eleven other occurrences of *sounen* meaning "to express, indicate," none of which refers to a dream, so the Chaucerian instance may be an isolated example.

20. See, e.g.. *Exodus* (164), *Elene* (28, 112), and *Judith* (206). The devil is described as a wolf in *Christ I* (256), and associated with carrion and savagery in *The Wanderer* (82) and *The Fates of Men* (12).

21. R. L. Venezky and A. diP. Healey, eds., *A Microfiche Concordance to Old English*, Publications of the Dictionary of Old English 1 (Toronto, 1980).

22. Caie, *op. cit.*, p. 2. Caie does not list the occurrences. I have found the following fourteen words that connote "pride" or "proud" in *Daniel*: *swiðmod* (100, 161, 268, 449, 528, and 605); *oferhygd* (107, 489, 494, and 614); *ofermedla* (656); *wlonc* (96); *modig* (105); and *heahheort* (539). *Anhydig* (604), though strictly denoting "resolute," could also suggest "arrogant," especially because it is parallel to *swiðmod* in the next line.

23. "Hie nihtes on frumslæpe on bestælan & þa burg mid ealle awestan" (Or 2 8 92.1) (At night, during the first sleep, they stole into the city and laid it waste entirely); and "[Stephanus] ða on þære ylcan nihte æfter his frumslæpe neodlice clypode biddende þæt man ðone bisceop to him gefette" (ÆChomII, 2 13.35) (Then on that same night after his first sleep, Stephen had to call out asking that someone should summon the bishop to him).

24. See, for example, Horace *Satires* 1.10.33, where he remarks that Quirinus appeared to him "post mediam noctem . . . cum somnia vera," "after midnight when dreams are true" (Loeb Classical Library, ed. H. Rushton [London and Cambridge, MA, 1966], 118).

25. *Commentarii in Somnium Scipionis*, ed. J. Willis (Leipzig, 1970), 1.3.7.

26. Pliny, *Naturalis Historia*, 10.211 (Loeb Classical Library, ed. H. Rackham [London and New York, 1946], 426).

27. Artemidorus, *Onirocriticon*, trans. Robert J. White (Park Ridge NJ, 1975), 21. White, 69, contributes other classical references to the effect of food and drink on the prophetic nature of dreams: "Philostratus (*Life of Appollonius* 2.37) records that dream interpreters did not hesitate to interpret a dream that came at dawn on the assumption that the soul was in a condition to divine soundly, since by then it had cleansed itself of the stains of wine." Later, he notes that Cicero (*De Divinatione* 1.115) remarks that "the soul will be in a condition to watch as the body sleeps only if moderation has been observed in eating and drinking."

28. An example occurs in the *Aeneid* (2.268) when Hector appears to Aeneas "quo prima quies mortalibus aegris incipit," "when the first sleep has begun for wretched mortals" (ed. R. G. Austin [Oxford, 1964]).

29. This can be inferred both from the prevalence of the distinction in classical literature and from the evidence of surviving manuscripts and booklists that attest knowledge of many of the classical works mentioned here. See J. D. A. Ogilvy, *Books Known to the English, 597–1066* (Cambridge, MA, 1967); Helmut G. Gneuss, "A Preliminary List of Manuscripts Written or Owned in England up to 1100," *Anglo-Saxon England* 9 (1970), 1–60; and Michael Lapidge, "Surviving Booklists from Anglo-Saxon England," in *Learning and Literature in Anglo-Saxon England*, ed. Michael Lapidge and Helmut Gneuss (Cambridge, 1985), 33–89.

30. Cf. Nebuchadnezzar's second dream, which terrifies him in both accounts. The OT has "quod perterruit me" (4:1), "which terrified me," and in *Daniel* it is called *egesa* (524) "terror."

31. "Miracle as Prophetic Gospel: Knowledge, Power and the Design of the Narrative in *Daniel*," *English Studies* 72 (1991), 129.

32. Farrell, *Daniel and Azarias*, 54, considers retaining the MS reading but rejects it as less likely than the emendation on metrical grounds, erroneously assuming that the emended *meted* would necessarily take the dative of the dreamer (a point which is discussed below).

33. Farrell, *Daniel and Azarias*, 113. *Metod* occurs in the poem twenty-six times, at lines 4, 14, 20, 36, 56, 92, 169, 174, 234, 283, 332, 334, 383, 398, 401, 442, 493, 537, 566, 578, 589, 624, 630, 647, 658, 680.

34. *Microfiche Concordance*.

35. Of the forty-one occurrences of *(ge)mætan*, twenty-four are with an

accusative referent, seven a dative referent, nine with the form *me*, which could be either accusative or dative, and one with a nominative referent.

36. A pun that modern editors, including Blackburn, Krapp, and Farrell, appear to have overlooked in their emendation of *metod* to *meted*.

37. Dan. 2:31–5 and 2:37–45.

38. Cf. the OE translation of Bede's account of the poet Cædmon, where a comment is added to explain Cædmon's departure from the beer hall, "for forscome" (Bede [4] 24.342.23), "on account of shame."

39. These lines support the claim that *metod* was intended in line 119, as they reiterate the meaning of the MS reading of that line, that the poet's main concern is how Nebuchadnezzar comes to recognize God.

40. Bernard Huppé, *Doctrine and Poetry* (New York, 1959), 225–27; Geoffrey Shepherd, "Scriptural Poetry," *Continuations and Beginnings*, ed. Eric Gerald Stanley (London, 1966), 32; and Roberta Frank, "Wordplay in Old English Poetry," Ph.D. Thesis (Harvard, 1968), 80–93.

41. This collocation in these examples is noted by Frank, "Wordplay," 84

42. The *Microfiche Concordance* lists seventy-eight occurrences (under the spellings *sefa*, *sefan*, *sefæn*), sixty-four of which are from poetic texts. Many of the prose examples are glosses to *sensus*.

43. M. R. Godden, "Anglo-Saxons on the Mind," *Learning and Literature in Anglo-Saxon England*, ed. Michael Lapidge and Helmut Gneuss (Cambridge, 1985), 295, argues that in Anglo-Saxon poetry, the idea of the mind, expressed with terms such as *sefa*, is associated with "emotion and a kind of passionate volition and self-assertion . . . distinguish[ed] from the conscious self."

44. Lines 110, 116, 118, 126, 129, 144, 148, 159, 165, 481, 495, 523, 528, 532, 552, and 653. It is evident from these references that the term was used and then repeated a few lines later, this patterning effect contributing to the repetitive nature of the work, and also emphasizing the cerebral venue of much of the activity of the narrative.

45. Lines 49, 84, 110, 131, 144, 268, 415 [MS *selfa*], 485, 535, 651, and 731.

46. Lines 14, 39, 98, 184, 361, 483, 521, 596, 624, 630, and 721.

47. The terminology of this passage brings to mind the famous call to courage enunciated in *The Battle of Maldon*, where it is used with a quite different effect:

> Hige sceal þe heardra   heorte þe cenre
> mod sceal þe mare   þe ure mægen litlað.   (312–13)

(Intention shall be the more resolute, the heart the keener, courage shall be the greater, as our strength dwindles.) Here, *hige*, *heorte*, and *mod* are given in the same order as in *Daniel*. The two citations suggest that these faculties comprised a literary trinity of human virtue and strength of character for the OE poet.

48. Fanger, "Miracle as Prophetic Gospel," 131.
49. The beauty of the tree symbolized in dreams is emphasized in a similar manner in *The Dream of the Rood* (4–7) and *Elene* (88–91).
50. Roberta Frank, "Some Uses of Paronomasia in Old English Scriptural Verse," *Speculum* 47 (1972), 216 [reprinted in the present volume—*ed.*].
51. For example, ÆHom 22 248, "to Danihels dom."
52. In *Cleanness*: "and al þurg dome of Daniel" (1325), and "ðat ilk dome þat Danyel devysed" (1756).
53. Cf. line 489, where Nebuchadnezzar is "oferhygd gesceod," "injured by pride."
54. If one accepts that the poet is primarily concerned with Nebuchadnezzar in the role of the humbled *swiðmod* king, this conclusion is indeed fitting, although perhaps a little unusually abrupt. While Farrell, *Daniel and Azarias*, 33, believes that the poem is complete as it stands, most critics favor the view that the poem is incomplete as the result of a missing leaf. Most recently and convincingly, see Barbara C. Raw, "The Construction of Oxford, Bodleian Library, Junius 11," *Anglo-Saxon England* 13 (1984), 187–207; see also Peter J. Lucas, "On the Incomplete Ending of *Daniel* and the Addition of *Christ and Satan* to Manuscript Junius 11," *Anglia* 97 (1979), 46–59; and J. R. Hall, "The Old English Epic of Redemption: The Theological Unity of Manuscript Junius 11, *Traditio* 32 (1976), 185–208 [reprinted in the present volume —*ed.*].

The Power of Knowledge and the Location of the Reader in *Christ and Satan*

RUTH WEHLAU

This essay first appeared in JEGP 97 (1998), 1–12.

Christ and Satan consists of three narratives taken from salvation history, the Fall of Satan, the Harrowing of Hell, and the Temptation, in that order.[1] Interspersed between the narratives are homiletic exhortations to the reader to make preparations in this life for judgment in the next.[2] It is generally assumed that the placing of the Temptation at the end of the poem and out of chronological order is a result of the need to conclude the poem with a model that the human reader might be able to emulate. Since at the Temptation, unlike the Fall or the Harrowing, Christ was believed to have conquered as man, not as God, the Temptation functions as a lesson and exhortation for human beings in their own personal battle against Satan. *Christ and Satan* is thus a poem whose structure has been organized around the position of the reader in the world, a position which is a function of the fact that although the cosmic battle between Christ and Satan is over at one level—Christ's conquest of Hell is the concluding confrontation—it continues in another form in the conflict between Satan and each individual believer.

In 1974 Jackson Campbell argued that the challenge to modern critics was to bring to Old English poetry the same typological and figurative thinking that the Anglo-Saxon audience brought to it.[3] *Christ and Satan* offers us one approach to this project; both its content and structure offer ample evidence of the poet's concern for the reader's response through its emphasis on the theme of knowledge, recognition and remembrance.[4] By examining the organization and use of these themes we may gather some evidence of how the reader was expected to respond.

The language of *Christ and Satan* makes clear the importance of its concern with knowledge and recognition. In reading the poem it is impossible not to be struck by the number of words relating to knowledge and identity, *seolf* ("self"), *cunnan* and *witan* (both meaning "to know"), as well as *gemunan* and other words of thinking and remembering. The word *seolf* alone occurs twenty-two times in the poem,[5] almost always referring to Christ or Satan as each identifies himself or is identified by others. The reader, who exists within time in a world in which revelation has already taken place, is in a position to take advantage of the power of knowledge. But since the Scriptures have already revealed the story of salvation history, knowledge need not involve the acquisition of new information. Rather it takes the form of recognition, both the acknowledgement of identity, and the literal re-cognition, or acknowledgment, of something already known.[6]

Throughout, Satan is presented as a foil to the reader, an example of what not to do. Each narrative episode revolves around this theme as Christ either reveals his own identity or that of Satan, and as Satan either purposely confuses his identity with Christ's or is made to recognize his own.[7] At the same time, the distance between Christ's knowledge and human knowledge is emphasized. Within this scheme, ultimate knowledge resides with God; he alone understands the design of the cosmos since it is he who made it. In the opening lines, the word *seolf* appears three times to describe Christ as Creator: He himself set the sun and moon in place ("Seolfa he gesette sunnan and monan," l. 4); he himself can see the whole of the sea ("He selfa mæg sæ geondwlitan," l. 9); and he himself set the number of days ("Daga enderim / seolua he gesette," ll. 12b–13a). In two of these instances the identity of God is expressly associated with his role as Creator through the alliteration of *seolf* with *gesettan*. The word *seolf* is capitalized in the manuscript on line 13, implying a need for emphasis on the identity of God as Creator.[8] Human understanding does not extend this far: "Hwa þæt ðe cunne / orðonc clene nymðe ece god?" ("Who is there that understands completely the design, except the eternal God?," ll. 17b–18).[9] But people must acknowledge the builder of the cosmos through his work, even if they cannot understand it. Thus the narrator, advising the reader to prepare for the Judgment, associates the believer's knowledge of Christ with Christ's role as the builder of the cosmos: "þæt is monegum cuð / þæt he ana is ealra gescefta / wyrhta and waldend þurh his wuldres cræft" ("That is known to many, that he alone is the builder and ruler of all created things," ll. 582b–584).

The poet emphasizes Christ's identity while asserting human limitations. In marked contrast, Satan assumes his knowledge is equal to Christ's and yet is unable to recognize Christ. In the first instance Satan purposefully confuses his identity with God's, misleading his followers and himself. After their fall, the rebel angels accuse Satan of confusing his identity with God's:

> Ðuhte þe anum   þæt ðu ahtest alles gewald,
> heofnes and eorþan,   wære halig god,
> scypend seolfa.   (55–57a)
> [It seemed to you alone that you possessed the power over all, over heaven and earth, that you were the holy God, yourself the shaper.]

Satan here is described as confusing himself with God the Creator or shaper (*scypend*), recalling the narrative of Creation at the beginning of the poem. Shortly after, the fallen angels rebuke Satan for telling them that he was God, the father of Christ: "Segdest us to soðe þæt ðin sunu wære / meotod moncynnes; hafustu nu mare susel!" ("You told us that it was true that your son was the creator of mankind. Now you have more punishment," ll. 63–64).[10]

In the second section of the poem, the Harrowing of Hell, the confusion of identity that is described in the narrative of the Fall of the angels is reversed. There Satan declared himself the father of "the creator of mankind" (*meotud moncynnes*, l. 64). Here the Son reveals himself again, but it is Christ's identity that Satan is made aware of, not his own. As Christ triumphantly enters hell, Satan declares "Hit is se seolfa sunu waldendes" ("It is the son of the ruler himself," l. 394). The scene is a revelation not only of Christ as God, but of the cosmic battle itself, as the narrator makes clear:

>   hæfde drihten seolf
> feond oferfohten.   Wæs seo fæhðe þa gyt
> open on uhtan,   þa se egsa becom.   (402b–404)
> [The lord himself had out-fought the fiend. The enmity was now revealed at the dawn, when the terror occurred.]

In the final section of *Christ and Satan*, the Temptation of Christ, the poem's concern with recognition is most noticeable. Here Satan makes several attempts to discover the incarnate Christ's identity. In the first temptation, he asks Christ to turn stone to bread "gif þu swa micle mihte hæbbe" ("if you have that much power," l. 672). Again, at the third temptation, Satan shows curiosity about Christ's identity in the comment, "gif þu seo riht cyning / engla and monna, swa ðu ær myntest" ("if you are the true king of angels and men, as you thought earlier," ll. 687b–688). But immediately after the third temptation *Christ and Satan* diverges from the exegetical tradition that Christ kept his identity secret. In Matthew, it is at this point that Satan leaves and Christ is ministered to by two angels.[11] In *Christ and Satan*, on the other hand, Christ reveals his identity to Satan: "Gewit þu, awyrgda, in þæt witescræf, / Satanus seolf" ("Depart accursed, into that cave of punishment, Satan himself," ll. 690–691a).[12] In this single statement Christ simultaneously reveals himself and unmasks Satan. He reveals himself partly through what Huppé calls his "incommensurate might,"[13] as evidenced in his punishing of Satan, but also through his knowledge, his ability to recognize Satan for what he is.

According to medieval exegesis, Satan's purpose during the Temptation was to determine the identity of Jesus, but since Christ conquered as a man, he was able to keep his identity secret.[14] But *Christ and Satan* emphasizes not the disguise of Christ, but his revelation, providing an unambiguous ending in which both Satan and Christ are unmasked; Christ condemns Satan to measure hell. The Temptation becomes thematically identical to the Harrowing—a battle in which Christ's identity as both God and victor is made manifest. Since the measuring scene is nonbiblical, it is clear that the poem's Temptation scene is not a representation of the literal truth of the Bible story, but a symbolic construction. Satan's measuring of hell not only represents his recognition of Christ; it also functions as a graphic figuring of self-knowledge. Although hell is, in one sense, a fief given by Christ, it is Satan's own construction since it is what he has earned through his own behavior.[15] Satan and his followers "establish" their home in hell, just as Christ has established the cosmos:

> Him ðær wirse gelamp,
> ða heo in helle   ham staðeledon,
> an æfter oðrum,   in þæt atole scref.[16]   (24b–26)
> [It worked out worse for them when they established a home in hell, one after the other, in that terrible cave.]

The devils are, in a sense, constructing their own cosmos, and so Satan's measuring of hell is parallel to God's measuring out the cosmos.[17] When Satan is told to measure hell, Christ instructs him to tell the fallen angels "þæt ðu gemettes meotod alwihta, / cyning moncynnes" ("that you have met the measurer of all creatures, the king of mankind," ll. 696–697a).

In commenting on this passage, Thomas D. Hill has pointed out the wordplay involving the words *metan* ("meet") and *ametan* ("measure"), so that Satan's measuring of hell is connected with his meeting of Christ.[18] Hill's identification of the relationship between the two words takes on extra significance if we see it as part of the theme of knowledge and identity that runs throughout the whole of *Christ and Satan*. "Uton cyþan þæt!" ("Let us make that known," l. 297b) says the narrator in urging the reader to think of the home that awaits the good soul. Knowledge already acquired is not to be ignored: "Deman we on eorðan, ærror lifigend, / onlucan mid listum locen waldendes, / ongeotan gastlice!" ("Let us on earth, the living, decide beforehand to unlock with skill the stronghold of the ruler, to comprehend spiritually," ll. 298–300a). In like manner, Satan is ordered to relay his new-found knowledge to his followers, the difference being that his knowledge is acquired too late to offer any hope:

> Ah ic þe hate   þurh þa hehstan miht
> þæt ðu hellwarum   hyht ne abeode,
> ah þu him secgan miht   sorga mæste,
> þæt ðu gemettes   meotod alwihta,
> cyning mancynnes.   (693–697a)
>
> [But I order you through the highest power that you do not offer hope to the inhabitants of hell, but you must tell them the greatest of sorrows, that you met the almighty creator, the king of mankind.]

Satan's own punishment is based on a revelation imposed by Christ:

> Wite þu eac, awyrgda,   hu wid and sid
> helheoðo dreorig,   and mid hondum amet.
> Grip wið þæs grundes;   gang þonne swa
> oððæt þu þone ymbhwyrft   alne cunne,
> and ærest amet   ufan to grunde,
> and hu sid seo   se swarta eðm.
> Wast þu þonne þe geornor   þæt þu wið god wunne,
> seoððan þu þonne hafast   handum ametene

hu heh and deop   hell inneweard seo,
grim græfhus.   (698–707a)

[Know then, accursed one, how wide and vast is the miserable hell-hall,
and measure it with your hands. With them take hold of the depths; go in
this way until you know the whole circuit, and measure first top to bottom
and how wide the dark vapor is. You will know then the better that you
fought with god, after you have measured with your hands how high and
deep hell, the grim grave, is inside.]

Unlike human knowledge of Christ, already known and needing only to
be reflected on, Satan's recognition of Christ's divinity is a form of
humiliation in which his own understanding is contrasted with Christ's.

The notion of measurement as self-knowledge is not without prece-
dent in the early Middle Ages. The same linkage of identity, measure-
ment, and hubris that we find in *Christ and Satan* also occurs in Gregory
the Great's *Moralia in Job*. Gregory's moral interpretation of Job 38:5
("Who hath laid the measures thereof, if thou knowest? Or who hath
stretched the line upon it?"[19]) sees the measures as mysterious lines
drawn by God that set the limit on human abilities. Every man has cer-
tain gifts, Gregory explains, but these gifts are limited and to try to go
beyond these limits is to risk a fall: "In praecipiti enim pedem porrigit
qui mensuraram suaram limitem non attendit. Et plerumque amittit et
quod poterat qui audacter ea ad quae pertingere non ualet arripere festi-
nat."[20] In light of Gregory's commentary, Satan's punishment is entirely
appropriate. As a created being, Satan is restricted by limits. His mea-
suring of hell is thus a literalizing of a patristic metaphor, a measuring
out of his own limits, limits assigned to him at the moment of his cre-
ation. Here punishment is knowledge; so is Satan made to "know" hell,
which he himself constructed, just as thoroughly as Christ knows his
own construction, the cosmos.

Satan's knowledge, acquired too late, is in perfect contrast to the
"unknowing" that Christ will perform on Judgment Day, when Christ
will refuse to acknowledge the sinners who have previously "forgotten"
(*forgeaton*, l. 640) him: "Astigað nu, awyrgde, in þæt witehus / ofostum
miclum. Nu ic eow ne con" ("Descend now, accursed ones, into that
house of punishment with great haste. Now I know you not," ll.
626–627a). The *witehus* here is an especially appropriate term since hell
in this poem is both a house of punishment and of knowledge. *Witan* ("to
know") and *wite* ("punishment") are distinguished by the length of
vowel, so, like *ametan* ("to measure") and *metan* ("to meet"), as

described by Hill, this too may be a play on words.[21] If so, it would, like the pun on *metan /ametan*, reinforce the connection between two important themes in the poem. Just as Christ's revelation to Satan is itself conquest, so knowledge acquired too late *is* punishment. *Christ and Satan* repeatedly contrasts before and after, *ær* ("before") and *nu* ("now"), as Satan and the fallen angels remember their earlier actions from their position in the eternal present, and as the narrator urges the reader to consider the afterlife while in this life. The resulting construction of time is based not on the chronology of the narrative episodes, but on these two opposing states. The reader exists in the period "before," while Satan is eternally "after."

The self-knowledge that Satan painfully acquires in *Christ and Satan*, as well as his forced recognition of the divinity of Christ, serves to guide the reader toward another kind of recognition: the ability to distinguish between true and false words. Satan himself is the father of lies, and at several places in the poem it is clear that those who have fallen— the rebel angels and Adam and Eve—have been lied to. Eve, at the time of her release from hell, expressly refers to the mistake she and Adam made in believing the lies that were told her by Satan: "Þa wit ðæs awærgdan wordum gelyfdon" ("Then we believed the words of the acursed one," l. 414). Likewise, the devils lamenting in hell comment on the lies of Satan: "ðu us gelærdæst ðurh lyge ðinne / þæt we helende heran ne scealdon" ("you taught us through your lies that we ought not to obey the savior," ll. 53–54). The Temptation, more than any other of the cosmic battles, is a battle of words, specifically of true and false readings of Scripture. In the biblical accounts of the Temptation, both Christ and Satan quote Scripture at each other. To each temptation Christ responds with scriptural quotation, beginning with the words, "It is written." Satan also quotes Scripture, attempting to persuade Christ to leap off the pinnacle by quoting Psalm 90:11–12: "For he hath given his Angels charge over thee: to keep thee in all thy ways. In their hands, they shall bear thee up in their hands lest thou dash thy foot against a stone."[22] This dialogue is interpreted by Jerome as a conflict between the true and false uses of Scripture. Satan, he says, is a bad interpreter who does not really know the Scriptures, otherwise he would not have neglected to mention the verse that immediately follows the passage he quoted: "Thou shalt walk upon the asp and the basilisk: and thou shalt trample under foot the lion and the dragon."[23] For Jerome, Christ's battle with Satan is pictured as a war of words: Christ "breaks the false arrows of the devil's Scriptures with the shields of the true Scriptures."[24] Hrabanus Maurus, following Jerome, comments that the devil is willing to mention the angels, but is silent about the verse that refers to himself—the trampling of the beasts.[25]

The Temptation, then, presents a battle in which Christ conquers not only as a man, but as a reader and knower of sacred Scripture. Like the Temptation itself, Scripture plays a part in the human battle against Satan, since the Scriptures are available to all, and are, in fact, a means of combat.[26] But the reader's position is quite different from that of Christ or Satan. The cosmic battle has already been fought, and although believers must constantly fight their own battle, they are able to draw on the knowledge of Christ revealed through the Scriptures. There are no secrets from the reader who, unlike Satan, is expected to recognize Christ's power from the beginning, as the poem's first lines make clear:

> Þæt wearð underne   eorðbuendum,
> þæt meotod hæfde   miht and strengðo
> ða he gefastnade   foldan sceatas.   (1–3)
> [It has become manifest to earth-dwellers, that the measurer had might
> and strength when he fastened the regions of the earth.]

Christ's might and strength are visible to all. Christ has already made known (*gecydde*) his strength and the reader is encouraged not to learn, but to remember or to consider (*gemunan*) this fact:

> He þæt gecydde   þæt he mægencræft hæfde,
> mihta miccle,   þa he ða mænego adraf,
> hæftas of ðæm hean selde.   Gemunan we þone halgan drihten,
> ecne in wuldre   mid alra gescefta ealdre;
> ceosan us eard in wuldre   mid ealra cyninga cyninge,
> se is Crist genemned.[27]   (199–204)
> [He made known that he had that great strength, great powers, when he
> drove out that mob, the captives from the high hall. Let us remember the
> holy lord, eternal in glory with the master of all created things; let us
> choose a home in glory with the king of all kings, who is called Christ.]

Remembrance itself is a form of action, a choice made that will protect the reader in the future life. For this reason *Christ and Satan* avoids the construction of tension or suspense that is a common function of narrative. The poem is iconic, creating symbolic images to be contemplated. This style of writing is not unknown in Old English poetry, especially the wisdom poetry or the elegies, which tend to repeat precepts or imagery. *Christ and Satan* is, however, a narrative poem in which the narrator effectively "gives the plot away" from the beginning as though the narrative itself were in danger of concealing what is necessary to know. This is in marked contrast to most Old English heroic narrative, such as *Beowulf*, where, despite the high degree of foreshadowing throughout the poem, Beowulf's individual fights are often presented as suspenseful.[28] The more iconic form of representation in *Christ and Satan*, in which the underlying symbolic message actually dominates the literal, is a function of the homiletic purpose of the poem. The symbolic is not only woven into the narrative, it actively distorts the chronology. Although unusual in Old English narrative, this style of represention does make an appearance in the tenth and eleventh centuries in what has been called "symbolic illustrations" in psalters. These psalters employ a series of images showing Christ (and David) in combat with the devil. Although the chief exomplum, the Tiberius Psalter (c. 1060), is later than *Christ and Satan*, they form a useful reference point insofar as the structure of the poem is concerned. The symbolic illustrations do not illustrate the events of the psalms, but rather create typological juxtapositions.[29]

As in *Christ and Satan*, the interest in theophany and cosmic combat is apparent in these psalters, especially in the Tiberius Psalter. This psalter shows a series of images, relating to the conquest of evil by Christ and David, including the Harrowing and the Temptation.[30] The illustrations for the Tiberius Psalter are similar to *Christ and Satan* in that they too are compressed versions of salvation history. They are also symbolic rather than literal representations of the events depicted. In the Tiberius Temptation scene, Christ appears with a cross staff, a sign of his role as victor over death. The achronology of this image is clear; Christ could not have had the cross staff before his death. It is a symbolic image, an image of Christ as victor, a revelation of his identity rather than a depiction of the actual event of the Temptation.[31]

Like the Tiberius Psalter, *Christ and Satan* relies on the reader's typological thinking to undermine the reader's sense of suspense. This iconic experience of the text can never be entire; all reading involves some sense of changing expectations, a "filling in of gaps" as described by Wolfgang Iser.[32] What is interesting about *Christ and Satan* is how much the narrative attempts to undermine this quality of reading. As much as possible it avoids leaving the reader to fill in the gaps. Rather, *Christ and Satan* attempts to control the reader's interpretation in a way that is not possible in traditional narrative structures. The hortatory passages, the achronological construction, the repeated revelations, all work to override what has been called "the pilgrimage of reading," the reader's experience of working through the text.[33] Instead, *Christ and Satan* offers knowledge to the reader as an immediate response, a memory as weapon to be used in vanquishing the devil.

The concerns of both the illustrator of the Tiberius Psalter and the author of *Christ and Satan* may be found in the Augustinian foundations of medieval theories of language. For Augustine language was both incarnation, the presence of God, and veil, mysterious and distancing, or as Marcia Colish describes it, "a necessary and inadequate means to the knowledge of God."[34] Faced with this dichotomy, the poet of *Christ and Satan* attempts to bridge the gap, to reveal, breaking down the distancing effect by focussing on the reader's present knowledge, rather than attending to the chronology of the narrative. Just as the psalter illustrator relied on symbolic images to show the reader the true Christ, so *Christ and Satan* removes the veil of historical time to reveal the incarnation and the cosmic battle that underlies it all.

NOTES

I had originally intended to thank Kathleen Openshaw for her help in reading this paper and for her advice on symbolic illustration in psalters. As a result of her sudden death in January 1995, this is no longer possible. I would, however, like to acknowledge her help and support over the years, and to dedicate this article to her memory. An earlier version of this paper was presented at the University of Western Ontario's conference, "Crossing the Boundaries," on March 12, 1994.

1. Originally this strange structure resulted in negative criticism, and the poem was often accused of disunity and lack of structure. One of the earliest to the see the poem as thematically unified was Huppé, who argued that the unifying theme was "the incommensurate might" of God. Bernard F. Huppé, *Doctrine and Poetry: Augustine's Influence on Old English Poetry* (New York, 1959), 227. More recent critics have followed Huppé's lead. Thus Charles R. Sleeth argues that the unifying theme consists of "the concepts '*cupiditas* brings abasement' and '*caritas* brings exaltation'" (*Studies in Christ and Satan* [Toronto, 1982], 14). Finnegan,

whose formulation provides this paper's point of departure, describes the structure of the poem as bodying forth "the dual theme of the revelation of Christ to man and man's moral obligation with respect thereto." See Robert Emmett Finnegan, *Christ and Satan. A Critical Edition* (Waterloo, ON, 1977), 36. Sleeth counters that revelation of the character of Satan is equally important (p. 13). For a discussion of previous interpretations of the poem, see Finnegan, 12–17. My own discussion is focussed on identity, as opposed to character, the former term implying not so much personality or qualities of character, as who one is in relation to others. For a discussion of the poem that focusses on the notion of *dryht*, see Constance Harsh, "*Christ and Satan*: The Measured Power of Christ," *NM* 90 (1989), 243–253.

2. The homiletic structure and purpose of the poem are admirably described by Finnegan. See "Christ and Satan: Structure and Theme," *Classica et Medievalia* 30 (1974), 490–551; and *Christ and Satan*; 17–36. On the placing of the Temptation at the end of the poem, see Huppé, 231; Finnegan, *Christ and Satan*, 35–36; and Sleeth, *Studies*, 24–26.

3. Jackson J. Campbell, "Some Aspects of Meaning in Anglo-Saxon Art and Literature," *Annuale Medievale* 15 (1974), 5–45 (p. 44).

4. Although I use the word "reader" throughout this paper, it is also probable that the experiences described were felt by a listening audience. Although reading a text oneself and hearing it read can be vastly different experiences, both involve the phenomenon of acquiring information according to a temporal sequence ordained by the text, and it is this element of the reading experience that I will focus on.

5. See Jess Bessinger, *A Concordance to the Anglo-Saxon Poetic Records* (Ithaca, 1977), s.v. *seolf* and *self*.

6. In this context, Jean Leclerq's comment on meditative reading of the Scriptures is helpful. The monastic reader must "pronounce the sacred words in order to retain them; both the audible reading and the exercise of memory and reflection which it precedes are involved. To speak, to think, to remember, are the three necessary phases of the same activity" (*The Love of Learning and the Desire for God*, trans. Catherine Misrahi [New York, 1982], 16).

7. On the revelation of the identities of Christ and Satan, see Finnegan, *Christ and Satan*, 32–36, and Sleeth, *Studies*, 13.

8. Finnegan, *Christ and Satan*, 8.

9. All quotations from *Christ and Satan* are taken from *The Junius Manuscript*, ed. George Philip Krapp, *ASPR* 1 (New York, 1931).

10. This passage has caused some confusion. Thomas D. Hill, "The Fall of Satan in the Old English *Christ and Satan*," *JEGP* 76 (1977), 315–325, takes the passage to be an Augustinian reference to Satan as father of

mendacium (p. 323). Finnegan argues that Satan is trying to usurp the place of the father (*Christ and Satan*, 27). I would agree, and argue this passage is an example of Satan's purposeful confusion of identity; he claims to have fathered Christ since he believes himself God.

11. Matthew 4:11.

12. Christ's command to depart "in þæt witescræf" echoes the language of a number of exegetes who complete the phrase "Vade retro Satanas" with "in infernum" or "in aeternum damnationem." See Wolfgang Huber, *Heliand und Matthäusexegese* (München, 1969), 141–142.

13. Huppé, *Doctrine and Poetry*, 227.

14. Jerome makes this clear in his commentary on the episode: "In omnibus temptationibus hoc agit diabolus ut intellegat si filius Dei sit. Sed Dominus sic responsionem temperat ut eum relinquat ambiguum." ("In all the temptations here the devil acted in order to know whether he was the son of God. But the Lord so phrased the response that he left him confused.") Jerome, *Commentariorum in Matheum Libri IV*, I, 342–45, ed. D. Hurst and M. Adriaen, *CCSL* 77 (Turnhout, 1969), 21. Augustine, commenting on Psalm 23:10, "quis est iste rex gloriae? Dominus exercituum ipse est rex gloriae," ("Who is this King of Glory? The Lord of hosts, he is the King of Glory"), explicitly connects the Harrowing and the Temptation in terms of the falsity of the devil, while playing on the words *tempto* and *tendo*: "Et iam uiuificato corpore, supra te pergit ille tentatus; supra omnes angelos tendit, ab angelo praeuaricatore ille tentatus." ("Now with his body brought to life, the tempted one proceeds over you; he extends over all the angels, that one tempted by the lying angel.") *Enarrationes in Psalmos*, ed. E. Dekkers and J. Fraipont, *CCSL* 38 (Turnhout, 1956), 137. Biblical quotations are taken from *Biblia Sacra iuxta vulgatem versionem*, 2 vols., ed. Robert Weber (Stuttgart, 1969; 2nd ed., 1975). Biblical translations are from the Douai–Rheims version.

15. On hell as a gift of land, see Sleeth, *Studies*, 16–17 and 90–106. The notion of constructing one's own home in the afterlife is not unique to *Christ and Satan*. It occurs in The Apocryphal Life of Thomas, and thus appears in Ælfric's Life of Thomas. Thomas is enlisted by the king of India to build a mansion, but instead of using the money for this purpose, Thomas spends it on good works. Eventually it becomes apparent that the money has gone towards building not an earthly mansion, but a magnificent palace in heaven. See *Ælfric's Lives of Saints*, vol. 2, ed. and trans. Walter W. Skeat, *EETS* 114 (London, 1900), 398–425. A similar concept is found in Alfred's Preface to Augustine's *Soliloquies*, where he describes reading as gathering wood in order to construct a heavenly mansion. See Alfred, *König Alfreds des grossen Bearbeitung der Soliloquien*

des Augustinus, ed. William Endter (Hamburg 1922; rpt. Darmstadt, 1964), 1.

16. The word *staðelian* means "to establish," "to found," or "to make firm," and is often used in the poetry to describe God's construction of the cosmos. See, for example, *Phoenix*, ll. 129b–131a: "siþþan heahcyning, / wuldres wyrhta, woruld staþelode, / heofon ond eorþan" ("after the high king, the maker of glory, founded the world, heaven and earth."). *The Exeter Book*, ed. George Philip Krapp and Elliott Van Kirk Dobbie, *ASPR* 3 (New York, 1936).

17. On the cosmos as God's construction, see Paul Beekman Taylor, "Heorot, Earth and Asgard: Christian Poetry and Pagan Myth," *Tennessee Studies in Literature* 11 (1966), 119–130; and Alvin Lee, *The Guest-hall of Eden* (New Haven, 1972), 179–180.

18. Thomas Hill, "The Measure of Hell: *Christ and Satan* 695–722," *Philological Quarterly* 60 (1981), 409–414.

19. "Quis posuit mensuras eius, si nosti? vel quis tetendit super eam lineam?"

20. *Moralia in Job*, 28.10.24, ed. M. Adriaen, CCSL 143B (Turnhout, 1985), 1414: "Indeed he reaches his foot out to the precipice who does not pay heed to the limit of his measures. And moreover, he even loses what he was able to do who boldly hastens to snatch those things that he is not able to reach." Gregory's interpretation of the measures might have had special interest for an Anglo-Saxon poet since earlier he explicitly refers to God as *mensor* ("measurer"), recalling the Old English epithet *meotod* (*Moralia* 28.6.16, CCSL 143B, 1408).

21. Hill, 411–413.

22. "Quoniam angelis suis mandavit de te, ut custodiant te in omnibus viis tuis in manibus portabunt te ne forte offendas ad lapidem pedem tuum." For the Temptation, see Matt. 4:1-11 and Luke 4:1-13. Jerome's comments had an impact on the author of Blickling Homily 3. Charles D. Wright, "Blickling Homily III on the Temptations in the Desert," *Anglia* 106 (1988), 130–137.

23. "Male ergo interpretatur scripturas diabolus. Certe si vere de Saluatore scriptum nouerat, debuerat et illud dicere quod in eodem psalmo contra se sequitur: *Super aspidem et basiliscum ambulabis et conculcabis leonem et draconem.*" *Commentariorum in Matteum libri IV*, I, 352–56, CCSL 77 (Turnhout, 1969), 21. ("Indeed, the devil interprets the scriptures badly. Truly, if he really knew what was written about the Savior, he would have been bound to say what follows there against him in the same psalm: You will tread on the asp and the basilisk, and you will trample the lion and dragon.") Also see Augustine's comments on the lying angel as quoted in note 14.

24. "Falsas de scripturis diaboli sagittas ueris scripturarum frangit clipeis" (*Comm. Math.* I, 360–61, CCSL 77, 21).

25. *Comm. in Matthaeum* I.iv, *PL* 107, 783.

26. For the scriptures, specifically the psalter as a weapon in combat with the devil, see Kathleen M. J. Openshaw, "Weapons in the Daily Battle: Images of the Conquest of Evil in the Early Medieval Psalter," *Art Bulletin* 75 (1993), 17–38, especially 19–21.

27. *Gemunan* and other words of thinking or considering, including (*ge*)*hycgan* and *geþencan*, are used repeatedly in the hortatory passages, urging the reader to remember truth and righteousness (1. 206), God's strength (1. 285), and the afterlife (1. 644), and encouraging the reader to obey Christ (ll. 593 and 642). See Finnegan's analysis of the hortatory language in *Christ and Satan*, 22–25.

28. See, for instance, Beowulf's fight with Grendel's mother, *Beowulf*, ll. 1518–1569.

29. See Kathleen M. J. Openshaw, "The Symbolic Illustration of the Psalter: An Insular Tradition," *Arte medievale*, II Serie, Anno VI, n.1 (1992), 41–60.

30. London, BL Cotton MS. Tiberius C.vi. Kathleen M. J. Openshaw, "The Battle Between Christ and Satan in the Tiberius Psalter," *The Journal of the Warburg and Courtauld Institutes* 52 (1989), 14–33.

31. Openshaw, "The Battle," 29, notes that the only other image of the Temptation showing Christ with the cross staff is the Odbert Psalter (*ca.* 1000). The theophanic element in this image may be connected with the image of *Christus miles*, an image of Christ as a warrior trampling the beasts, which is usually associated with Psalm 90:11–12 (see above). For a description of the *Christus miles* type and the image of Christ over the beasts, see Fritz Saxl, "The Ruthwell Cross," *Journal of the Warburg and Courtauld Institutes* 6 (1943), 1–19, especially 10–13; and Openshaw, "Weapons in the Daily Battle." The close relationship between the image of the conquering Christ over the beasts and the Temptation is apparent in the ninth-century Carolingian Stuttgart Psalter, and in the Odbert Psalter. In each, the illustration of Psalm 90 amalgamates illustrations of the Temptation with the image of Christ trampling the beasts (Openshaw, "The Battle," 26–27).

32. According to Wolfgang Iser, all reading must involve a constant state of changing expectations necessitated by the way in which readers repeatedly create and revise their understanding of the text as they read: "We look forward, we look back, we decide, we change our decisions, we form expectations, we are shocked by their non-fulfillment, we question, we muse, we accept, we reject; this is the dynamic process of recreation" ("The Reading Process: A Phenomenological Approach," in *Reader-Response Criticism*, ed Jane P. Tompkins [Baltimore, 1980], 50–69, at 62). Also see Iser, "Interaction between Text and Reader," in *The Reader*

in the Text, ed. Susan R. Suleiman and Inge Crosman (Princeton, 1980), 106–119. About listening Iser has little to say, but it should be noted that due to the fact that listeners have little opportunity to "go back" through the text or to skim it (admittedly an unlikely strategy in a monastic context), they are even more dependent on the process of expectation and mental revision that Iser describes.

33. Peter Travis, "Affective Criticism, the Pilgrimage of Reading and Medieval English Literature," in *Medieval Texts and Contemporary Readers*, ed. Laurie Finke and Martin Shichtman (Ithaca, 1987), 201–215.

34. Marcia L. Colish, *The Mirror of Language*, rev. ed. (Lincoln, NE, 1983), 54.

The Wisdom Poem at the End of MS Junius 11

JANET SCHRUNK ERICKSEN

Christ and Satan is the last of four sections in the Old English collection of religious poetry in Oxford, Bodleian Library Manuscript Junius 11. That the poem is different from the others in the manuscript has long been established: it focuses on Christ, while the preceding poems are all based on Old Testament material; it is written in two or three hands, while the preceding poems are written all by a single hand.[1] At its conclusion, moreover, appears the phrase "FINIT LIBER II. AMEN," suggesting that *Christ and Satan* was considered by at least one scribe or the compiler as a unit separate from the implied book one consisting of the poems on Genesis, Exodus, and Daniel. The section numbers in *Christ and Satan* underscore the break by starting anew at one, while the section numbers of the earlier poems are continuously numbered. The distinction is even clear in broad visual terms: *Daniel* is on quite clean vellum; *Christ and Satan* is on worn-looking pages, with more corrections and more densely written text. That *Christ and Satan* is to some degree distinct, then, from the other poems in the Junius 11 manuscript is not debatable. How distinct, where the distinctions lie, and their potential significance to an Anglo-Saxon audience are less clear. The physical condition of *Christ and Satan* indicates that it was handled differently than were its companion poems; one possible explanation for this is that the poem was understood and approached in distinct terms, associated perhaps with its affinities with a category of literature, wisdom literature, not shared by the other poems in the manuscript.

Its distinction from its companion pieces contributed to the predominantly negative critical view from which *Christ and Satan* suffered in the nineteenth and first half of the twentieth century. Early judgments of the poem, such as Conybeare's in 1826, condemned it as "an accumulation of detached fragments" rather "than [of] any regular design."[2] A hundred years later, Krapp comments that "[o]ne may lament the literary judgment of the person who added *Christ and Satan* to *Genesis*, *Exodus*, and *Daniel*."[3] The standard response has now swung the other direction, focusing in the last twenty-plus years on the poem's own coherence and its connections to the Old Testament poems that precede it in the manuscript.[4] At issue in part are the narrative units within *Christ and Satan*, units that occasionally have been considered as distinct poems; the sections offer a rather homiletic overview of the actions of divine and once-divine figures at three significant moments in Christian history: first, the fall of the angels; then the harrowing of hell and the ensuing resurrection, ascension, and anticipated last judgment; and, finally, a chronologically out of place account of Christ's temptation in the wilderness. The relationships among these three pieces have been variously and exten sively explained as, for instance, a rhetorical display of the "incommensurate might of God," a "demonstrat[ion of the] various aspects of Christ's power in the context of a comparison of the forces of good and evil," a "celebration" of "Christ's long-ago victories on the planes of heaven, hell and earth," an exemplum–exhortation, and a comparison between Christ who abases himself and exalts humanity and Satan who exalts himself and earns condemnation.[5] These readings point up not only *Christ and Satan*'s focus on Christ, but also its lack of a clear, relatively continuous narrative; both distinguish *Christ and Satan* from its companion poems in the manuscript.

The dominant view of *Christ and Satan* in relation to the other poems of Junius 11 begins with J. R. Hall's arguments that the manuscript is thematically unified. Joyce Hill deftly sums up the claims of coherence:

> there was at least some moment in time, in the early eleventh century, when some Anglo-Saxons read these poems as an interlocking scheme, one which could be perceived morally (tracing patterns of disobedience and obedience which shape the sequence of fall and redemption), typologically (with the Old Testament material of the first book anticipating the more directly presented redemptive patterns of the second), liturgically (in echo of Lenten, Passiontide and Easter texts), and as an epitome of Christian history, which Hall proposes as the generic model for the manuscript's compilation.[6]

Such connections, however, may reflect the interests and expectations of the manuscript's compiler more than the responses of its early audience(s).[7] Recognizing the intellectual unity of the manuscript may not, in other words, be the end of the story, for doing so does not fully address the material condition nor the literary distinctions that separate *Christ and Satan* from the poems that precede it.

The opening eighteen lines in particular of *Christ and Satan* reveal an affinity with wisdom literature, a popular and multigenre category, that the other poems in Junius 11 do not share. The introductory passage in *Christ and Satan* describes divine power in terms of the physical world and ends with the question: "Hwa is þæt ðe cunne / orðonc clene nymðe ece god?" (Who possesses pure intelligence except eternal God?); the same kind of question and answer can be found in such works as the Old English *Solomon and Saturn*, which includes questions such as "Tell me what is God," with the answer, "I tell you he who has all things in his power is God" (SS 4).[8] In *Christ and Satan*, the answer to the question identifies in enumerative form the extent of God and Christ's "pure intelligence"; the narrator lists the things that God "gesette" (placed) and then suggests the totality of divine knowledge:

> Seolfa he gesette   sunnan and monan,
> stanas and eorðan,   stream ut on sæ,
> wæter and wolcn,   ðurh his wundra miht.
> Deopne ymblyt   clene ymbhaldeð
> meotod on mihtum,   and alne middangeard.
> He selfa mæg   sæ geondwlitan,
> grundas in heofene,   godes agen bearn,
> and he ariman mæg   rægnas scuran,
> dropena gehwelcne;   daga enderim
> seolua he gesette   þurh his soðan miht.
> [He himself placed sun and moon, stones and earth, the current outside the sea, water and cloud, by his wondrous might. God in his power encompasses the deep circuit of ocean and the whole world. He himself can look around the sea (and) the foundations in heaven, God's true Son, and He can count the drops of rain, (number) each drop. He himself appointed by his true power the number of days.][9]

The list and the pursuit of knowledge that it advocates associate *Christ and Satan* with apocryphal literature, to which the poem has already been connected by Merrel Dare Clubb, in the abundant notes for his edition of *Christ and Satan*.[10] In the apocryphal books of Ezra, Baruch, and Enoch, for instance, reference to the "number of the drops of rain" (II Baruch 59:5) appears, like *Christ and Satan*, in the context of stressing the power of divine wisdom.[11] In the book of Ecclesiasticus, too, appears the list that opens *Christ and Satan*, but with a more riddling form that stresses the pursuit of wisdom: "harenam maris et pluviae guttas et dies saeculi quis dinumeravit altitudinem caeli et latitudinem terrae et profundum abyssi quis mensus est sapientiam Dei praecedentum omnia quis investigavit" ("Who has numbered the sand of the sea, and the drops of rain, and the days of the world? Who has measured the height of heaven, and the breadth of the earth, and the depth of the abyss? Who has searched out the wisdom of God that goes before all things?") (1:2–3).[12] Michael Stone describes the function of such lists in apocalyptic literature "as summaries of information revealed . . . at the high point of visionary experiences"; as a whole, the "interrogative lists take their origin apparently in the interrogative Wisdom formulations such as Job 38," a text "designed primarily to state either things which God alone can know, or things which man cannot know" until revelation.[13]

The emphasis on wisdom in *Job* includes a version of the list of revealed things found in *Christ and Satan*, with more emphasis on revelation but with the same reference to calculations of the physical: "ipse enim fines mundi intuetur et omnia quae sub caelo sunt respicit qui fecit ventis pondus et aquas adpendit mensura quando ponebat pluviis legem et viam procellis sonantibus" ("For he beholdeth the ends of the world: and looketh on all things that are under heaven. Who made a weight for the winds, and weighed the waters by measure. When he gave a law for the rain, and a way for the sounding storms") (*Job* 28:24–6). The reference in *Job*, while less complete than the enumeration in Ecclesiasticus, occurs after Job's insistence on his innocence, in an explanation of how God's wisdom is the only true wisdom and exceeds in all ways human industry; it is part of the answer to the question posed in *Job* 28.12, "sapienta vero ubi invenitur et quis est locus intellegentiae" ("where is wisdom to be found, and where is the place of understanding")?[14] The ultimate source of the list of revealed things is, unsurprisingly, obscure—Stone identifies connections in apocalyptic vision materials, in wisdom literature, and in hymns of praise.[15] Perhaps by a variety of paths, the list becomes part of the wisdom literature that flourished in the Middle Ages. Though the Old Testament wisdom books first acquired the modern label of wisdom literature, the term, as Vivien Law neatly defines it, expanded to refer "subsequently to other ancient and medieval texts concerned with purveying moral precepts and reflections upon human existence. It is not a genre but a content-based category, a class to which texts in a large number of genres may be assigned."[16]

Law, in her study of the seventh-century Virgilius Maro Grammaticus, identifies one strand of wisdom literature as a "popular tradition which relied on an unselfconscious, though by no means unsophisticated, use of language to awaken its hearers to awareness of the wisdom permeating Creation." Within this tradition, "[r]iddles and enigmata heighten awareness of Creation: mundane objects or beings are invested with mystery, as the listener glimpses the elements at war within a humble cooking-pot or learns to marvel at the water-spider. The natural world plays a vital role in bringing the common man to recognise God's wisdom."[17] The list of revealed things that begins *Christ and Satan* functions in this way, as does the same list in the often apocryphal question-and-answer material of wisdom texts such as the *Joca monachorum*. The "monks' jokes" are Latin dialogue texts, a form of popular wisdom literature; they offer assortments of wisdom drawn from a range of materials, from obscure details of the Bible to secular proverbs.[18] Two examples of *Joca*-style material include lists nearly identical, within a much more extensive array of partial parallels, to that at the beginning of *Christ and Satan* and, in addition, might have connections to Anglo-Saxon England.[19]

While not directly part of the group usually identified as *Joca monachorum*, the *Collectanea pseudo-Bedae* has much in common with it.[20] It includes brief wisdom pieces of the sort found in the *Joca*, as well as texts on numerology and "miscellaneous hymns and prayers."[21] The history of the *Collectanea* is uncertain, but Michael Lapidge suggests "that the majority of its datable contents are most plausibly assigned to the middle decades of the eighth century" and "the majority of its localizable contents originated either in Ireland or England, or in an Irish foundation on the Continent."[22] Whatever the origin, the *Collectanae* include an abundance of passages "demonstrably related to medieval dialogue-literature or riddle material."[23] "Of fifty-nine questions in the Old English *Solomon and Saturn*," by Martha Bayless's count, "thirteen are paralleled in the *Collectanae*, and of these, four are 'rare,' " that is, among a "small number . . . found in very few other dialogues" and having distinctly "Insular connections."[24] One of those parallels James E. Cross and Thomas D. Hill connect to *Christ and Satan*. Item 15 of the prose *Solomon and Saturn* and item 123 of the *Collectanea* ask, in part, who "was baptized after death"; the answer is Adam, whose body, Cross and Hill explain, was understood as having been baptized at the Crucifixion by the blood of Christ as it sank through the ground. The "fulwihtes bæðe" in the Crucifixion account in *Christ and Satan* (545) suggests that

> [at least] one other OE writer knew of the tradition about Adam's baptism. The poet of *Christ and Satan* certainly filled out scriptural statement with apocryphal story . . . [and] [t]he "baths of baptism" [there] could well be for Adam, in view of the persistent emphasis on apocryphal tradition in this poem.[25]

Cross and Hill's yoking of the three texts, the *Collectanea*, *Solomon and Saturn*, and *Christ and Satan*, is echoed in a similar link, this time in the list of revealed things, that occurs in the *Collectanea*, *Adrian and Epicti tus* (like *Solomon and Saturn*, a trivia dialogue), and *Christ and Satan*.

Item 46 in the *Collectanea* asserts that no one but God can count "the sand of the sea, the drops of rain, the days of the world, the height of heaven, the number of stars, the vastness of the earth, and the bottom of the abyss and the hairs of the head as well as the race of men and pack animals: these are to be numbered by God alone" (Arena maris, pluuiarum guttae, dies seculi, altitudo caeli, multitudo stellarum, profunditas terrae et imum abyssi et capilli capitis siue plebs hominum uel iumentorum: haec non nisi a Deo tantum numeranda sunt).[26] The Latin *Adrian and Epictitus* dialogues, which, like *Solomon and Saturn*, derive their title from the names of the voices in the dialogue, contain material probably derived from *Joca* texts. While the surviving manuscripts are mostly from the later Middle Ages, Suchier places their origin as early as sixth-century Gaul, deriving from Greek models.[27] One version includes a nearly identical list and premise: These things "sunt difficilia que nemo novit nisi Deus: arenam maris, pluviarum guttas, altitudinem celi, numerum stellarum, profunditatem terre, pruna abyssi" ("are difficult, which no one knows except God: the sands of the sea, the drops of rain, the height of heaven, the number of stars, the vastness of the earth, the fire of the abyss").[28] Both dialogue texts imply, by the list and their attention to the pursuit of wisdom, that to those who seek and apply what right knowledge they can, God's wisdom is made clear, although the full extent of knowledge, the actual number of raindrops and sand grains, must wait until heavenly revelation.

The currency of this kind of text in Anglo-Saxon England is suggested by Bayless, who notes that "the trivia-dialogue sections" of the *Collectanae* "have clear affinities with a group of texts circulating in the early medieval period," and among the closest identified links between trivia-dialogues, related texts, and the *Collectanae*, "the overwhelming proportion are Insular or have Insular connections."[29]

The list of revealed things is among items in the *Collectanea* that Bayless identifies as "not typical *Ioca* questions," but nevertheless ones that "do find parallels in unusual *Ioca* texts."[30] A wider wisdom context, one beyond the trivia-dialogue genre, is suggested by two other occurrences of the list with Insular connections. One is in the biblical commentaries of Theodore and Hadrian; the other is in the pseudo-Isidorian *Liber de ortu et obitu patriarchum*. In the Theodore and Hadrian Second Commentary on the Gospels, in what appears to be a preface to comment on Matthew 10:30, comes the list in form nearly identical to its appearance in *Adrian and Epictitus* and in the *Collectanea*, and strongly echoed in *Christ and Satan*: "Septem sunt difficilia quae nemo nouit nisi Deus: harena maris, pluuiarum guttae, altitudo caeli, numerus stellarum et profunditas terrae et ima abissi et dies saeculi" ("There are seven unfathomables which no one knows except God: sands of the sea, drops of rain, the height of heaven, the number of stars and vastness of the earth and the depth of the abyss and the days of this world") (EvII 19).[31] The substance of Matthew 10 is wisdom, specifically the directions Christ gives his disciples as he disperses them to teach; in verses 29–31, Christ is reiterating the extent of God's power.

Christ's power is the core of the "Christus" chapter of the *Liber de ortu et obitu patriarchum*, a collection of "[s]hort biographical notices . . . on fifty-nine great heroes of the Old and New Testaments," which McNally describes as a "compact handbook valuable for Scriptural studies, especially for biblical history."[32] Like the *Collectanea*, this pseudo-Isidorian text has Irish connections. According to McNally, the *Liber de ortu et obitu* "originated about the middle of the eighth century in southeast Germany, probably in the wide circle of the Irish bishop of Salzburg, St. Virgilius."[33] Chapter 42, in itself a "tract on Christ," includes a fairly lengthy account of the extent of God's powers, including the enumeration that appears in *Christ and Satan*:

> Infernum sub terra et aquis potentia posuit et penetrat. Cardines celi ac terre terribiliter terminat. Latitudinem celi metitur palmae. . . . Mari mirabiliter terminum posuit. Duodecim ventos varios de suis abditis

eduxit. Cursum solis et lunae et siderum sublime statuit. Arenam maris et stellas caeli, pluviae guttas et dies seculi earum numerum solus agnovit.[34] [The abyss under the earth and waters His power placed and set. The center of the clouds and also of the earth He fixed, awesomely. The breadth of the clouds is measured by His hand. . . . He placed, marvelously, the bounds of the sea. The twelve various winds he produced from their concealment. He fixed the sublime course of the sun and the moon and heaven. He alone knows the number of the sands of the sea and the stars of the sky, the drops of rain and the days of the world.]

Both the *Liber de ortu et obitu patriarchum* and the biblical commentaries of Theodore and Hadrian, like the dialogue texts, suggest that the list of revealed things was found particularly effective in contemplating the bounds and extent of human and divine wisdom, and in encouraging the pursuit of wisdom.

The list of revealed things occurs not only in Latin didactic texts, where its significance is perhaps clearest, but also in vernacular poetic texts; besides *Christ and Satan*, it turns up in the Old English poems *Exodus*, "The Creed," and *The Descent into Hell*. In the *Exodus* account of the test of Abraham's faith, lifted from the book of Genesis, the angelic voice that stops the sacrifice of Isaac goes on to describe God's wisdom in terms of sea, stars, and the expanse of earth and heaven. The passage is a reworking of the biblical account of Abraham and Isaac that substitutes the list of revealed things for the angel's description of how the race of Abraham will multiply: "benedicam tibit et multiplicabo semen tuum sicut stellas caeli et velut harenam quae est in litore maris" ("I will bless thee, and I will multiply thy seed as the stars of heaven, and as the sand that is by the sea shore") (Gen. 22:17). The Old English poem's interest in divine knowledge is introduced early, when the narrator speaks directly to the audience about Moses's history; the first time that God spoke to Moses, "He him gesægde soðwundra fela, / hu þas woruld worhte witig Drihten" ("he told him many marvelous truths—how the wise Lord created this world, the earth's ambit and the sky above"), things that, along with the name of God, "ær ne cuðon / frod fædera cyn, þeah hie fela wiston" ("the wise race of patriarchs did not know before, though they knew much") (ll. 24–5, 27b–29).[35] The story of Abraham elaborates on this idea, in a curious suspension between an account of the order of the troops marching into the Red Sea and, in part because of a lost section, the gory description of the slaughter of the Egyptians. The heavenly voice tells Abraham that

Ne behwylfan mæg   heofon and eorðe
His wuldres word,   widdra and siddra
þonne befæðman mæge   foldan sceattas,
eorðan ymbhwyrft   and uprodor,
garsecges gin   and þeos geomre lyft.   (427–31)
[Heaven and earth cannot cover over his glorious word, which is farther
and wider than the surfaces of the world, the earth's orb and the sky, the
sea's great depth and this sad air can encircle.]

The extent of God's knowledge thus described is then amplified by its
contrast to limited human knowledge:

             rim ne cunnon
yldo ofer eorðan   ealle cræfte
to gesecgenne   soðum wordum,
nymðe hwylc þæs snottor   in sefan weorðe
þæt he ana mæge   ealle geriman
stanas on eorðan,   steorran on heofonum,
sæbeorga sand,   sealte yða.   (436b–42)
[men on earth will not be able with all their skill to say in certain words
the number—unless there be someone so wise of mind that he alone can
count all the stones on the earth, the stars in the heavens, the sand of the
sea-cliffs, the salty waves.][36]

Divine knowledge, as in *Christ and Satan*, is defined in terms of the vis-
ible, divinely ordered world and in relation to a narrative in which right
and wrong knowledge plays a pivotal role. While the Abraham and Isaac
passage as a whole "emphasizes the renewal of the covenant between
God and the Israelites," as Lucas puts it, the angel's invocation of the list
of revealed things works as in the Latin examples, where reference to
"[t]he natural world plays a vital role in bringing the common man to
recognise God's wisdom."[37]

    In *The Descent into Hell* and "The Creed," the object of the count
varies, but a clear parallel to *Christ and Satan*'s framing list remains vis-
ible. *Christ and Satan* describes God as having "gesette" the "stream
uton sæ"; the "Creed" similarly asserts that God "garsecges grundas
geworhtest" (created the seas' depths) (7).[38] *Christ and Satan* and *The
Descent into Hell* share the subject of the harrowing of hell as well as the
material example of God's expansive wisdom. In *Christ and Satan* is the
assertion that "ymbhaldeð / meotod on mihtum . . . alne middangeard"
("God in his power encompasses . . . the whole world") (7–8); in John

the Baptist's perspective from hell in *The Descent* is the comparable acknowledgment that God possesses the ability to "ymbfon eal folca gesetu" ("embrace all the dwellings of people") (115).[39] God, according to *Christ and Satan*, "ariman mæg rægnas scuran, / dropena gehwelcne" ("may count the shower of rain, each drop") (11–12a). In *The Descent*, in a parallel cited by Clubb, God is described as able "to count the sands of the sea" ("þu meaht geriman, rice dryhten, sæs sondgrotu") (116b–17a), and in the "Creed," He counts "the multitudes of the splendid stars"—"þu ða menegu canst mærra tungla" (8).[40] God's knowledge of creation is exhaustive and exact. In both *The Descent* and "The Creed," as in *Christ and Satan*, the enumerative passages use reference to the natural world to help characterize the supreme extent of divine wisdom—and to offer a potentially humbling glimpse of it.

We can all count drops of rain, but only the misguided or the spiritually blind will fail to see that God or Christ alone can count them all, that only the author of all creation can reckon such multitudes. *Christ and Satan* not only invokes this wisdom with its opening use of the list of revealed things, but goes on to make it a central concern. Ruth Wehlau has argued that *Christ and Satan* both makes clear that "ultimate knowledge resides with God" and that the reader is encouraged to seek and use whatever knowledge is obtainable to fight against temptation and sin; the reader, "unlike Satan, is expected to recognize Christ's power from the beginning, as the poem's first lines make clear," and to use it to assess both Satan and Christian living.[41] If the list of revealed things posits a frame of mind for the reader in which an active, investigatory response is expected (from the reader or in the text), then the poem as a whole might be understood in connection to the didacticism and the concerns of popular wisdom literature.

The recognition of divine wisdom figures prominently in *Christ and Satan*, despite Satan's attempts to obscure the truth by asserting, for instance, that he is the father of Christ. By the end of the poem, Satan's lies are fully exposed and punished, and Christ's powers are, correspondingly, made clear: Christ assigns Satan the task of measuring hell—and in a wonderful detail reminiscent of the question-and-answer minutiae (though unattested in it), he tells him to complete the task in two hours (709). Before this command, the connection of divine wisdom and revealed knowledge occurs in language that echoes the opening list at least four times, and the link is demonstrated in the stories themselves, as they recount the fall of the angels, the harrowing and resurrection, and the temptation of Christ. References to right thinking and revealed knowledge are particularly thick in the middle section of the poem, that which recounts the harrowing of hell and describes the resurrection, ascension, and last judgment. The narrator proclaims, at the end of describing the resurrection, that "Us is wuldres leoht / torht ontyned, þam ðe teala þenceð" ("To us, those who think rightly, the brilliant radiance of heaven will be revealed") (555–56). In the final part of the ascension piece, the idea appears twice, first within a description of the heavenly kingdom: "Þæt is monegum cuð / þæt he ana is ealra gescefta / wyrhta and waldend þurh his wuldres cræft" ("It is known to many [not all] that he alone is Maker and Ruler of all created things through the might of his glory") (582b–84). The narrator then concludes the ascension account by encouraging his audience, reminding them in language nearly identical to that in at the end of the resurrection piece, that "Leaðað us þider . . . þær is wuldres bled / torht ontyned" ("Thither he invites us . . . where the glorious splendour of heaven is revealed") (592b–93a). The references here correspond to a more subtly phrased reinforcement of the poem's opening passage that occurs in the earlier fall of the angels section, in one of the narrator's expositions on his story: "Uton cyþan þæt! / Deman we on eorðan, ærror lifigend, / onlucan mid listum locen waldendes, / ongeotan gastlice!" ("Let us make it known! We must consider on earth, beforehand, when alive, [how to] unlock with skills the Ruler's stronghold [or mystery], we must understand [this] spiritually!") (297b–300a).[42] The remark is perhaps the most direct encouragement of the pursuit of wisdom in the poem, but the references overall indicate the necessity of doing so even as they, and the poem's opening, emphasize the gulf between human and divine knowledge.

References to knowledge obscured rather than revealed make the same points from a different direction. That Satan has, despite his attempts, so utterly failed to unlock the Ruler's locked-up knowledge is demonstrated not just in the fall and in hell itself, but in his companions' and his own lack of understanding. Satan's fiendish companions accuse him, " 'Þu us gelærdæst ðurh lyge ðinne' " (" 'You convinced us by your lying' ") (53); " 'Segdest us to soðe þæt ðin sunu wære / meotod mancynnes' " (" 'You told us as a truth that your son was the creator of mankind' ") (63–64). Satan's own inability to perceive clearly is reflected in his comment, as he looks around hell, that " 'Ne mæg ic þæt gehicgan hu ic in ðæm becwom, / in þis neowle genip' " (" 'I cannot understand how I came into that, in this abysmal darkness' ") (178).[43]

All that is now clearly revealed to him is the enormity of his wrong: " 'Nu is gesene þæt we syngodon / uppe on earde' " (" 'Now it is apparent that we sinned in the dwelling above' ") (228–29a). A sharp contrast to this incomprehension occurs in the striking speech by Eve, in the poem's subsequent account of the harrowing of hell. The *Christ and Satan* narrator asserts that Eve must repent aloud before Christ will free her from her hell. In doing so, she demonstrates the awareness that Satan lacks, a connection underscored by a repetition in phrasing: " *'Nu is gesene þæt ðu eart sylfa god / and ece ordfruma ealra gesceafta' "* (" 'Now it is apparent that you are God himself and the everlasting Author of all created things' ") (439–40).

The opening "catalogue of heavenly secrets" reverberates throughout *Christ and Satan*; the idea of wisdom which, as Stone puts it, "will be revealed eschatologically to the righteous," is never lost sight of and the opening formulation is most pointedly reiterated in the concluding emphasis on measurement.[44] What Christ requires of Satan is that he know hell, which he himself constructed, just as thoroughly as Christ knows all Creation. Satan must reckon in numbers his punishment:

> Wite þu eac, awyrgda,   hu wid and sid
> helheoðo dreorig,   and mid hondum amet.
> Grip wið þæs grundes;   gang þonne swa
> oððæt þu þone ymbhwyrft   alne cunne,
> and ærest amet   ufan to grunde,
> and hu sid seo   se swarta eðm.   (700–3)
> [Know you also, cursed one, how far and wide the dreary vault of hell is, and measure it with your hands. Take hold of the abyss; go then so until that you know the whole circumference, and first measure from above to the bottom, and how wide the dark air is.]

"The devils are, in a sense," as Wehlau phrases it, "constructing their own cosmos, and so Satan's measuring of hell is parallel to God's measuring out the cosmos. When Satan is told to measure hell, Christ instructs him to tell the fallen angels 'þæt ðu gemettes meotod alwihta, / cyning moncynnes' ('that you have met the measurer of all creatures, the king of mankind') (ll. 696–97a)."[45] Satan recognizes only the vastness of the task and not the lesson in it: "þa him þuhte þæt þanon wære / to helleduru hund þusenda / mila gemearcodes" ("Then it seemed to him that from there to the gate of hell was a hundred thousand miles in measure"). Other critics have noted the appropriateness of the fact that "se

mihtiga het / þæt þurh sinne cræft"—his wisdom—"susle amæte" ("the
Almighty through his skill commanded that, to measure misery").
Thomas D. Hill has argued that the wordplay in *ametan* and *metan*, "to
measure" and "to meet," adroitly emphazises the punishment; as Satan
meets Christ, he acquires the new task.[46] Wehlau suggests an accompa-
nying word play in *witan* and *wite*, "to know" and "punishment," for
"knowledge acquired too late is [itself] punishment"; the knowledge that
Satan's action will reveal to him "is in perfect contrast to the 'unknow-
ing' that Christ will perform on Judgment Day, when Christ will refuse
to acknowledge the sinners who have previously 'forgotten' him."[47]
What the audience desiring salvation can do, according to narrator and
narrative, is actively seek and see God in everything, every drop of rain,
every grain of sand. Though the knowledge thus revealed will only be a
fraction of what is known to God and Christ, it will serve, nevertheless,
to clarify God's power and wisdom. The opening passage in *Christ and
Satan* not only incorporates the list of revealed things but also, by doing
so, invokes association with wisdom literature that uses the same formu-
lation. From the start it thus encourages the audience to be active seekers
after right knowledge; they can pursue, and must, for salvation, right
knowledge through the Church's wisdom—and perhaps the poet was, in
a sense, advertising literary means to that end, in such texts as this poem
and the *Joca monachorum* or other wisdom literature.

In its affinity with wisdom literature—as well as in its three-part
structure and its focus on Christ—*Christ and Satan* moves away from
the biblical paraphrase that more strongly guides the poems preceding it
in the manuscript. If Junius 11 was normally or primarily read consecu-
tively, the "interlocking scheme" outlined by Joyce Hill would seem to
have been apparent, but given the literary distinctness of *Christ and
Satan* in the manuscript, the possibility that readers went to the final
poem either more often or with a different set of expectations than for
the rest of the manuscript becomes more plausible, and might help
explain the physical condition of the manuscript's last gathering. Despite
thematic connections the compiler may have had in mind, Anglo-Saxon
readers may have identified *Christ and Satan* as a revealed-wisdom
poem and may, in turn, have read it not as the conclusion to the sequence
begun with the *Genesis* section, but on its own. How carefully or fre-
quently any of these poems was read is impossible to discern with cer-
tainty, but the manuscript does offer some intriguing material clues that

underscore the possibility that an audience just might have read *Christ and Satan* more often or with a different eye than the poems that precede it in the collection.

On the whole, the status of the manuscript seems to have declined during its production.[48] Not only are the illustrations limited to *Genesis*, with blanks for full and half-page illustrations continuing through *Exodus* and *Daniel*, but *Christ and Satan*, at a glance, looks the least prestigious of its contents.[49] Krapp, in his edition of the Junius 11 poems, hypothesizes that

> interest in the manuscript as a piece of fine bookmaking had fallen off after the completion of Daniel . . . [or] perhaps a fully thought out plan was never formed for the whole manuscript. . . . Certainly even the plan as first made was not carried out with rigorous oversight, since after p. 96 there are many blank spaces left for illustrations and some for capitals that were never inserted.[50]

In visual terms, the pages of *Christ and Satan* appear rather splotchy, stained and worn, with margins of varying sizes; while the two or three hands are still beautiful, none of the scribes of *Christ and Satan* are the single scribe of the preceding poems, and they have been regularly corrected or revised.[51] The addition of one more line of text per page—twenty-seven, in comparison to the preceding standard of twenty-six—adds, too, to a sense of a more cramped page, as do the slightly smaller letters of the first hand and, most noticeably, the increasingly cramped letters of the second hand.

Peter Lucas has argued that *Christ and Satan* shows evidence of having circulated independently before being bound into Junius 11, and his claims would explain the wear in this section without reference to the other poems in the manuscript. Barbara Raw, however, counters this claim with a minute and persuasive examination of the stitching and binding of the manuscript, which leads her to conclude that *Christ and Satan* was "a fairly early afterthought" in the construction of the manuscript and, as such, was copied expressly for Junius 11 rather than being incorporated as an existing unit. Raw attributes the "extraordinarily dirty and crumpled state of the last gathering"—that containing Christ and Satan—to the thirteenth-century devaluation of Anglo-Saxon books. She offers no explanation for the clear crease in this gathering—"why this part of the manuscript should have been folded remains a mystery"—although she dates the damage to *ca.* 1230, "the time of the re-sewing of the manuscript."[52] That one gathering could have been so "seriously mis-treated" (Raw's assessment) while the poem immediately preceding it, and, indeed, all the poems that precede it, look quite clean is baffling, particularly since the damage occurs not just on the outer pages of the gathering, but throughout it.[53] Simple neglect seems an insufficient explanation for the physical condition of *Christ and Satan*. Particularly in its visual contrast to the relatively clean vellum containing *Daniel*, the condition of the pages containing *Christ and Satan* instead might be read as signs of use, before or after binding, if indeed the damage occurred after the vellum was written on, as seems to be the case.[54]

The most prominent visual aspect of the pages containing *Christ and Satan* is, indeed, the horizontal fold that led Lucas to propose that the inner part of this final quire was once a folded booklet. Striking, too, is the increase in the quantity of ink on the page, largely the result of cor-rections done in one or more hands other than the scribes'.[55] The *Gene-sis* and *Christ and Satan* sections are the most heavily corrected; Krapp describes "the number of corrections in *Exodus* and *Daniel*" as "very small, and practically all of them were made by the scribe of Liber I in correction of obvious errors as he wrote."[56] The corrector's goal in *Christ and Satan* was both simple correction of errors and "normaliza-tion" of the poem's Anglian exemplar, according to Charles Sleeth, "into late West Saxon."[57] The corrector's work, as Clubb notes, varies, becom-ing less plentiful "after line 125, where the second scribe, who did most of the normalizing himself, begins to write," and it is not limited to changes in word forms; the corrector also attempts to clarify passages, with rewriting or explanation, sometimes following on erasures. Clubb deems some of this work of "questionable value" and asserts that "most of his changes are unnecessary," but they still reflect active interest in the text.[58] Clubb, like Gollancz, finds a few corrections that appear the work of a second corrector, in addition to the distinct hand usually identified as that of the annotator.[59] The work, even if done immediately after the scribe's work, surely indicates some expectation or evidence of ongoing use, which is borne out in the only written evidence of ongoing reader-ship of the whole manuscript, what Raw identifies as "two marginal notes in hands of the twelfth century," one on the last page of *Daniel* (p. 212), which is in the same gathering as *Christ and Satan*, and one in *Christ and Satan* (p. 219).[60] If this final section of the manuscript attracted separate attention, or, at least, was judged in need of comment in the twelfth century, it may have done so in the eleventh as well. Certainly in the eleventh century it was already visually distinct from the preceding poems.

The multiple hands in this section of the manuscript, none of which is that of the first three sections, and the folded pages contribute most forcefully to the sense that inner pages (213–28) of quire 17, those containing *Christ and Satan*, were treated differently than preceding pages. The smaller marks and the impression of wear, however, heighten that sense. *Daniel*, in sharpest contrast and closest proximity, did not require the corrections deemed necessary for *Christ and Satan*, and its pages show not only few extraneous marks, but also little of the blurring and staining that has affected the pages of *Christ and Satan*.[61] Raw's codicological assessments tie the last quire to the rest of the manuscript, but still, *Christ and Satan* does not look like what has been designated "Book I," and not all of its condition surely can be attributed to the time of the rebinding.[62] *Christ and Satan*, then, shows material evidence of both being part of and distinct from the rest of the manuscript.

If *Christ and Satan* was understood by an Anglo-Saxon audience as a poem of a different nature than its predecessors in the manuscript, perhaps it was approached and used separately from its companions before being bound into the manuscript, a possibility that addresses both the distinct visual condition of the poem and its literary category, and that does not conflict with Raw's careful examination of the lining of the pages and the sewing of the manuscript. Raw notes that, because it shares stitch marks with the rest of the manuscript, *Christ and Satan* "had already been added to the rest of the manuscript by the time that it was first sewn and that if this text had an earlier, independent existence, as Lucas has claimed, it was used unstitched."[63] Ælfric's letter to the monks of Eynsham in Corpus Christi College Cambridge MS 265 (Ecclesiastical Handbook from Worcester) appears to have been used in just this way. As Mildred Budny describes it, "The first recto and last verso of Quire 17 (pp. 253 and 268), which contains the second and final quire of Ælfric's abridgement of the *Regularis Concordia*, are darkened and stained, probably from exposure while a separate unit."[64] While CCCC 265, as a "[m]iscellaneous collection of canonical, liturgical, legal, and other texts," is distinct in character from the thematically connected poems of Junius 11, it does provide roughly contemporary evidence of a manuscript "assembled in stages" but with some continuity of design and construction: the Ælfric section, section 3, like the texts before and after it, is "laid out in single columns of twenty-six lines."[65] Copies of the Gospels may have been actually designed to be used separately before binding even when clearly designed as a unit and actually written by a single scribe, as in Oxford, Bodleian Library MS Bodley 441. Not only does each Gospel begin on a new page, but the last leaves of Mark, Luke, and John are lost, suggesting that the four gospels were read separately for some time.[66]

Raw argues that *Christ and Satan* was an early addition to the manuscript, yet, even so, Junius 11 shows signs of some degree of assemblage in stages.[67] Its illustration cycle, by two artists, remains unfinished, and one might wonder if binding was held off until it became clear that the spaces left for illustrations were unlikely to be completed. The shift in hands in *Christ and Satan* likewise might be read as evidence of production in stages—the single hand of the first part working at one time, and the hands of *Christ and Satan* working at another.[68] While Raw's arguments are strongly against a wholly independent existence of the *Christ and Satan* section of Junius 11, the manuscript does appear to have been completed in stages, and *Christ and Satan* does appear to have generated some different responses than did its companion poems. *Christ and Satan* could have been both "added before the manuscript as a whole had been sewn" and used separately before the manuscript had been sewn, perhaps because of an interest in it as wisdom literature and independent of its role as the culmination of a coherent series in the manuscript.[69]

Both the enumerative opening and the larger narrative concerns of *Christ and Satan* connect it to the variable-genre, "content-based" category of wisdom literature, and, more specifically, to an assortment of similar or identical revealed-wisdom material that appears in both Latin and vernacular texts, and which may be associated with Anglo-Saxon England.[70] The physical appearance of the poem, particularly in contrast to the poem that precedes it, *Daniel*, indicates at worst wear associated with devaluation and at best an audience interested in updating, improving, and reading *Christ and Satan*. Together, the material and literary distinctions of the poem suggest that while the compiler of MS Junius 11 may well have had a plan, the Anglo-Saxon readers or audience may—like many a modern reader of collections—have made their own, non-sequential choices; in the case of *Christ and Satan*, a choice might well have been made to read the wisdom poem at the end of the collection without reading the biblical poems that precede it.

NOTES

1. The fullest description of the manuscript as a whole may still be that by Israel K. Gollancz in the introduction to the facsimile, *The Caedmon Manuscript of Anglo-Saxon Biblical Poetry, Junius XI in the Bodleian Library* (Oxford, 1927).

2. John Josias Conybeare, *Illustrations of Anglo-Saxon Poetry* (London, 1826), 189.

3. George Philip Krapp, ed., *The Junius Manuscript*, ASPR 1 (New York, 1931), xii.

4. See J. R. Hall, "The Old English Epic of Redemption: the Theological Unity of MS Junius 11," *Traditio* 32 (1976), 185–208 [reprinted in the present volume—*ed.*]; Robert Emmett Finnegan, *Christ and Satan: A Critical Edition* (Waterloo, ON, 1977); and *Charles R. Sleeth, Studies in Christ and Satan* (Toronto, 1982). See also Judith Garde's chapter, "The Junius Codex: A Vernacular *Heilsgeschichte*," in *Old English Poetry in Medieval Christian Perspective: A Doctrinal Approach* (Cambridge, 1991), 25–56, especially 31–34.

5. Bernard F. Huppé, *Doctrine and Poetry: Augustine's Influence on Old English Poetry* (New York, 1959), 227; Constance D. Harsh, "*Christ and Satan*: The Measured Power of Christ," *NM* 90 (1989), 244; Garde 49. See also Sleeth's chapter, "The Work and the Question of Its Unity" (3–26).

6. Hill, "Confronting *Germania Latina*: Changing Responses to Old English Biblical Verse," in *Latin Culture and Medieval Germanic Europe*, ed. Richard North and Tette Hofstra, Germania Latina 1 (Groningen, 1992), 71–88 [reprinted in the present volume—*ed.*]. See also Phyllis Portnoy, " 'Remnant' and Ritual: the Place of *Daniel* and *Christ and Satan* in the Junius Epic," *English Studies* 75 (1994), 408–22.

7. Modern response to the poems has often begun with the simple distinction of whether they deal primarily with the Old or New Testament (see, for instance, in Stanley B. Greenfield and Daniel G. Calder, *New Critical History of Old English Literature* [New York, 1986], 183–226).

8. James E. Cross and Thomas D. Hill, *The Prose Solomon and Saturn and Adrian and Ritheus* (Toronto, 1982), 63.

9. This and all subsequent citations of *Christ and Satan*, unless otherwise noted, are from Krapp's edition of *The Junius Manuscript*. Translations,

unless otherwise noted, are my own; here, both "the current outside the sea" and "count the drops of rain, [number] each drop" are Thomas D. Hill's translations, in "Apocryphal Cosmography and the 'stream uton sæ': A Note on *Christ and Satan*, Lines 4–12," *Philological Quarterly* 48 (1969), 550–54.

10. Merrel Dare Clubb, *Christ and Satan* (New Haven, 1925).

11. In Baruch the counting of raindrops is mentioned in connection with wisdom given Moses; in I Enoch 60:21–23, the numbering of raindrops appears again. See Michael E. Stone, "Lists of Revealed Things in the Apocalyptic Literature," *Magnalia Dei: The Mighty Acts of God. Essays on the Bible and Archaeology in Memory of G. Ernest Wright*, ed. F.M. Cross et al. (Garden City, NY, 1976), 412–52, esp. 420, 433–34. In II Baruch 59, as well, appears the idea of the "measures of heaven" (Stone, 424).

12. *Biblia Sacra, iuxta vulgatam versionem* (Stuttgart, 1983); Douai-Rheims translation. All citations from the Bible are from these editions.

13. Stone 435, 432.

14. Clubb, *Christ and Satan*, cites Job 28:11, "Profunda quoque fluviorum scrutatus est," for ll. 9–10, but not 28:12 for ll. 11–13. He points instead to "[g]eneral similarities" in Isa. 40:12 and Job 38:16, 36:27, 28:26 (48).

15. Stone, 431.

16. Law, 23.

17. Law, 25–26.

18. The term is W. Suchier's, taken from a title in the ninth-century MS Schlettstadt Stadtbibliothek 1073 (Suchier identifies it as "JM E"); see W. Suchier, *Das mittellateinische Gespräch Adrian und Epictitus nebst verwandten Texten (Joca monachorum)* (Tübingen, 1955), 83, 90. See also the *Clavis Patrum Latinorum*, ed. E. Dekkers and A. Gaar, 3rd ed. (Turnhout, 1995), no. 1155f (ii–vii). The editors Cross and Hill identify the OE prose *Solomon and Saturn* as part of the *Joca monachorum* tradition; closely related is the dialogue-based *Adrian and Epictitus* group, from the names of the two speakers. Together, Martha Bayless terms the groups "trivia-dialogues," in order to distinguish them from the so-called "more serious" group of "proverb-dialogues" (13). See "The Collectanea and Medieval Dialogues and Riddles," *Collectanae Pseudo-Bedae*, ed. Martha Bayless and Michael Lapidge et al., Scriptores Latini Hiberniae 14 (Dublin, 1998), 13–24. For discussion of the tradition of question-and-answer dialogues, see L. W. Daly and W. Suchier, *Altercatio Hadriani Augusti et Epicteti Philosophi*, Illinois Studies in Language and Literature 24, 1–2 (Urbana, 1939), especially ch. 2–3.

19. Charles D. Wright first pointed out to me parallels between *Christ and Satan*'s opening list and other examples of such enumerations; I am grateful for his generosity in sharing his findings.

20. James F. Kenney, *The Sources for the Early History of Ireland: Ecclesiastical* (New York, 1966), 680. CPL 1129 (Kenney refers to the collection simply as the *Collectanae Bedae*; the work is also referred to as *Excerptiones patrum* and *flores ex diuersis*). The Book of Cerne, an English-owned prayer book with Irish material and/or sources, includes four prayers/hymns that also occur in the *Collectanea Bedae* and includes "[a]n apocryphal *Descenus ad inferna*" (Kenney, 721). Cross and Hill cite the *Collectanea* for parallels to nine questions in the OE prose *Solomon and Saturn*.

21. Michael Lapidge, "The Origin of the *Collectanae*," *Collectanae pseudo-Bedae*, ed. Bayless and Lapidge, 2–3.

22. Lapidge, 12. In addition to containing five of Aldhelm's *Enigmata*, the *Collectanae* have close ties to Anglo-Saxon material in at least six other items, including a calf riddle, the closest parallels for which are in Eusebuius and the Exeter Book; see Lapidge, 4, and the commentary on item 194 (243).

23. Bayless, 13.

24. Bayless, 20, 17

25. Cross and Hill, 76–79. The SS passage reads: "Saga me hwæt wæs se acenned næs and æft bebyrged was on hys moder innoðe, and æfter þam deaðe gefullod wæs. Ic þe secge, þæt was adam" (Tell me who was he who was not born and afterwards was buried in his mother's womb, and was baptized after death. I tell you, that was Adam). Cross and Hill's commentary traces the extensive tradition of this " 'enigmatic question.' "

26. Bayless and Lapidge, 126.

27. Suchier, 101–2.

28. Suchier, 47–49; the list occurs in the version of *Adrian and Epictitus* that Suchier labels AE_1b, which begins, "Septem sunt difficilia," but only six items follow. See also *Clavis*, 1155f (i).

29. Bayless, 21.

30. Bayless, 16.

31. Michael Lapidge and Bernhard Bischoff, *Biblical Commentaries from the Canterbury School of Theodore and Hadrian*, Cambridge Studies in Anglo-Saxon England 10 (Cambridge, 1994), 400–1; see also the note on 511.

32. Robert E. McNally, S.J., " 'Christus' in the Pseudo-Isidorian 'Liber de ortu et obitu patriarchum,' " *Traditio* 21 (1965), 170.

33. McNally, 168–69. If the *Liber de ortu* did come out of the circle of St. Virgilius, moreover, it may well have close connections to one more occurrence of the list of revealed things. Bischoff describes an eighth-century formulary from Salzburg in which the list is used as the opening salution of a model letter: "eine überschwengliche Freundschaftsadresse mit

Bruchstücken von Hexametern aus dem Carmen paschale des Sedulius" (17). See Bischoff, *Salzburger Formelbücher und Briefe aus Tassilonischer und Karolingischer Zeit* (Munich, 1973), III.12. In Sedulius' Easter poem, the enumeration idea does not occur, but only reference to the fact that God "rules the universe, seas, lands, and stars" (*On Christian Rulers, and the Poems*, transl. Edward Gerard Doyle, Medieval and Renaissance Texts and Studies [Binghamton, NY, 1983], 173).

34. McNally, 178 (ll. 140–42). McNally edits the relevant chapter of "the oldest manuscript, Colmar (Murbach) 39 fols. 28r–37r (s. VIII–IX)" (174). A full edition of the *Liber de ortu et obitu patriarchum* appears in CCSL 108 E, Scriptores Celtigenae, edited by J. Carracedo Fraga (Turnholt, 1996); the quoted section is from 42.6.

35. *Exodus*, ed. Peter J. Lucas (Exeter, 1994). All citations of *Exodus* are from this edition.

36. J. R. Hall argues for translating "sæbeorga sand" as a kenning ("Old English *saebeorg*: *Exodus* 442a, *Andreas* 308a," *Papers on Language and Literature* 25:2 [1989], 127–134). Lucas, in his notes to these lines, asserts that "[t]hese lines are an expansion of Gen. 22:17 under the influence of 13:16; cf. also Heb. 11:12" (130). Lucas also refers to E. B. Irving's comment that the Old Latin phrasing of Gen 13:16, "si potest quis enumerare harenam maris," might have yielded "sæborga sand." See Irving, "New Notes on the Old English Exodus," *Anglia* 90 (1972), 289–324; see also Paul G. Remley, *Old English Biblical Verse: Studies in Genesis, Exodus and Daniel* (Cambridge, 1996), 190–94. J. W. Bright, "On the Anglo-Saxon Poem Exodus," *MLN* 27 (1912), 13–19, identifies possible biblical sources for the comments in the first section on God's extensive knowledge, among them Mark 13:31 and Luke 21:33.

37. Lucas, 124; Law, 26.

38. See Hill, "Apocryphal Cosmography," for discussion of the possible meaning and source of the phrase "stream uton sæ." Quotations from "The Creed" are from Elliott van Kirk Dobbie, ed., *The Anglo-Saxon Minor Poems*, ASPR 6 (New York, 1942).

39. Quotations from *The Descent Into Hell* are taken from George Philip Krapp and Elliott Van Kirk Dobbie, eds., *The Exeter Book*, ASPR 3 (New York, 1936).

40. Clubb identifies a possible source for this count in Psalms 146:4, "Who telleth the number of the stars, and calleth them all by their names" (48, note to ll. 11–13).

41. Ruth Wehlau, "The Power of Knowledge and the Location of the Reader in 'Christ and Satan,' " *JEGP* 97 (1998), 1–14 [reprinted in the present volume—*ed.*]; the quotation is from 7.

42. See Finnegan, 103–4.

43. Or "how I came to be there," as Clubb translates it (76); the reference is presumably to the *laðan ham* Satan mentions just before (177).
44. Stone, 425.
45. Wehlau, 4.
46. Thomas D. Hill, "The Measure of Hell: *Christ and Satan* 695–722," *Philological Quarterly* 60 (1981), 409–14.
47. Wehlau, 6.
48. The manuscript now has 116 vellum leaves, numbered pages 1–229 by a modern hand (The frontispiece, a blank at what would be p. 116, and an unnumbered blank p. 230, the verso of 229, are unnumbered). As Barbara Raw has demonstrated, it quite quickly lost leaves, perhaps a victim of vellum swiped for a more pressing project; see Barbara C. Raw, "The Construction of Oxford, Bodleian Library, Junius 11," *ASE* 13 (1984), 187–207; see especially 191ff. The full manuscript may be viewed, page by page, online at the Bodleian Library (http://image.ox.ac.uk/pages/bodleian/MSJUNI~1/preliminary.htm).
49. The illustrations in Junius 11 appear to be the work of three artists. The first illustrator runs from p. 1 to 62 and is responsible for thirty-eight drawings; illustrator two contributes ten drawings, running from p. 73 to 88. Artist three pops up briefly on p. 96 with an unfinished drawing, and scattered throughout the manuscript are are also several dry-point or metal-point doodles or partial illustrations. Raw argues that spaces for continuing the program of illustration once existed in *Christ and Satan* (203).
50. Krapp, xi–xii.
51. In a note, Raw suggests that only two hands are at work in *Christ and Satan* (189, note 7).
52. Raw 203, 202, where she argues that the book has been bound only twice, once initially, around 1000, and then again around 1230. Lucas argued for a twelfth-century date ("MS Junius 11 and Malmesbury," *Scriptorium* 34 [1980], 198–99).
53. I am very grateful to Martin Kauffmann of the Bodleian Library, Oxford, for allowing me to examine MS Junius 11, and to Timothy Graham for helpful suggestions regarding it.
54. Disagreement exists about whether the fold happened before or after the writing. Raw, for instance, believes it to have occurred at the time of the resewing of the manuscript (202), as did Clubb (xv), although for different reasons; Finnegan, like Gollancz, describes it as having happened before the copying (10). The ink does seem to be more worn at the fold, and this supports the idea that the fold occurred after copying. See also Lucas, on the idea that the ink is so worn in places as to suggest multiple folding and refolding: "On the Incomplete Ending of *Daniel* and the

Addition of *Christ and Satan* to MS Junius 11," *Anglia* 97 (1979), 46–59, 49.

55. The purpose of the accents in the manuscript, many of which are now so faded as to be hardly discernable, remains unclear. G. C. Thornley suggested nearly fifty years ago that the accents, though perhaps by different hands, might have been added for a single, "liturgical recitative" purpose, that is, "to assist a lector who was intoning the poems"; no more persuasive explanation has since been offered (G. C. Thornley, "Accents and Points of MS Junius 11" *Transactions of the Philological Society* [1954], 178–205; quotation is from 183). One difficulty with such a claim, however, is the uneven distribution of accents. The final pages containing *Daniel* (210 and 212), for instance, have only seven and eleven accents, respectively, while the first page of *Christ and Satan* has fifty-nine accents in what might be two (or more) hands—the ink color and shapes of the marks vary. This pace is not maintained; p. 225 of *Christ and Satan* has only three accents, showing how marked are the variations in this poem in particular. Thornley's suggestion implies that a hand other than the scribes' was at work in Junius 11, and it appears as if at least some of the adding of accents occurred separately in the two sections of the manuscript. At least two different shapes of accent marks appear in the manuscript; these Krapp describes as "a long slanting accent which is found throughout Liber I and not at all in Liber II, and a shorter and less slanting accent, which in Liber I is found only in the first thousand lines of *Genesis* but which occurs regularly throughout Liber II" (*The Vercelli Book*, ed. George Philip Krapp, ASPR 2 [New York, 1932], liv). In both accents and points, the color of ink is distinct from that of the text in *Christ and Satan*, and Thornley suggests the notations here may have been added in two stages, with dots being first added, then changed to various kinds of punctuation (Thornley, 189). The dots in *Christ and Satan* may be "the remains of metrical punctuation," and Thornley argues that although the pointing, like the accents, is incomplete, the marks above the dots look like various punctuation marks: "[t]his evidence makes it likely that the text of at least one poem in the MS. was prepared, or was in the process of being prepared, for use with the liturgical recitative, or for reading aloud according to the rules of the Church" (Thornley, 185–89). On the pointing in the manuscript, see John Lawrence, *Chapters on Alliterative Verse* (London, 1893), 14, and Clubb, xiv.

56. Krapp, xiii. See also A.N. Doane, *Genesis A: A New Edition* (Madison, WI, 1978), 14–16. Doane suggests that the corrections in *Genesis A* by a hand other than the scribe's might have been in preparation for recopying the manuscript (14, n. 24); this may also be true of the heavier corrections in *Christ and Satan*.

57. See Friedrich Groschopp, "Das ags Gedicht 'Crist und Satan,' " *Anglia* 6 (1883), 248–76, and Theodor Frings, "*Christ und Satan*," *Zeitschrift für deutsche Philologie* 45 (1913), 216–36. Sleeth provides a detailed analysis of the corrections in *Christ and Satan* (34 ff.).

58. Clubb, xvi–xvii.

59. Clubb, xvi, note 17; Gollancz, xxix. Finnegan identifies only a Corrector and an Annotator (5).

60. Raw, 204; on the date, too, of the corrections/annotations, see Clubb, xvi. Finnegan ascribes the p. 219 "omnis homo primum bonum" to the *Christ and Satan* annotator (5). There are, as well, "two twelfth-century drawings. The first of these (p. 31) is not related to the text but that on p. 96 shows the messenger telling Abraham about the capture of Lot, an incident described on p. 94 of the manuscript (*Genesis A* 2018–23). The drawing dates from the second half of the twelfth century and shows that the text was still considered to be of interest at that date" (Raw 204).

61. In the forty pages, including blanks, that contain *Daniel* very few extraneous marks appear: xb (crossed b) appears on p. 183 and on p. 190; on p. 181 is a pair of double horizontal lines in margin (slightly longer than those that turn up earlier in the MS), and on p. 185, the letter "f" is rewritten in margin where blurred in line. The word "innan" turns up as the sole inhabitant of p. 211 (besides a slash just before it). The discolorations are also minor, including only such things as some stains along the outer edges of pages and two small drops of red, as well as three smudges that just might be the faint residue of diagonally placed fingertips on p. 191. It is impossible, of course, to date any of these marks.

62. Remley offers a very neat summary of the evidence usually brought to bear in arguments about the status of the *Christ and Satan* pages (22–23, n. 34).

63. Raw, 189. Lucas argues that *Christ and Satan* was created independently and circulated as a folded booklet; see "On the Incomplete Ending of *Daniel*." In P. R. Robinson's terms, this means "a small but structurally independent production containing a single work or a number of short works," and he describes a number that were folded ("Self-contained Units in Composite Manuscripts of the Anglo-Saxon Period," *ASE* 7 [1978], 231–32). See also Bernhard Bischoff, "Über gefaltete Handschriften, vornehmlich hagiographischen Inhalts," *Mittelalterliche Studien* I (Stuttgart, 1966–67), 93–100.

64. Mildred Budny, *Insular, Anglo-Saxon, and Early Anglo-Norman Manuscript Art at Corpus Christi College, Cambridge* (Kalamazoo, MI, 1997), 605. See also M. R. James's description of the manuscript in *A Descriptive Catalogue of the Manuscripts in the Library of Corpus Christi College Cambridge Part IV* (vol. II, part I) (Cambridge, 1911).

65. Budny, 599, 602.

66. R. M. Liuzza, *The OE Version of the Gospels*, vol. I, EETS 304 (Oxford, 1994), xx–xxi. My thanks to Roy Liuzza for the reference.

67. Raw, 203. Raw's account of gathering 17 suggests that even it might have been completed in two stages: "the real division is between the outer three bifolia (pp. 211–16 and 225– 9) and the inner sheets (pp. 217–24). The three outer bifolia were pricked in both margins like those in the rest of the manuscript; the central bifolium (pp. 219–22), on the other hand, is pricked in the outer margins only" (200).

68. Finnegan notes that "[t]hough the styles of the scribes differ, they do not do so in any degree that would allow us to suppose that a significant interval separated their work" (4). Scribal similarities lead Clubb to assert that all three worked within the span of no more than a single generation (xii).

69. Raw, 203. Clubb argues that by the late eleventh century, at least, the collection existed as a unit, based on his belief that "there are traces in the *Genesis* of the hand of the Late West Saxon Corrector who was so active in *Christ and Satan*" (xv), a claim that Gollancz found unsupportable (xxix) but Krapp developed (xiv–xv).

70. Law, 23.

Index

CPSIA information can be obtained at www.ICGtesting.com
Printed in the USA
LVOW040426280112

265870LV00005B/301/P